Pre-publication endorsements for

THE EDUCATION OF CHRISTIAN FAITH
Critical and Literary Encounters with the New Testament

"Kenneth Cragg is not the first theologian to have made the processes of learning and growth central to the experience of historical Christianity – both Lessing and Newman were, in their own ways, before him – but he has a greater sense than either of the complex transactions between sacred text and secular literature. This is a work as impressive in the bold sweep of its thesis as it is in its constant illuminating asides. Indeed, he seems to have read everything, and seems equally at home in the biblical languages, Islamic tradition, Hindu thought, the European Classics, French, German and English literature. Moreover, as a poet himself, he has an instinctive sympathy with the anarchic and polysemous nature of literature, and makes no attempt to bend writers to fit his theological programme. I was particularly struck by his sense of the changing context of religious thought, from Hooker's unquestioned post-Constantine assumption that Church and State should constitute an all-embracing unity, to the problems and opportunities presented by modern pluralism. This is not merely a profound theological work, it is also a significant contribution to cultural theory – in its proper sense."

Stephen Prickett
Regius Professor of English Language and Literature
University of Glasgow

"Written in a strikingly subtle and penetrating style, this volume reveals an immense erudition, and a truly extraordinary moral and religious sensitivity, theological acumen and critical awareness, literary and other. On the basis of New Testament texts, Bishop Cragg presents Jesus of Nazareth as having undergone, during His ministry, a gradual process of education: He learned through suffering what it meant to be Messiah, not only to be Jesus but to become Jesus Christ. A similar process of education was demanded of His followers in the church. This process is illustrated through the cares of Christian Scholarship and the works of seven representative modern literary figures: Richard Hooker, Oscar Wilde, John Henry Newman, Robert Browning, William Faulkner, Rudyard Kipling, and Friedrich Nietzsche.

This fascinating volume is of importance because of its substantive quality and distinction and because, at this millennial time, it is by implication a very necessary and telling corrective to any exclusive and excessive concentration on the apocalyptic or eschatological Jesus. THE EDUCATION especially emphasizes the fundamental moral and spiritual dimensions of the Jesus who became the Christ and of the demands on His followers. This volume adds lustre even to the work of Bishop Kenneth Cragg."

W. D. Davies, Emeritus Professor, Duke University

Kenneth Cragg's intricate and suggestive prose has never been turned to better account than in his lucid and persuasive presentation of Christ as one who *learnt* through suffering, and of the early church as a fundamentally *learning* community. Bishop Cragg, fully acquainted with the trends of recent New Testament scholarship, makes a significant contribution to the study of the historical Jesus. The book excels equally in its scholarly account of "quintessential Christianity", its bold selection and exploration of examples of personal struggle with it, and its grasp, born of the author's long experience, of the constraints and possibilities of Christian witnessing in the plural society of today.

The Revd Dr Anthony Harvey

THE EDUCATION OF CHRISTIAN FAITH
Critical and Literary Encounters with the New Testament

The Education of Christian Faith

Critical and Literary Encounters with the New Testament

Kenneth Cragg

SUSSEX
ACADEMIC
PRESS

Brighton • Portland

2 4 6 8 10 9 7 5 3 1

First published 2000 in Great Britain by
SUSSEX ACADEMIC PRESS
PO Box 2950
Brighton BN2 5SP

and in the United States of America by
SUSSEX ACADEMIC PRESS
5804 N.E. Hassalo St.
Portland, Oregon 97213-3644

British Library Cataloguing in Publication Data
A CIP catalogue record for this book is available from the British Library.

Library of Congress Cataloging-in-Publication Data
Cragg, Kenneth.
The education of Christian faith : critical and literary encounters with the New Testament / Kenneth Cragg.
p. cm.
Includes bibliographical references and indexes.
ISBN 1-902210-49-2 (hc : alk. paper)
1. Christian biography. I. Title.
BR1700.2 C685 2000
270'.092'2—dc21
99-048132

Printed by Bookcraft Ltd, Midsomer Norton, Bath
This book is printed on acid-free paper

Contents

Preface

"Here endeth the lesson" is a familiar directive to readers in the Church of England. "Here beginneth . . ." also when the passage starts. One soon registers that "lesson" has moved on from when it meant "lection". Meaning drawn from a text is something other than its hearing when read aloud. In this modern sense the church lectern is surely where "the lesson" should *not* end.

The reason for the form of words is not far to seek. In the days of non-literates in the pew it was important they should know that what they were hearing was authentic Scripture, innocent of all embellishment from the lore or the liberty of the clergy. Hence the careful rubric enjoining precision in start and finish.

The formula may well go back to Hebrew patterns. When the lector in the synagogue read from the scroll in his hands he was duty bound to keep his eyes firmly fixed on it, even though he knew it well by heart. This was to demonstrate that the text was in entire control. As and when he paraphrased or expounded, recruiting insight from the Targums, he had first to close the scroll and avert his eyes from it. These actions made clear the radical distinction between the reading and the exegetical roles. Likewise, in Christian architecture, the pulpit is a different place from the lectern.

"Lesson" as now an archaism for "lection" hides a fascinating theme, namely how, in readership, text becomes meaning with riches at risk. The whole business of exegesis belongs in the vagary of terms. Where reading concludes, comprehension – hopefully – begins. Scriptures, Jewish or Christian, assert their canonical status by rubric directives so that readers and hearers alike are subdued to things textual. Holy words, however, are at the behest of commentary and homily. Voicing, public and oral, and faithfully "begun and ended", issues into discernment of its content that is mental and personal. "Lection" proceeds into the aegis or the jeopardy of "lesson". The given of the one is at stake in the taken of the other. What is textually sanctioned with due care waits on precarious reception.

Coming to *The Education of Christian Faith* this way anticipates the query that this book is aspiring to an odd thing, bringing together incompatible themes by proposing some useful juncture between New Testament studies and miscellaneous biography. Why associate the document of the Christhood of Jesus with seven widely selected figures in literature whose responses to the Christ of the New Testament text were highly idiosyncratic?

Reflection may perceive how the two realms of interest consort well. They are certainly in line with the "lection/lesson" situation about things given and things taken, the Christ in his story and that story's story in personal reckoning. The theme of "learning" unites them.

Its point of departure is the play on words in the Greek of the Letter to the Hebrews (5: 8) about the Christhood of Jesus' – *emathen, epathen* – "He learned in that he suffered". It is clear that there was a learning at the very heart of his Messianic achievement as the New Testament presents it. It issued, in turn, into a learning as the very shaping of the Church. It spelled an intention for the world, embracing "Jew and Gentile" alike in the wounded hands of the Cross. All had to do with a conscious interpretation of Messiahship, first by Jesus in ministry from Galilee to Jerusalem and then by the Church – in its own coming to be – reading its logic as the act of "God in Christ". What brought Jesus into accomplished Christhood made his disciples apostles to the nations. In turn came the documents, the literature called "the New Testament", making textual both stories – Christ's and theirs.

At the heart of this double event lay the theme of suffering. The active ministry of Jesus headed into confrontation with "establishment" on vital counts, serving for him as, cumulatively, the very school of Messianic meaning – "the cup my Father gives me". It was the active meaning of his Sonship. "Messiah" in those terms gave birth to the community of recognition, thanks to what the terms had been.

"The sin of the world", "the contradiction of sinners", were the words in which they identified what Jesus crucified had undergone. By the manner of his "enduring" these measures of a humanity in the wrong he had inaugurated a Gospel set to belong to all humankind.

This school of the learning Christ and of the learning Church was the education in which Christian faith began. It constituted for inclusive human cognizance the self-disclosure of God. For it had to do with the most divine task, namely love in action precisely where human wrong had exacted, in his crucifixion, the crucial place and cost of it. Perceiving it so gave being to the Church: its vocation was to verify it for the world.

It is right to take this drama of Christ-learning into the meaning of the familiar words of Matthew 11: 28–30: "Come to me . . . learn of me . . . all you who are heavy-laden." Mysterious in their incidence, they have long been ringing true in human yearning. There was paradox in their invitation to "rest" by dint of a "yoke". The imagery was familiar in Jewish ears of the "yoke" of law as "burden". Whatever the immediate setting of the invitation in Matthew, who yields no clue, its final reach is surely where we have located it in the title-deeds of "God in Christ reconciling the world", the world that learns its long Good Friday.

Ta mathemata ta pathemata are words as old as Herodotus, in his distant unawareness of *emathen epathen* in a New Testament letter. Both are here our script and score: experience is the school of faith, even as faith is the disciple of experience. Having for our learning, first the original and then, Church-wise, the incorporate Christ, is the lively warrant for linking to New Testament study a clutch of life concerns. They can truly inter-depend. The dyer's hand betrays where it has dipped. In their diversity our representative modern figures afford case-studies in Christ-learning that by their variety and fervour serve our own education well.

Doubtless – all western and white – the choice is easily indictable and also haplessly haphazard. Yet Richard Hooker and his heirs to companions of Oscar Wilde and *De Produndis*, via John Henry Newman, Robert Browning, William Faulkner, Rudyard Kipling and Friedrich Nietzsche, have no mean range of relevance. They concern major realms of yearning and misgiving in the things of faith. Some squarely, others only obliquely, relate their muse to Christ and Christ to their perplexity. Lay figures, non-ecclesiastics, predominate – poets who are story-tellers or dramatists, a radical philosopher and, from the deep American South a novelist of rare penetration into the human dark.

Invidious as selection may seem it will be found to take in significant fields of religious and philosophical quest, whether of "rest" or "discipline" or "discovery". In the proxies of imaginative writing we can probe anxiety, take purchase on costly secrets or register the forfeiture of disavowed illusions. Biographies personify the stakes in truth. They measure the onus in belief and interrogate the will for it. What, when truly known, could never be merely academic becomes the stuff of crisis, of integrity yearned for and found – or perhaps for ever elusive. With our mentors we are back around the lectern asking where the "lesson" ends – in heart and will.

What St. Paul called the "persuadedness" of the first faith, the confidence so characteristic of the New Testament, meets the less persuadedness, the unpersuadedness, of dubious minds – and the encounters aid our learning. So doing, they present a strange paradox. The Scripture on the lectern has its sacred status as both text and Canon – categories to be jealously reserved their proper rights. Yet, hallowed as they are with authority, they derived from an active Christ-learning on the part of apostles and evangelists. Should the words ever have assumed, *qua* Canon, a status that worked to exclude ongoing believers from the same learning/textualizing process by which they had themselves arrived? The fact of the Canon holds this strange anomaly, in enshrining Christ-learning and yet curbing or conditioning its persisting into the future. More exactly, should a limited realm of reliable learning have acquired its closed prerogative over what Christ-learning should evermore comprise?

Being itself "the learning of the lesson" ought the New Testament text to enjoy a documentary status somehow disallowing any further continuity of that "education", at least in the form, and of the rank, the Canon alone enjoys? Clearly education into Christ *was* taken further via Tradition, the Fathers, the Creeds. For the faith that acquired its Scripture awaited other minds bringing their perceptions. Given the Canon, however, what writ and mandate had these?

The questions bring us squarely to the central "heavy-ladedness" of John Henry Newman. He is for some the most significant religious figure of the 19th century: for others a man strangely overrated. He lived in urgent terms the point at issue concerning a Christ through and beyond the Scriptured Canon. He yearned for a resolution of his problem which had authority. His sensitivity of soul sought definitive escape from faith-perplexity, in total contrast to his contemporary, Robert Browning and a faith accommodating doubt.

Newman's disquiet about authority escorted him through an early evangelical piety, via (as he came to see them) the inadequate credentials of the Church of England, into the reassuring bosom of the Roman Catholic Church. He judged it capable of guaranteeing the truth of Christ by the weight of its prestige and the sound hierarchy he held it to possess. Faith-verification through the "Vicar of Christ" could exempt him from the faith-onus he most dreaded, namely the exercise of "private judgement".

He was not in fact relieved of that onus. He exercised it in opting for the Church he chose, by assigning to it the decision he shunned making in himself. He shifted the onus for "being authentic" from the heart in its own cognizance to the institution. A personal opting for the referent was still entailed, turning now on ecclesiastical credentials – taken as adequate to dispense with weighings that might have remained within his own reckoning. He took such certitude to be the due and proper shape of faith, whereas Browning came to see the demand for certitude forever incompatible with the liberal sense of things which Newman abjured.

Yet patiently to live and think with John Henry Newman, to sense his ardent personalism and his unresting anxiety, is to have extra-canonical

Christ-learning with the urgency it deserves. That is true for those who can never approve of his conclusion. The choice is between yearning for mind-security and homing on convictions open to ripening revision. Newman wrote that he was for ever occupied with "two supreme realities" – "God Almighty and John Henry Newman". Because of each he was hungry for a third – a right Church.

So, in his judicious way, was Richard Hooker. His *Laws of Ecclesiastical Polity* discoursed in eminently sober terms on "Christian statehood" for Elizabethan England. He argued an attainable unison of things spiritual and political for the health and sanity of both. At odds, in his own day, with "recusants" and "free-thinkers", his *Laws of Ecclesiastical Polity* are still more at odds now with a prevailing secularity that threatens to leave Cathedrals, as Nietzsche saw them, as mere "monuments of God" surviving only anachronistically as relics of a lost tradition. Yet in England the forms of constitutional "Establishment" continue.

Large questions remain as to how an honoured concept of the political hallowed in the spiritual can or will survive. It stems from the Biblical tradition of a good creation entrusted to responsible creaturehood in custody of the good earth and in care for *humanitas* rightly ordered and duly governed in righteousness and truth. That meaning remains vital to our sanity. Sacred and secular must for ever inter-penetrate. Society only ceases to desecrate when it learns to consecrate and only duly technologizes where it humbly celebrates.

For the secular factors which have so far distanced us from Richard Hooker's *Laws* belong squarely with that human autonomy or "dominion" explicitly sanctioned by the Biblical doctrine of human stewardship. The power dimension is, therefore, central to at least a modicum of well-being, justice and the common good. For it embodies in the round the obligation of conscience in the self. It has been remarked that the parable of the Good Samaritan makes no reference to any policing of the road. Islam is foremost among religions in urging the necessity of rule and power. But how are these preserved from their inherent snares and made dedicate to truth and right? Hooker's shape of Christ-learning belongs with our contemporary scene in caring for a polity of laws and in thinking them "ecclesiastical" in that they are referable to transcendant ends for which their means are meant. Hooker-wise we can no longer be. But to grapple with his vision, as notable successors did well into the 19th century, is to be in living exegesis of the New Testament and its whole pre-Constantinian, pre-Charlemagne, pre-Christendom perspective.

What, though, always, of "the unruly wills and passions of sinful men", of the dire insanities that oppress our human life? In few territories might the invitation of Matthew 11: 28–30 be more desperately heard than in Yoknapatawpha, that county of the darkened human soul created by William Faulkner. In the southern State of Mississippi, its topography drew a map of human depravity and degradation. It is right to think Faulkner's portrayal of human self-wronging, lust, insanity and crime proliferating across the generations, as belonging duly with the significance of Christ.

By reason of its origin no faith is more realist than Christianity concerning human perversity. No one can understand Gethsemane and be sanguine about humankind. All Faulkner's scenes and characters come where the weary world is. His panorama of pathos is a hinterland where the New Testament penetrates.

The poems and stories of Rudyard Kipling are in a different idiom, while his sense of "Empire" has kinships with Richard Hooker. Kipling was burdened with the theme of power, which he saw in imperial terms. These were "heavy-laden" with private griefs through youth and age, drawn from loneliness as a child and sorrow as a father, from vicissitudes in India and Sussex.

Often misconstrued as a crude trumpeter of Empire, he became more truly the accuser of arrogance and a warner against delusion. It would be proper to associate his idea of power imperial, of a *Pax Britannica* (or *Americana*) with current ideas of a "world-order" – a writ of "human rights" across all frontiers, of an inclusive mandate the myth of separate sovereignty should not exclude on the claim that what goes on within "our" holy borders is no one's business but "ours".

The right to make this good belongs now to the United Nations which, however, does not possess the power unless by the "grace" of powerful member states. These can too readily turn the means they afford to their selfish ends. Kipling's vision in his own day had some kinship with this sense of necessary power in trust with comprehensive cares worldwide. Such was "the white man's burden", the vocation holding "dominion over pine and palm". Honour could not "stoop for less". Advancing technology and globalism have rendered "world-order" more vital than Kipling ever sensed, thanks to the sophistication of nuclear war-forms and the chronic elusiveness of peace in the growing obsolescence of "nation-states".

Pretentious as Kipling's Empire was, with his early vision its celebrant, there was dignity in its heart for "all the subject peoples". In maturity he was able to detect the temptations of power and register the snares around political dominion. These he knew well how to indict. His racialism was capable of a humanism in inclusive terms. It was not his style to theologize. Yet there is more than a furtive Christ-learning in his tales and poems, their accents of pathos and of pleading. When he wrote *Recessional*, a poem modelled on hymn and liturgy, he threw it first into a waste-basket in despair of its meaning in the grim world. Retrieved by a friend to be printed in *The Times*, its "Lest we forget" came to be inscribed on a vast array of "War Memorials". Learning Christ he surely was, out of a *De Profundis* of his own.

Oscar Wilde's soul-confession with that title, and its reiterated "only what is realized is right", was at far remove from Kipling. Wilde drew his self-reproach from the image of "Christ, the suffering servant", as clue to the costliness of grace and forgiveness. The issue of Wilde's homosexuality was central to his story, though the litigation in the famous Trials concerned only formal libel on which ground he was imprisoned. He "realized" his own self-ruin and told it in the folly of a misguided trust in treacherous friendship physically transacted.

Wilde's tragic story was far more than evidence of the latent evils of homosexuality and homophobia alike. The fascination of his lively wit, his self-ostentation and theatricality made his a *cause célèbre*. Wilde knew, and told with poignant honesty, how much deeper went his tragic muse. The haunting allusions of *De Profundis* and *The Ballad of Reading Gaol* reveal how near his own Gethsemane came to the meaning of Christ's. They can then be read as living entry into the New Testament.

In the light of Oscar Wilde's "what is realized", what do we say of Friedrich Nietzsche? They were so nearly contemporary. On his own showing, Nietzsche had the godliest of human fathers, deep in the Lutheran tradition. A mental genius of rare powers, the son measured the range of Christ-learning by the very vehemence of its rejection. He saw the will to Christian belief a fickle, frail and foolish thing that sought in futile piety the fraudulent solace of a deluded theism. He countered it by a strenuous will to disbelief in which his revulsion was complete.

Around his "will to power" he risked large misconceptions into which many fell whom he mystified or appalled. His writings probed Christ-learning with so thorough a repudiation that its essentials were the more tellingly defined. Yet there were points where his copious aphorisms seem to be counter-witnessing against his theme. He has his place here if we would know the New Testament aright.

What, finally, of the poetic doubt of Robert Browning? The legend of a buoyant optimist does him little justice. For all his leisured elegance, his romantic love-match, his seemingly complacent aura, he was – like a parallel Walt Whitman – no stranger to dark thoughts. He was alert to misgivings around New Testament faith spawned by David Strauss and other critics. The novelist George Eliot, translating Ludwig Feuerbach from the German, made him aware of the view that took theology as mere human subjectivity, projecting an image of its own wistfulness.

We can esteem him as a Victorian doubting-Thomas, delighting nevertheless in the charm of subtlety in words and a poetry indulging eager verbal sword-play. He excelled in dramatic monologue, shaping both sides of an issue as if debating with his other self. But imaginary discusants were honestly contrived. They reflected his capacity to make all consent to faith fully liable to the reach of doubt. Browning rightly perceived that the New Testament invites a lover's, rather than a pundit's, faith.

Thus he stands as a complete foil to John Henry Newman, allowing deep conviction to "love remaining questions", not banishing them in lust for guarantee. In this he was alive to how the Holy Spirit's action in the soul is never superseded by the forms of doctrine. Rather the Spirit moves in the private mind, the personal soul, for the sake of the integrity that can live in these alone.

Perhaps, then, in a miscellany of pens and minds, "the lesson continues". "Only what is realized is right." Wilde's words could be written across New Testament Scripture. The ministry of Jesus "realized" the Messianic Cross. Its summons into community and witness was "realized" in the nascent Church. Divine Incarnation was "realized" in a preaching intention for the world in a trans-ethnic wideness and a reach of catholicity.

"What was realized was right" – the verdict and the venture one. The Canon that installed the primary referent as "holy Scripture" had not thereby imposed a rigorous rule of thumb. It had garnered the first-fruits of a believing situation in apostolic Letters and the Gospels. These bequeathed themselves as the prior document of faith on the lecterns of the Christian world to serve as a paradigm of ongoing "realizings" of the faith in the fabric of new times and places.

It follows that the siftings of a probing scholarship can ally with all faith-biographies. These take us where "the lesson" never "ends". The newly printed, "chained Bible" amid a cluster of illiterates waiting for a reader, was a familiar image in the 16th century. We now enjoy more copious access to the text, or we register "chained-ness" of another order in the preoccupations of our own indifference. For us there are many means and shapes of legibility. At all events, what is laid open for the scholar in study is laid open for the disciple in obedience. "Christ in the Learning" was ever – and still remains – the task and the experience of faith. Faith means responsible possession of its text and responsive surrender to its Lord. Only so are we "disciples indeed".

Kenneth Cragg
OXFORD, APRIL 2000

ἔμαθεν ἀφ' ὧν ἔπαθεν

Son as He was, He learned obedience in that He suffered.

The Letter to the Hebrews

All you who are weary and heavy-laden in heart, take My yoke as yours: learn of Me . . . you will find your souls' rest.

Jesus according to Matthew

Far other is the lesson you have learned from the knowledge of Messiah, if indeed it was his voice that you hearkened, if in union with him you were taught your lesson – truth as it is in Jesus.

The Letter to the Ephesians (A. S. Way translation)

I will tell the no-telling . . . recount what I cannot count . . . All unskilled in the telling I make God's great acts my theme.

Psalm 71: 15, playing on words

To me that story – ay, that life and death
Of which I wrote "It was" – to me it is,
Is here and now. I apprehend nought else . . .
And as I see the sin and death, even so
See I the good and glory consummated thence . . .

Robert Browning

Awake, my lute and struggle for thy part
  With all thy art.
The crosse taught all wood to resound his name,
  Who bore the same.
His stretched sinews taught all strings, what key
Is best to celebrate this most holy day.

George Herbert in Holy Week

THEN AND THERE

ONE

Jesus in His Christ Experience

I

"Learn of me" is familiar enough through all the Christian centuries as being the invitation *of* Jesus. "Jesus himself learning" as the steady theme of his own ministry might seem to have a dubious ring. Traditionalists might wonder how it could belong with divine Sonship to be in the throes of hard decisions stemming from a gathering crisis and spelling sharp anxiety. Yet so it was and however theology proposes to understand "incarnation" the "agony" must be part of it. For it was implicit from the start and became steadily more explicit as Jesus' encounter with the world of his time and place unfolded.

Some decades after the climax, a Christian thinker in the Letter to the Hebrews (5: 8) made a play on words with his Greek verbs, *emathen . . . epathen*: "He learned as he suffered", "suffering he learned", "obedience" being the clue. The twin verbs incorporated the whole story, very much as the later Latin Creed was satisfied with the bare "suffered" to tell the career of Jesus. It must always be remembered that while "Jesus" was the personal name, *Christos*, "the Christ" was a title denoting an office, a role, or – more vitally – a task. It meant *being* "the Messiah" by *reading* what Messiahship required and both in the givens of the living situation which ministry presented to him for decision.

It is this "Christ-experience" we have, in this chapter, to comprehend in all its cumulative meaning. The whole might be known as a "Jesus agonistes", drawing the term from classical drama where the *agon* meant both the issue as exacting for the mind's discernment and arduous in the undergoing.[1] The cares scholarship properly needs to take around this perception of what is central to the New Testament are deferred to CHAPTER FOUR. Here those perplexities are taken as read in the terms that follow.

Our study has one immediate duty. Familiarly we read the Gospels with hindsight. We know how the story ends and begins anew. We come traditionally appraised of the meaning of the Incarnation. We assume ourselves having to do with "the Word made flesh". We are "in the know" of what faith tells. It needs, therefore, a deliberate effort of mind to remember how the story was lived and known by Jesus only as it progressed. Properly understood, the "divine-in-the-human" situation which faith – only *post facto* – confesses was realized and transacted in the fabric of events. The governing term of "obedience" in Hebrews and elsewhere tells a dramatic, not an abstract, Christology – the term the Greek language yielded for the comprehending of what was, by its very essence, eventful – a life-told significance and never an arcane ideal or idea.

We need, then, to see what we have in the Gospels as a "coming-to-be" of the Messiah, the patterning and achieving of an identity in a concrete situation the full measure of which had to be taken step by step as the preacher's encounter with his reception mediated into Jesus' mind the shape of Messianic vocation. To this, as faith believes, the whole of his instincts in Sonship were bent. Their ready-ing for decision could only happen in the developing context of a growing *antilogia*, "a contradiction of sinners against himself".[2] This his teaching and his personality were apt to generate, but not arbitrarily to fit a scheme or devise a theoretical salvation. Rather, there ensued from his presence and his words the contours of a destiny to suffer, in which both the meaning and the price of things Messianic would be attained. The mind that learned to know it so was the measure of the Sonship. We find what faith confesses in the Incarnation by starting, not with the formula that came to house it, but with the history through which, in deed of suffering love, it came to pass.

II

From tentative to cumulative Messianic decision went. Since there were contradictory conceptions attending it, these meant that Jesus could only fulfil Messianic hope by radically revising it. The question "whether" about Messiah had long entailed the questions "when" and "how". The third would always be the key to the other two. The "who" of identity must plainly turn on the "how" of achievement.

It is necessary to take the whole Messianic theme back into the Biblical understanding of creation. For it was this sense of a willed universe that gave significance to the history that ensued from it. For this the created world set an open-ended arena. Natural history, the sequences of seasons and centuries, gave occasion to ethnic, social and political histories. The Biblical "dominion" which creation intentionally bestowed made for cultures, cities, civilizations in its fulfilment. The garden, not a desert, was the symbol of the human habitat. All was understood as being set for human occupancy and a creaturely entry upon a perennial inheritance. Jesus' parables echoed with this trusteeship perception of human affairs and for the same reason, Paul and John firmly linked "the light" they recognized as Jesus with "the light" that was "let be" at creation – the light of an intelligible world for an intelligent peopling. Faith could in no way abrogate the role of history,[3] however vexing to hope, and devious with truth, history threatened to be.

It was out of the emerging panorama of human obduracy and perversity, beginning with the fratricide in the first generation, that yearning for rescue ultimately transpired as somehow "expectable" from the Lord whose will underlay creation. However, there was a sharp privatization in the Biblical history of both the concern over wrong and the incidence of rescue. Both were confined, for the most part, within the parameters of a "chosen people". Adam, or generic "man", had handed the test-case of creation – and so its history – to Abraham and thence to Moses, Joshua and David. Noahid covenant of universal natural fertility gave way to Sinaitic covenant of unique ethnicized destiny.

It was not that this tradition in any way ignored or minimized the incidence of human evil outside its own race and story. On the contrary, it was only too well aware of the perversity of pagans and other breeds outside Mosaic covenant. But its instincts were always to assess those evils in relation to themselves, in terms of obstruction and enmity *vis-à-vis* Hebraic special status. Only slowly, via the integrity of the great prophets of the 8th century and later (BC), did the Hebrew mind more intelligently internalize the mystery of a recalcitrant history and begin to read hope for the future in terms of their own purification rather than only of the discomfiture of their national foes.

When hope of these, its broadest terms, began to be focused towards a single figure, a divine agent or agency by whom it would be implemented, the theme still remained essentially nationalist[4] whether in terms of the purity of a divinely sanctioned people or of their political hegemony. These twin, and sometimes competing, ideas stemmed from the Davidic mythology of "a holy nation and a royal priesthood", which came to hold great fascination in Israel's story.

The concept was chastened and, in part, refined by the bitter experience of post-Solomonic forfeiture, by the division of the kingdom and the ultimate exile, first of the northern and then of the southern régimes. Then a foiled history forced upon the people an intensification of the Messianic dream. The long story through the prophetic, the restoration and the Maccabean periods, might also be seen as a gathering mystification of what an elusive "Davidism" could conceivably hold. What precisely could "promise" mean in the successive worlds of dominant non-Jewish powers, Babylonian, Persian, Greek, Seleucid, Roman? Was a *David Redivivus* feasible? Why had the Maccabees with their power and priestliness failed to make it good? The greater the perplexity for some the sharper the ardour, for others the deeper the despair. The Idumeæn compromise under the notorious half-breed, Herod the Great, did nothing to redeem Messianic hope by the emotions his magnificent buildings aroused with the Temple itself as a hardly subtle effort to curry popular favour. By the time of Jesus, Roman governors of the Pilate-type controlled Jerusalem and Judea. Zealots became the more zealous with their will to a fanatical Messianism: purists by various pleas and means yearned for a peoplehood somehow capable of a corporate redemption of themselves by the purity of their sabbaths and the patience of their souls. Theocracies by election and covenant were far to seek and inherently liable to their own frustration.

III

There can be no doubt that Jesus' ministry moved in this climate of Messianic expectation, at once hazardous and contentious. There has been prolonged debate among scholars concerning how the clues from the Gospels should be read in reckoning with his response. Much has been written on the alleged "Messianic secret", according to which Jesus "concealed" from the world at large his real Messianic consciousness – which is then held to explain why the disciples only comprehended it fully after the resurrection.[5]

But the bewilderment recorded of them during the ministry is surely far more credibly explained, not by any conspiracy of silence but by the sheer tangle of misconceptions – theirs and the people's – in the midst of which Jesus walked. It is clear enough that the title "The Christ" belongs with the world of the New Testament Epistles and that "Jesus", "Lord", "Master", predominate in denoting him in the Gospels; and clear also that, with significant exception, Jesus sedulously avoided the "Messiah" term throughout his ministry, preferring the more elusive "Son of Man".[6]

The reason is not far to seek and needs no subtlety. To have publicly announced or claimed Messiahship would have been to step into the chronic confusions he had first to disentangle. These distorted and imperilled the only rendering of Messiahship compatible with his Sonship and meant for his obedience. Painfully and blunderingly, as we must see, the disciples were to prove bewildered parties to that education.

Accordingly, any exposition of Jesus as "Messiah" needs to set down the evidences – as far as the Gospels yield them – of his inner awareness of the role, its progress within his own consciousness in steady reaction to the evolving experience of "learning" drawing on his ministry and, finally, the sources in prophetic antecedent of the clues by which he read and resolved all he underwent. Such exposition must keep steadily in view the impact – and the imponderables – of the charismatic healings which figure so largely in the Gospel narratives.

Indeed, these constitute a telling point of departure into such Messianic exposition. For, in their light, what might a "Zealot" type Messianism have achieved had Jesus been minded for it! Pilate would have had more to do than wash his hands, had the healer Jesus chosen to rouse the exuberant mob about his ears. There is no clearer index to the Messianic reticence of Jesus than his sustained refusal to capitalize on publically thrilling charisma for political or insurrectionist ends.

Never was the healing charisma, or grace-possession, of Jesus presented, still less exploited, as contrived for publicity or right for credulity. To be sure, his repeated injunctions not to tell or "noise abroad" could hardly avail in an excited and gossipy world. "He could not be hid." Yet insistently his "works of grace" were perceived, and meant to be perceived, as "signs" or tokens of "the kingdom" in its liberating, restoring and enlivening power. Galileans were not unaccustomed to wandering charismatics. Their potential for political agitation – and also for personal charlatanry – was well known among a credulous and volatile population. They were not all "moved with compassion", but rather by other inducements a probing psychology might explore both in them and their retinue and the prestige they enjoyed.[7]

The Gospels see it, and tell it, in Jesus quite otherwise. There was a summons in his dealings, a mission in his method, things symbolic in his caring. Readers of the story of Jesus' testing in the desert, hard on the heels of his acceptance of commission at the hands of John the baptizer, must rightly wonder from where the story came and how the text came by it, if not somehow from communion with Jesus. The point will recur in the chapter following. Whatever we should conclude concerning its transmission the fact that, transmitted it was, is eloquent of its persistence in the mind of Jesus in the long sequel. Luke says as much in noting that "Satan left him for a season" (4: 13).

In that encounter with the whole implications of a potentially Messianic destiny, Jesus decisively rejected supposedly Messianic devices that would have ministered to naked credulity, the blithe perpetuation of mere economic plenty, side-stepping human perversity therewith, or arriving airborne into the Temple court from its highest pinnacle leaving the credulous no option but a gaping wonder. In this context it must follow that to speak glibly of "signs" as "miracles" is clumsy, unless we take the latter only in the shape of the former, and not as extraneous cogs on the gears of belief. Were they such they could only betray both the living Christ and the nature of faith, being alien to the entire meaning of "the kingdom of God".

That central theme of Jesus' preaching intimated in subtle ways the open question of its "king". For, without a king, there is no "kingdom". The wide accessibility of healing, and yet its careful economy, told both the generosity and the patience of its siege of human hearts. On both counts its meaning came to be seen as bound into the preacher's personality. Always, with those who purport to speak from God or for Him, lurks the question not only: What is he saying? but: Who is he that he should presume to do so? All the prophets knew this sequence of query from the word they brought to their capacity in doing so. Authority for the content inevitably entailed the authority of its bearer.

The crucial point about Jesus is that this situation came in heightened – faith says uniquely perceived – terms. The Gospel he brought in words belonged in the person he found himself *learning* to be. We must concede that we are in the presence of something indefinable – the bond between "these that I say" and "this that I am". It is a theme which needs to be pondered for how it transpired for the disciples, which is the concern of CHAPTER TWO. Here it must be studied in the interior consciousness of Jesus himself, keeping steadily in mind, as we do, the mental context of Messianic dimensions in all their ambiguity.

The theme of Jesus' Messianic consciousness has to do with what is implicit in all thought of God, namely the association between divine being and divine agency. Such association apart, faith in God has no content. Only in relationality is God known. Jewish faith had several ways of expressing this situation of Yahweh's "being" shown or told in Yahweh's "doing". Always within the divine unity, there was nevertheless a discernible "other", like sound in its echo, by which divine action was at once distinguishable, yet not distinguishable, from the divine nature.

"My presence will go with you," was the divine assurance: "Lift upon us the light of Thy countenance," the psalmist's prayer, "the Name of the Lord a strong tower" his sometime boast. Such language clearly discriminated within a divine reality that was both beyond and transcendent yet present and known. The distinction had its meaning in relation to humanity and history, such relationship being explicit in the divine initiative only because it was implicit in the divine nature.

This perception of divine "presence" or "wisdom" or "face" only seems subtle when we try to formalize it away from the necessary metaphors it employs. These long and tried Hebraic usages point forward to the kind of "God in . . ." language Christian faith came to require in its understanding of Jesus. They went back vividly to the formula Moses received in Exodus 3: 14: "I will be, as there I will be." The two pronouns "I" spell out this twin unity of doer and doing, of identity in its credential.[8] The God who could "presence" Himself in the event of exodus might "presence" Himself in the event of incarnation. History, as humans can receive and read it, is where God is both giving and given in His own terms.

Before, however, we can intelligently make this recognition of faith there is need to study divine "agencies" that were entirely human and could only instrumentally be read as divine "presence" by a commissioning of messengers and prophets. It will then be necessary, and – in hope – possible, to see how the Messianic consciousness of Jesus moved through the instrumental to the incarnational, from the "servant" to the "Son". No such study sequence should fail to recognize how Messiahship *per se* incorporates in necessary earth-found agency the heavenly obligation of the eternal Creator to the history, the broken history, of His creatured world. Messiah would always *ex officio* be "more than prophet". Yet what appertained to prophethood, both of servanthood and suffering, might be the clue by which Messiah might know himself and be known – a truly "learning Messiah".

IV

We could take an interesting point of departure for the link between prophet and Messiah from the words in Psalm 105: 15; "Touch not Mine anointed and do My prophets no harm."[9] They have in mind the patriarchs in their wanderings long before the sojourn in Egypt. Warned off molesting them are the tribes through whose lands they passed – all a far cry from the ultimate role of the Isaiahs and Jeremiahs of the Hebrew world. The "Messiah" word, clearly, could have many uses. Two ideas are central. The one is divine agency through "anointing" which the patriarchs are seen to possess merely as progenitors of the later kings and prophets. The other is the immunity they should properly enjoy as those whom "anointing" must make inviolable.

It is that second notion that throws the light of paradox on the almost uniformly violable, that is, vulnerable, experience real prophets underwent. In their time and place, it was their own kith and kin, not marauding alien tribes, that dogged their steps with malice and hounded their way with scorn. The careful student soon notes that these notions of "the anointed" had their place in the traditions of Jesus that have come down to us. There were early moments in which the notion of vindication, of indubitable success and assured destiny was to crown Jesus' story, when, in Galilee, it was "good to be there". Equally there were moments at the end when "coming down from the cross" could have shown in a dire reversal how divinely inviolate he was. Neither were consistent with "the kingdom of heaven". Clearly, on the principle of "Touch not Mine anointed and do My prophets no harm" there could have never been a Christianity.

It is evident that the issue of what could *truly* belong with human means to divine action in the world preoccupied the ministry of Jesus. "The prophet of Nazareth" was among his honoured titles. His sermon in the Nazareth synagogue – a pivotal event – laid claim to a personal parallel with the commission in Isaiah 61, "the place of the Scripture where he read".[10] When, at length, the so-called triumphal entry into Jerusalem brought a solitary departure from studied non-publicity as his set of soul, the imagery he invoked of "one riding on an ass" drew on the clearest of allusions to a gentle, lowly Messianic picture.[11]

That event was, of course, a culmination which requires us to see that the entire logic of the antecedent ministry was leading towards it. In that logic we can see emerging two frames of reference strongly coinciding. The one was the precedent of prophetic non-immunity – for Jeremiahs were never spiritually quarantined patriarchs: the other was the striking parallel of hostility characterizing Jesus' own experience and reception. Jesus' Galilean perception of Jerusalem was of a city used to "killing the prophets", not realizing "things belonging to her peace". The Elijahs and Elishas of the old tradition might have contrived their own security, not so the great prophets of the full tradition. From Amos and Hosea onward, because of their words, "they came through great tribulation". Ridicule, enmity, persecution, inner anguish – these were the price their fidelity paid.

The reasons are not far to seek. It was as spokesmen for the divine rule that they incurred obloquy, were threatened and reviled. Silence could have rescued them but loyalty forbad. Thus they were a sort of proxy-bearers of the disavowal which, via their persons, was meant and intended for God. Their experience took the instrumental role we earlier noted into dimensions anticipating what the cross would be for Jesus.[12] And, in those terms, they linked him with precedents his own ministry was steadily indicating as one becoming imperative for him.

While some scholars dispute the role of prophetic example in the shaping of the Messianic consciousness of Jesus (for whom CHAPTER FOUR must care), the echoes in his discourse – assuming we can rely on them textually – are clear and strong. His road to Jerusalem is marked by anticipation of "the Son of man suffering". He speaks of "being set at nought" and of "giving his life as a ransom", in evident echo of Isaiah

53. He invokes the imagery of the vineyard so dear to psalm and prophet as a symbol of "Israel in the land" and tells a parable of the sending of "the son" whose errand is continuous with that of "servants" yet alone can vindicate the ultimate claim of ownership. The parable interprets a situation of cumulative rejection plainly analogous to what has attended his own preaching. His hearers too understand its implications and it sharpens their hostility.

It seems, therefore, possible to read clearly enough what perception of his ministry and of himself Jesus was reaching in the setting as it yielded how and where he was *learning* the "contradiction of sinners", the *antilogia* of a religious world. The precedents of prophethood and hazard were there deeply in his inherited tradition. The suffering inherent in them could then be the clue to being Messianic, the key by which to resolve all those contentious notions of nationalist, racialist, purist, Davidic, priestly and other Messiahships.

Indeed, the "servant songs" in Isaiah 42 to 53 had already conceived that same equation between a human agency of suffering sublimely fulfilling the divine serving. The prophetic quality of Jesus was never in doubt. It was in that quality his Galilean retinue acclaimed him in Jerusalem as "Holy Week" began. It was in that capacity he had incurred the disavowals with which the establishment – in Luke's graphic word – had "murmured against him". By the single role of "agency" for God, might not prophethood foreshadow Messiahship and, by the common factor of suffering, confirm for Jesus the vocation and the meaning of "Sonship"? Then, in the sequel, the Church would be right in confessing "the Christ and him crucified".

But the whole was no formal scheme, no arbitrary fate-like destiny. It was alone worked out in the harsh immediacies of an unfolding drama where a Christ-calling would engage with the full expression of representative human wrong. We need to understand the travail of the growing conviction with which it came to be realized, first in mind and then in will and deed.

A crucial point where we may do so is in what the Gospels tell (Matthew most fully) about Jesus with the disciples at Caesarea-Philippi. More from the disciples' angle, it will concern us closely in CHAPTER TWO. Why is Jesus asking them whether "the people" think him Messiah and whether, further, the disciples have an opinion? The occasion is clearly a watershed. They are withdrawn far from usual haunts. The ministry, his and theirs, is at mid-point. There is both retrospect and prospect.

Plainly, this cannot have to do with omniscience wanting to be informed, nor with some vulgar preoccupation with a pride-inducing reputation. Jesus is not coveting adulation or soliciting from sycophants. He uses no leading words to prompt them, only the familiar "Son of man" and the private pronoun. If one can argue from the answer he received, it must be that all minds were occupied with the Messianic questions. Must it not be that Jesus – if not consulting with disciples – was unburdening to them his own preoccupying thoughts? How should he read his ministry thus far? How interpret a logic to which it was leading? Was his experience a process of *learning* the shape of its likely climax?

In that case, what could be more fitting, indeed more incarnational, than to sound out his devoted followers, the inner circle of his companions whose presence with him, if not their frame of reference, had given them a perspective from which to report their mind? "Report", according to Isaiah 53: 1, had always figured in reputings of "the servant". It could not be otherwise, given the perplexing conflict of views that would be, and had been, current, around that much-awaited, long-debated figure. In any event, expectations would be the context in which even their consternation would be taking place.

If charismatic ministry was heralding the "signs" of the kingdom, if even crowds were capable of repentance, if old patterns of travail were emerging, would not Jesus' own reading of those other "signs" of a rejecting scene move him to relate with the disciples in "*learning*" his way? Had he not "called them to be with him"? Companionship is always two-way.

The outcome did not ease his burdens: it only enlarged them. It transpired that, around the crucial word, they were sharing his thoughts, while in no way sharing his perceptions. These the encounter could only deepen as the mingled confirmation and incomprehension in Peter's words gave Jesus to know how urgently posed his questions had been. If Messiahship was indeed coming to be fused in the popular mind with his story, all the more pressing became the need to let that role have its way while disavowing what they all thought it to signify. Hence the severity of the rebuke to Simon Peter. Hence, also, the "setting of the face to go up to Jerusalem". The conversation at Caesarea-Philippi had closed a Messianic inauguration in ministry and opened the Messianic climax in suffering. It had tied them into one whole.

V

Our earlier themes of divine "presence" – the human relatedness of divine being as twin aspects of the divine unity – and the human instrumentality that prophethood fulfilled are understood in Christian faith to have come together in the person of Jesus as the Christ. It finds in

Jesus' learning to be the Christ an experience which is at once human and divine. The thread of prophetic servanthood is there, and there virtually, but what is being transacted is seen, by faith, to be of an order to entail the divine presence in the more than servanthood sense. There is that, we might say, for which only God – and not proxies, however ready, can avail.

It is this perception of Christian faith which underlies its theological reading of Jesus-being-the-Christ, precisely in having been enacted historically. In turn historical enactment is the ground of the theological perception. Together they belong with the historical/theological meaning of the fusion, in Jesus, of "the servant" and the "Son". This fusion informs the text of the Gospels and is the steady witness of the Epistles in their ethical Christology. It was in learning his servanthood that Jesus taught us his identity. For it was in the one that the other was fulfilled.

The movement into faith's interpretation of him is thus in line with that of Jesus into Christ-experience, which is why "learning Christ" is so appropriate a phrase. Jesus, we can say, became the Christ he was, the divinely definitive Messiah, because – as we have seen earlier – Messianic action could proceed only from the nature of God. Thus, "becoming" in its historical incidence was not innovative about the God it revealed. For it derived from His eternal being as the responsible architect of all things. This deriving, as Christian faith understands, necessarily had its counterpart in the consciousness of Jesus precisely in the context of the story in which he was anxiously wrestling with, and in entire volition moving to, the actual meaning of that Messianic task.

It was precisely here that Christ became, as Hebrews has it, "the pioneer', "the captain", the *teleiotes*, of faith.[13] It is here, too, that we must locate the meaning of "Sonship" mysteriously present in the whole fabric of events. Since what Messiah was set to achieve in redemption proceeds from the divine nature, the divine nature was engaged in and through it. "My father is always at work, and so am I."[14] Sonship, therefore, assumes the instrumental role of the prophets and shares its sorrows, yet – being therein divinely Messianic – is essentially "more than" instrumental, more than prophethoods could be. It must fall to CHAPTER THREE on the Mediterranean dispersion to study the faith telling how it understood this "Christ-learning".

Here we stay with "Sonship" in the immediacies of Jesus in his Christ-experience. The Messianic issue as we have traced it was bound up with Sonship. The terms "servant" and "Son" were often almost identical in Hebrew context: in the Greek *pais* they are one and the same.[15] They are seen to be synonymous in Jesus, Messiahship being a "servant" role that only a "Son" can fulfil. Always in the New Testament the task is primary, the status its corollary. It is in the "doing" of ministry and suffering grace that faith is both invited and required to acknowledge the divinity these possessed. All was antecedent in the eternity of God. For otherwise the Messianic deed-in-history could not have happened nor been what it was. It was only, however, in the deed as it was that we know it so.

Faith must, therefore, read and revere the Sonship of Jesus as the interior awareness of mind and will inside the actualities through Galilee to Gethsemane and beyond. This is the context in which the Gospels present it – a sense of "my Father's",[16] the intimacies of communion, the gentle term "Abba", the presence of a constraining "mind" moving within his own at the supreme points of outward crisis. Hebrews 5: 8 has it exactly: "Being Son, yet he learned . . . as he suffered." It could not be otherwise. Only "in flesh and blood" it happened: only from eternity could it have been the thing it was.

It follows that it is pointless and crude to ask, as some have querulously done: "Did Jesus think he was God?" in the sense of some kind of self-deification or that he imagined some *coup d'état* or usurpation in heaven. Since "God was *in* Christ" there could be no supersession. The "Father/Son" language, being within the unity of will and deed, said as much. The Messianic task ("I came to save the world")[17] – if we rightly measure it as the Creator's liability to His own earth-ordered, human-vested, history – is big enough for God and God alone is big enough. It must, however, be accomplished in the history it concerns and this means a "someone", more than angelic, more than proxy, more than prophet. Christ the Son is whom it means.

We might make the point – though only in a legal-style analogy – from the crucial parable, noted elsewhere, of the vineyard and the husbandmen. That it was extremely pointed all its hearers understood. It certainly clinched official resolve to arrest Jesus when ways could be found.

It might seem highly imprudent to risk sending "the son" after the "servants" had been so roughly handled. We have to understand, however, a descending spiral of conspiracy. Absentee landlords – it might be argued – bred ambitious tenants. Occupancy, after all, is half the battle. Begin by demurring about rents, test the absentee's patience, refuse the dues, manhandle his agents, manoeuvre to gain possession. This was the way things were, as Jesus' hearers well understood.

In such deteriorating situations only the lord's son and legal heir could defy the flouting of rights and assert continuing ownership. Servants could only come for dues. Hence the son's advent, squarely joining the emerging issue between recalcitrants and owner, between contractual right and defiant wrong. The sight of the son coming excites the idea that perhaps by a speedy murder, subsequently "fixed" and exploited, the tenants can suppress the owner's rights and claim possession.

How sharply the scenario fitted the divine/human situation was plain for all to recognize. History was a similar tale of accumulating perversity necessitating the inclusive divine response, where – confined as it is to rights in law – the parable breaks down. Messiah is seen to be, representatively, the point of climax, the crux of what is at issue in the economy of God and His dealings with the human world. Incidentally, we learn how far from zealotry was the Christ who could employ this parable. For absentee landlords were the prey and the bane of ardent nationalists.

Essentially, the parable only hints obliquely at the cost the paying of which takes everything far beyond its own silences and the reach of legal things. Nothing is said about the emotions of "the son", who must know well enough the grim reasons why the situation has necessitated his going. The evil is now beyond the range of "messengers", whose sufferings have only maximized the peril he alone runs in sonship terms. He is at once a larger quarry for the tenants' hatred, a more inclusive prize in their conspiracy. The paradigm of the crucifixion is plain for all to see, as the focal point of a human story of divine rejection. But now see how "the parts shift" and redemption displaces requital when the death of the victim is in the terms of Calvary – still, however, "a Son's doing", no longer in the merely legal claim but in fulfilment of a Fatherhood that was never an absentee.[18]

We are closest, then, to understanding the Sonship of Jesus in the "flesh and blood" realities through which the Gospels trace his path. What philosophers call ontology can come later when a Greek-minded church yearns to state this "sending" in the Father's mind, this coming in the Son's will, as a theology might formulate it. That yearning, and its fruitions, have their place. They affected the telling of the story, most markedly in the Fourth Gospel. But their warrant was, is and always must remain, in the deed and act of Sonship.

VI

It must be clear how this perception of things truly fits the language of Jesus about "the cup my Father gives", "the will of Him that sent me which I came to do", "no one knows the Father save the Son", "Father, forgive them . . .", "Father, into thy hands . . .". All these, springing from living situations, are the breathings of a society that might be told in the words: "As in heaven, so on earth."

That is certainly the import of the much-pondered passages identifying, at baptism and transfiguration, "the beloved Son". "In whom I am well pleased" is an obtuse translation if it is taken to mean some benign satisfaction as of a delighted observer. The meaning has to do with a congruence of wills, precisely as enshrined in the entire concept of "obedience" sought and brought. It tells of concurrence of wills in either part of a mutual intention, either party to a shared end. "To be well-pleased" is to find a mutual acquiescence of desire. There is a comparable significance in the word "well-beloved". The term "only begotten" in this context comes only in the Johannine writings and the Letter to the Hebrews, and there rarely. With "firstborn", it might seem to bring an abstract formalism into the active case we are making – no doubt the reason why the Creeds resound with it. It needs to be held firmly within the sense of a designer and the design, of the work that tells the workmanship, the architecture the architect. We will return to it in CHAPTERS THREE and FOUR, and its bearing on "not made". Meanwhile, we might almost contradict and say that the ministry and passion of Jesus were "made in God" and in the "making" Jesus humanly made of them. His "well-beloved-ness" was simply the seal of that eventfulness. A full Christology is better, and earlier, known in Gethsemane than at Chalcedon.

This sense Christian faith has concerning the divine-ness of Jesus in "grace" and, therefore, in "truth", in being who he was in the suffering he undertook, is no arbitrary thing issuing inscrutably from some diktat. It belongs inherently with the nature of God. That is why the Sonship has always to be traced back into the Fatherhood of its origination. How darkly do Shelley's lines distort it:

> On way remains.
> I will beget a son and he shall bear
> The sins of all the world; he shall arise
> In an un-noticed corner of the earth,
> And there shall die upon a cross, and purge
> The universal crime; so that the few . . .
> May credit this strange sacrifice, and save
> Their souls alive . . .
> E'en as a parish demagogue.[19]

They do so on two counts. They read all as some mere strategem where no heart was, and they scorn the world-inclusive-ness on which, in Christ, the heart was bent. Had Shelley lived longer there is no doubt his genius would have probed deeper and his ardour refined its quarrel with the Church. It was not only during and at the climax of his ministry that Jesus was vulnerable. His meaning has always been so since. It is the measure of his divinity that his Father also suffers the wounds of disesteem. That is should be so is further measure of their unison.

The thought takes us to the theme of vindication. Reading this active harmony of "God in Christ" from within the mind of Jesus, how should Messianic suffering relate to divine sovereignty? The question had certainly been present in respect of the suffering of prophet messengers. For when these incurred enmities and threatenings were they not bearing them instead of God? As proxy spokesmen the hostility was theirs for God's sake. Silence might have saved them but they kept faith with the word and so became victims. Thus their travail was vicarious, God being – as it were – a debtor to their suffering.

It seemed, therefore, imperative they should be vindicated. By the logic of Psalm 105: 15, "doing prophets harm" could not be tolerated. Even if only posthumously, God must "justify" them and their travail.[20] But in what terms? "Reprieve me" had been the bitter cry of Jeremiah.[21] "Prove us right" might be another. But it would seem that "the suffering servant" – or rather those who pondered the story – discerned a different vindication. It would consist in the undefeatedness of the truth in his witness. "In his fidelity the servant would live" in the sense that evil did not pass without rebuke, did not have the last word, did not escape the ultimate challenge which the sufferer made to it in resisting even to the death.

By such travail sin-bearers in their prophethood were vindicated in the community of repentant recognition they brought to birth. "We esteemed him not," men learned to say "and how wrong we were." Guilt saw its own image and the "servant" saw "of the travail of his soul". His fidelity was vindicated in that "not being overcome of evil", good could overcome the evil and release forgiveness to answer penitence.

This insight would pass into Christianity in the Pauline shape of "justification by faith".[22] Our immediate concern, though, is this perception in the Christ-experience of Jesus. Did his sense of suffering as "the cup his Father gave" see beyond it in these Isaian terms? Certainly, in the event, his disciples did. It would be strange to think that it was only by lights of their own they did so and not from his education of them. He used the "ransom" language. He spoke of "the good shepherd" whose patterns in the shepherding equation went far beyond the prescripts by which shepherds, in employ, were held responsible.[23] He was aware that popular Messianic expectations had place for a Messiah's future tense in what, as "pioneer", he might initiate, and that a "yet to be" might belong with a "This is he".

There has been much speculation about Jesus having moved towards the climax of his suffering in expectation of an immediate, even cataclysmic, vindication. We must take up the question among the cares of scholarship in CHAPTER FOUR. It has, of course, against it the hard fact that it did not happen and that the disciples – as we must see – if not serenely at least imperturbably outlived the disappointment of a non-*parousia*, or reigning-return of Jesus. That might suggest they had grounds from memory of him for their ultimate long-range vision of his posterity and of the kingdom.

We have the perennial problem of how far the Gospels have perspectives that do not belong to "the days of his flesh". With the dark apocalyptic warnings, there are reminders of "long patience" and "times the Father had in His own power" which it would be both faithless and impossible to know. It must always be a sane stance to take the consensus of the New Testament Letters as the soundest referent for "the mind of Christ", inasmuch as they were intent to share that "mind" as the clue to their whole being and belonging.

VII

Our study of the Christ-experience of this "learning Jesus" has its holiest duty in the event of the Cross itself. Most of all – what is the lesson of the loud cry: "My God, my God, why did you forsake me?" heard out of "a darkness over all the land"? How does it belong with the other words from the Cross, so confident, so gentle? Should that "forsaken" read: "Did you . . ." or "Have you?" Did the cry close a travail that gave way to peace? Or did it tell an unrelieved despair? If the latter, how did it belong with Luke's words from Jesus? Could it mean that Jesus in fact died in unrelieved anguish, as finally abandoned, disillusioned in "his Father", deserted in his entire Gospel?

There are those who read it that way, pointing to the abrupt, perplexed end of Mark's Gospel which has no other words to record.[24] In both Matthew and Mark, the saying is Aramaic (unless the vocative alone is Hebrew). As for Matthew, it seems clear that there is a close alignment of how he tells the entire story of Jesus with his manual of citations from the Psalms. Scholars differ as to which controls which. Is the narrative in fact conforming to where its author finds precedents apt? Or is the event factually requiring them to illuminate its meaning? The *lama sabachthani?* is quoted from the opening of Psalm 22 which, along with Psalm 69, echoes (or supplies) many of the circumstantial details of Matthew's telling of the Passion.

But Psalm 22 ends triumphantly and its opening words are not to be taken there as blank desolation. Confidence is latent, for Jewish idiom attested elsewhere,[25] in the very extremity of what seems to refute it. Such is the nature of the mind of Hebrew psalmody and prophet. With these Jesus was perfectly acquainted. He breathed their whole ethos.

Here, perhaps more than anywhere else in the Gospel record, "authorities" take what their predispositions induce them to read, and believers are not immune. It is part of discipleship to be ready to allow that situation, since it makes faith stay alert. Some have taken *sabachthani* to show that Jesus, having staked all on apocalytpic intervention, if only he precipitated it by self-immolation, found himself deserted, left to die in utter, frantic disillusion and defeat. Such readings have much to do reconciling their presuppositions with all that they ignore.

Some theologians, too, have latched on to *sabachthani* to sustain some real divine "forsaken-ness" of Jesus required by their arbitrary theories of atonement, holding Jesus as somehow divinely "scape-goated", thrust into a wilderness of wretched isolation from the Father. Contriving exegesis by their prior clues drawn from incongruous rites with animals and entrails, they make havoc of divine Fatherhood itself, and of "God *in* Christ", where a vicarious travail joins Son and Father in one reconciling grace.

We are left with the significance so well caught in the terms of the writer to the Hebrews, namely a Christ-learning that "trod the wine-press alone", where the experience yielded to the joy of a truly unbroken divine intimacy. Gethsemane had wrung from Jesus the plea; "If it be possible, let this cup pass from me." Possible it had not been. The human travail lay only – and only lay – through the divine purpose. How could he have ceased to be "the well-beloved Son" at any point, least of all where the vicarious experience reached, in death, its sharpest length, its fullest register as his in God and God's in him? "By the things he suffered he learned obedience." Only through the Cross was Christhood fulfilled.

If "Christ for the learning" is a theme well suited to the kind of exploration around Jesus this chapter has intended, plainly it awaits a variety of sequels. The first of them must be the accompanying "learning" of Jesus' disciples, their experience as companions, misconstruers, devotees and minor characters in the same drama. For a master who, seemingly, never wrote, they as his prime documents in evidence were crucial for all we know of him. Not only so, their human foibles, the tensions in their loyalty and the factors in their tragic desertion, are the steady accompaniment of the Jesus story.

Thought, then, must pass to that "first world of Galilee", meaning to have it inclusive also of the Jerusalem to which it led, yet also contrasted with the second world of the Mediterranean into which the New Testament record takes its way. There in turn a world of shores and towns, of itinerants and markets, of strangers and proselytes, had an education into grace, moving infectiously, if also precariously, through the mental and social landscapes of Greece and Rome. Church history ought not to want or assume some special status, immune from the doubts and pains of other histories. Indeed, how the church "learned" to be itself – whether, authentically, it ever did – must be one of the hardest explorations in history, monitored as it must always be by the theologians. The three following chapters have a hard ambition.

TWO

The First World: Galilee and Jerusalem

I

The famed Leo Tolstoy, supreme in Russian literature, was accused by his younger contemporary, Gorky, of arranging his own version of the Gospels in order to forget "the contradictions in Christ". Others, too, have laboured long over what they see as the enigmas in Jesus of Nazareth. We cannot hope to escape if we are intending to dwell awhile in the learning world of the first disciples in the Galilean movement which Jesus inaugurated. Galilee will always keep the honour of having been its initiating locality, the territory to which its founding memories returned and whose speech betrayed its origins when the wider Church was born.

CHAPTER FOUR will have to undertake the several issues of scholarship which must always attach to the formation of the Gospel narratives and to the portrayal they offer of the tensions behind their story. If it was a right instinct, in the preceding chapter, to read "Christ-experience" as the vital clue to the career of Jesus of Nazareth it must follow that the disciples' story has to be read as their would-be loyal yet confused responses to the central theme. If "the Master" was "learning by suffering", that crucial lesson could hardly fail to be – in their own terms and from their own perspectives – the central criterion for our understanding of his followers and the story as their school.

His being – but also coming to be – who he was through the actual sequence, and logic, of the encounters his ministry underwent was clearly in mutual relation to their companionship. It could hardly fail to be the vital circumstance of their discipleship. We have seen already how this was pointedly so in the crisis-conversation at Caesarea-Philippi and his "whom say you that I am?" The mingled confidence and confusion, ardour and consternation, of that occasion are read here as vital evidence of what was always latent in the disciples' response to his recruitment of them and its puzzling course. They were "his" and they were "with him", yet always by the cross-purposes of their perceptions and his destiny.

Mark, with his usual brevity, sees their vocation as being to "companionship and a preaching mission" (3: 14). The latter was always conditioned by the former and would be steadily enlarged by what the companionship entailed, and entailed most of all in its final seeming tragedy. Being "with him" by the Lake, among the crowds and in the Upper Room on either side of Easter, would forever inform what their preaching could attain to say. Throughout, it would be "the Gospel of the Kingdom", yet *learning* finally to know itself only through the trauma of the crucifixion as divinely underwriting the first exhilaration of the Beatitudes. It was about a "kingdom" which had its ethic in sayings, parables and sermons on the mount and in the plain, and found its redeeming warrant in the Gethsemane to which these took the master-teacher.

These, dovetailed in the mosaic of grace, together made "the first world of Galilee" the learning world it was. We have then to study how Jesus' experience of being the Christ shaped the experience of being discipled to him. They are two sides of the same coin in the utterly different idiom of the pioneer and the recruit. A "disciple" – as Latin says – is *in statu pupillari*. The story was the school, the school the story. The learning of the disciples moved with "the learning of the Christ", but only fitfully and through crises of perplexity and final desertion and discovery.

II

Our task with the Gospels is not to edit out the contradictions with Tolstoy, but to have their significance in full measure. The disciples' eyes are the surest way to see into them. For they were many. A divine "kingdom" and a "Messiah" to bring it into history were deeply Jewish hopes, yet there was about Galilee an intriguing "Gentile" quality. The Jerusalem élite felt they had good reason for considering Nazareth uncouth. The region, known as "Galilee of the nations", was characteristically cosmopolitan. One has only to note the Greek form of the names of most of the disciples, while *Petros* linked to *Simon* and *Boanerges* to the two brothers are eloquent of how much bi-lingualism there was in Galilee.[1] It is fascinating to ponder the likely Greek-usages of Jesus' speech, though the Greek Gospels treasure the memory of his *Talitha Qumi* and his *Ephphatha* in their actual Aramaic, so that the needed interpretation may signify how all belonged primarily with Jewry.

So the first irony in the disciples' education was the interplay in their whole story of Hebraic exceptionality and "Gentile" relevance. Gospel writing itself is involved in the tension – for tension, truly, it was. We have later to concern ourselves with the textual aspects of this issue between the Jew-centred and the universal, as New Testament scholarship debates them. It is clear from the context that Jesus' saying: "I was sent only to lost sheep of the house of Israel" (Matt. 15: 24) was not absolute, either in that context or elsewhere.[2] Otherwise, he would hardly have been "in the coasts of Tyre and Sidon", so far from Jewish populations. The query from his detractors: "Will he also go among the Gentiles?" (John 7: 35), whatever its provenance in John's context, hardly rides, even as gibe, with firm exclusion zones.

Moreover, that "certain man" refrain in so many parables in no way demands only Jewish shepherds, Hebrew housewives, wayward "sons of Abraham". It has about it the universal ring of the meanings it carries about repentance and grace. The anger told of Jesus concerning the cluttering of the Temple precincts had to do with "the court of the Gentiles", the area prior to the forbidding, and forbidden, exclusion zone to cross which was "pain of death" for non-Jews. To be sure, problems remain around the Jew/Gentile question during the Galilean ministry, to be decisively and finally resolved beyond the crucifixion in the entire openness of salvation. Meanwhile, the first world of Galilee was both apt context and apt pupil of the things at issue. The education of "Simon-Peter" and of "James and John Boanerges", proved to be as dual as their blended names.

For all its testing nature, this theme of the particular Jewish and the universal "Gentile" merged into a tension, bewildering for the disciples, around the parables of "the Kingdom" as Jesus told them. It might be described as a contradiction between the luminous and the scandalous. The stories were incredibly "down to earth" and had a sharp educative thrust, yet they were disconcertingly bold and adventurous. "Common folk" were both astounded and alerted to new stretchings of the mind. Could it really be that an "unjust judge" yielding, not to the nature of the widow's plea but to the nuisance of its reiteration, spelled any education into the nature of God or the meaning of prayer?

Or, what were hearers to make of a proposed analogy for "the king of heaven" in those often rapacious absentee landlords who sent servants to claim the fruits of their tenants' toil? Was not this an over subtle use of the Isaian similitude of Israel as a vineyard? As and when "the son" was sent because only the heir, and not mere servants, could represent the lord's right of possession which, by implication, the tenants were flouting in their treatment of the servants – could this be any proper imagery for the inner paradox of divine compassion?[3]

Or, again, in what sort of world could a bizarre defiance of market forces be tolerated, when an employer recruited "men idle in the marketplace" even at "the eleventh hour" and awarded them the same wage as those who had entered the vineyard at dawn? To make havoc of differentials and bargaining counters in this way, in the name of an idiosyncrasy of the heart, was to defy all economic laws in some fond and foolish transvaluation of values.

Or that canny steward astute enough to ingratiate himself with his master's debtors by adjusting their accounts – did all Jesus' hearers get the hidden point? "Selling" notional goods and agreeing to "re-buy" them at a future date and a higher price was a familiar way of evading the prohibition of usury and concerting loans and the "interest" they could yield.[4] The steward was merely acting on his boss's own connivance with a dubious ethic and not, in fact, robbing him. He had been legally "unjust" in the first place by consorting with his agent's guile. The accrued goodwill from the "debtors" had the virtue of sophistication. If they shared this virtue listeners to the story were regaled with an intriguing commentary on human subterfuge, told with a nice irony.

It is evident on every hand that disciples, and others, in that first world of Galilee, were in a lively school. What could they have made of a – supposedly Jewish – wayward young son getting as low as "the swine-trough" in the extremity of his hunger in a "far country"? The metaphorical distance was further still. Did they register the grim humour also? It was a humour latent also in the excuses of absenting invitees from "the great supper". Would one buy a plot of land and not first inspect it, or a yoke of oxen one had not first tried? As for "marrying a wife" – that might exempt a man from military service for a time but hardly from a banquet to adorn his protracted honeymoon and present his bride.

For all their evident earthiness, there was also a quiet subtlety about those parables. Jesus' hearers would no doubt be sufficiently aware of Galilean family etiquette so take the point of the father "entreating" his son, against all the usages between the generations. They would know, too, the difference between "a kid" and "a fatted calf", and between the "servants" who had honoured tenure and the "menials" paid by the hour.[5] They knew well enough not to build on the sand of a wadi liable to sudden floods, and how to savour the hyperbole about "planks" in the eye or millstones for sure submersion in the waters.

This was not a manner of teaching that sought refuge in the citation of authorities, drawing from the dust of ancient tomes. It lived and moved in the open air, from the sights and sounds of the daily round. It belonged with a world where housewives hunted for lost coins from their necklaces and merchants, by contrast, traded goodly pearls; where peasants might take out a neighbouring grudge by sowing a crop of tares. It could make even excrement teach the truth of "what indeed defiles". Nets and flocks, and sickles, sheep and birds, and lamps and weddings, were all occasions for truths through the imagination.

But it was finally the central theme of all this sage simplicity that was so arresting – that of the self-expending reality of God. "One there is who . . ." was the characteristic note, followed by the predicate, Aramaic style, of One forgiving, caring, providing or – in those terms – ruling and reigning. The faith concerning incarnation which the disciples were to reach concerning the person of Jesus himself, in the full retrospect of their experience, could be anticipated from the very manner and motif of his teaching. The words, like "the Word", belonged with flesh and blood, with the highways and the byways of the same Galilee. Both were about human means in divine ends. They would prove at length a single education, at once both luminous and scandalous – the former for its cogency, the latter for the human intimacies as the ready condescension of divine transcendence. God should be known, according to this Jesus, as the seeking shepherd, the waiting father, the patient investor, the generous host, the vigilant guardian. For all its surprising confidence and its seemingly daring analogies, there was often about Jesus' teaching a note of: "How could you not have known it so?" He took all warrant out of doubt, by the assurance of his own communion with God. It may have needed the strange theophany on Mount Thabor for Peter to declare: "It is good for us to be here . . ." yet, for "here", one might read the whole of Galilee.

III

Whatever they were *learning* in a mountain-top theophany, the three disciples were soon down again to all that was sordid and sullied in the plain. A distraught father stood pleadingly among their helpless comrades face to face with human tragedy: "Master, it is harrowing for us to be here!" said only in the mind. The company of Jesus was always strenuous. We need to probe to know in just what terms the disciples were enlisted and why they volunteered. Was there not a wry humour in that hearty comment to the fishermen: "Don't fear, Simon: you'll be catching men soon!" (Luke 5: 10)?[6] For persuading humans to faith is a far cry from taking fish in a net. The metaphor was only not remote in its aptness to the immediacies out of which their rugged quality was being recruited.

We have no record of the disciples preaching until they became apostles after Jesus' Resurrection. They were commissioned to "preach repentance" in the proximity of "the kingdom of God", which could, in some urgent but still cryptic sense, be dependably announced. They were, for the most part, a very local band with Simon's house (or was it his wife's mother's?) in Capernaum the first headquarters. There would seem to have been itineraries in which they were on their own. Otherwise, we find them on the road with Jesus. Their education proceeded in attention and interrogation. It is evident that they were throughout student-teachers only slowly assimilating inwardly what they were to echo around.

The themes themselves were about expectation. In varying degrees of intimacy, they stood in the tradition of John the baptizer but were aware of a different texture of discourse when they took up with Jesus. It was of something still awaiting definition, a meaning steadily unfolding and yet somehow also eluding them, a magnet to their allegiance while also a puzzle in their souls.

The urgency of repentance which had been John's exclusive theme they found carried forward into the positive redemptiveness that belonged symbolically with Jesus' works of healing compassion and was salient in the import of his parables. As, steadily, they companied with him on the roads and through the villages they became compellingly aware of kindling hope and a livening enthusiasm, checked by Jesus from time to time by warnings of sobering risks ahead. It seems clear from the record that they felt puzzled and chastened by these portents of the tragic.[7]

Eagerness and bewilderment conflicting in their education surely belonged with their ambiguous Messianic expectations. There can be little doubt that – for all its tentative confusions – the core theme of their discipleship, their recruitment, was Messianic. How else, in the entire context, could they have read what they saw and heeded what they heard? Yet the ambivalence both of their enlistment and its ideology was to persist right up to its resolution in the Cross itself, and how they came to their Easter.

One factor in that conjectural quality about them all lay in the individual contrasts they presented. They were a diverse group with Simon the Zealot and his possible fellow in Judas of the *sicarius*[8] readily consorting with Matthew the reprobate tax-gatherer. Their partnering together in feasible harmony is a clear testimony to the reconciling instincts of Jesus. It would seem that Thomas was the intellectual among them or perhaps the easily despondent. As for the fishermen, and the extended cousinry among them, they had the virtues of their trade – rough, ready and robust. While three of these formed the inner circle, others were obscure enough to need to be paired in calendars anon to merit mention.[9] It seems that the Messianic "banquet" figured at times in their waking thoughts.[10] Who shall say what was mirrored in their dreams?

This significant diversity and their rapid transit through the sequences of ministry taught and tested their perception of themselves and of their mission. The Gospels offer no record of how they preached when sent forth on their own. We are beyond the Resurrection when we hear from them as vocal. Returning, they were warned against being sanguine about their success. Meanwhile, being in his own society was meant as preparation for their ultimate mission into the world beyond the time and place of Jesus in "the days of the flesh".

During this time, it is surely intimate companionship and a certain mutual reliance we should understand and visualize in reading the Gospels. There have been film – and other – versions of a Jesus striding majestically ahead and mysteriously beyond the disciples and they in straggling intimidation.[11] That imagery may owe something to the Johannine portrayal, the implications of which are a concern of CHAPTER FOUR. Broadly, in the Synoptics, it is the education of comradeship that most marks the story. "That they might be with him", is the Markan formula as the warrant of their being "sent out to preach" (3: 14). As noted earlier, the "whom say ye that I am?" in the peak event in Caesarea-Philippi has to be read as no fond query but as a genuine consulting of their thoughts, their reading of the retrospect and prospect, of the arena from which they had withdrawn and to which they would return.

The quick assurance of Peter's reply betrayed the ardour of their verdict and its impercipience. Their experience of itinerant ministry, with its signs and sermons, was schooling them in only part of the equation. They had the theme but not its measure. They had learned the breadth of his significance but not yet its depth, the things Messianic that could be vocal, popular and gradual, not those of anguish and the night.

Already, and more sharply after Caesarea-Philippi, they were tense with their surmizing, strained by the risks they were running, the conflict of hope and apprehension. Even in Galilee, Jerusalem cast a long shadow. Is it here that we should seek the meaning of one of the great riddles of the New Testament, namely the "historical geography" of Jesus' mission? The Fourth Gospel is emphatic about an early, indeed a frequent, locale in Jerusalem on which the other three are largely silent, depicting a prime Galilean theatre and a Jerusalem climax. The problem as such we must defer to another place. In present context, it may be right to read a strategy of presentation in the shape of the Johannine story.

If we can assume that the fourth evangelist is consciously presenting an interpretative picture turning on the steady theme of Jesus face to face with confrontation – a picture "developed" (in a photographic sense)[12] only after retrospect – then his strategy brings Jerusalem into the frame almost from the beginning. The positioning is then the index to the focus. His reading of the Galilean accent in the Synoptics is that it was destined – for all its spring-like gladness – to be at ultimate grips with the harsh authoritarian reality housed in the capital city and the awesome Temple.

Such a view still leaves us with issues of precise history as scholarship requires them but historical portrayal is always more than chronology. Locale has symbolic as well as literal claim on mind. Things proleptic are involved. If, for example, those fishermen-disciples were recruited in terms of: "Behold, the Lamb of God", as John 1: 29–37 has it, then how could they have been so incomprehending about Jesus' Messiahship in the terms that Mark, Matthew and Luke present? The literalist will say: "You cannot have it both ways." Here is an "either-or". Not so the discerning reader, if we appreciate what the fourth evangelist is doing. The terms that would only *become* theirs in the sequel were already implicit in he to whom their first response was made in forsaking their nets to follow.

There are several other clear occasions of this quality of theological historicism in the Fourth Gospel. Whatever the precise data – if we can ever ensure them – about the ministries and sequences between Galilee and Jerusalem, it is evident that a "Jesus in mission" in the former is a "Jesus on trial" in the latter.[13] Our immediate concern is with how the two merge imperceptibly in the experience of the disciples. There is a deep and telling irony in the fact that when Peter is critically tested in Jerusalem outside "the judgement hall", he is interrogated about being "a Galilean". If the disciples had been echoing a summoning of the "heavy-laden" to a yoke, the crux of their own experience might be expressed in the same words.

IV

May we not then conclude that the story-school we are studying was a gathering initiation into self-sifting and self-awakening, a tuition through crisis into truth? Beyond the stress of inter-compatibility across diversity of skill and character, it is clear that the implicit Messianism provoked a climate of ambition, of expectations rich with personal possibilities. Impatience about delay in their fulfilment or misreading of their basic nature may well explain the tragedy of Judas to which we must return. Devotion itself was always at risk from its own fragility in them all.

"Can you be baptized with my baptism?" (Matt. 20: 22; Mark 10: 38): "You know not what manner of spirit you are of" (Luke 9: 55): "Why could not we cast him out?" (Matt. 17: 19; Mark 9: 28) – these were waymarks in their education. Informing all was the sense of status belonging to their destiny. Subsequently at least, it is evident that "twelve" had a mystique significance. Their calling, to that total, is in all the first three Gospels though John, in hallowing the number (6: 67, 70, 71 and 20: 24), omits a listing. Some echo of "the twelve tribes of Israel" could hardly have been serious to them *in situ* unless in wildly Messianic dreams. We may doubt how far they were alive to what, in his later portrayal, Matthew presents as a Moses on Sinai renewed and superseded in Jesus ascending "the mount" giving a new law as "his disciples came to him" (Matt: 5: 1).[14] Yet, clearly, they were in a critical *learning* situation where their own subjective identity was precariously at stake.

Plainly, too, there was hierarchy involved: within the twelve, the chosen three were Peter, James and John. Around these, if we can read from Acts 1: 21, "a whole group of men" were said to have "companied with the Lord Jesus" throughout the ministry and thereby qualified to yield a candidate for replacing Judas. It is clear also that there were numerous other, un-named disciples – "the one whom Jesus loved" (he would seem to be a late recruit and a Jerusalemite), the owner of the upper room, and the woman with the precious ointment, as well as named ones like Nicodemus and Joseph of Arimathea. Yet the sense of rank the inner circle had could not fail to confront them with the crucial mystery of all discipleship, namely how, at one and the same time, to devote – and yet also abnegate – the self within. The contradictions around the very meaning of their mission, entailed in the Messianic issue, only accentuated the desperate learning process.

It would ultimately engage them in an inward conflict with their exclusive Jewishness. The emphasis "Jesus the Jew",[15] so properly right in recent Jewish scholarship, involves the sharp question of its definition. Issues we have seen in CHAPTER ONE as crucial in the self-consciousness of Jesus – authority, the law, the Sabbath, covenant, divine magnanimity – belonged, with lesser clarity and, therefore, more distracting incidence, in the reckoning of disciples. The loyalty they brought was at times more dogged than undaunted and, in the end, "they all forsook and fled". "Finding rest" through "learning of him" could be no idle story. When the evangelist has Jesus telling them that they had "been with him in his trials" (Luke 22: 28) it was literally but hardly imaginatively true. That there was often a kind of mental absence in their very presence is clear on many counts. That the fact did not escape them was no small part of their burden. Was there not a sense in which they found Jesus un-followable, despite the earnest sincerity of their following?

It is the consternation they underwent from time to time which is here our concern. There had been an early occasion in the reading and the sermon in synagogue at Nazareth (Luke 4: 16–32). Lately broached in Capernaum, Jesus' movement had come to his home-town. The Nazarenes were roused to wonder about their "native-son". Reading from Isaiah 61 with its vision of "the anointed one" to bring good news of liberation, sight, healing, grace and jubilee, Jesus read himself into its meaning. The fascinated, rivetted audience hung on his words with glad surprise.

Their tribute of acclaim was rapidly reversed when, pursuing his theme, Jesus threw open the privacy of relevance they had assumed about its Jewish import. Provokingly, he reminded his hearers of Sidon and Syria providing solitary beneficiaries of divine mercy in the days of Elijah and Elisha, thus responding to their half-gibe, half-envy about his having made their Nazareth lesser than Capernaum. Their anger at a perceived insult fomented into near murder.

What "rest to their souls" were the disciples "finding" here? Exultation, doubtless, about the destiny of Jesus stemming from the pages of Isaiah, their rapturous enlistment in its programme and yet the stark evidence of its contradiction, its self-endangering truth. The disciples' side of the exchange at Caesarea-Philippi renewed the dimensions at that later point in a glad sense of goals and of his person as one hope, yet with a shudder of bewildered fear about the price.

At what point did they sense the *descensus Averni* ahead?[16] that their ministry would be read by history as prelude to a passion narrative? "Can Satan cast out Satan?" If so, how should his "kingdom stand"? The questions were answered by accummulating experience of the reality of evil. Their Jesus was plainly at odds with rigorism and, echoed by others as some of his precepts were, his teaching was under no illusion about an easy amenability of humankind to counsels of compassion or the law of love. There could be no refuge for his hearers in a legal complacence nor a satisfied conscience. "The kingdom of heaven" was no Utopian call. The revolution in his meaning would not omit the most revolutionary dimension of all, namely the "righteousness within". Evil was evil and would not be overcome by dreaming it illusory, or pliable to law, or neutered by precept, or subdued by writ, or negotiable by compromise. The forms in which it schemed its empire in men's souls and their societies were defiant alike of religious order and of covenantal status.

There were two striking experiences that underscored this truth of things – the first for only the chosen three, the other for the numerous following of Galileans. The one was the event on Mount Thabor, known as the Transfiguration and, with it, the heavy contrast of the scene into which Peter, James and John came down with Jesus from the summit. Faith, not to say history, has always been perplexed how to read this clearly pivotal occasion, recorded by all but the fourth evangelist, whose whole Gospel might be read as commentary (Matt. 17: 1–13; Mark 9: 2–8; Luke 9: 28–36). Jewish tradition was used to theophany – divine visions or insights in encounter with revelation. What was significant about Thabor was that, in symbolic converse with Moses and Elijah, supremely representative of law and prophethood, the theme was Jesus' dying in Jerusalem.

It was as if the unfolding logic of his ministry was being interpreted as the climax to those two structures of Jewry from which the Messianic meaning had derived. When the cloud – always the symbol of frontier on transcendence – dispersed "they saw Jesus only with themselves" – telling emphasis on the sole decisive role of suffering in the economy of grace. This law and prophet had foreshadowed but could not achieve by their precept and example. The world that then awaited Jesus and the disciples was *in extremis*. The vision was for a time to come.

There was no David on the Mount of Thabor. That name, however, rang through the acclamations at the Palm Sunday entry to Jerusalem – the other puzzling event and prelude to the Passion. Its drama surely brought together that long relation between Galilee and Jerusalem. This time there was no privacy of a chosen three. Rather disciples in multitude were on hand to register their possessive gratitude as they explained to the staring locals of Jerusalem: "This is Jesus, the prophet of Nazareth of Galilee." Their demonstration told, quintessentially, the outward ministry of Jesus – as Charles Wesley's hymn discerned.[17] For this was "a train of the triumph" of Jesus' active compassion, attesting his healing, liberating story.[18]

"Hosanna to the son of David coming in the name of the Lord." What did Jesus mean to signify by so uncharacteristic an invitation – indeed incitement – to public acclaim? Analysts and historians are no less perplexed than around the Transfiguration story. Was the cleansing of the Temple a desperate shift in policy, a deliberate provocation, a signal for insurrection, or – rather – an inclusive imprinting on to Jerusalem of the whole import of his teaching since that Nazareth sermon?

The surest clue is in the contrast at the day's end. Never was a demonstration more abruptly broken, more apparently aborted. We ask where Jesus was when night fell? back below the ridge of Olivet, a sort of fugitive, the excitement spent, the multitudes dispersed and the die cast for an issue totally at odds with the seeming of the morning. It is right, here at least, to read things by their sequel. Issues had been dramatically joined. In the midst of their keenest celebration of hope the disciples had been initiated into their deepest travail. One event had crowned their following and would register the entry on their anguish.

V

Before passing to that climax it is not enough to perceive it as having had its antecedents plainly all along. It is necessary to go back and read the other side of the coin in Jesus' steady nurture of the disciples in the art of prayer. For this communion with the Father – and its language – would become the secret of their capacity, beyond the trauma of the Cross, to grow into the apostles of the Resurrection.

The – for us – all too familiar "disciples' prayer", as we might more properly call it, came – according to Luke (11: 1) – in response to a request of theirs, stirred by his own example. "Lord, teach us to pray", they said in sequel to his own practice. His careful synagogue attendance was familiar enough by their sharing in it. The habit of personal devotion did not preclude the claim of public liturgy. Indeed, they had a mutual kinship. Yet the danger of ostentatious piety was plain enough from Jesus' parables about Temple worship and his dicta about the closed door and the private shape of soul-language. Learning to pray was a school of inwardness and it was, we may guess, on that score that the disciples sensed their need to be thus schooled.

The "Abba, Father" language of Jesus' habit in prayer is evident enough. Even in the darkest hour it did not desert him. It sprang from his perception of the divine solicitude for all things human, the outgoing-ness of divine compassion. It was the experimental meaning of his own sonship, the voice of a relatedness the Church would subsequently formulate in the faith of "the Word made flesh". All that this faith came to confess as the truth of him "in one being with the Father", which disciples could not then have identified in those terms, was nevertheless implicit in the Father–Son converse which was the hallmark of his ministry. The order of experience is always prior to the order of doctrine, because the prior order of being comes through the evidence of knowing.

That might seem to make Jesus' experience of prayer an unsharable thing. Yet, if the Incarnation is a truth of humankind as well as of God, then "Beloved now are we the sons of God" can be the hope and ground of all our spiritual learning to be articulate, with awe and ardour, in the divine presence.

The "Our Father who art in heaven . . ." the disciples learned from Jesus breathes exactly this assurance, this reverence, this discipline.

How endlessly it has been repeated, how devoutly expounded, down the centuries. "Forgiving and seeking forgiveness",[19] "bread" sufficing for "this day", and "Thine the kingdom . . ." – all are familiar enough, with the "hallowing of the Name" and – in "the kingdom" – the "doing of the will" to sanctify the whole. What is not always clear to us now is how far Messianic all these petitions are. The disciples, in the aura of all we have examined, must have read several petitions in a way that now eludes us. The three opening ones clearly fit into that context, with their yearning about that which is "not yet". "Thy will be done" – so often equated with "thy will be suffered" in passive submission – means precisely that caring compassion, that struggle against evil, which had characterized the ministry of Jesus.

The three clauses echo the Aramaic Prayer that concludes the synagogue liturgy:

> Exalted and sanctified be His great Name in the world He created according to His will. May He let His kingship rule in our time and in the lifetime of the whole house of Israel, speedily and soon.

In Jesus' prayer, "Our" – capable of inclusive, not restrictive meaning – suffices, we may wonder, to de-ethnicize "the kingdom", consistently with "as in heaven" about the divine will.

Yet, that the "happening" of what God wills should turn on humankind, should be a theme of their spoken willing, takes us squarely into that realism about evil which we see attending the whole story of Jesus. It is still further latent in the seemingly simple but sharply cryptic words: "Give us this day the bread of the coming . . .". The "coming" what? *epiousion* in the Greek. The word is unique and has a ring of futurity. Some have referred it to manna at evening and made a moral precept about dependence a day at a time. The separate word *semeron* for "this day" or "today" would seem to make *epiousion* unnecessary if merely translated: "daily".

Jesus said elsewhere that "his bread" was "to do his Father's will" (John 4: 34) or, reportedly as a boy in the Temple, "to be in his Father's . . ." (an open phrase) (Luke 2: 29).[20] If that "bread" or "meat" was the Messianic task, then this clause of the Lord's Prayer might be paraphrased:

> Let us know today as our very bread the work of him who comes in the Name of the Lord. Let us in expectancy participate this day in that which is yet to be.

Impatience might well misread that as hope to have the Messianic banquet without delay, exempt from all the task insistently entailed. If so, then "Do not bring us to the time of trial but deliver us from the evil" would at once renew the true perspective of present hope only found in present strife.

"Temptation" in the popular text is teasingly ambiguous. "Trial *qua* test" is the only sense and must be always held in firm tie with "deliver us from evil". For the two clauses must be seen inseparable. The hope of Messiah's coming was generally linked with an end-time of ultimate iniquity. It would be fatal if Messiah came before wrong was ripe for final overthrow. For then its worst would post-date his alleged victory and helpless awaiting would be left with a failed eschatology.[21] This pattern of thought explains the Messianic "Woes" – as they are known – which also echo in the Gospels.[22]

When we transpose such thinking from a mere time calendar the clauses "lead not . . . but deliver" can take us to the crisis – as in the ministry of Jesus – which belongs with redemption in the Spirit. Then "the time of trial" may be seen as perpetual but also as where, being "delivered" (i.e., "not overcome of evil"), we may "overcome evil with good". This sense of the Lord's Prayer belongs with the very heart of the crucifixion and finds its place in Paul's meaning in writing to the Romans (12: 21). For the "bread" of that Messianic "future" has to be also the "daily bread" that consists in "doing the will". It is in this way that their Master's ministry recruited them just as, after the Cross, it claims to recruit all.[23]

"After this manner, therefore, pray ye" has this unitary meaning with all else in Christ-learning. With that in place, we are free for all the other devotional meanings of moral duty and spiritual aspiration we catch from *imitatio Christi* in personal prayer. The New Testament Letters become in turn a school of prayer drawn from Jesus in his prayers of dawn and darkest night, his withdrawal to the hills, and domestic sanctuaries with shut doors.

VI

All the preceding via the preaching, the itinerating, and the praying as the school of the disciples brings us finally to the climax of the Passion, the experience of the Last Supper and the burden of Gethsemane. Here, the sense is of things grimly impending that Galilean fidelity, for all its dogged quality, could neither comprehend nor follow. The ultimate lesson of discipleship was to learn its own collapse, as the price of its renewal.

Collapse is epitomized where it is most tragic, namely in Judas, who "handed him over". It is well to remember that the Greek verb that gives us "traitor" also yields "tradition".[24] The meaning becomes sinister only in respect of the intention. Of that in the mind of Judas speculation has been baffled as well as baneful. The story of his exit from the final meal deepens the apprehension, enigmatic as it remains. The likeliest clue must be impatience at Messianic delay on Jesus' part, intensified by such manifest futilities as the anointing by the weeping woman. How could such extravagant and embarrassing emotion belong with the urgency of God's coming kingdom? The more entire Judas' devotion to the cause, as his criteria saw it, the more exasperating Jesus' failure to get its climax in hand.

It may be safe to conjecture that Judas calculated on provoking Jesus into active political decision by confronting him with a situation in which all would be at stake. If so, the realization that Jesus, once and for all, was not that sort of Messiah, would explain Judas' inconsolable remorse – the penalty of a fearful miscalculation. The kiss was the normal inter-male Palestinian greeting. In the dark it would help to identify and so facilitate arrest of the right quarry. But it could also have been occasion for some wistful appeal. The "innocent blood" he had "betrayed" was known such only on the far side of the Gethsemane Judas had neither shared nor understood. The words could only mean that Jesus was "innocent" of the militancy Judas had envisaged (by this reckoning) and of the cost to many it would have engulfed – as thirty years on (in the Jewish war) – the Zealots would show only too well.

By this light we can exonerate Judas of the charge of mere cupidity over "thirty pieces of silver". They can be read as a fee-pledge lest his resolve should weaken, turning a perhaps troubled volunteer into an accomplice. It was always difficult for the later Church to reconcile about Judas. For his more outright and obvious wrongdoing was a sharpened image of the desertion by them all. That bitter finale has to be read through the significance of the Passover meal.

All the Gospels agree on the event in "the upper room", i.e., the reception hall (cf. "the inn" in Bethlehem)[25] which an unnamed friend made available for Jesus. Interpretations, however, leave vital problems open. There is a brooding sense of crisis. Jerusalem is alive with rumours and a restless fever. Conspiracy is afoot. The ministry of Jesus has ripened, by its own inner logic, into ultimate encounter. The Passover has brought its ritual of "exodus", of collective memory through the emblems of deliverance. Are these somehow merged into the dimensions of the awaited Messianic banquet? Yet, why a meal, with bread and cup and blessing, where there is no victory – only shadows of defeat? The table acts of Jesus were familiar enough though scholars worry over whether the cup precedes or follows in the old tradition.

The essential theme revolves around a consummation of suffering on Jesus' part and of disciples coming to their ultimate despair. The table acts with bread and wine that will pass into the abiding Eucharist of the Church have their immediate context in Jesus' perception of what waits for him and in his disciples' initiation into meanings yet to be understood beyond their dereliction. The memory that will forever scar them has its interpretation in the given retrospect of the cup from which they drank. What, for both him and them, it anticipated it would also symbolically disclose. They would find themselves again by the tokens that marked their first deep incomprehension.

Readers familiar with the Gospels and the passion story may fail to remark their patent honesty. There is no palliating the role of the disciples. After the scuffle in the garden and the chosen three sleeping through the agony of Jesus, "they all forsake and flee". The plain, stark sentence spells a sentence indeed. Yet is it not as much bewilderment as disloyalty? How is a master to be followed who has no will to be aided and rescued in the only terms you understand? What conduct is proper, or feasible, when your Messianic hope is wrecked in its very core by its own exponent?

Peter is portrayed as staying around – not to share but to eavesdrop. Then his distance deepens into betrayal. His Galilean accent gives him away as belonging to where it all began and telling how now it ends. The bitter tears confirm the double anguish of a desertion compounded by denial. It is as if Peter's repudiation of all connection figures the confusion of all his hopes. "I know not the man" is loaded with unnoticed irony. In what eventuates he can in no way identify what he had from the outset awaited.

Other disciples, if less in focus, less compromised in word, are remoter still in craven dispersion. None are recorded as present at the crucifixion, except that Jerusalem recruit, the other John. Their absence is the eloquent truth of their self-abandonment as disciples. It is not only that in them Jesus forfeits loyalties: it is that loyalty itself is forfeit, being seared and withered in its very tasks. Christ-learning came to them only through the bitterest grief and what might have remained perpetual guilt.[26] How it was not so is the meaning of the Resurrection.

VII

The sequel here has to wait its full dimensions in the chapter following about the Mediterranean dispersion of the disciples, now "apostles". In turn the critical issues of that experience extend to CHAPTER FOUR. Here the only adequate measure of what followed has to be the depth of despair in what preceded. The Resurrection, as historically understood, can only be comprehended in the resurrection of the disciples – a resurrection whose antecedent was the total ruin of their vision and the devastation of their personal world.

It was a nadir so complete that the self-repossession that ensued could only have been as dramatic as the collapse, as evidently real as the guilt had been abysmal. This was the transformation the empty tomb epitomized. It is right to see it in those terms, rather than engage in the elucidation of a detective mystery. One may argue that no corpse was ever located (or so it would seem): surely an urgent and certain way of authority stifling the new preaching. That no such corpse-location ever happened might underwrite the story but would in no way underwrite or vindicate what the disciples became. At best it could be only a negative argument, yielding not relevant assurance, but only grieving perplexity.

As a symbol, however, a "not-there-ness" about Jesus and sepulchre, could readily be the language of a conviction rooted, otherwise, in the dawning realization of his followers that, precisely in what had so direly shattered their Messianism, Messianic reality had supremely transpired in "him crucified". The "integral" of their despair and guilt became the sure "integral" of their new apostolate.

How this discovery eventuated must be left in the silence where history has it – how the disciples rallied, mused, perceived and believed. The Gospels tell it in the conviction of his living presence identified by the wounds that first had been only the desperate index to futility. The narratives condense, invoke symbols of days and signs, through which we can read the essentials of realized Messianism moving with seeming swiftness and testing discipline into a world-sense of vocation and destiny. It was in them that the vindication of Jesus as the Christ had happened. The Gospel about him was itself a "learning" – a school that from Galilee to the garden and the Cross ushered its first sorrow-stricken, hope-born pupils into the education of the world.

There is in Jesus' admonition to Peter, according to Luke 22: 32, prior to the tragic denouement, an intriguing hint of this entire sequence. "When you have come round . . . give a hand to your brothers". The verb *epistrepsas* might be rendered – in the context of Peter's "sifting" – "when you have rallied, recovered" then "share your being 'stablished' with your brothers".[27] The from – and to – of that "coming round" was the credential, in them, of Jesus' Resurrection. It was set for an ambition into all the world. What they had realized was meant for disclosure to all.

THREE

Into Mediterranean Dispersion

I

A tuning fork might well be the symbol we need – a stem carrying two parallel arms whose vibration sounds the note the stem will strike. The great original is the Christ-event. From it came two derivatives extending from it and returning to it. Together they constitute what could not be, without them both. The one was the community of Christ-faith, the other the document of the Christ-story. They belonged together with extending time and place, the twin creatures of a wide dispersion.

It was a dispersion impelled out of experience of Jesus as the Christ, experience inherently creative of community and requiring to be told in text and thought. An ongoing history, seeking out to the Graeco-Roman world, was the setting for an ongoing education into the entire significance of a Christhood crucified. The apostolic Christ-learning found the opening world for its school. That world, as the due sphere of apostolic witness, gave occasion to the documentation by which the Church learned to know itself as community in Christ's truth. It happened in the forming of a literature by which it both possessed and presented him. The fact of Epistles and Gospels is evidence enough of this double situation and the clearest index to their understanding of Jesus as set to take in the world and how, so doing, gave itself the form of Scripture. Their believing was their going and their going their believing.

There are many open questions about early Church history. The gaps are serious, the hazards difficult. Some will have to concern us in the chapter following. It is no part of honest faith to overplay the hand due enquiry yields it in the interests of secure doctrine. What is not in doubt is that a destiny towards humanity at large was being obeyed and that, in this obedience, the impulse it had found in Jesus Christ duly learned his meaning. The New Testament text itself is proof enough of how taxing, how precarious this schooling was, how beset with human frailty. It was an education in which, in measure, the very pupils had to be their own tutors. That was part of the meaning of the Holy Spirit "guiding into all truth". In a careful sense, there was "a process theology", seeing that only as they went did they comprehend, only as they told did they participate.[1] The founding story, from Galilee to the Mount of Olives, had to be cherished for its defining quality as vital for the undergirding of the extending discipleship in the widening circle. Living memory being a diminishing treasure in the passage of time, memories-in-text had to take its place. The oral had to find a way into the written, the written into circulating recognition. Community was both the matrix and the means. There is no more eloquent clue to the nature of Christianity than the context in which it scriptured itself and the impetus by which it did so.

II

Through all that must remain conjectural or hidden in this story of the early Church finding itself in learning its Lord, two motifs emerge beyond all question. There was a reaching into a theology concerning God and humankind proper to the fulfilled Messiahship as identified in the whole person of Jesus and the drama of his story. There was the joyous, yet hard, vocation to make good an inclusive people of God. The first meant wrestling with the "wisdom of the Greek" which, for all the paganism of popular Greek religion and the cults of the Roman world, was the primary intellectual context of apostolic mission. The second meant translating the heritage of "Yahweh's chosen people" into the new idiom of a "peoplehood" in which the stubborn, harsh Jew–Gentile distinction no longer obtained.

It would be possible to assemble all the traumas and tensions from Matthew to John of Patmos, the strains in the Fourth Gospel most of all, under this double destiny. Both tasks were likely to be stressed by vagaries of passion and perplexity, the wiles of prejudice and aberrant enthusiasms. The first was prone to the pitfalls of speculation, the partisanship of sects. The second gave occasion to controversial pride and the obfuscation of clear issues by wilfulness and contention. Controversies are always ugly when consciousness is at war with interpretation. Where things old are entrenched things new go hard with them. The early Church had its growing pains precisely where its antecedents had their vested interests. It could only make its way with the painful reproach of its hinterland in Jewry. The anguish for all parties around a new peoplehood in Christ was only the more acute for the fact that its main mentors and architects came from the originally "covenanted nation".

Given that a time-and-place expansion was the context of the documenting of Messiah Jesus – or at least of that faith concerning him – it may be well to take the geography first and the theology second. CHAPTERS ONE and TWO have already set the Messianic theme in focus in its prior to dispersion terms. We can have the New Testament literature duly, in sequence to the travelling story from "Jerusalem to uttermost parts".[2]

That the faith was set for "telling to the dispersion" was inherent in its Messianic conviction and in how it had "learned its Messiah". The heart-question was whether this telling was for the widespread Jewish dispersion only, or whether it belonged, of right, to the "Gentiles" and belonged to them in a way that made that term of discrimination irrelevant and obsolete. Given that the tellers were, initially, all of Jewish birth, the issue was essentially an inter-Jewish one. What is sometimes seen as "anti-Semitism" – as for example in the Gospels according to Matthew and John – is not such in any modern sense. It stems from a tension between Jews as to the significance of birth and circumcision *vis-à-vis* "the Gospel of the kingdom". As such, it could not avoid to be sharp and heated, reaching – as it did – into the very soul of Jewry.[3]

That an exclusively Jewish dispersion, already wide and richly Hellenized, was a vital positive factor is evident enough. Its relevance could later be enshrined in The Letter to the Hebrews. But it was also a powerfully adverse one, as is clear from the tribulations of Paul. All around that Jewish diaspora was the "Gentile" world, abounding in "proselytes" drawn to Jewish mores but deterred by the – to them abhorrent and appalling – ritual of circumcision, a sort of "identity by mutilation".[4] The converse of that feeling lay in circumcision being a badge of pride for Jewry.

Apostolic Jewry – for such it was before there were any evangelizing, as distinct from evangelized, "Gentiles" – had perceived an inclusive Gospel ignoring the Jew/Gentile divide. The decision, and the controversy, are written deep into the New Testament. It was intellectually and emotionally costly for both parties, both those who would include the "Gentiles" and those who would perpetuate their exclusion. Its being a deep infra-Jewish anguish – and in no way a contra-Jewish thing – is undeniable.[5]

Why should it have been so? Answer has to take us into a long *mise en scène* of history and theology, to the Exodus, the covenant, "chosen-people" status, "the fathers" and Sinai. These were a *privilegium Judaiorum* never to be yielded into any larger, fuller magnanimity of Yahweh, who was their ethnic patron, their exclusive mentor and their guardian Lord. This defining conviction by which Jewry knew itself was ensured against all self-scepticism by being essential for "Gentiles" themselves. For only by its inviolable perpetuation could "the nations of the earth be blessed". Any notion that specialness might be transcended would mean that "Gentiles" also forfeited their best – indeed their only – hope of "light" and its benediction. It would do the non-Jewish world no good, no favour, were Jews themselves to rethink or ever relinquish their exclusive significance as Yahweh's only people. Nor, in Judaic terms, could other people aspire to, still less attain, some comparable role as "light to other nations". In both its interior and its exterior meaning the destiny of Jewry was *sui generis divini*.

It might be fair to say that Jewry has never really resolved the "Gentile" theme. Apostolic Jewry at the birth of the Christian Church did so by perceiving an ongoing Jewish particularity participating in a new inclusive "people of God" and doing so undiminished, except in one dimension, namely that a divine "servanthood" could now belong with any and every human ethnic, territorial and linguistic identity. "The nations of the world" might "bring their glory and honour into the kingdom" – as they had never done before. Israel could prove the pioneer of open "peoples of God" and this would be the true fulfilment and confirmation of its ancient identity.

In the event, outside apostolic – and thus Christian – Jewry, ancient Israel did not read it so nor permit the reading. At stake were two radical issues – the one deeply theological, the other tragically historical. The former involved the understanding of monotheism. Many, in the Jewish tradition, have insisted that in fact the ultimate monotheism belongs to the Jews only.[6] Only they, in covenant terms, "know and worship" Yahweh for the reason that only in the Jewish context is Yahweh "known" – or indeed "knowable" in that the intimacy which is "immediate" to Jewry only alone affords authentic "knowledge".[7] But could that mean what Nietzsche once called "monotono-theism"? Or is it not in fact, monolatry and not monotheism at all.[8] For if the Hebraic: "I will have no other people but you" is the counterpart of: "You shall have no other gods but Me", then monotheism itself seems in question. For must not the "Oneness" of God mean the oneness of humanity under God? There is a questionable "unity" where there is a divisive distinction within God known *qua* Sinai and God *qua* non-Sinai, between the covenant of Abraham and that of Noah, between "the people of the land" and dwellers outside it.[9] That cannot be "one worship" of "the One worshippable" where thus radically differentiated. Has Jewry, in this sense, been monolatrous all the time in saying: "Blessed be the Lord God of Israel."?

That vital theological issue, needing to be frankly faced, underlies the founding Christian perception of a Messiahship, a divine "agency in history", required to be humanly inclusive in its scope and import.

According to Acts 15: 11 we find Peter, as a Jew, saying: "We believe that we (Jews) shall be saved even as they ('Gentiles')." "We even as they." Not simply: "They as we . . ." as though it were some inherently Jewish thing condescendingly bestowed on others, not some truly universal thing belonging to all by equal right, Jewry most emphatically included.

Given this truly inter-Jewish issue in earliest Christianity, it is confusing to talk, at least until well after the Fall of Jerusalem, of any "Gentile" monopoly of the faith that spread into diaspora. Such "Gentilizing" came by the end of the first century and into the second, partly by Jewry turning away from a profferred destiny through the trauma of Temple forfeiture and partly in response to the claims on its integrity from the ministries of Greek culture. Even after those developments, it is evident how Jewishly solicitous the faith was – witness, for example, the Matthean Gospel in its passion for citations from Hebrew Scripture to sustain its case. Some of these are suspect for their ingenuity. Even so, they witness to an ardour for a Jewish credence. It has been surmized that the evangelist may have let a hand-list of passages shape the very pattern of his authorship.

This honest care about the Jewish dilemma is even more expressive in the Fourth Gospel, with its highly structured and self-aware authoring, whereby its episodes offer a "spiritual" presentation, reflecting essential issues in a serial depiction. In CHAPTER THREE the Jesus of the evangelist's cognizance is narrated in conversation with "a ruler of the Jews". This "Nicodemus" intends to relate to Jesus in terms of teaching, of ethics and Torah in a purely Jewish context that is affable and discursive. He is abruptly told: "You must be born again." It is seldom realized how "out of order" such words were between two Jews. For Jewish birth had already set Nicodemus within the covenant. That assurance was itself being directly challenged. "We shall be saved even as they," that is, by the universal work of grace.

III

Saul of Tarsus is clearly the pivotal figure in the New Testament diaspora as the biographical embodiment of its tensions and travail. It is well to come to him and his emotional burdens from two retrospects. The first is how entirely Jewish – as we have learned in CHAPTER ONE – was the interface of divine being and divine doing, via human agency, and how ripe this theme was for the "hypostatic" formulation that Greek thought instinctively recognized in it.[10] To this, via "Gentilizing" of an inherently Jewish Gospel, we will return.

The other is how far burdened, even perhaps embarrassed, were the great Hebrew prophets and some psalmists with their covenantal peoplehood and "elect" identity, how wistfully they dreamed of some universal human-ness under a world-yearning Yahweh. A tribal deity had truly become, in their reckoning with human space and time, a "God of all the kindreds of the earth". "Look to Me all the ends of the earth: for I am God," Isaiah 45: 22 has Yahweh crying, while 49: 6 has Him telling "His servant" that "exalting the tribes of Jacob" would be so far "a lesser thing" than a mission of "salvation to the ends of the earth". Psalm 72 visualizes a Messianic kingdom that will be acknowledged by a well-nigh universal celebration of "dominion from sea to sea . . . to the ends of the earth".[11] It might almost seem that the Jews had gladly foregone their prized particularity, their cherished privacy as Yahweh's only people.

Yet these visions seem always to have been checked by a throwback to their instinctive ethnic and mental differential as something instinctive also in their God. Or there lurked the ambivalence as to whether "salvation to the ends of the earth" had to do with a wholly Hebrew dispersion, a bringing home of the scattered "children of Zion". Were those Yahweh-worshipping "nations" authentically now "His people" too or was it that they were summoned to acknowledge some Hebrew coronation of a Davidic successor, as was the case with the strangely strident Psalm 2?[12]

That issue, often hard to resolve, is ambiguously captured in Psalm 87 – often hailed as the most signal celebration of inclusive peoplehood under God.

> His foundation on mountains of holiness Yahweh loves . . .
> I will declare Egypt and Babylon as among them that
> know Me. Behold Philistia and Tyre, with Ethiopia
> This one was born there. Each one shall say (of Zion)
> He was born in her.
> The Lord shall declare when He writes down the peoples:
> This one was born there.

Do we understand that Yahweh is registering these "alien peoples" and counting them as having Zion for their birthplace? Or is "this one" a prince of the royal Jewish dynasty whose accession (or right to it) is being heralded? Should we read a vocative: "Look, Philistia, Tyre etc. this Zion-born one you are to salute in tribute"?[13]

It was this deeply Jewish, sharply Biblical issue that New Testament Christian Jewry – the first disciple-apostles of Jewry – finally and categorically resolved in favour of the-all-people-inclusive grace and sovereignty of God, of God in Christ. They did so out of the prerogative they believed they had to do so from the meaning of Jesus as Messiah.

We need not wonder that what had been a tense theme for prophet and psalm while it was glimpsed but unresolved, became an even more sharp and agonizing argument once resolved in New Testament terms for which there were "no more Gentiles" but only "fellow citizens in the household of God" (Ephesians 2: 19). "Saul, who is also called Paul" became the unique, yet representative, focus of that trauma of re-written, still continuing, Jewish identity and, is therefore, central in the New Testament literature. By the same token, he is the most readily maligned and distorted.[14] His Jewish credentials have been scouted and his logic impugned. Yet the integrity of his "Gentile" mission is proven beyond all doubt by the fervour and the tense arguments by which he affirmed his Jewishness. To explore these is to penetrate to the heart of Mediterranean diaspora "in Christ".

The famous Damascus road narrative, three times repeated in the Book of Acts, whatever the issues attaching to its details, embraces the heart of the Messianic theme and, with it, the impetus towards a world faith both in the personal destiny of Paul and in the larger Church. The drama of his persecuting zeal may, perhaps, be overdrawn – like the hyperbole about "the chief of sinners"[15] – but in "the heavenly vision" there is a double theme that rings insistently true, namely Messianic identity in Jesus *and* its extension into the infant Church

Saul's psyche is gripped by a fervid hostility to the Christian claim as to "Messiah crucified". By the "pricks" metaphor it is clear he is resisting misgivings infiltrating his antagonism. Inward struggle against them only intensifies his zeal to quell them. It is not seldom that a suspect passion grows the more adamant lest it should capitulate. The arresting voice from heaven exactly fits this psychic situation. Was not Messiah supposed to be "riding on the clouds of heaven"? Thus *where* the voice originated would have caused any pious Jew no shattering surprise – only great adoring wonder. But *who* the voice identified was utterly confounding, disqualifying all Saul's ardour, overwhelming his psychic world. "I am Jesus . . .". Whatever the blinding flash, this was the disconcerting truth. The words came from where Messiah should be: they belonged to Jesus.

Discerned in post-traumatic terms this was the essential faith-crisis. Messiahship had been attested in the crucified Jesus through a truly Jewish imagery and ambience.

The crucial point was underwritten by ". . . whom you persecute". Saul's ardour against the Jesus–Messiah story was continuous with the Cross in which that story culminated. There was this ongoing identity between the suffering of Jesus and the community of faith in its meaning. For the whole exchange had been opened with the question; "Why are you persecuting me?" – a leading question indeed! since it anticipated where Saul's returning enquiry would convey him: "Who are you, Lord?" – the quarrel in Saul's whole journey, the clue to an inner revolution.

There is no need to argue further how and why this Saul/Paul experience launched his sense of mission and directed it into its Mediterranean dispersion, its intention for the "Gentiles". Their inclusion in *this* Messiahship – as we must argue in more theological terms later – was determined by the sort of Messiahship it was. But the cost to Paul, both in the soul and in the mind, was agonizing. To portray him, as some have done, in renegade terms as a blatant "Gentilizer", is never to have known him as the agonistes he truly was. Nor is it to have known the stresses of the straining, even strained, logic by which he strove to cling to Jewish exceptionality and reconcile two loyalties in Christ.

The yearnings that find voice in Romans 9 to 11 – so evidently an interlude in the sequence from 8: 39 to 12: 1 – may not succeed in holding together "this Hebrew of the Hebrews" and "this apostle to the nations", but they fully attest the integrity that made them one. The imagery of "the olive tree" (Jewry) and the "grafted-in wild branch" ("Gentiles") is oddly contrived in that the main root is (temporarily) "rejected".[16] There is a similar curious anomaly in Galatians 4: 22–23 where Sinai – and presumably its covenant (exclusively Isaac's Jewry) – is "Hagar" to be cast out. Meanwhile the Abrahamic people, via Isaac and Jacob, find Sarah's people now to be the profusely "Gentile" progeny of grace. Yet was it not for an exclusive, single Sarah-progeny that the actual Hagar was sent to languish in the desert? To align Sinai with Hagar was a strange reversal of roles. Yet, if here and in Romans 9–11, Paul tied himself in ingenious knots, which have had unhappy mystifying consequences, it is only a measure of how intense the Jewishness of his inclusive mission. "Truths of imagination", as S. T. Coleridge insists, require mere logic to defer to them.

Nor is Saul/Paul a solitary in the inter-Jewish dialogue. The Johannine New Testament tradition is comparably a discourse about the very destiny of Jewry. It could not be a Gospel and be otherwise. So often read as "anti-Judaism" it is more rightly seen as intra-Judaic discourse.[17] This is not less the case because – perhaps in the mood of Malachi 1: 11 – it is reaching for engagement with Plato. For such intellectual duty was part of the very dilemma of Jewish exceptionality. Nicodemus we have already noted. That "once-for-all" Jewish birth theme, so personal to him, is found inclusively shaping the thought of the Prologue. "Children", or "people", incorporated as "God's", are such – according to 1: 12–13 – "not by human womb and wombing" but "by faith in the divine Name", such faith being accessible to all the diversities of humankind as the sole condition of inclusion. "As many as received . . . them . . ."

The entire notion of "divine peoplehood" is copyrightly Jewish. It remains for ever – and Christianly – in place. But it is now de-privatized. On both counts, affirming it so could not fail to constitute an inter-Jewish debate as to what could warrant it and whether – so warranted – it could keep its Jewish provenance. The radically Judaic character of that issue is not diminished nor deniable by the obvious fact that what would come more strictly to be denoted as "Judaism" was itself in formulation by the very presence of the issue at its heart. When, by the trauma of the years of the Jewish Revolt and its aftermath, mainline Jewry opted for the rejection of Pauline/Johannine reading of Jewish fidelity, it would be odd to call the situation "Gentilizing" except insofar as "Gentile" preponderance in New Testament faith inevitably followed from such Jewish opting.

The usage "the Jews" in the Fourth Gospel requires note in this context. "Waterpots of the Jews", "salvation is of the Jews", "a feast of the Jews", "the Temple where Jews always resort" (2: 6; 4: 22; 5: 1; 18: 20) denote an entire people. Elsewhere, as in 7: 11, 9: 22, 18: 12 *et al.*, the term clearly relates to a more official or sectarian grouping bent on pressing their hostility to the length. When 19: 20 notes that "many of the Jews" read the inscription over the Cross, since the place was very public, it would seem to intend both categories. Were the inner-circle ones the more angry because Jewish "kingship" was placarded incongruously in Greek and Latin as well as, mockingly, in Hebrew? If so, Pilate's irony about what was "Jewish" would be the more complete.

For "what was Jewish" stood sharply at stake then and later, though the Evangelist is writing from within the tensions that persisted when it had become more categorically clear that "his own received him not". But it was some of "his own" who had thought and said that "Receive him they should". Christianity, like Jesus himself, came from a Jewish home. When, in the last book in the New Testament the seer of Patmos ponders "the new Jerusalem", the old formula is there of "God and people" but now an open humanity. "The tabernacle of God is with men and He will dwell with them and they shall be His people and God Himself shall be their God" (Revelation 21: 3) When he comes to doxology the same emphasis is clear in the deliberate – otherwise unnecessary – profusion of terms – "kindred and tongue and people and nation" (5: 9; 10: 11; 14: 6 *et al.*). There must be no mistaking the inclusive newness, the new inclusiveness, however reluctant Jewry might be.

The loved Pauline formula "in Christ" has the same provenance. Grammatically a "locative" it signifies that "the place of the Name", the rendezvous ground, is no longer territorial but historical. It has passed from a land and/or a city: it has become an event, the Christ-event, where the locale is of divine encounter and so, in turn, of authentic worship. In this conviction, all lands are equidistant from the Cross in that all are severally near.

Further, the unison figured in Paul's vision on the Damascus road informs the First Letter of Peter and the Letter to the Hebrews, namely that the suffering of the Lord extends into the suffering of the Church. "Why are you persecuting me?"[18] This meant that the same paradigm had to obtain. The memory of the Cross, far from being an incentive to hostility, had to be taken for a clue to the things undergone by disciples. If their faith and theology had been shaped by its meaning, so also must be their conduct and their ethic. "Christ suffered . . . leaving an example . . . you are partakers of Christ's sufferings . . . as Christians, glorify God in this name" (1 Peter 2: 21, 4: 13 and 16). Hebrews 2: 9–11 and 13: 12–13 make the same point in their own distinctive idiom.[19] All is in line with the prime case made in Philippians 2: 5–11, the *Carmen Christi* and early credal/codal liturgy.

> Let this mind be in you as it was in Christ Jesus, Lord . . . wherefore work out your own salvation . . .[20]

When, in such terms, the first Christian faith was "Gentilizing" in its geographical expansion there is no doubting the Jewish fidelity with which it did so. If it could seem to be jeopardizing, or even betraying, the original "chosen-ness", in truth it was prospecting for it a new destiny and doing so in good hope.

IV

"In good hope", and also in good faith in that its reach into "Gentile" society was resolute about ethical loyalty to Torah concepts. So much of Jewish demur about conceding a new destiny sprang, not merely from retention of privilege as being the only acceptable loyalty, but from fear for the proprieties of human behaviour – moral, social, sexual and personal. Had not the analogy of "pearls before swine" been used by Jesus himself? Even if circumcision were ceded as "the mark in the flesh", ought the norms of Biblical behaviour to be put at risk from the vagaries of "Corinthian" licence, the crudities of pagan idolatry, the libertinism of a lusting society?

It is clear from the Letters in the New Testament that the new movement shared those concerns but had a lively faith in the "salvation" it preached, a confidence about the redeemability of all humans and the sufficient availability of divine grace. It had due cognizance of the human reach of evil in the criterion of the Cross itself and was under no illusions about our human perversity both of mind and will. But part of its evidences in Christ was that this perversity did not reside unilaterally in any single culture nor was any culture uniquely exempt. That realization was the counterpart of its foregoing of "chosen-ness", "chosen-ness" not as a vocation but as an unshareable prerogative. It did not adopt a Jewish condescension towards "the good Gentile" in "the life to come", but had him participating in the here and now in divine service with acceptance before God.

If "whoso-ever would might come" then "whoso-ever came might attain". The emergence of Christian leadership in a context of pastoral nurture explains the epistolary shape the first Christian literature has. Groups meeting in individual homes and involvement in a much travelling world required mentors and monitors, men and women who could attest their migrating members as *bona fide* and take note of the credentials of those similarly commended from elsewhere. The beginnings of Christian ministry, and then hierarchy, were practical as well as conceptual. Hence, too, the habit of apostolic address by circular letters whereby diversity could, in some measure, be disciplined and inclusive community around local grouping be realized.

Even here there were significant Hebraic continuities. Divine "peoplehood" could inherit concepts of structure and order, not now in "twelve tribes of Jacob" but twelve "apostles of the Lord". Its Gospel meant that this new society must organize its discipline around the given Christ-event, even as the other had derived from Sinai and covenant. As it aimed to do so under the taxing constraints of its expansion it brought doctrine and morality together so that believing legislated behaving. This we have noted already in the *imitatio Christi* theme in 1 Peter and Hebrews. It is built into the more treatise-like Romans. Reading Chapters 9–11 as a parenthesis, it is evident that the clarion call of 12: 1: "I beseech you, therefore . . ." resounds from the ringing climax at 8: 39 where doctrine ends in doxology – as such doctrine always must. Yet doctrine and doxology can only continue in discipleship, where alone they walk in sandals and energize wills and think in minds.

If it is fair to think all the kindred of the Letters doing so in Jewishly moral terms, it is only with a realism *vis-à-vis* the "Gentiles". We can discern it so in the New Testament in three realms, namely the rescue from idolatry, the defying of Emperor worship and the translation into Greek terms of the Hebraic theme of "divine agency" in human history.

V

Intellectually, the New Testament dethroning of idols was no problem. The doctrine of divine unity and the Biblical theme of an ordered creation fitted to a human "dominion" left no place for a superstitious "demonizing" of nature nor for tribal deities of local patronage. Emotionally, among traditional pagans, the liberation from idol-tyranny was more strenuous. Idol-names were in common parlance: streets carried them; oaths were made by them; shrines abounded to them. Market practices of meat-slaughter spelled anxiety for the timorous.

To all these realms of soul-bondage the Gospel brought a robust mastery. The implications of divine unity were borne in upon pagan minds not, by and large, like the "philosophy with a hammer" of Nietzsche, but a gentle weaning away from fiction and fear.[21] The Thessalonians "turned to the living God from idols" (1: 1–10), emancipated into a new allegiance. The closing verse in the Johannine Letters bids the readers to "keep themselves from idols". In between these first and last passages on idols came Paul's firm but gentle handling of "idol-meats" in 1 Corinthians, and the warning in Colossians against esoteric sources of false worship. According to Lucan versions of apostolic preaching in Lystra or Iconium or Athens there was vigorous disavowal of credulity at shrines, whether crude or philosophic (Acts 14: 11–18 and 17: 22–31). Most dramatic of all was the celebrated encounter between Paul and the silversmiths of Diana in the theatre at Ephesus (16: 19). These craftsmen knew where their vested interests lay in the prestige of their city's patroness and how inimical to her, and it, and them, was this Christian Gospel. Then there was the careful ruling of the Jerusalem Council to the "blessed uncircumcized" that "they keep themselves from idols". In this dimension of their Jewishness the apostles kept good faith with their Jewish Decalogue 1, 2 and 3. For the erstwhile superstitious a radical faith-crisis was soundly negotiated.

There was a similar tenacity in face of Emperor worship. Unlike continuing Jewry developing its Judaism, the Christians enjoyed no *religio licita* status. They were, therefore, under obligation to acknowledge "deity" – in some sense – in the likes of Nero and Caligula. Their rubric, according to 1 Peter 2: 17 was: "Fear God, honour the Emperor" – in that order. As a small despised movement the Church was in no shape to challenge imperial power – and in no will either. Deferential subjects they were ready, as well as obliged, to be. From the Passion of their Jesus they knew how much could be at stake – or at risk – in the justice, or injustice, of the Empire. But, by the same token, they were determined to "let God be God" however much Emperor-worship might be read as no more than a political fiction to be equated with citizen loyalty. But the rights of God were paramount. Hence the long trauma of the persecutions. Again the new community fulfilled its defining Jewishness.

VI

The third demand on mind and spirit of the Mediterranean dispersion belongs with what is so often held against nascent Christianity, namely a "Hellenizing" that involved a forfeiture of Jewishness. There is need of patience in disentangling this knotty contention.

The two preceding chapters have pondered the Messianic setting and implications of the ministry of Jesus and the shape of the disciples' final awareness of him in Messianic terms. The antecedents were squarely in the activism of Yahweh (if we may so speak) according to Hebraic tradition. We noted the constant theme of divine "agency", means employed by Yahweh for divine ends consistent with His character as His people's guardian, patron and sovereign. These – His "capacities" – were historically operative in His people's experience. There had been, crucially, the Exodus and the land entry and, at length, the Davidic kingdom. All were perceived as sure tokens of His "presence" – a term, like "face", somehow other than the ineffable "Name" and yet the same. The Hebrew mind was not given to mental curiosity concerning how Yahweh at work and Yahweh as "being" related within Himself.

It is fair to say that the Greek mind was so concerned. While Greek religion was chaotically pluralist, needing the Christian corrective of a sane theism, Greek philosophy loved to enquire, to prob discursively the meanings it received whether from the senses or the intellect. Moving from its Jerusalem/Palestinian locale across the Aegean and beyond, early Christianity was required to translate a Messianism of inherently Hebraic provenance into the heritage of Greek metaphysics.

Such "Hellenizing", far from betraying things Hebraic in their Christian form, was serving the very core of responsible integrity. The task might be captured in the two ways of reading Exodus 3: 14. The point, as the context surely requires, is a pledge about action: "I will be as there I will be".[22] Only in the Exodus will the God of exodus be known. There can be no advance guarantee, only a call into trust. In that sense the famous words are a paradigm of the entire Hebraic tradition – waiting on the fidelity of Yahweh, even without rime or reason other than His being Yahweh.

For every Greek instinct, however, the "I am that I am" formula could not be repressed or ignored.[23] The Socratic mind, with its *Sapere aude* ("dare to think") loved to press discursive reason whereever it might lead. The faith about God in Messianic action, taking itself into the Greek world, could not escape the obligation to subject its divine activism to enquiry about divine being. If "the presence" was there in a history: how – metaphysics had to ask – was "it" there in eternity?

If divine will and word had been activated in events, in creation and redemption, how did they belong with the Logos, the principle of heavenly reason underlying all things? If, as later times would think to say, Christianity was a Platonism for the masses, the Hebrew/Christian Messiah could not fail to find due interpretation among Plato's heirs in that first Christian century and beyond. The "going into all the world" which the faith understood to be its duty was more than geographical travel. It had to be cultural immigration. To talk of "Hellenizing" as if it were some betrayal or distortion would be to deny – or simply to mistake – the inherent world-measure that belonged with the Messiahship of Christ crucified.

For, in the reading of it that generated the Church, exclusive or private assumptions had been rescinded and left behind. "Christ crucified" did not mean an eschatology of which one might still dream.[24] Nor an apocalyptic for an ever-receding future. Nor was it an élitist vision fulfillable only for an ascetic community immured in the desert. Nor was it a political passion bent on national autonomy. None of these would have had cause to obey a preaching vocation across all human frontiers. All would have been immersed in their own privacies of hope or destiny. Supra-Jewishness belonged to where "all might be drawn to him".[25] Yet precisely in that quality, as we have seen in CHAPTERS ONE and TWO, Messiah Jesus had been a supremely Jewish event. It follows that its essential, effective relevance to all – if it meant "Hellenizing" – also meant Jewish/Christian sincerity, in keeping faith with the impulses of the Greek mind. For these surely had their place in the economy of God.

The question whether it is right to have the Messianic theme as truly the central clue belongs to CHAPTER FOUR below where it constitutes the very core of the familiar issue between – as the phrase runs – "the Jesus of history and the Christ of faith". For the present the very terms "Christian" and "Christianity" suffice to indicate in what capacity worldwideness happened and from whence it came.

One important factor in the *sapere aude* of the Gospel in apostolic Jewish hands and among "Gentiles" was the presence of various sects of Gnosticism with their esoteric "wisdom" and the cult of dying and rising gods. There is controversy as to the precise dating and diffusion of their lore and influence. Alongside the "dare to think" in a Christology that kept positive faith with Greek thought, there was the duty to guard that Christology from gnostic-style aberrations incompatible with genuine theism and, in cultic terms, a source of endless confusion. The emerging Eucharist in its sacramental meaning, as well as the integrity of theology, were endangered in this Gnostic context, as the Letter to the Colossians explains.

One serious aspect of Gnosticism, at least among Docetics, was its fondness for mythicization, calling in question the historical order of event, in time and place, seen by the Church as central to faith. Hence, in due course, the credal emphasis: "Very God of very God", to rule out the twin notions that the actual could never be in truth the spiritual or the spiritual incarnate in the historical. By any Christian reckoning "charade", or "fantasy", or "supposition" about "God in Christ" would have been the denial of God and the death of Christology. One could not have the faith of "God in Christ" without the entire inter-relevance of God and Christ. It was precisely that conviction which Gnosticism, in both its cults and its concepts, crucially disputed, and – precisely in resisting it – Christianity among the Greeks affirmed its Jewish loyalty.

How then, we might ask, was it "foolishness" to them? Not – the answer must be – in its Logos-theology of "the Word made flesh" but of that Messiah "crucified". The more they might be capable of learning about a "Logos" in history, the more incapable of allowing "the form of God" (using the language of Philippians 2: 5–11) taking on "the form of a servant . . . obedient unto death on a cross". On either count, it is the Messianic theme according to Jesus and *via* the Church which determines all else. What can be in glad negotiation with a culture proves to be also in radical dispute with it. The encounter anywhere is always critical.

VII

The engagement we have been studying of the nascent Christian faith with the "Gentile" world of its Mediterranean dispersion prompted sustained engagement with its origins. It is immediately obvious that the New Testament is only about origins because it is about consequences. It has Gospels with a story because it travels in mission outside their place and beyond their time. Messiah as Yahweh's "agency" has to be interpreted into philosophical minds, via *hypostasis*, as expressive of God only because a time and a place are perceived to have "staged" that self-expression.[26] If Christians are saying that God used the ministry and the Cross of Jesus to define Himself, then a travelling Church needs its documenting literature. Thus the need for, and the origin of, the four Gospels belong squarely with the event of expansion. Time meant the lapsing of contemporaries of Jesus, the passing of an apostolic generation, the possible dimming of memory. The world clearly owes the record of the words and work of Jesus to the going-out of the Church from the place of its genesis in Jesus. For only so were records both possible and necessitated. The Achilles heel of all dispute about "the Jesus of history" is that it depends on the literary traditions it purports also to discount or despise.

Debate is deferred to CHAPTER FOUR over how this Church-perspective affects, for good or ill, the documentation it contrived. That Church issues from Asia Minor and Europe and from the decades of Gospel-formation influence the Palestinian portrayal is readily absorbed into any critical Christian confidence in its own texts. If perspective – undeniable as it is – was the one the prime event had itself created, it may well be the one most likely to be right. Caveats and contraries we can await. In present context, it is enough that divine "agency" at work in Jesus as the Christ is known through divine "agency" at work in the world as continuity through memory and memory into continuity. The Gospels are both the root and the fruit of mission.

Likewise, and no less obviously, the Epistles are a literature of dispersion and – only so – a literature of emerging discipline and authority, and so, in turn, of structure and unity. With the Gospels they give substance to the concept of "the body of Christ". For this is discerned as the ultimate "temple", "the place of the Name", and thus also where "members" belong, meet and pro-exist.[27] That will to solidarity reaches back into where it knows its debts are. Hence, for example, Matthew's frequent citation of Biblical passages and the habit of the Hebrews Letter to recruit evidences of Hebraic ancestries.

But all is now quite de-territorialized away from the old sense of a "promised land". Jerusalem is only nostalgically loved.[28] All is now quite de-ethnicized – witness the tensions in the mind to have it so. The New Testament itself is a Greek language book. Its whole shape, casual as it must often seem in its provenance and pattern, conforms in that very quality to the journeying – and journeyman – circumstances in which it came to be the thing it was.

Through all there is no mistaking that it was perceived Christhood in Jesus that took mission into the world and firm conviction about Christhood being in one crucified and risen which energized the movement in face of its great odds. If it is inapt to call Jesus "the founder of Christianity" it is due and right to hold Christ-Jesus as "the mentor of Christianity".[29] It was not in terms of an itinerant Galilean miracle-worker that Jesus had his way to Philippi and Rome. We do not hear of Hanina ben Dosa gathering disciples to a breaking of bread in Thessalonika or Corinth.[30] It was not as a wandering charismatic that

Jesus was hailed in the Philippian *Carmen Christi*.

Pliny, the diligent Roman governor in Bithynia, during the second decade of the second century AD, reported to his Emperor Trajan on "a pestilential sect" that met before daylight and "sang hymns to Christ as god",[31] and thanks to whom, as he reported, temples were largely deserted. They were law-abiding except in terms of Emperor worship and, if they bound themselves by oath, it was to hold themselves free of crime, abstaining rigorously from adultery and theft.

It was thanks to such as they and to what had scattered them so far that we savour the Beatitudes at all and can educate ourselves in the wisdom of the Parables. The new "Torah" of the Sermon on the Mount reaches us only by way of the crucifixion of the preacher. The creed has sure reason to name Pontius Pilate. For his was the verdict that sealed the climax that launched the story that made the Church. The teacher Jesus inherited his global world as the Saviour Christ. The New Testament sense of "one people of grace", indifferent about circumcision and fully accessible to faith, was owed to Messiahship as Jesus had lived and died his patient learning of it.

VIII

"His global world?" Does the New Testament not require us rather to say "his western world"? We come finally to the strange irony of a Scripture about a world's redemption that confines itself, almost totally, to the Mediterranean dispersion. That there were other diasporas to Egypt, to Numidia, Armenia, India is evident but the New Testament is Europe-tied. It makes for a strange anomaly, canonizing only what is westward. The Ethiopian in Acts 8: 39 may have gone "on his way rejoicing", but into what future, what sequence in life?[32] The story seems meant to confirm how central was the Messianic theme and to link Christ with "the servant" in Isaiah but could this high official have been left to a churchless, individual discipleship? Luke ought to have been more thorough.

If this situation is not the usual "riddle of the New Testament" it remains one.[33] Perhaps we should think of it as analogous to Jesus never writing so that we have him – as Master and Lord – only in the "These presents"[34] witness of the New Testament writers, Pauline, Johannine, Petrine and the rest. They are his "mediators" to us evermore. Comparably must not the shape of western dispersion, its vicissitudes, its lessons, its paradigms, suffice for us as vehicles and precedents for what dispersion of the faith in all other directions faced – and still faces. Given the three languages of the inscription at Golgotha, the "Hebrew,

Greek and Latin" of the placard, there was perhaps a certain justice in faith's missionary sequel into the cultures they served. That can only be, however, if such triple particularity in faith's document-as-scripture from Galilee to Rome is taken as symbol and servant of what can only belong with "the uttermost parts".

From this final perplexity, and through the primary emphasis we have laid on the Messianic theme as where the clues must be, we have left ourselves with large liabilities. The faith-crises we have studied in three chapters open out into the long cares of New Testament scholarship through two late centuries. To these CHAPTER FOUR belongs before giving way to a miscellany of ventures through belief and unbelief where "learning" and Christ have strangely come together.

HERE AND SINCE

FOUR

In the Cares of New Testament Scholarship

I

The title of The Acts of the Apostles is initially reassuring. Their travels, adventures and teachings, to be sure, but "acts" has a decisive ring. The word is so akin to "facts". But what of these, if Church history is not to enjoy advantage or privilege over other history? And what of the "facts" of the Gospels with the "fact" of the Gospel and then the issue in the same word "Gospel" denoting both the singular thing itself and the fourfold records of it?

Three preceding chapters have remitted far-reaching problems for which good faith and sound scholarship have to undertake due liability as tests of integrity. That liability has been extensively explored in "criticisms" – textual, historical, literary, sociological and doctrinal – prolific in industry and ingenuity in the last two centuries. It is hard to think of any academic territory of similarly limited dimensions so thoroughly and meticulously scrutinized as these Christian Scriptures. Indeed, the sedulous activity seems at times almost to revolve inventively around itself. The whole, however taxing for the unprofessional mind, is at least evidence of a will to honesty whether informing belief or unbelief, sober reliance or radical agnosticism.

Two recent centuries were in no way innovative in this activity. It is false to think of "ages of faith" that modernity has left behind. Ever since the dubious Thomas, incisive minds have probed Christian faith and tried to love the questions if the answers seemed elusive.[1] What is new about the modern "cares" is that they have been advantaged by new techniques of science, by gathered resources of archaeology, not least from the Judean desert, and by more refined sophistication in the disciplines of a proper criticism. It is fair to say that the New Testament has thus been an area of faith-crisis more strenuous and far-reaching than any other Scripture.[2] There have been total casualties, conviction-wise like Friedrich Nietzsche, partial ones like George Eliot relinquishing doctrine while still wistful about ethics, and buoyantly retentive ones like Robert Browning. To him we come in CHAPTER SEVEN but can here savour him as a genial example of Victorian response to misgivings about New Testament faith.

After quitting the intolerable crudity of a perspiring evangelist and wandering through the high splendours of a mystic, mythic Rome, the poet takes himself on Christmas Eve into a lecture hall in Halle – is it? – or Göttingen. Clearing his throat, a bespectacled professor proposes

> . . . tracing back into Christianity . . .
> Inquiring first into the various sources whence
> This myth of Christ is derivable,
> Demanding from the evidence
> How these phenomena should class?
> Whether 'twere best opine Christ was,
> Or never was at all, or whether
> He was and was not, both together . . . understanding
> How the ineptitude of the time,
> And the penman's prejudice, expanding fact into fable . . .
> Had by slow and sure degrees, translated it
> Into this myth . . .[3]

Browning had a robust resilience of his own to survive that "Professor's grave voice". Hardly so Matthew Arnold in his now celebrated "Dover Beach", written on his return from a European honeymoon and likening the receding tide of faith to the ebbing waters silvered by the moon rising over the naked shore.

> The sea of faith . . .
> Retreating to the breath
> Of the night wind down the vast edges drear
> And naked shingles of the world.[4]

Even so, elsewhere, in tribute to his famous father, Thomas, he could go "on to the city of God", beyond "the bound of the waste".

There were other reasons via Darwin, Sidgwick, Bradlaugh and Huxley for the erosion of Christian faith but uncertainty about the shape and theme of the New Testament was a major factor. There was a curious irony in that even those who had no "desire to be breeders of heretics" nevertheless held that beliefs did not merit compassionate protection.[5] Thus they contributed to misgivings either way, no less than the most destructive purveyors of aggressive doubt.

The story of explicit or implicit agnosticism concerning the Gospels – Paul, John, Peter and the rest, their Letters and their themes – is complex and confused. That the faith and the Church had documented themselves in a hazardous way was evident even on a cursory view. Some of the factors have been with us in CHAPTER THREE. From Matthew to Revelation, the New Testament was not from an engineer's drawing board nor the product of an authorial synod. It belonged with the road and the working day. It derived from community and memory, from storied retrospect and pastoral discipline. Aspects of it were as haphazard as the meeting of friends and the impulses of a beleaguered society. Its formation occupied turbulent decades cherishing receding recollection and slowly letting it distil into collective nuclei of tradition, citation and narrative, both retentive and vulnerable. Fidelity forbade caprice but could not ensure uniformity. Imagination now needs to listen for the silences and bring a discerning eye to a fascinating heirloom, whether of Gospel content-in-context or of apostolic correspondence. The whole speaks from ongoing community shaped precariously in a hostile Roman and a contentious Jewish world.

These circumstances, as the hinterland of the scriptural documenting of Christianity, we have earlier reviewed. They require us to love the questions they set us. For they belong to more than scholarship. Yet scholarship must neither disclaim nor diminish its business with their credentials as being, in truth, all we possess whereby to identify Christianity.[6]

Even casual readers soon realize that the first three Gospels (in present order) are "synoptic" having much in common as well as significant differences. Who then relied on whom? Did all rely on something antecedent, now "lost" in what they present? These three, further, have very strange compatibility with the fourth, so idiosyncratic and perplexing in the different Jesus it depicts. Yet it clearly ties into much of the same history and – for all its distinctive aura – *is* a gospel and not a theosophy.

But, further, why *these* four? Others exist but were not allowed into *this* New Testament. And those *ad hoc* epistles – how do they constitute "Scripture" from heaven, being merely letters to sharply local situations? Why is the single figure of Paul so dominant even if we concede that some writings, like the unattributed Ephesians, are more "pauline" than Paul's? How reliably does The Acts link the two worlds of gospel and epistle, being itself so selective or eclectic, so negligent of things it could have included? And what can anyone wisely make of the Revelation on Patmos to conclude a testamentary whole?

The more the questions press the more they make us realize the kind of task that scholarship faces. With so much in hand contributory to so much more that remains unknown or imprecise, it is vital to locate the essential witness, to identify the defining significance. Only so can we contain the open questions that must remain such. Only so can we bear with the loose ends of inconclusiveness on minor points at issue. That this situation is compatible with the very nature of faith confirms it as also congenial to the documents of faith. If, finally, "the Word of God" is Christ and only derivately the Scripture, then the sundry questions about "synoptic harmony" or default of it, about the strange distinctiveness of John or the bias – if such we find it – of Acts, will be carried in and by the larger whole.

The familiar disciplines of synoptic study, for example, form criticism, redaction criticism and narrative criticism, strive to detect source tradition, owed maybe to prior texts, but discernibly identified by comparing the texts we have. Or by redaction, editorial nuances or attitudes may be located and assessed. Or by narrative criticism we can move away from such fragmentary treatment and conceive of a more inclusive authorship at work beyond the piecemeal items.[7]

Such fascination with Gospel formation and the making of Acts in their familiar shape have fulfilled a necessary duty but only inside a whence and whither of what existed to be "scripturized" at all. What is found in words found words for itself. What we can meticulously study as "record" arises only from what we must perceive originating it. How the Scriptures are – as all due criticism takes and finds them – ensues from why they should emerge to have the shape, and the problems, they do. The more incisively we mean to assess them, the more crucially we confront Christ, not thereby begging the question of faith but knowing where, for good or ill, faith finally comes home. "These are they that testify of me" (John 5: 39). Is not this precisely why concern with the document as Scripture has so often constituted a crisis of faith? It follows that the ultimate confidence must be *via* the text but *in* the Lord between its lines. Those whose trust is in what they hold to be the central clue will be wisely open to all they may gain from the scholarship that does not share it.[8]

II

The "learning" theme has already made clear that this central clue, the heart of all else, turns on Messiahship. It is there in the very name of the nascent faith. It is crucial to the cumulative course of Jesus' ministry. It is continuous with the underlying logic of prophethood in its experience of rejection and adversity. It was clear from the sequence between Amos and Jeremiah how vulnerable to enmity, how "crucifiable" the prophets were as the conscience and mentors of a wayward and obdurate society. Their woundedness, actual or mental, could hardly fail to register, *via* "the suffering servant" theme – for all its riddles – with Messianic anticipations, however prone these were to political or national triumphalism. Moral suffering, vicarious heart-ache over human wrong, "a wounded spirit", were hallmarks of that great prophetic tradition. Through all its moods and accents, the Messianic hope concerned the same divine vindication, the sovereignty for which prophethood yearned and suffered. It could hardly fail, therefore, to anticipate a comparable. cost.

We have seen earlier how this line of spiritual logic also belonged to the "learning" by Jesus as the course of his ministry renewed a similar pattern of *antilogia*, of "contradiction". Seeing that "ministry" – charismatic, wandering, "sign-bearing" or however we opt to characterize it – was pivotal, Messianic implications could not be absent from it. Yet, in whatever terms present, they were at risk to multiple popular misconception and in need of radical correction.

It is true that much New Testament study has been sceptical, if not dismissive, of this – in present context – central clue. It is all, of course, bound up with the familiar formula concerning "the Jesus of history" developed, distorted or distanced into "the Christ of faith". That very formula, nutshelling all else, captures the point. If "faith" is entailed it is about "the Christ": if "the Christ" is truly had, it is faith that has him. Making Messiahship central as key to "the Jesus of history" resolves the problem in the formula by accepting it as an equation in the making. "The Jesus of history" emerges into history, in the final event, as "the Christ of faith", seeing that "a Christ for faith" was potential and present in that Jesus.

"An equation in the making" is a phrase that aims to describe a potential in a process. Both are germane, either to the other. "The Christ of faith" *came to be* seen as such – that being the process. Its happening fulfilled the potential in "the historical Jesus". That an "equation" existed to be "made" deserves consideration, on any count, even by those who find reason to disown it. For what things ensue from antecedents *may* be significant indication of what those antecedents were, though giving these no exemption from investigation. It might be cynical to observe that "Jesus preached the Kingdom of God and what came of it was the Church". But if he was *duly* called "the Christ" and "the Church" "Christian", cynicism would have to be dismissed from the comment.

It is worth noting that the phrase "the Jesus of history", whatever revisions, riddles or scepticisms it presages, is caught in the same dilemma as high Christology – or low. For "history" in the clause is always ambivalent. Do we mean what – as we say – "actually happened" or do we mean what historians say of it?[9] For "saying" is always reporting or interpreting "what happened" from the historian's perspective. If we want the "actuality" we had better simply say "Jesus" (though even this will attract some agnosticism). For adding ". . . of history" will at once entangle us in our own verdicts, whether they posit a mere charismatic, an itinerant healer, a wandering ascetic, an ardent Zealot, or an unfortunate maverick. Be it F. C. Baur, D. F. Strauss, A. von Harnack, Albert Schweitzer or Geza Vermes – all move in their parameters and what they take to be the referents of the "history" they are both relating and shaping at one and the same time. This shared situation gives the "equation" that New Testament "faith as to the Christ" made (as a "Christian" Church itself coming thus to be) no immunity from the countering it has from these other verdicts. For they, in "un-making" its "equation" are no less caught in the ambivalence in the two senses of "history". None are exempt from the instincts of their own selectivity. We have to resort to asking about the instincts most attuned to the actuality.

Was it not out of this disputable "equation-making" that Rudolf Bultmann was minded to move radically out of history altogether and take refuge in an existentialism that willed "the Christ of faith" to be authentic, aside from all the "whether or nots" of history? These could be discarded as irrelevant. It need not matter who, how, whence, whether Jesus really was. Certainty would be for ever elusive. It need not matter to conclude as narrators or historians. History, being so open to debate, so far always at issue, could never be taken as a proper venue for faith. Theology must assert its independence of historians and opt – as knowing itself a life or death commitment – into the decision of faith. It must find in the *preached* Christ the only ground of faith. It must do so in response to the inner personal need to decide. For life did not admit of perpetually open options.[10]

In so far as the Gospels (pl.) mattered in relation to the Gospel (sing) Bultmann's thought moved, not from Jesus to Christ, but from Christ to Jesus. The Gospels (John's least of all) did not give *historical* warrant for the Christ-*kerugma*, the theme of faith. Contrary to the case we are making, the "Messianic" in Jesus did not lie in his "learning" ministry or its factual sequel. It lay in its proclamation by the Church, in a Christology that summoned humanity to belief as answering the predicament of all existence in its yearning for faith-anchorage. Only in the word of preaching did Christ meet the human world. What we have in Scriptures are "testimonies" on which we must rely. They are not "sources" by which we might be persuaded after fair examination.[11]

This malign twist to faith-crises purports to relieve the mind of the textual cares we are accepting. As such it spells a pseudo-exoneration. It cannot disembarrass us of the Gospels in the embrace of an existential Gospel of only a preached Christology. It does not itself escape the toils of history.

Whether or not we vindicate the process, we have to enquire how this all-in-preaching arose historically. It found existence before it encountered existentialism. To be sure, legitimacy of faith is not wholly in the lap of history.[12] There are truths of the imagination. But the Creeds were rightly explicit about events "under Pontius Pilate". We cannot be satisfied to say that Jesus was historical only in his influence (identifying that "influence" as being in the *kerugma*). It is precisely what we see his influence to be that confronts decisions of faith. The Gospels and Epistles, anyway, are replete with time and place. They have their *mise en scène*. It was these that preaching itself had to interpret and commend. How, for example, could the preaching of the Cross be negligent about the measure of the antecedent trial? Had Jesus been, as Vermes thinks, simply acting misguidedly, doing "the wrong thing, in the wrong place at the wrong time",[13] how would we have at issue "the sin of the world" – so crucial to the very preaching of the Cross?[14] If "the historical quest" is doomed to failure, preaching of its climax must be a pretentious illusion.

That will not mean that "quest for the Jesus of history" is set for indisputable success. The faith-principle Bultmann enthroned on the preaching comprehends the whole story and the bond between them. Beliefs indeed do become "facts" in themselves – facts of the situation, that is. They cannot do so in indifference to the events out of which believing came. A confessional faith is one thing: faith only confessional is another. Bultmann's crisis-of-faith solution returns us to history, to how and why Jesus/Christ, faith/history, could be conjoined. We are back to Messiahship.

III

Here it is well to note how insistently Jewish perspectives on Jesus, in long regarding him as the "renegade" possession of misguided Christians, have also turned away from the Messianic theme. Prominent modern Jewish exponents of it tell us that Messiah identified must mean Messiah betrayed. So Martin Buber, while Gershom Scholem, revered historian of the Messianic idea in Judaism, interprets it as a "perpetual futurism".[15] Messiah never "comes" so that he may be forever awaited. The concept is a symbol of perennial hope – but only hope. Apart from 20th-century Zionist and political Messianism (in whatever terms secular or religious Zionists perceive it) Messiah has broadly receded from Jewish thinking. In something of this disinterested mood, Geza Vermes writes, of the Christian Scriptures, in terms of

> . . . all their subsequent theological colouring about Messianism and redemption still allow(ing) a genuine glimpse of a first century AD Jewish holy man, portrayed as a preacher, healer and exorcist delivering special moral exhortations concerning the impending arrival of "the Kingdom of God".[16]

The "Messianic", then, is "Christian colouring", as such to be "discounted" as the aberration in a "pocket book" of "myth", to be classified as such by "a single-minded search for fact and reality . . . undertaken out of feeling for the tragedy of Jesus of Nazareth". "Historical and linguistic analysis of the titles borne by Jesus in the Gospels" leads Vermes to "prophet, lord and son of God". "Messiah" is not among them – though he is appealing to the Gospels.[17]

Unhappy reductionism as this stance is for the Christian mind, its avoidance of Messianic centrality, in line with other Jewish thinking, is closely relevant to the vital "historical quest". Geza Vermes has contributed to it with acclaimed erudition and sustained industry.

However, he insists that there are two incompatible pictures of Jesus in the Gospels, namely the picture just quoted and "the religious speculations of the primitive Church".

> When one sketch is super-imposed on the other, it becomes clear that they have hardly anything in common.[18]

One would need to be reluctant so to conclude if one had any adequate place for the Messianic in the ministry, passion and death of Jesus. It is a strange position to hold about "Jesus the Jew" whose Jewishness was never in intelligent doubt. The phrase leaves the specific Jewishness of Jesus (for there are many shapes and accents) in question and, with it, the Messianic theme.

Being "religiously detached", and finding virtually no interface between "charismatic holy man and exorcist" and "the Christ of Christian myth", Vermes opts unilaterally for the first. Figures like Hanina ben Dosa from that 1st century Galilean world, and its "popular charismatic Judaism of prophetic derivation", are taken as sufficient to underwrite and establish a verdict on "the Jesus of history" exactly in parallel – though "incomparably superior . . . in profundity of insight and grandeur of character". The caveat itself relies on the Gospels' evidence.

Questions of Messiah aside, this radical solution to "the Jesus of history" raises sharp puzzles of its own. Obviously we are not troubling ourselves concerning "the Hanina ben Dosa of history". To ask why we are so troubled concerning Jesus must bring back the Messianic theme as the terms in which history wrestles concerning him. Even in discounting the Gospels as plagued by bias, Vermes, like all "quest of Jesus" writers, necessarily appeals to them. Only by these Christian "learners" were the priceless teachings and parables made available for admiration. The denigrated source itself becomes priceless for what it conveys.

It is true that Vermes and his peers believe they have established adequate alternative sources to the Gospels, from which to pursue, widen and deepen the search for Jesus in his time and place. Their scholarship deserves to be gratefully saluted. But do their Judean desert – and other Judaic – findings require to be so confrontationally deployed against alleged Christian mythology? Can all parties not transcend the things emotive that colour language and spell derogatory signals?[19] Even more importantly, are there not several features from the scholarship of "The New Schurer (*History of the Jewish People in the Age of Jesus Christ*)" – the seedbed of Vermes' other writings – that could align with the Messiahship so central in the Gospels?[20] The "prophetic derivation" he traces for his characterization of "Jesus the Jew" would far more pointedly belong to a suffering Messiah. Had the healing, the exorcism, the enlisting of disciples, the journeying features – which the Gospels fully portray and in no sense discount – no Messianic implications? Could "the Kingdom of God" lack its signs and tokens? Even negatively, these in their popular impact could have brought much more trouble around Pilate's ears than a bother in a courtroom, had Jesus chosen to employ them in mob-arousal. Might that non-development in the story indicate a Messianic issue actually resolved in terms firmly unpopular and deeply Isaian?

We are not intelligent about the whole hinterland of what came to be the Christian perception of "Jesus the Christ and him crucified" (the hinterland, that is, in his active ministry) except as incorporating those very features Geza Vermes identifies. Rightly related to what he ignores or excludes they have legitimate place. What they need for legitimate integration is the Messianic perception.

A brief parenthesis is needed at this point to preserve the case from obtuse confusion. It concerns the so-called "Messianic secret" in Mark, which has been used to suggest that Messiahship was only affirmed after the Resurrection, and had no native place in the actual story.[21] Its alleged absence is explained as "kept a secret" by Jesus from the disciples. The assumption is that Messiahship had no place in sources Mark used, that recognition of it was post-Easter and that "secrecy" – in some sense – accounts for why the disciples, earlier, had been so uncomprehending. On this score, weight is thought to be added to the view that Jesus as "the Christ" – subsequently written into the Gospels – had in fact no place there. Thus the case would be strengthened for "a healer-teacher" Jesus and steered away from Christology. Then the Messiah dimension, so prominent in Mark and the others, as we now have them, might be firmly detached from "the real Jesus". Messiahship would be a post-Resurrection import into the narrative (when alone it could be comprehended as a mythic conviction) whose excision would demolish any sound Messianism as an authentic clue and undo classical Christianity.

Aside from what is speculative about pre-Markan sources, the hypothesis has surely miscontrued what seems a very self-evident situation. Messianic concepts and anticipations were dangerously confused and contradictory. Jesus could only fulfil them by transforming them. To have openly claimed Messiahship, except when directly challenged at the close, would have played into the hands of zealotry and ignorance. Hence, it would seem, the fondness Jesus had for the more enigmatic "Son of Man", with its elusive, lively implications. The Gospels portray the disciples themselves as caught in misconception – which could be another factor in the caution of Jesus and his patient education of their minds.

If CHAPTERS ONE and TWO were earlier in "a right mind" here then we know what meaning to attach to "secrecy", and are in no way required to see the Messianic factor as other than crucially dominant in the gathering logic of Jesus' ministry. The puzzlement of the disciples which, as we have seen, finally underlay their "treachery", was real enough (Mark 9: 9–10 and 8: 30). How could they have come to it after the Resurrection – given the awesome, assumed veto on it of crucifixion itself – if it had not been powerfully present almost from the outset as a capacity Jesus had accepted at his baptism? The parenthesis must conclude in a reinforced return, not to the secrecy of a "hidden" Messiah, but to the veracity of the Messiah Jesus.

IV

A strangely paradoxical "veracity" – and with it a deep personal crisis – belonged with Albert Schweitzer's reading of Jesus. The very language about "the Jesus of history" setting a "quest" came from the English title of his influential work. He posited either a total scepticism about the recovery of any veritable Jesus or the view that took him as urgently expecting an apocalytic intervention, prior to which his whole teaching was an "interim-ethic". Yet, on the latter ground, there was an invitation to "follow" him in a costly discipleship that would "know Jesus in an ineffable mystery".[22] Jesus had heroically turned the failure of apocalyptic hope into a sublime acceptance of suffering to fulfil it in the different shape of crucifixion. This supreme gesture of divine trust bequeathed its immortal spirit as too authentic for mere historicism.

> The abiding and eternal Jesus (was) absolutely independent of historical knowledge and could only be understood by contact with His Spirit . . . still at work in the world.[23]

This was a very different sort of Messianic "secret". Schweitzer himself obeyed his own Jesus-vision in a deliberate abandonment of the profession of theology for prolonged medicine in Africa.[24]

As works of able scholarship, his books breathed romantic mystical conviction but, so doing, left vital issues wide open, perhaps "white clouds" mistaken for "distant mountains".[25]

Schweitzer read Matthew 10: 23, and the mission of the disciples expecting persecution, as imminent prelude to the "coming of the Son of Man". When it did not happen, Jesus came to think himself called to suffer death and precipitate thereby the Kingdom's advent, being himself its "Messiah". This was his heroic error: but the tragically wrong apocalytic for which he gave his life was accompanied by the teaching of the Gospel of love, a love to emulate when the ideas of Jesus' time had long faded.

There was much in the Gospels about which Schweitzer was ready to be cavalier. He had to improvise, as many with contrasting theses have done when dealing with passages awkwardly inconvenient, and regard them as showing composite sources, or as evidence of honest confusion in that they were allowed to remain, or as insertions to be disregarded. He needed to believe that Jesus somehow engineered the course of the "trial" that condemned him. He read a precipitate "zeal" into Jesus' ministry that scarcely suited the humane gentleness of Galilean scenes and attentive crowds. That there was urgency, Mark, most of all, leaves us in no doubt; but the appeal was patient not coercive. Did Schweitzer somehow imprison Jesus too drastically in the 1st century mind-set of impatient hope, via eschatology, and so doing, circumscribe "historical quest" itself? He jettisoned the whole emerging verdict of the Church whose ideas of a spiritual Kingdom he saw as imposed on a Jesus to whom they never belonged. Even so he had to argue from the Scriptures that Church, and only that Church, afforded to him.

Most important of all, Schweitzer's exclusive preoccupation with apocalyptic obscured the transforming spiritual outlook Jesus brought, via sermon and parable and practice, into the world of 1st century Judaism.[26] Further, the contrived character he imposed on the self-offering of Jesus and his condemnation altogether reconceived the redemptive terms in which sacrificial suffering belonged with

Messiahship in "the mind of Jesus". "The cup my Father gives me", "not as I will but as Thou wilt" – these have no place in Schweitzer's *Quest*. Nor does the resultant opening out of grace towards the "Gentiles" – itself, as we have seen, the logic of Messiah Jesus crucified – find any warrant in his scheme. "Christ-learning", as Hebrews 5: 8–9 told it and Matthew 11: 28–30 invited into it, was of a different order. Could we say that Schweitzer's scholarship around the "stranger in Jerusalem" had not walked the Emmaus road in the hearing "in all the prophets of things concerning him" nor stayed to "bread and wine"? "Crisis" was indeed paramount but only in the full dimensions of the real Gethsemane.[27]

V

Albert Schweitzer's perspective on the Jesus of the Gospels, dated as it now is, at least illustrated the wide range conjecture could take concerning Christology. He found in Jesus an ethical timelessness yet made him hostage to a highly limited time-vision. "Historical" as applied to Jesus became itself controversial. Where (or when), we have to ask, did he really belong, in how narrow or how wide a time-realm?

Moving on from these debates, and alerted by them, we need to have Messiahship reach back far from the narrow confines of Schweitzer's work and forward to the measures of a whole New Testament. Keeping Messiahship central, this means having it linked with "the suffering servant" and the old prophets and, beyond these, with the long saga of "covenant" and the human dignity of creaturehood. For these are where its lineage belongs. Forward, it means seeing the sequel to the Passion (as we have done in CHAPTERS TWO and THREE) finding its way towards *Carmen Christi* and a confessional Christology. These were, in truth, its whence and whither. That Jesus came to be Christ in such "confession of his name" and by the Church's mind, while not self-warranting, has certainly to be allowed into the equation. Taking our way to Qumrân should not mean ignoring, still less disowning, the Damascus road.

Ripening the "quest" language about Jesus in his history to what had better be the "measure" language, we find both the Gospels and the Epistles of the New Testament setting his Messiahship in the whole orbit of creation, human creaturehood, Noahid and Mosaic "covenant", a "pilot" history ensuing in Israel, prophethood and exile and hope of redemption. From the climax of all these perceived in Jesus as the Christ of God, the whole carries forward into the being of the Church in these fulfilment terms. We have that *Carmen Christi* within a quarter century between the Cross of Jesus and Paul taking his pen to write to the Philippians.

That there are lacunae, silences, queries, in that story is evident enough but the broad theme contains them as the major key. History can be truly eventful in being only strenuously ascertainable. Finding it so is appropriate to the things of faith. One can be absolute for meanings in being amenable to questions.

On that ground we have two definitives in one – Jesus in his Christhood and the open people of God by an open faith. The one is the received consequence of the other. If Jesus knew his Christhood in his "obedience as Son to the Father", the Church's openness was its responsive "obedience" in like kind. It had its only motive and impetus in its reading of the significance of Messiah-Jesus. Hence the wit of folk in Antioch in the coining of its name (Acts 11: 26). It was an openness in which its Jewish pioneers emphatically meant to include themselves, fulfilling "chosen-ness" in the discharge of their task as also something continuously theirs with new partners in an equal peoplehood, equally "bound over" to the world's serving.

What is at stake here may be illustrated in negative terms. Commenting on Isaiah 56: 7 – "a house of prayer for all nations" – which figures importantly in the Gospels, H. M. Orlinsky writes:

> Only those foreigners [sic] who have already converted to God's Torah and accepted the covenant are welcome to His house . . . Not one of all those peoples apart from Israel were God's covenanted people . . . Yahweh (is) a universal, but not an international, God, a national God, the God of no nation in the Universe but Israel. He is the God of Israel exclusively.[28]

It was this perception – here explicitly frank but implicit in many other writers [29] – that Judeo-Christian faith amended its heritage so that, while honouring particular ethnic vocation, the privilege of it could be inclusively shared by each and every ethnic, cultural and temporal particularity. Both the logic and the motive came from the Messiahship of Jesus and the inclusiveness of his Passion.

It is little wonder that the Jewish heirs of such a tenacious particularity as that of Jewry, with so much committed to its charge, should have found this development unhappy, distressing and – in the end – anathema. That the struggle is written agonizingly into the texture of the New Testament is evident enough. It was not merely that instincts of self-perpetuation in the old terms prevailed. It was also that the admission of "Gentiles" into the saving community which, in some sense, had always been part of Messianic hope, would dispossess Jewry of its unique identity. The concreteness of this "Christian" Messianic realism would also deprive them of their distinctive role as custodians of the principle of hope and irreplaceable witnesses to their Yahweh-fidelity. Christianity, inviting them into another role as mutual witnesses to a given, actual Messiah, seemed to spell their "internationalization".

It is well to register the tensions of the New Testament from this perspective. Jewishness, so deeply rooted in historical experience (exodus and land-entry, monarchy and exile) as the context of theological faith, had necessarily possessed a deeply Messianic religion.[30] Events had certainly given Jewry their teleology, their sense of Yahweh's purposes. But the Christian sense of the "end" realized in Jesus and his Christhood proved at length uncongenial to their tenacious self-perception in its "old" terms. Instead of an open salvation by grace they clung to the sanctification of Israel, foregoing blood sacrifices after AD 70 and the loss of the Temple. Torah community then became their watchword leaving Christ as the Torah to Pauline, Johannine and other deviants with their "Gentile" associates. So much we have seen in the previous chapter.

What, then, of that dual Christian acknowledgement of "God in Christ" and all faithful therein "the people of God"? Being the New Testament theme, was it misguided and wrong? We say Yes! if we are embracing a final cynicism or a weary scepticism about any historical Jesus. Yes! also if we are insisting that divine action has no bearing on divine nature and that, therefore, no theology belongs with "the Word made flesh". Yes! again, if we conclude that Messiahship was never the central theme in the significance of Jesus and that finding him "the Christ-Lord" was either delusory or perverse.

With what, however, would such disavowals leave us? The answer has to be – enormous problems! How could such a deep and entire aberration have ensued on the Jesus of purely hortatory, charismatic, exorcist dimensions? As E. C. Hoskyns argued seventy years ago:

> The words and acts of Jesus must possess a significance adequate to generate and sustain the faith of the primitive Church. There is no event or utterance recorded of Jesus which does not wholly proceed from a conception of the Messiahship smelted . . . from the ore of the Old Testament Scriptures.[31]

Sequels have to enter into a full reckoning with origins.

One might dis-authenticate the sequel by ascribing it to cults of dying–rising gods like Tammuz or Osiris, or to some Latin fascination with heroes in the heavens – highly dubious suggestions in a context (albeit also "Gentile") steeped in things Judaic. Or one might suppose that the disciples in the act of becoming apostles were compensating for tragic disappointment by a construction of reassuring imagination –

two developments that seem to cancel out each other.

But there are deeper reasons still for the authenticity of what transpired. If the Messianic theme belongs squarely with God as the reality of cosmic responsibility, as witnessed to in the entire faith as to creation, the human privilege, covenant and prophethood, then a fully cosmic responsibility is not fulfilled in exorcism, or preaching charisma or itinerant exhortation. It belongs in deed as well as word, in word as deed, in the love that suffers to redeem. Ernst Bloch, contemporary philosopher, says of Messiah: "He haunts the deepest depths in all of us" and asks: "What does Messiah do when he cannot appear or redeem?" His answer is: "He weeps."[32]

Is it not this ultimate pathos in the human predicament that Matthew 11: 28–30 had in mind and that must finally decide the necessary dimensions of Messiah? It was the clear conviction of the first Church that these had been made real in history in the person and Passion of Jesus Christ. Only in such concreteness (as Jewish writers love to use the word and concept to express their own history) can a divine, cosmic responsibility be measured and known, not in esoteric ascetic piety or verbal wisdom.[33] It is well to go to 1st century Judaism with scholars like Geza Vermes to overhear the contemporary world of Palestinian society, its hopes and fears. It is then the more imperative to perceive, in that same world, the shape of a Christhood that answered both hope and fear in terms that could be worthy of God and comprehensive of all humankind.

VI

It remains to consider one other factor before turning finally to all these scholarly cares which New Testament studies entail. It centres on the Fourth Gospel whose distinctive style and "high" Christology have been a large factor in contributing to scepticism about the Gospels and the Gospel. It has also seemed to some responsible, in a major way, for the speculative, mythicizing tendencies which they deplore as falsifying the real Jesus. It therefore needs a sophisticated readership alert to the demands it makes on their perception of *how* it is at once a Gospel, a narrative centred on a personality in time and vivid place, and yet also a kind of theological symphony in movements of its own.

There are three areas of literature from which we might draw careful light on the Fourth Gospel. They are the poetry of Wordsworth, the habit of the Greek historians and the dramatic quality of a Shakespeare or a Dostoevsky, all recruited with due caution. William Wordsworth is known to have sometimes found the very flow of his lines from the "observations" of his sister, Dorothy, and so was in debt to "hiding places ten years deep".[34] There was something of this order – many years more than ten – in how what was erstwhile eventful in the synoptic tradition was represented in the Fourth Gospel from the angle of maturing faith in the glorified Christ.[35]

It is important in Gospel study to realize that even in the Synoptics we do not have the words of Jesus as tape-recording now allows a voice to be heard again. There were no such devices around. What we read was filtered through retentive memory and oral transmission. That filter is still more mentally possessive – as well as retentive – in what is Johannine. Though distant and otherwise no parallel, the likes of Thucydides can help us. The speeches he gives us on the lips of protagonists caught up in great events are obviously *from* him. He had no means of knowing that they ever precisely uttered those words. But the literary method he uses sets the reader realistically at the heart of the action and mediates the very feel and meaning of the occasion. It is his way of communicating vividly and dramatically what the event meant *within itself*. It is Thucydides' way of being an adequate historian by participating with his own kindling imagination in the meaning of what he tells. Something of his order has happened in the Fourth Gospel. If, in either case, you ask: Were these precise words actually uttered as sounds in ears, we cannot say Yes as we could if we played a tape. But, if we mean, do these words convey the real perception of an event's significance we can venture a discerning Yes.[36]

This authorial responsibility for the shape of the document and "the lie of the land" of the history in the Fourth Gospel is thus truly Shakespearean in having a very deliberate "plot-management" concerned with a crowning theme. There is a dramatist fully in charge of his *mise en scène*, moved by an intention that has a vision to fulfil and an import to deliver. "John" is a dramatist doing with the theological meaning of what happened around Jesus what Shakespeare did for the human predicament in what happened around Hamlet.[37] In either case, the theme is there – all authorship apart. We are not dealing with fiction. But the perception, as his possession of the theme, is all his own. It is the theme alone which makes him the maker of the telling by which, through him, the theme is ours.

What our Johannine dramatist presents is "a gospel". In being different in so many ways from the Synoptics, he is still an evangelist. What he gives us has a clear Palestinian milieu, is concerned for chronology and anchored in a shared tradition, yet he assumes an authorial freedom to set the stamp of his own perception at all points. It is, therefore, urgent for all users of the Gospel to appreciate this situation for what it is and not attempt a simple "harmony" of the four

Gospels as if their obviously common story could be neatly dovetailed into one sequence.

If we try to do this and ignore the angles of vision we only minister to perplexity. The commanding serenity, for example, of Jesus in the "farewell testament" of John 17 cannot be reconciled with the Gethsemane of Matthew, Mark and Luke.[38] The discourse in the Synoptic parables contrasts sharply with the discourses in John. These, for example in Chapters 3, 4, 5 and 9, start from potentially synoptic-style "interviews" but pass into deeply allusive and theological realms where the immediacies of a "ruler by night" or "a man born blind" give way to principles of divine truth keyed into decades of Church experience and authorial reflection. What ensues on the feeding of the crowd in Chapter 6, heavy with allusions to the Eucharist, would have been incomprehensible as a sermon echoing in the Galilean hills. In that first context, Jesus had no cause to reproach the eager folk about not "coming to him, while eating his bread". They were only too avid for his presence. The reproach had a different ring when, in Jewish antipathy to the Eucharist, "his own received him not". On the hillsides there seems to have been no antipathy to "table fellowship" around "broken bread".

Instances of this shift of perspective are too numerous for detailed exposition here. The primary point is to take the fact of it and to perceive the shape of the Johannine portrayal as incorporating what "the glory of Jesus as the Christ" had come to mean – where it could only come to mean – in the experience of his ongoing community as that community reacted with, feared from and yearned over, the parallel indecisive and finally negative hardening posture of ongoing Jewry concerning both him and it.[39]

There is thus a kind of bi-focal situation throughout the Fourth Gospel's narrative. The perspectives of the early Church, maybe as late as the nineties of the 1st century, characterize but do not submerge the Palestinian scene in its local incidence. It is not that something "unreal" is contrived: it is that its first reality is mediated as retrospect came to reread it with the advantage of sombre experience of the same issues, as these were perpetuated and embittered in the inter-Jewish tensions waiting on the "Gentilizing" of the Christian outreach. In the words of C. F. D. Moule we can perceive

> . . . good traditions of the actual controversies of Christ's own life-time, preserved and re-set in such a way as to be entirely topical to the evangelist's own circumstances . . . a genuine piece of dominical tradition is being retold in the light of the prevailing conflicts.[40]

If so, the situation – though at much longer range – is akin to the implication of Paul's Damascus road vision, namely that what was happening in Church history extended what had happened to Jesus. There was this continuity "in the body of Christ" in both senses of that phrase – "the days of his flesh" and the corporate community.

Luke, for example, is very aware of the Samaritan question. The tensions in Luke 9: 51–56 are re-minted in John 4, with its subtle imagery about where "right worship" happens, its allusion to the controversial Pentateuch and the female role in the exchanges with its soul-harvest sequel.[41] The atmosphere in John 9, around the blind man's "now I see", his being "put out of the synagogue" and his parents' fence-sitting under interrogation lest the same thing should happen to them – all is redolent of the writer's own immediate context.

Similarly, in 6: 60–66, were there hesitant Jewish Christians in, say, Ephesus, returning to the synagogue while the evangelist was calling for a forthright commitment to the Church? How readily could that situation be superimposed on the circumstances of Jesus' immediate ministry. Defections under pressure were familiar enough in either situation. Moreover, it seems clear that the Johannine community's time and place belonged to the late eighties when a reworded Birkat ha-Minim, or "cursing of the deviators", was introduced by the synagogue authorities into liturgy. The aim was to force these individuals into the open and expel them from the Jewish community. There were also serious civic risks in holding on to Christ. In all such situations of confrontation, indecision, still more neutrality, become impossible. Moreover, they conduced to spying and inside "informing", so that pseudo-members stayed in place to inform on waverers. Such religious "espionage" invited counter-espionage by crypto-Christians hovering in Jewish midst.

The sundry references in the Fourth Gospel to "his own receiving him not" (1: 11), "the world has hated them . . . even as me" (17: 14), and "many went back and walked no more with him" (6: 66) become intelligible in this context. Yet they tally, in measure, with what locally happened also in Galilee. Similarly, the point about "a true Israelite" in 1: 47 (cf. 3: 10) in contrast to the cunning Jacob, or the Messianic symbol of "peace under vine and fig tree", or the contrast in 9: 28 between "disciple of Moses and of Jesus".

The same sense of crucial encounter between loyalties arose also around the now forfeited Temple and "the Temple" that Christ's body had become to the inter-Jewish/"Gentile" new people for whom, in dispersion, he constituted the saving rendezvous with God. This may also explain how so many of the "sign-carrying" discourses in this Gospel occur at Jewish festival times and may suggest overtones with ritual worship.[42] "Other sheep, not of this fold" (10: 16) whom "the good (true) shepherd has" and the contrast with "the hireling whose own the sheep are not" would seem to belong to the same salient issue in the Johannine world.

The double situation, then and now, there and here, about this Gospel could well be captured in the words: "There was a division among them because of him" (7: 43, 9: 16, and 10: 19). The reproach, too, in 7: 35, about "going to the Greeks" echoes the same issue. Other Gospels, to be sure, have something of this same interplay between the then and there of Jesus in his ministry and the here and now of the evangelists' world. How, for example, could the refusal of the elder brother in the parable to share the father's welcome to the wayward son not resonate also in a church harassed for its "Gentilizing" of Christ? However, in the Fourth Gospel these inter-associations are quite deliberately taken to the core of the presentation, which is a presentation of – we might say – the "issue joined between Jesus and his world" set in a serial drama gathered around events and conversations and controversies in which he, Jesus, is "on trial" for what his ministry signified in its historical course and in its apostolic sequel in the care of his loyal, or misguided, heirs in the making of the Church.

VII

"For crisis I came into the world" (9: 39) yet "not to judge but to save it" (12: 47). The Johannine witness holds the two together. Judgement was ever the road to redemption. The crisis Jesus brought intended the salvation. Light, as the Prologue knows it, engages with the "darkness" men prefer but the darkness does not prevail. Was it, perhaps, to heighten this "saving crisis" that – using authorial liberty – John brings the cleansing of the Temple forward to an early point in the story, whereas it is elsewhere the climax that precipitates the end? Is it why also, in a proleptic way, he has the disciples from the start recognize "the lamb of God" on first acquaintance with Jesus?[43] With his forward knowledge he can employ a backward vision. So doing, his supreme purpose is to hold together "the glory of Christ" and the earthbound-ness of Galilee and Jerusalem. The theological meaning of "Ascension" imbues the incidents. It is the Cross and Passion which alone sustain the significance everywhere. The Fourth Gospel intends reader-faith in writing from within the faith apostolic. It uses narrative to convey symbol. It abounds with overtones and nuances and carries back into original situations the significance of their Christological future, completing in terms of a Gospel the gathering perceptions of the New Testament Letters that had moved tellingly in the same direction.

Nowhere is the Fourth Gospel so prescient with its own idiom than in its presentation of the Passion of Jesus to which, with discourses, it devotes Chapters 13 to 20. This will bring us back to our emphasis on the central theme of Messiahship. While the actual term "Messiah" is rare in this Gospel, the drama before Pilate in the Judgement Hall, with its ambiguous word "King", illuminates the whole vocation and its Jesus-fulfilment. For there, truly was "the crisis of this world". To paraphrase John 18: 28–38 is to measure its meaning. After the hearing has alerted Pilate to an issue he cannot refer back into Jewry, he opens his interrogation of Jesus with the query:

"Are you the king of the Jews?" brusque, soldierly and Roman. Jesus replies: "Are you using this word "king" as you would as a Roman might, or are you quoting a report from another context?" Pilate, impatiently: "Don't equivocate! What have you done?" Jesus, still pausing over that "king" word: "My kingdom is not the kind you Romans have in mind when you hear the word. Had it been so, I would not be standing here now before you without a fight. But it is no kingdom of that sort."

> PILATE: "So you are a king then?"
> JESUS: "King is your word . . . I bear witness to the truth . . ."
> PILATE, angrily at a loss: "What is truth?" and reports "No fault in him . . . but something of a harmless riddle."[44]

In this highly-charged political scene Jesus insists on "the sense of the word Messiah" transforming the aberrant notions which underlay the trial itself into "truth witness drawing to itself a truth-community". It was a climax crowning the whole thrust and significance of his ministry. In the dire quality of final drama, it sealed the entire New Testament witness to "the Christ-mind of Jesus". It was the mind which taught and sustained the world-minded-ness of the Church. The Fourth Evangelist achieved a presentation by which both dimensions could be seen at work – and that in the very crucible of hope and adversity. This discernible unison of Jesus in history and the Christ for faith constituted the "title-deeds" of Christianity.[45] Many, like Thomas in John 20: 24–29, have "doubted", hesitant or unpersuaded about "the God with wounds" of whom that union tells. Maybe it is fitting it should be so. For faith betrays itself if it craves for guarantee. Many open questions remain in the minutiae of the New Testament. That the story issued into the faith, conceptually and institutionally, cannot be gainsaid. That it credibly did so, not infallibly so, makes reliance on its veracity at once the more firm and the more gentle, inviting both confidence and humility sealed with patient gratitude.

By the same token, it is a situation which scholars remain free to handle with a specific or a total scepticism,[46] and insofar as scholars do so they involve more than themselves in the vicissitudes of faith. For, depending on their time, place and intellectual task-perception, they function *vis-à-vis* an *ecclesia*, an "established" faith-system with disciplines that are more, or other, than intellectual. The authority of a *magisterium*, or hierarchy, will be crucially aware of stakes in their findings. While New Testament scholarship may rightly claim and duly exercise complete autonomy, it is finally impossible to professionalize what belongs to religion. For so to think to do is to violate the ultimate dimensions of what engages academic pursuit only by also transcending it.

Historically the issue here has been painfully acute within Roman Catholic Christianity, though not exclusively so.[47] The interests inherent in hierarchy, pastoral concerns for the due piety of the laity, fears for the sinister connivance of a subtle secularity inside academic freedom – all these have contributed to a vigilance to curb what dogma can concede to critical studies. The consequences have been tragically painful to many whose scholarship has laboured under sharp duress. Doctrine itself (and more, its custodians) have been compromised by unreadiness for an honest exposure to research. Supposed "findings" of academic ingenuity have then been liable to enjoy a status they did not deserve. The faithful may have been usefully protected but the form of the protection called its purpose into question. The long-term effect has likely been either a less than worthy faith-allegiance or the creeping advance of weary agnosticism. Or – perhaps least acceptable of all – some theory of the foregoing of intellectual liberty as a devout sacrifice on the altar of due submission. That form of lay-obedience should surely be anathema to any ecclesiastical authority that understood its own mission and mandate.

It cannot well be that only "churchmen" should be theologians and only theologians historians where history bears on their theology. Yet the open-market principle in scholarship has to remember that, by definition, the commerce of "theology" belongs with "the love of God". "The knowledge and love of God" – in the long tradition of Christian benediction – are forever coupled and require to co-exist. How this translates into the inter-duty of study to pulpit, of pulpit to pew, of the academic to the credal, of the credal to the liturgical, of the liturgical to the privately spiritual, remains the hard vocation.

Paul's passionate theology had no leisure for havens of research yet his fervent intellect led him to a pastoral model for their emulation.

> Love is never boastful, never conceited, never rude, never self-willed, never quick to take offence. Love keeps no score of wrongs, takes no plea-

> sure in the sins of others but delights in the truth. There is nothing love cannot face: there is no limit to its faith, its hope and its endurance.

How to "delight in the truth" – patiently, perceptively, positively – has always been the hard onus on ecclesiastical authority, its temptations often contrasted with those of the critical scholar.

VIII

How the quality of "the meek and lowly in heart" goes with the yoke and the learning has preoccupied us from the start. Reviewing the Christ-learning of Jesus himself led to that of the first world of the disciples and then to the education of an expanding Church carrying the storied meanings into the Mediterranean world. The geographical limits, perpetuated in the Canon, seem a strange anomaly for a world-wide society of faith. They can only now be conceded if used to yield precedents and guidance far beyond their European borders.[48] From that first diaspora with its apostolic formulation of a Christian theology and ethics we over-leaped the centuries to the sundry learnings and unlearnings of New Testament studies concerning all the foregoing in the crucible of critical scholarship. It has conveyed us finally to pained questions obtaining between dogma and research, between things confessional and professorial.

These are most at issue when known within a single heart. From so many personal mentors of the inner tensions of faith and integrity, of believing and belonging, isolated choice is haphazard. Yet in Alfred Loisy (1857–1940) there avails a striking example a brief resumé of whom can fittingly conclude this chapter. Aiming to capture the stresses we have summarized, it can also serve as prelude to a miscellany of Christ-learners in the eight chapters following.

Many of the issues have been refined since Loisy's day but he remains a poignant example of the travail that can belong to the cares of a believing and critical scholarship. As a Roman Catholic pursuing textual study at the rigorous behest of the *magisterium* in the Vatican, he experienced the near impossibility of the honest loyalty he sought to *both* his roles. Could loyalty to a Church be honest in holding to a Church which seemed not to prize it in the reverent scholar? Could a conscience pursuing Biblical evidences stay conscientious about a Church sharply circumscribing where that other conscience might arrive? It may be that Loisy's personal temperament contributed to the tense nature of the anguish he suffered. Nor was his generation eased by the sort of relaxed familiarity later times have reached, if only at the price of caring less about integrity or, perhaps, about what integrity can mean.

He exemplifies many of the aspects waiting on any resolution of the things at issue between the autonomy of scholars and the dogmas of church authority. There are those, like his own first teacher, Louis Duchesne at the Institut Catholique, a Church historian, who stay in "safer" areas and avoid perilous ones, or those who see some degree of deliberate obscurantism as the prudent policy in retaining either priesthood or tenure. Yet Loisy believed sincerely in the hope of a resilient Church, sustained in some measure by the stance of Pope Leo XIII, and in Newman's concept of "development" as enabling a genuinely compatible "liberalism" inside orthodoxy. Though deprived first of his teaching tenure, then his priesthood and finally his faith, Loisy mounted a spirited disavowal of Harnack's radical "de-Christologizing" of "Christianity", reducing Jesus' significance to his moral sonship to the Father. His *L'Évangile et L'Église* (1902) argued strongly for the validity of the ecclesiastical order and the doctrinal shape the Gospel found in the tradition of the primitive Church.[49] By these lights he had wanted to see – and prove – himself as a loyal believer tuning his scholarship to the vindication of his Church, but a Church constrained to recognize precisely that role as being legitimately exercised within it. It was not to be. His work and later ventures on the Fourth Gospel and on the Synoptics were treated as subversive of orthodoxy and he was never reconciled to Rome, finding extra-ecclesial fields of teaching in the history of religions.

There is no doubt that the bitterness he experienced was deeply felt, sharpened perhaps by temperamental strains in his character. Pioneer as he was, it is not finally the merit of his case-making but the travail of his mind that symbolizes for present context the care of faith in the cares of scholarship.[50]

That these – the care and the cares – hinge on the Messianic theme is central to all else. It has been so urged here from the beginning.[51] It is there in the very name the new faith and society had for itself as "Christian". It stems from the cumulative significance of Biblical prophethood.[52] Its Christology is surely inseparable from a theology adequate to divine relevance and responsive to the human situation. On all these counts, we can hold that the Christ-learning into which Jesus invited the weary and heavy laden truly was – and is – our sure graduation into "the knowledge and love of God".

FIVE

In the Ebbing of "Ecclesiastical Polity" – with the Heirs of Richard Hooker

I

If the cares of New Testament scholarship have posed for many in recent generations a searching crisis for faith, the same is no less true in respect of "ecclesiastical polity". The far-reaching impulse of contemporary secularity would seem to have made a strange anachronism of Richard Hooker's assured treatise of that title in Elizabethan England in the closing years of the 16th century.

> Let it stand for our final conclusion, that in a free Christian state or kingdom, where one and the self-same people are the Church and the commonwealth, God through Christ directing the people to see it for good and weighty considerations expedient that their sovereign Lord and governor in causes civil have also in ecclesiastical affairs a supreme power . . . the light of reason doth lead them to it, and against it God's revealed law hath nothing . . .[1]

The confidence of his sonorous prose is undermined on almost every count. Subjects and believers, citizens and communicants, are no longer "one and the self-same people". His "good and weighty considerations" related to an England which he saw to be "according to the pattern of God's own ancient people", in contrast to "the state of pagans" and vigilantly preserved from "where the bishop of Rome beareth sway".[2] As for "the light of reason and God's revealed law", present times could hardly stay with him on either ground.

That "polity", the civil and legal ordering of human society, could still be "ecclesiastical" in Hooker's terms, has been steadily rescinded in the course of two centuries by the rise of secular thinking, the growing awareness of pluralism and the trend away from acknowledged doctrine to private options of belief and behaviour. "The Christian religion, as by law established" no longer sustains the former role of monitor of the mores of society nor has in single custody the elusive "spiritualities" of a confused and partly agnostic people.

Perhaps the ambition had always been presumptuous even given the urgency for it in the Tudor times for which Hooker wrote. Yet there – and in the sundry other forms "ecclesiastical polity" assumes from the time of the conversion of Constantine in the second decade of the Fourth century – it could claim a powerful logic. Its force was captured by John Donne, Hooker's near contemporary, writing in his Third Satire:

> That thou mayest rightly obey power, her bounds know. Those past, her nature and her name is changed. To be then humble to her is idolatry.[3]

If political authority was so liable to break out of its due confines in God-fearingness, what better remedy than to have it tied into unison with religious warrant and behest, to hold it consecrated in spiritual terms to an office seen as divinely anointed and mystically bound to righteousness and sanctity. If it were thus endowed with "divine right" would it not be secured on both counts – duly guarded from subversion by false pretensions and the ever-present temptations of power when free for its own corrupt devices and, by the same tokens, preserved by its holy status from violation from without? Let the due submission of the subject be thus religious and the due religious status of the ruler sacrosanct. Could it not then follow that society itself would be truly hallowed and power beneficent? "Being interjacent . . . each could cleave to the other and so all continue one."[4] To hold power as from God could authenticate due obedience from below and enjoin all righteousness and humility within, power itself being an anointed trust and its exercise a hallowed mandate.

That reciprocal perception of divine prerogative and holy sanction surrenders both its logic and its polity where secularity has eroded its explicit theology of "all things under God" in a "kingdom of priests and a holy nation". What can survive from it under the contrasted auspices of prevailing forfeiture of its mind-set takes us in this present chapter to what, in response, the "yoke" of "Christ-learning" has to mean. That caring spirits have reason to be "weary and heavy laden" by the issues is evident enough. For they reach into the heart of things. There are those who would cling tenaciously to an old order in love of what it once connoted. There are others who would readily admit its demise and believe otherwise "to see – and serve – the goodness of the Lord in the land of the living", confident that the crisis of their faith is not finally any *regio/religio* equation but the power-free theme of the apostolic Church, "the wisdom of God – in Christ".[5]

Leaving still open here the many issues around "ecclesiastical polity" ever since Constantine, it is well first to have the primitive Church in clear perspective. There is certainly a sense in which the current situation in western secularity has returned today's Christians again to it in that – the remnants of old Christendom apart – they are on their mettle, their ultimate asset being in their convictions alone with their obedience to them no longer privileged by dint of state-establishment. There are aspects cordially to welcome in that shape of events. Yet the memory of the long centuries of Christendom means that the Church can never be innocent of what they contained or fully recover the experience of its pre-Christendom existence. It is, therefore, all the more important to measure what that first reality was.

II

Chapter three has explored the world-seeking quality of that first Christian diaspora. Its Gospel-faith did not go into the world as some "nation" into exile from a land of its ethnic necessity or out of a polity which mourned the loss of power. It did not hang harps on willows in Greece or forbear to sing its Lord's songs in imperial Rome. It travelled as a community of faith across both geographical frontiers and ethnic divides. Being world-concerned, it was not land-based, except insofar as ancient cities were springboards of its mission.[6]

The significance of Constantine's "take-over" of the Church was that it became, for the first time, a territorial expression. His adoption of the Church as the faith of the Empire made it a state-sponsored religion with a sanction such to be whereever the Emperor's power reached. The principle of territoriality emerged as defining the Church in political terms. Undoubtedly vestiges of paganism long persisted – as the brief resurgence proved under Julian the Apostate. For it was not the faith and Church that had comprehensively persuaded the Empire: it was the Empire that had seen fit to adopt the Church as the prospective new principle of its unity and cohesion both East and West. It was as if the old pagan divinization of the Emperor (the form of the subjects' submission to his power) was subsumed into the Pontifex Maximus of a now Christian power-realm. Hence, no doubt, the imperial concern for the credal definitions, via the Councils, lest disputes should jeopardize imperial cohesions. Thus even controversies assumed a political significance with great risk to their intellectual integrity.

Thus the principle of territoriality supervened on a Church which had neither known it nor coveted it earlier. After long decades – some twenty-six by the time of Diocletian – of bitter, intermittent persecution and survival by trauma, it would hardly have been possible for the faith to repudiate this strange turn in its fortunes or anticipate all that it could entail. Why should it not be feasible still to sustain that claim in the Letter to Diognetus about being "everywhere alien" while now, surprisingly, so differently "at home"?

That the cost in the spirit would prove so heavy only serves to demonstrate the vital character of pre-Christendom. When, three centuries later, Islam was territorialized in the form of the Caliphate, power had both its warrant and its thrust in the Hijrah of Muhammad himself from Mecca to Medina and his triumphant return eight years later to his birth-city. The power-structure was his own direct, and founding, legacy whereby he was "free in the land".[7] The concept of *Dar al-Islam*, "the realm of the faith", was a fully territorial reality. Its being reciprocal to kindred concepts of Christendom contributed vastly to the tensions and conflicts of the two faiths down the centuries.[8]

The point of present relevance is the first Christian non-territoriality *qua* power and politics, thanks to its diaspora spirituality *qua* evangel seeking humankind. Then it could invite only into religious community. It could offer only pains and troubles. It could be free of the additive to faith that belongs with sanctions other than its own appeal, sanctions which can displace conscience and compromise integrity. It was healthier for being socially at risk. Statehood did not infringe its witness to the transcendent Lord. It was truer in not being "the public truth" of some imperial establishment. Yet it was in no way "a private option" to be secretly cherished by folk under no obligation to hold it commendable to all. Rather it willed to embrace all in a situation that held no easy inducements equating faith with advantage.[9] The lack of privilege was its great negative asset.

In the limited sense in which Christians today can feel that the climate of secularity has – by a strange paradox – "re-established" their initial situation by the very process of broadly dismantling "establishment" as Christendoms knew it, finding it so must sound a *Sursum corda* now. There is abiding encouragement in the primitive history, in recollecting that Jesus himself was a politicians' victim and that political identity came late to a Church that had known itself strenuously authentic in the quality of its faith alone without the benefit of power, the "benefit of clergy", that Constantine set ambivalently in train when the 4th century was underway.

III

Even so, the legacies of long centuries persist. Vocation now in the ebbing of "ecclesiastical polity" may be fortified by the example of pre-Christendom but the Christendom tradition sustains a deep nostalgia and carries historical, if not also legal, weight in many quarters. It cannot be conjured out of strong cultural and physical accompaniments in art, literature, architecture and education where its writ ran and its meanings were transacted. The trust of its past, even if we concede it superseded, has to be positively served in engaging with what the poet called "the naked shingles of the world".[10] The secularity, the diversity, the privatization of belief which are assumed to have displaced it remain, even so, in yearning and confusion. The task of an "ecclesiastical spirituality" abides.[11]

Facing it requires that we appreciate what the old ideology was. The territoriality which Constantine introduced into the being of the Church was finalized, centuries later, by Charlemagne in "Holy Roman Empire". The imperial ruler was God's anointed agent as a sort of "theocracy at one remove". Pure theocracy, the direct rule of God, being impossible, in that "God is Spirit", there must needs be divine agency in deputy-ship on the divine behalf. "Things duly rendered to Caesar" must be seen as duly "rendered to God" via imperial means to the divine ends. The concept carried down to the national states which by the 15th and 16th centuries had broken free from the imperial bond. Régimes still loyal to the western Papacy and those harnessing reformed religion to national identity, alike, perpetuated the territorial theme of church and people in mutual identity. In Elizabethan England Hooker's thesis took this single identity for granted. With all his heart he wished it so. For he had shown his debating skills as Master of the Temple on controversy with "sectarians" who either defied the religio/regio principle or – as did Rome – invoked it only for themselves. His rugged faith in "natural law" and "holy reason" led him to hope that he could persuade such "sectaries" – by their own lights – to concede that his Anglican Church was consistent with Scripture and eminently open to all "men of good-will". "If only" – that perpetual formula of religious confidence – men would share his mind, in its soundness so patiently expounded, then "comprehension" of all but those incorrigibly partisan to Rome, or elsewhere, could peaceably and beneficently obtain, "all such things being lawful and honest".

Yet this ardent optimism was his Achilles' heel. He acknowledged that if society was *not* one in its believing allegiance to faith and Crown then "comprehension" in Anglican terms could not hold.[12] History steadily demonstrated that diversity must prove incorrigible and that "ecclesiastical polity" in Hooker's terms – which were essentially amicable – could not forever ignore the factors set slowly to erode it. It had been proposing a potential inclusiveness on its own terms and other notions of "tolerance" refused to concede its vision.

In England, the Restoration of 1660 restored King and Church but in subtly different terms from those of Charles I's bid for absolutism and Laud's rigorist Episcopacy. Acts of Supremacy, Acts against "conventicles" and of "occasional conformity" would still prevail but steadily pressures of inter-Christian – and later secular – diversity would claim and enjoy recognition. The "Englightenment" in the 18th century came to temper faith-assertion and open doors to emancipation, freedom of worship and liberty of conscience, in due time to inaugurate the climate of agnostic secularity. The story is familiar enough and does not call for recounting here.[13] Something of it is comprised in the biographies to follow, just as one of its main factors had place in the previous chapter.

Yet if all that was symbolized in *Ecclesiastical Polity* was too sanguine to be viable in a realist's world was there nothing authentic in its aspiration? Lost causes are not always insignificantly lost. If the nation-state cannot be *simpliciter* the realm of "established" faith, is it thereby irrelevant to "the things of God"? Leaving behind all that was immediate in the anxieties of Hooker's work – Spanish Armadas threatening precarious native sovereignty – there were yearnings in his logic and his scholarship worthy of the Apostles themselves. If their 4th-century successors had been providentially entrusted with a territorial role and history in so many shapes had steadily bequeathed it, ought it not – like all things Christian – to be redeemed? Was the first powerlessness Constantine had ended – and itself what history had contrived – necessarily the only form of Christian destiny?

In any event, modern secularity, for the most part, was not reinstating that physically oppressive condition. Its indifferentism, its lofty disdain or careless negligence, called for a different kind of durability. Once expressed in territory and franchised (in some sense) within "commonwealth", Christian faith would be obligated in ways a persecuted excluded Church had never been.[14] The increasing secularity of the modern state would make "Christian politics", as distinct from Hooker-style "ecclesiastical polity", a more subtle and exacting liability.

IV

Both subtle and exacting because it brings to the Christian dimension of society an exercise in relinquishment which is yet not relinquishment and thus, in a double sense, a crisis of faith. The old – and in its context the splendid – ambition to have all things under God can no longer obtain yet there can be no abandonment of conscience concerning the due subjection of the political order to "the rule and sovereignty of God", nor any foregoing, by Christian conscience, of how that sovereignty was identified in the Christ of the Cross and Resurrection.

Such Christian obligation and its "mental fight" have now to be somehow shared with secular, humanist ideologies or perceptions and, in some measure also, with the moral resources of other religions present in the plural population. It is in conceding and fulfilling such sharing that faith-crisis consists, seeing that this reading of the present world chastens all sense of a self-sufficient or unilateral aegis and, so doing, raises searching questions about finality and a theology of co-existence. Something ideally valid yet essentially flawed – namely the comforting unison of a Hooker-style world – has been properly forfeited but nostalgia has never been appropriately Christian. Nor was the complacence that thought society and believing could ever be coterminous. For such confidence, however appealing, had never recognized the private openness of the faith-option (as the New Testament knew it) nor the non-coercive genius of the Gospel.

On both counts, it was a genuinely "Christ-learning" vocation to acknowledge the claim of religious liberty and to acquiesce in that steady process whereby, often as a result of ecclesiastical controversies and their distastefulness, the Bunyans, the Miltons, the Paines of this world staked their right to tolerance and equal citizenship. In the climate of such gathering demands and their legitimacy by primary Christian criteria it was urgent, however, not to forsake the ancient vocation for a "righteous Caesar" whose "things" were always vigilantly ordered within "the things of God".[15]

Christendoms, then, whether in Constantinian or any national order had to be foregone yet, given their long history, there was no returning to the primitive centuries.[16] Legacies had been too long. The relinquishment of privilege was a different kind of destiny from the haven of the catacombs. The one proved to be a slow and tedious ebbing: the other was a shifting tide of enmity and threat. A reluctance to be diminished was a different trial from that of ever precarious survival.

If, indeed, "God fulfills Himself in many ways", it is significant that "judicious Hooker" himself made the case by which his own "polity" was undermined. Failing, as we have seen, to register the vital difference between the Hebraic pattern of "king and priest" as strictly ethnic, and the open "faith-criterion" of the Christian society, his "polity" had always hinged on that criterion being nationally – and indeed notionally – fulfilled. He was ready to allow that it might be dubiously assumed to be attained. Hence his laborious efforts to win over the Puritan "sectaries" by his "pleading reason". He recognized that time might change the scene.

> In these things the experience of time may breed both civil and ecclesiastical change from that which hath been before received, neither do later things always violently exclude former, but the one growing less convenient than it hath been, giveth place to that which is now become more.[17]

He was even ready to concede that "the Church is so much troubled about the polity of the Church". The trouble lay in how "our private discretion, which otherwise might guide us in a contrary way, must here submit itself to be that way guided".[18] He could thus be almost describing what has irreversibly happened. "Private discretions" which are "contrary" do not "submit to be (Churchwise) guided". For him there could not be "as many supremacies as there are congregations".[19] Now it would seem that either all are or none can be. How painfully Hooker posed the issue his "ecclesiastical polity" sought to resolve!

> Many talk of the truth which never sounded the depth from where it springeth and therefore when they are led thereunto are soon weary.[20]

Or perhaps not "weary" but only contentious or sanguine. While fearing the alternative of chaos – and social malaise – he yearned as many still do for a "public truth Gospel". Yet uncannily he may have foreseen a time when "change" would make that theme "grow less convenient" and those who knew "whence truth springeth" and could "lead to it" would need to co-exist with others who differently assumed the same competence and with those who doubted any such competence anywhere. Could it ever really be that "no truth can contradict any truth"?[21]

It is uncanny how far Hooker's perceptive honesty foresaw what could undo his system. "Some truths there are the verity of which doth alter," and

> For men to be tied and led by authority, as it were with a kind of captivity of judgement, and though there be reason to the contrary not to listen to it . . . this were brutish.[22]

Yet when such "brutishness" was relinquished he was right that bodies politic have duties ethical and spiritual, and that vagrant, malicious, bewildered human nature needs both curbs and disciplines only bodies politic can establish.

His yearning to have his England a "Respublica Christiana" found wistful echoes long after his time. Edmund Burke held that:

> In a Christian Commonwealth, the Church and the State are one and the same thing, being different integral parts of the same whole.[23]

All branches of non-conformity ought to enjoy toleration, the "conspiracy of atheism" apart, whose practitioners were "outlaws from humanity" and "the most horrid and cruel blow to any civil society".[24] Opposing any repeal of the Test Act, Burke was ready to replace the sacrament with an oath renouncing all hostility to "the Established Church", as one with three other "establishments", namely monarchy, aristocracy and democracy, each in the degree that it exists and no greater.[25]

Meanwhile, his near contemporary Samuel Taylor Coleridge held that "Not without celestial observations can ever terrestrial charts be accurately constructed."[25] The first he found in "Christ the Logos" as the centre of convergence without which we would entirely lack all historical sense.

> To divinity belong those fundamental truths which are the common groundwork of our civil and our religious duties . . . indispensable to a right view of our temporal concerns.[26]

Under the name of theology all else was disciplined and contained. He saw a "national clergy" as the "clerisy" inside a larger realm of learning as the *Nisus formativus* of the body politic, and vital to the weal of the realm.

It was evident that even in the sober rationality of the 18th century "establishment thinking" died hard. It was vibrant in the younger Gladstone until the middle of the next but steadily as the 19th century progressed a stronger ebb set in.[27]

V

No late 20th-century theologian or day-to-day Christian could fail to register the problematics of "holding to" their faith or "holding on" to its active commendation in the climate of the West. "Preaching", *per se*, is suspect as "axe-grinding" in a time when all options must be open and non-intrusively left in private worlds of convenience or illusion.[28] Authority, in any field outside demonstrable or strictly empirical sciences, is considered either a cracked or muted bell. Some vested interest or hidden prejudice waits on its tones. "Private spirits not safely to be allowed" in Richard Hooker's world are now the preferred tribunals for the adjudication of truth. The sheer confusion of auspices laying claim to truth-credentials, and the unlovely guises in which they do so, deter the honest seeker and go far to make the seeking seem forlorn or futile. Life, doubtless, must be somehow lived but its ultimate meaning, with its immediate lights, can only dimly bear upon its present management.

On "these naked shingles" of secular uncertainty there is a strong temptation for faith-custodians to fall back on sharp assertion – perhaps even as the condition of their own assurance. For when anxiety about unwantedness threatens the inward confidence of belief it is liable to let a subtle resentment into its witness. Its concern for a right persuasion may then be forfeit. The pain of indifference may spring the trap of impatience. The errant world must be "confronted". It is destroying itself and unless a halt is called society heads towards its own doom. The very urgency of impending ruination calls for an uncompromising counter-action of truth-propagation. If, in the last analysis, the world thinks that the Christian Gospel is no more than "a faith-in-faith", then so be it. Let faith fall back on the unargued force of its credentials and join issue around authority *for* by a passionate claim to authority *with* the given "Word of God". Let open questions be answered by the conviction that is the clue duly closing them.

It is from such thoughts that the claim emerges for the Christian faith as being "public truth". Early in the 20th century the stance could be identified in the paradoxical banter of G. K. Chesterton. It was more staidly put by J. N Figgis in *Civilisation at the Crossroads*.[29] The very will to be agnostic, he argued, had to be confronted. If civilization had effectively abandoned Christianity, it must be told there was "death in the pot". Self-salvation, by the same token, was impossible. The chronically sick do not heal themselves. It was the task of Christian faithful not merely to repudiate the trend to secular folly but to require it to know its sins and return to the ever faithful, ever "public", truth of "God in Christ".

Lesslie Newbigin has been foremost in renewing this shape of Christian response through the second half of the century.[30] The Gospel must affirm itself as "public truth" and claim the adherence to it that such "truth" expects and demands. Justly deploring what he sees as the "demoralizing of politics" and the subordination of inclusive spiritual values to the relativism of cultural flux, he affirms – denying all charge of "arrogance" –

> . . . the unique decisiveness of God's action in Jesus Christ (as) . . . the enduring bulwark against the arrogance of every culture to be itself the criterion by which others are judged.[31]

This "canon" of revelation and salvation" means that we have to start – and finish – with "where the Gospel has placed us". For it has done so "publicly" and to locate ourselves firmly within it is a truer posture in the tumults and confusions of our age than to "entrust a secularized society with tolerance". Ours is no time "to rescind Christian uniqueness and the public validity of religious truth claims".[32]

Those whose Christian mind and conscience read vocation in these terms have right to their verdict in that all are bound over, in the Holy Spirit, to the one Master and Lord. The problem lies in the concept of "public validity" and – in that last citation – the fact that "religious truth claims" are far from underwriting "Christian uniqueness". For these are widely various, even contradictory – and there is ever more urgently the far-away-ness of secularity.

Christian faith is certainly not "public truth" in the sense that numbers, added, divided, multiplied avail to be, nor in the way that geometry states that "the sum of the angles of a triangle equals two right angles". Euclid has demonstrated such "public truth" and architecture splendidly proceeds upon it. Nor can any faith-doctrine see itself like some "Highway Code" which, being publicly legislated, demands conformity, having also – in the nature of the case – built-in-sanctions in that deviance endangers the deviants. Faiths may well put unbelief into jeopardy but never in those condign and self-evident ways.

The parallels are eloquent precisely in being trite and obvious. The thinking of Lesslie Newbigin and others of his mind obliges us to reach for an urgent distinction. The Christian Gospel is, indeed, "public truth" but only for those interior to its grace and power. It is, indeed, "a faithful saying and worthy of universal human recognition that Christ Jesus came into the world to save sinners". So the writer in 1 Timothy 1: 15 states. So also the unanimity of the long Christian centuries.[33] But that inward conviction can only be urged on a world's "acceptance" as authentic as an invitation, a response to which alone enthralls us into the truth of it. "I am persuaded . . ." – Paul's wording – is the shape of its truth-presenting quality as something never presuming to enforce the consent for which it waits. It is only in freedom that it comes: only freedom that it addresses.

Or, in other words, its truth becomes intrinsic in the experience ensuing on its acceptance and can only be claimed for it in advance as that which free response will be given to know. That priority gives pause to the idea that the Gospel can well be asserted as "public truth" if – so doing – we do violence to "the meekness and gentleness of Christ" by obviating its own strategy of "the patient siege of human liberty".

It follows that all assurance as to Christian truth comes to be intrinsic within what Paul called "acceptation". The Greek word *apodoches* carries the sense of what you can be "heartily hospitable to". But, like all hospitality or embrace, the impulse to it can only be private (i.e., personal). "Acceptance", in that sense, can never be "public truth", being for ever within the liberty of the personal heart and will. "Reliance" – which also fits the sense – is likewise within spontaneous personal will in a way that is necessarily different from one's acceptance of a chemical equation or of a finding in the laboratory.

The truths of faith are intrinsic to the experience of belief and, since this is obviously how it is inside all religious allegiance, their claims to be "public truth" – whenever made as such – are plainly competitive, none having the exclusive right to a unilateral public accreditation. That there are available alternatives to each of them is evident enough. Practically, it is not within their power to claim that "there is no alternative". Yet a conclusion of that order is precisely what "public truth" means to reach.[34]

To realize that "the faith in truth and the truth in faith" are always on their mettle for genuine acceptance is to recognize that there is an indispensable "private conviction" quality about the "public truth" status they properly claim. To ignore this situation would be to forfeit the nature – in this realm – of both truth and faith. To think the one to be compulsive and the other subjugated would be comparable to saying that friendship was axiomatic, the personal dimension being always inherent – and pivotal – in its public quality.

It follows that the commendation of Christian faith, of the grace in the Gospel, must locate itself in its very content and not be transferred deliberately or unwittingly to an authority other than its own worth. Our study of Newman in the chapter following illuminates how readily this can happen. His yearning for a Church that could relieve him of personal truth-onus by the sheer weight of its custodian status did not relieve him – as we shall see – of "private judgement". It simply diverted the theme of it from Christ to Church, the second having the indefectible role as guarantor of the first. He was in sharp contrast to his contemporary, Robert Browning, asking himself: "Has it your vote to be so if it can?"[35]

This is not to say that custodian tradition, heritage, times past, garnered and garnering institution, have no place in the authority of faith. No one is beginning from isolation and loneliness. But all such authority betrays itself as custodian if it covets an allegiance of which it has not wanted to be worthy by the quality of its own deference to the patience of the truth itself.

It follows again that Christian truth-commendation, seeking this lowly way to the personal heart and will, becomes at once a more strenuous and yet more hopeful enterprise. It is more strenuous in that it is pledged to interpret "the fulness of Christ" and not to stop short of this by recourse to a proxy or approximate substitute that, at best, could only be servant, at worst, a substitute. It is more hopeful in that it may find unsuspected allies in other faiths and among seculars who might well be recruited to its meanings but would likely be deterred or alienated were the appeal coming from institutional investment or dogmatic insistence.

For is it not these that too often deter or even repel outsiders to the systems or citadels that address them from what seem, to the unaware or the prejudiced, to be vested interests of prestige or structures of arrogance? Such prejudice can only be surmounted by having whatever is honest in its reticence or its scepticism actually recruited into a commendation that had registered these as legitimately entering into its duty. This means a ready "negotiation" with every shape of human unpersuadedness.[36]

It follows that Christian communication is itself a learning process by which the very ministry of witness kindles a right perception of its dimensions. If the experience of belief allows itself its proper confidence it must remain alert – even wisely conciliatory – towards the levels of contemporary bewilderment. It must be ready to feel within itself how many and how potentially devastating these are. For they derive so variously from whether any transcendence exists, from distrust about the capacity of Biblical history to yield satisfactory findings, from the sundry relativities of psychic and social conditioning, and – more recently – from the sense that language itself deals only artificially with the "reality" it purports to handle.[37]

Since religion, dealing as it must with what is ultimate, cannot be content with less than a final conviction (if one always honest about where it "rests and stays"), it is tempted to make itself arbitrary and authoritarian in what it holds and tells. But then it renders its very authority unworthy and undeserving of any right recognition.[38] Our personal, private witnessing experience of faith only well becomes "public truth" by the quality of its negotiation with all that supervenes to daunt, delude or dominate the public domain.

There are two human factors which must sustain this unremitting task. The one is the human faith-capacity, the other is the human nemesis in defiant evil. The very freedom which belief-commendation addresses is inherently both volitional and deployable. Theology could well call this its anthropic principle. Faith in Christ is not addressing a cypher or an enigma or a captive.

> As a moral agent [man] is potentially capable of entering into a real fellowship with God the Creator, and such fellowship is mediated . . . by an activity which is in miniature like that of God . . . he enters into a sphere of activity all his own, a microcosm of God's macrocosm.[39]

Assumption this may, initially, be. But it is at once a joyous and a credible one to make, seeing that without some assumption we can never begin – a fact no less real for those who would start with denial. Thinking humankind "meant-for-faith-ness" in these Christian terms may seem like circular argument if then taken as the case for faith. Yet there is a similar circularity in the contrary argument asserting that humans have no option but a secular doubt, therefore secular doubt is the truth of them. Old Richard Hooker makes the positive point with characteristic verve. "God and man should be very near neighbours." "Touching God Himself hath He anywhere revealed that it is His delight to dwell beggarly?"[40] There is a magnanimity transcending, which deserves an answering magnanimity in a love of which we humans are arguably capable both in mind and heart – capable that is, as their fields are to magnetism. *Magnificat* was always two-sided in this way – the singer made splendid in the sung.

To see humankind this way has its nether side. In all betrayal of truth there is a betrayal of the self. "Self-wronging" is the deep reality of all depraved living, all sexual distortion, all atrophy of the good.[41] The human wastage and wreckage that ensue for society in self-wronging, in their pathos and their urgency, are what prompt – as we saw – a reaching for "public truth" to "uphold and enforce the peril we are in". William Faulkner's fiction (CHAPTER EIGHT) portrays it well. But dredging through the dregs which life and literature will darkly register is the surest witness to the countering truth of our being entirely otherwise meant. Our tragedies are the surest evidence of our proper destiny. The psalmist's "I was even as a beast before You" is the verdict of his cry in faith: "Whom have I in heaven but You" (Psalm 73: 22 and 25). The Christian witness to grace and redemption has to hold both in one, to tell the human reproach in the positive case-making of salvation. The human story, panoramic and private, will be the plainest "public truth" of "yesterdays lighting fools to dusty death".

> The eternal note of sadness . . .
> Sophocles long ago
> Heard it on the Aegean, and it brought
> Into his mind the turbid ebb and flow
> Of human misery . . .[42]

Matthew Arnold's "Dover Beach" held universal truth for him that sombre night as he mused: "Ah, love let us be true to one another!" "The moon lay fair" and – reassuringly – "the cliffs of England stood". It was because of these that he registered all else. What then should we make of the lingering "Establishment" that still survives from Richard Hooker's world in the realms of this "retreating sea of faith"?

VI

It is a survival which – according to Nietzsche (see below) – is mainly architectural. Cathedrals and abbeys in major towns, church steeples across rural landscapes – these persist, "the tombs and monuments of God" where the living worshippers are the dwindling devotees. A modern poet saw them as

> Luxury liners . . .
> Holding to the East their hulls of stone,
> The high, thin, rare continuous worship
> Of the self-absorbed.[43]

Insofar as the inference is just, the obvious task is to end the self-absorption and exchange it for a self-expending care beyond the sanctuaries.

If, relating to a "Church of England as by law established", we turn from the poets to the constitutional lawyers we must leave them also, for present purposes. For whatever may ultimately transpire from their discoursings on behalf of Crown and people falls within issues more taxing still concerning the spiritual meaning of nationhood.

Even the most lively recognition of an ebbing tide of habits of worship must know that legacies still signify. To consent that "ecclesiastical polity" survives only formally is not to seek relief from what its vision meant, namely the due consecration of the State to justice and compassion, to righteous conscience in all its policies and ends. There are things, like friendship, which only exist and persist because they are willed. The State is one of them. Its quality, never static, is ever in the making. It lives by the will to believe concerning its concepts and fulfilments. If these are no longer to be willed in abandoned Hooker-terms, they must pass into other mentorship and monitoring. To assent to "dis-establishment" in bland surrender to temporal flux would imply that this vital task is forfeit, that the State is out from under any constraints to its own – thus unbridled – ways and means.

The ongoing task requires some careful widening of that constraining aegis to embrace at least a more inclusive Christian ecumene of thought and life and, as far as may be, the wisdom and relevance of other faith-systems and of secular humanism. What is outmoded about Establishment – unless we deem politics an absolute realm of its own – is not its vision but its partial institutional form. That form no longer registers the diversity of the population nor the secularization of the public mind.

Surely, however, in the meantime, with this prospect ahead, a still constitutional "national Church" is in no way reduced – or reducible –

to a "notional Church". Recent diversification of the population does not undo centuries of history. Nor does secularity reverse the significance of Shakespeare with his genius, Milton with his *Areopagitica*, Bunyan "with a book in his Pilgrim's hand", Burke with his "Thoughts", or Clare, Cowper, Wordsworth and all the lyricists of the English countryside. All these and their sundry peers are in the fabric of the nation's soul. They duly belong with its continuing identity. Their legacy abides in the very process of "willing the selves we are" which time in its passing for ever imposes.

In such willing it could be that those very "monuments of God", the architectural tokens that, being stone, survive better than their rites, may still hold us to the living task. Even a sceptical mood can recognize in them "a serious house, on serious earth – a place fit to grow wise in".[44] Museumize them? If we will we may. For there is something insistent about their sheer physical survival, even when in ruins, that mistimes the incidence of human frames of mind. What once yearned to rear them can still surprise us.

If the State is always in the making of the human will to it, so also is the Church. "The love that endures all things" is never static. The liabilities it faces have to be read as the assets it must redeem. Judicious Hooker always sought to persuade into lively being the widest possible consensus, the tolerances that a patient rationality might induce in honest minds. That temper of the Church whose single-hearted advocate he became has comparable current tasks far from the perspectives of his Elizabethan world. How right, for example, of the Buddha and of Buddhism to set the riddle of the human self at the centre of the religious quest, how strange to resolve it by surmising that selfhood only ever existed as an illusion to be voided. For must not that mean forfeiting the more inclusive mystery of history at large? Yet, from that verdict came a way of moral discipline, a path of self-awareness not unlike – on quite contrasted premise – the crisis-meaning told in Christian baptism.[45]

How wise in the Hindu to perceive that there is a bias in our birth, that past wrongs carry their entail into the future. How sad that these should be read as incapable of love's retrieving action as crucial to the very logic by which they mattered. What deep converse the Christian has with the majesty of Islamic theism and its inclusive sense of the dignity of humankind in sure entrustment of liable custody in the good earth. How crucial, in turn, the Christian's perception of the Cross of Christ to the confessing of *Allahu akbar*.

The Christian's quarrel with the secular humanist is not that we can conclude that "we are on our own".[46] It is that this very liberty so to conclude is the very evidence of how magnanimously it is not so. For so a divine generosity may be discerned in the very neglibility of God in all our thoughts. That may be read as a sure token of the infinite risk of love and ride well with the crisis urgently constituted in and by our selfhood. Thus the "sacred" is not some arbitrary imposition but rather the responsible destiny of the "secular", just as the "secular" in turn may be known, in all its risky wonder, as the raw material of the "sacred".

Such summary thoughts are not to suggest that Christian faith "trumps" every case it faces, with no listening will, no conscious reticence. They are to say that there is a motion towards Christ in every inter-religious, inter-cultural encounter, a resonance in the Gospel when doubts and diversities are intelligently heard and, indeed, loved for their own sake and not as subjects to a propaganda. There will, we may assume, always be more than enough Christians of a mind to witness from arbitrary assertion and requiring submission to a given dogmatism. All the more urgent place, then, for a Christian presence amid such "strife of tongues" and aches of heart that knows itself "ambassador", whose credentials come as "presentable" by a courtesy alert both to what it tells and where it comes. For such, with all his vigorously controversial bent, was Paul's favoured word – "commendation", the Greek *sustatikos* from *sunistemi*, meaning "to establish together", "to cause mutually to cohere" "to find common consistency of mind".[47] There will be enough examples, if not of this art, then of realms in which it may be practised and know itself skilled, in the chapters that follow. For such is their intent. There can be "Christ in the learning", "a learning through Christ" in every dimension of society and of experience. There is one final consideration. It has to do with what, both theologically and experientially, undergirds all such schooling.

VII

It consists in how divine self-expending, central to the entire Biblical understanding of creation, comes to climax in the self-offering of Jesus as the Christ and continues in the ever-vulnerable ministries of the Holy Spirit. All belong with "the God of patience" (a term characteristic of New Testament faith) where these three dimensions – purposing, redeeming and hallowing – all combine in divine *kenosis*, where "being passes unreservedly into giving".[48] "Emptying" misleads us if some quantity is in view so that, when emptied out, it is no longer "there". There *is* an emptying where a quality is more present in being more risked, more itself in being more "spent". Such "spending and being spent" is the cardinal dimension of Christian theism. It can be partially grasped by an analogy from "status" – something inherently self-regarding and self-protecting, like rank, dignity, office, prestige – which in other realms proves its true quality in putting all these in doubt the better to fulfil its real nature.

To think the very sovereignty of God of this self-foregoing order – befitting and fulfilling sovereignty *per se* – is where "Christ-learning" came and for ever comes, seeing that in and from the Cross God teaches us to think into His nature, the truth of "Who He is". It follows that the Church that has this sense of things is summoned into a parallel truth about itself, in that "being-in-giving" has to be the clue to its life.

At once we can see the implication for that surrender of privilege and the possible prejudice of pride which old "Christendom" afforded to long centuries of the Church. It is not simply that secularization in the West restores us to something like the condition of the early, totally vulnerable, Church. The intervening centuries cannot be undone. Their legacies cannot be rescinded. Yet, within all that recollection of them retains, their habits of mind have to be yielded up. Their instincts are superseded by all that intellectually confronts us, and more radically and societally disadvantages both liturgies and ethics.

Cannot, then, the whole experience be read as falling within the age-long vocation to *kenosis*, to accepting an "unselfing" in one order which spells a truer self? It is useful to recruit from an Iris Murdoch novel to illuminate the meaning. For, as we have seen, she was no sanguine purveyor of religion. In *Henry and Cato*, she has a character wrestle with what is her perpetual theme, namely "the long, long task of unselfing". He deplores "the tissue of illusions" with which we delude ourselves. The chief of these is self-perception, our sense of having an importance no one should violate. From this all our tiresome resentments derive. We can hardly endure being mocked. Yet, in our absurdity "mockedness" is what we need to understand and accept, since, when we arrive to saying: "There is no one there", perhaps you are on the brink of an important truth".[49] Christ, too, was mocked.

The lesson is clear. We must be ready for "self-noughting" – ready in the most inclusive sense. Murdoch over-mounts the case. She makes even a sense of guilt and a will to be forgiven tokens (as sometimes they may well be) of our inveterate egoism. The will to self-forgetfulness, which she so admires, has no place of attainment, if "there is no one there", no self to be "selfless". Plainly the empirical ego-hood, i.e., our being as such, has to be distinguished from the chronically acquisitive version that, ethically, it is for ever constrained to be. If that constraining as potentially perverting all things, even love, penitence, kindness, hope and desire, is "all there is" of me, then the very selflessness Murdoch so steadily admires has no habitat, no life, no arena, no ground, no will. Selfhood is indispensable to any quest of selflessness.

Mutatis mutandis, is it not this way with institutions? They have the same destructive appetite for glory, place, honour, recognition, and – in those terms – "establishment". Being collectives, these prideful things in them are fortified by the personal lusts of office, rank and esteem amid their private members. Religions are most of all in need of due "unselfing" and precisely in being religions find the destiny so hard, so uncongenial, so seemingly contradictory to all they have to be in deliberate power and resonance.

The Christian story has, in God's own *kenosis*, the sufficient corrective. Faith in a self-expending Lord cannot well argue a self-admiring, self-imprisoning organ in its name. In due perspective, it will be proper to read in contemporary secularity a hint, if not a summons, to such interpretation of our calling. To safeguard wrongly is to forfeit justly. The divine *kenosis* at the heart of Christian theology has to be the evident mentor of "ecclesiastical policy".

Do not the New Testament writers draw theirs from "Christ-learning"? The *kenosis* passage itself is prefaced by: "Let this same mind be in you which was in Christ Jesus". Elsewhere, Paul writes of "bearing in the body the dying of the Lord" (2 Corinthians 4: 10) as how "his life is manifested". He may be alluding first to physical costs in his mission, from persecution and tribulation, "carrying in the body" some affinity to the Cross itself. His own inaugural vision en route to Damascus had brought together, in one "persecution", the mortal Church and the Christ in heaven. But there was more to his words.

Death, seen as the most self-noughting thing in our human awareness,[50] becomes the most telling analogy, for institutions, of their ongoing authentic life in the shape that such "dying" preludes. There are things of which we rightly say: "It is expedient that they go away." So Jesus assured his own first disciples in respect of their clinging fascination with post-Easter experience. So it remains in all the generations.

This truth was no more eloquently expressed than in the comment the Fourth Gospel attributes to Jesus in response to the enquiry of "certain Greeks". "Except a corn of wheat fall into the ground and die, it abides alone but, if it die, it brings forth much fruit" (John 12: 24).[51] The ebbing of "ecclesiastical polity" may only show to agnostic mind "the naked shingles of the world". To heirs of the Gospel it may open the shore to new tides of vocation.

Matthew Arnold's metaphor, anyway, was ill-judged. For ebbing alone was never the manner of tides. But to be alert to what *has* receded in our recent generations, to be realists at the "dis-inklings" about truth, worship, prayer and attention to God, we must know where we are. There are ways of reading Jesus' precept about "the corn of wheat" which lose sight of the fruit abiding out of the apparently lost. The historian Arnold Toynbee, for example, believed that "Easter was premature". Jesus remained forever in Gethsemane. The world stayed always in Good Friday in that truth and love, somehow, forfeited their final mystery if ever "triumphant".[52] One may say that some more recent Jewish thinking absents itself from Christian hope on similar grounds.[53]

Any such thinking would be valid if the Easter of the Church was understood without the ongoing meaning in its being the truth of the prior Gethsemane. It is no "happy ending" fit to be distrusted as merely gratifying the clamant demands of human solace. It was – and is – the evidence of that "other side" whence *kenosis* came. For that reality of "self-given-ness" has no point in lowliness without its source in majesty. The word itself is doubly significant – both whence and whither. "Mercy and truth are met together". Or, in the language of doxology: "The Lamb is in the midst of the throne." Theology and Christology describe one circle. "The crown of glory" and "the crown of thorns" together tell "the God of patience".

We now turn from the large, documentary "chapters in faith-crisis" to explore in literature and biography more personal measures of their meaning and their continuity.

SIX

Amid the Irony of "Kindly Light" – with John Henry Newman

I

"Kindly light . . . lead thou me on . . .". There is more than a poetic justice in coming to John Henry Newman in the words of his most celebrated hymn. "Lead, kindly light" was never meant for public singing yet it established itself as a most evocative symbol of Victorian Christian piety. Few could have known – perhaps not even Newman himself – where he located "moor and fen", his "crag and torrent", nor to what his "garish day" referred. His early nurture had been devout enough, and sheltered, and he had emerged – if not without mishaps – into academic pastures congenial to his mind and mood.

If there was deep irony in the destiny of the hymn there was deeper irony still in his reading of "encircling gloom". For, while its immediate reference was clear enough in the shadows of the contemporary liberalism he so hated, it was one which, more intelligently identified, he could never escape or not, at least, by any "*kindly* light". The supreme lesson of Newman's biography is that to seek certitude in religion for the sake of certitude is never to attain it, seeing that the ultimate faith must always leave room within itself for doubt of itself. The things of faith have to be as Newman's contemporary, the historian J. A. Froude, was to write of Tennyson and Carlyle: truth lovers have "to let the uncertain remain uncertain".[1]

This, beset with thirst for a sure haven, an impulse to soul-security, Newman found both impossible and inappropriate. He needed to convince himself that the revelation of God, if it had given itself into the human scene, could not have failed to identify the institution to which it had been assuredly entrusted. To have neglected this evident requisite would have been to betray the whole. When he became distrustful of his first youthful repository of this indispensable incorporated *vade mecum* of divine truth, he sought and found another.

Yet his whole subsequent career found itself caught in the fallacy that cost him dearly. His will for "guarantee" had shifted the onus from where in truth it belonged to where it could not properly be had. It was as if he had paraphrased the words in 2 Timothy 1: 12: "I know in whom I have trusted . . ." to have them read: "I know where I have resorted . . .". It was a revision that – as we have studied in earlier chapters – ran counter to what the New Testament, by its very nature as a document of faith, could credibly underwrite. It would qualify for the rebuke that said: "You have not so learned Christ". The "learning" that had been the faith's own story had not come in those guaranteed terms. Indeed, the ensuring institution for which Newman opted to warrant his Christianity owed itself, in more pristine shape, to the very Gospel which now needed it as copywriter. His intensely private poem – for such it was – addressed the "kindly light" as "Thou" yet, in retrospect, his appeal was institutional. Christ may not be thus displaced as the theme of the trustworthy. None can well desire security by other credentials than Christ's own.[2]

Thus abruptly to state the significance of John Henry Newman in the company of Christ-learners is to acknowledge duties of argument to be offered in the sequel. The baldness is deliberate. We shall encounter in the following chapter a reckoning with doubt, on the part of Robert Browning, that may illuminate by contrast. Meanwhile, let us return to "kindly light" and "encircling gloom".

II

When Newman wrote the lines he was returning on shipboard in the Tyrrhenian Sea by Sardinia, from a long and perilous travel saga. He had been close to death in Sicily, nursed precariously back from delirium by a devoted servant. That part of his eastern travels had been intensely lonely.[3] There were brooding issues awaiting his return to his cherished "dreaming spires" of Oxford. "Dawn" with "the angel faces" was far to seek, however piously awaited. He had been face to face with himself, his ardent ambitions, his love–hate relation with controversy, his musing and gropings in the Church Fathers and his effort to insert their ancient controversies into immediate bearing on Oxonian tensions.

"Encircling gloom" may have been brought into the lines by sea-mists enwrapping his vessel. More thickly he saw them ominously clouding the ecclesiastical landscape at home. The "gloom" was the liberalism, as he reproachingly dubbed it, which was gathering pace in tune with the Great Reform Bill of 1832. That measures of Catholic Emancipation, on which so much in Newman's own future was to turn, would be his benison was hardly then apparent. But had it been, it would not have deterred him. It was merely to be another irony in his story.

It was enough that a reforming Parliament, in a creeping yet still tardy democratization of the suffrage, was laying secular hands on Mother Church. That unethical Irish Bishoprics deserved to be amended in the interests of justice and compassion towards a Catholic peasantry they exploited and oppressed, had not deterred John Keble from identifying "national apostacy" – no less – in these reforming gestures of a potential "national righteousness". It was enough that the autonomy of the "spiritual estate" was being challenged in terms that violated holy status and divinely ordained privilege. Things sacrosanct invaded anywhere would be threatened everywhere.[4] Hallowed structures were no quarry for unholy hands.

Anticipations and auguries more personally urgent were also laying siege to Newman's soul. Doubtless in retrospect on the turbulence of his inner journey, he could cry: "I was not ever thus". Yet where was he pleading to be led? The "light" he held was "kindly". Was that gracious to his foibles or akin (as "kind" by origin must be) to his nature? He had always been aware, as he said, of "only two realities – Almighty God and John Henry Newman".[5] It was a strange form of words, but wholly congenial to his mind. Goodly, and godly, upbringing had smiled on him and, despite uncharacteristic near failure as an undergraduate, fortune, or the Lord, had given him the coveted Fellowship of Oriel, then eminent among Oxford Colleges. Newman's tenure there, with its vicissitudes of status and temper, tested the deep, evangelical fervour with which he had first experienced the shape of an intimacy between those two supreme realities.

He grew increasingly alerted to what emerged for him as the central problem of authority – authority at once credal and ecclesial. Clearly the pair were intertwined. To know "whom one had believed" (if using that Pauline language) was to need to ascertain by what paths, on what grounds, one had come into the ken of it. True believing had to turn on sound receiving. His studies in Arianism had made him aware of how significantly doctrine could mistake itself and how its vagaries – as "orthodoxy" came to perceive them such – could distort original and definitive faith. Yet one would need to ask how faith had ever been "original", how it was becoming dependably "definitive". For those vital measures of discipleship had never been the creatures of an antecedent institution warranted to authorize them in any independence of their meaning. On the contrary the two – faith and community – were one emergent experience. The authority for belief could not be other than inherent in the story and the grace that had engendered it. It was not, finally, the "right" institution that had to be identified as authenticating the faith. For the faith had not generated its institutional custody in terms of any such external referent.

It was here that the fundamental error of Newman's urgency for right-church refuge belonged. The fear of heresy doubtless had its grounds. Vigilance is no enemy to sincerity. To "know whom one has believed" is not to be exempt from care to confess Him worthily and truly. But one does not do so by effectively shifting the onus to "where one has accepted to belong". The two may well come to be sensed as one but never so that the allegiance which reposes in a church takes over from the conviction informing mind and heart.

The latter has need to be perpetually alert and reverently revisable. Its "negative capability" means that it wrestles patiently with its own uncertainties and, therefore, looks for and dwells with the kind of authority that, as a structured institution, assumes and anticipates such perception of its role. It knows that neither faith nor church were meant for "infallibility". The lust for it, however circumscribed by subtlety, will violate the open nature of faith. Only "He in whom we have trusted" is able to keep, to guard and undertake what we have entrusted of our hearts and wills. The organs by which He does so – be they theologies or creeds or powers of order, discipline and means to meaning – are alway subject to His Holy Spirit so that they are never sufficient to themselves. To want or think them so is to violate their nature. To be anxious about their validity on any other terms would be a sort of "unlearning" of Christ and of the "rest in our souls" He promised.

It is not that, in all this, we are thrown back on the "private judgement" with which Newman was so obsessed as unwarranted individualism. We are not left to optionality, or random personal choosings, which he rightly saw to be inconsistent with the nature of Christian faith. "Knowing whom we have believed" is not of that order. Yet the faith is such that the personal equation is never absent from its confession or its recognition. It seems not always to have been evident to Newman that if we finally place the onus on identifying and then for ever heeding "the right Church", we have not avoided an act of "private judgement". We have exercised one and done so even more categorically in thereby opting out of ever resuming the task that led to it. We have changed the centre of gravity of faith.

The point at issue is not, immediately, whether we were wrong to do so: it is that, in so doing, we have not escaped a personal judgement, a decision in our personal will. It is we who have decreed that "the right authority" must exist, be ecclesial, and require our capitulation and that the implicit option we had is one we should explicitly conclude and surrender in this way. A reckoning on our part has necessarily been there. We have said, in terms different from the first meaning of

Newman's hymn: "One step enough for me".[6] It has been our step. It is evident that a critical "private judgement" has been made – but made in surrender to a Church identified, by credentials we have weighed, as "right".[7]

Are we then, was Newman, essentially different from a Luther saying "I can do no other" in precisely the opposite sense of disavowing the same authority? One soul's refuge becomes the other's repudiation, but both have concluded from within themselves. In either case, the authority that avails turns on being personally assessed. The case for an authority that addresses, lives with, but does not lust to override this situation of inherent personal liability for faith, employs the temper of the Anglicanism which Newman decisively renounced. There were painful aspects in the sequel of his Roman Catholicism that deeply interrogated his choice.

III

In thus formulating the core of Newman's significance we have run ahead of dimensions in his story to which we must return. First it is well to note how the very shape of the New Testament as an original Scripture puts a question-mark around the sort of primacy Newman's decision gave to church-institution. The documenting of Christianity in its New Testament form as a canonized Scripture certainly came only from and with community in faith. Yet it did so in strangely haphazard and seemingly fortuitous fashion. We have explored the circumstances sufficiently in CHAPTERS THREE and FOUR above. The Letters and the Gospels came from no "General Synod" and with no *Imprimatur* from a Holy See. They belonged squarely within the expanding outreach of faith-communities and with the lapse of generations in their possession of time. Something like a *Nihil obstat* might be read into their eventual canonization but not before apostolic mind in pastoral education had given them being as an exercise in a truly ecumenical ethics. For the way in which the one in Christ was becoming "many" across the lands required how that "many" should also be one in its discerning of Christian behaviour, that behaviour stemming with discipline from Christian doctrine.

The Gospels, as means of "living in a story" where that story had so widely reached, sustain the same point as the Letters. They may have clustered round particular communities, even noted cities, but they were not the promulgations of dogma in citadels. Their purpose was to enshrine in words "the Word made flesh" and they drew their *raison d'être*, and so their character and their authority, from no other intent. It is, therefore, impossible sanely to receive and heed them as more properly church-prescribing than Christ-presenting. In any event their haphazardness (as contrasted with how the Qur'an presents itself as heaven-dictated) belongs more with the freedom of the Spirit than the aegis of a hierarchy. Things synodical only came later attesting and affirming the antecedent status they possessed of themselves in the process of the Canon.

Is it not clear that these Christian Scriptures do not have the Church predominate over the prior theme of there being any church at all because of the reality of "God in Christ"? In the mutual entrusting that happens Godward and manward within the Christ-event, preoccupations around authority, structure and security, though not excluded, are subdued to the immediacies of grace and redemption as the first and last theme of faith. It is surely on those immediacies of "God in Christ" and "the Christ in God" that we must place our inclusive trust and esteem the Church as no more than their custodial creature and servant. In that due role it could never, in concept or effect, pretend to be substitute for them. Known in those terms, the issues, so crucial for Newman, concerning that Church's licence for that creaturely role take on a duly relative and subordinate character. It would be strange to think we have to agonize about the messenger when this sufficient Christ is the message.

It is painfully plain that Newman's mentality did not see it so. Insofar as the reasons were theological rather than temperamental,[8] they had to do with the vexed matter of truth and time, or – in one word – finality. Could the New Testament as the founding document be trusted to present the "fulness" of "the Word" that was "God in Christ"?[9] Or were there dimensions of an ultimate whole, only then implicit, which only the "right" Church could subsequently "develop" into explicitness over long centuries? If so, then clearly the credentials of that validator of "development" would be crucial and a legitimate anxiety in scrutiny might attend the faithful.

The idea of "development" had central place in Newman's thought and stemmed, in part, from his careful study of the early and later Fathers. It went far to precipitate his drift towards Rome. The other side of this coin, of course, was the Anglican principle of "the sufficiency" of Scripture. The term had a double import. It excluded the idea of "infallibility" or "inerrancy", so leaving necessary, indeed urgent, place for perceptive exegesis and an authentic role for scholarship. But it also held that the New Testament in its entire and apostolic provenance had sufficed to document and commend the founding "fulness" in Christ. To be sure, it had not formulated the Nicene or Apostles' Creed, still less Chalcedonian definitions. These had only been latent in its "fulness".

There had been "development" but it had occurred – and out of "sufficiency" could still occur – under the constraints of what was already and for aye, "the fulness of God". It was a defining "fulness" awaiting a possession determined by its finality in the liberty of its own authority.

In terms of scholarship and of devotion this was at once a more lively and a less pretentious quality in a Scriptured faith. Newman's keen mind, in his long Roman Catholic years, was often dismayed over the inhibited scholarship of allegiance in Roman terms – a scholarship which was not allowed to rely on that "sufficiency" in its ranging implications. And he was sometimes in spiritual strain over aspects of the workings of the rigorous principle of Church-auspices of "development" allegedly only latent – if not omitted – in Christ's "fulness".

The alleged need for, and presupposition of, those auspices explained a paradox of his career. For they engendered the anxieties about them, and their criteria, which interrogated his Anglicanism until they seemed to oblige him to forsake it. Yet when the right auspices – and their indispensable task – satisfied him institutionally he found himself often painfully at odds with what they yielded – strictly by leave of the *Magisterium*.

For, if they implemented what the New Testament had told as "the fulness", they could also be seen to compromise or imperil it. It is here that we reach the crux about "Christ-learning" in the Newman story. Did the paradox of "developing" the "fulness" – as the Roman condition of somehow ever rightly possessing it – imply that "fulness" was not adequately there initially? If not, had the Incarnation somehow not transpired? Had we been too long saying "Very God of very God" when there were yet more vital affirmings to "develop"? Was "learning Christ" – always a progressive discipleship in the soul – also a revised curriculum? Could an "infallible" Church ever be appropriate to a "sufficient" Christ, or ever come crucially to amend a once for all "fulness of God"? Instances of the question were many. With some, Newman's mind and temper came to be entirely at home. With others he was ill at ease. Either way, always central was the issue about "the fulness of Christ" as translating into "the sufficiency" of the Church via its Scripture. Might additives become essentials? Might original essentials find themselves made relative, not by total supersession but by an altering co-existence? If misgivings were to arise, as they did with Newman about aspects of what submission to Rome entailed, was it well to let that submission extenuate the moral or the intellectual disquiet and include an uneasy conscience in the meaning of the allegiance? If so, had faith not forfeited integrity?

Deferring sharp occasions of this order with Newman, the central point about the "fulness/sufficiency" equation can be illustrated in areas of the converting allegiance with which he was entirely at ease. Is the cult of Mary as "the Queen of Heaven" rightly "developed" from the "fulness of Christ"? Or would it be fair to ask, as it were with Paul: "Was Mary crucified for you?" There might be many impulses to her "coronation" – cultic, cultural, feminist, popular and mythopoeic. But must not Christ's "fulness", from a manger to the Cross, require that the "sufficient" mystery of Mary was her being "the handmaid of the Lord"? The Incarnation needed a human yieldedness enabling it. Mary, in the words of St. Bernard, had "that one thing to do", namely "offer what was hers and receive what was of God". It is "that one thing" which must belong with "all generations calling her Blessed". Mary is not well honoured in ways that take from her, and take her from, the lowly terms of her own surrender. Nor is she rightly "magnified" or "hailed" against the tenour of her own *Magnificat*, if we learn aright what "annunciation" meant.

Emmanuel, the vision said,
Here seeks nativity:
The travail of your low estate
His own necessity.

It is His love's prerogative
To come by need of you.
In every enterprise of God
Some human part is due.[10]

Newman knew himself aware of the danger of Mary coming between the soul and God but in his *Apologia* he expressed it in terms that seemed to ignore its superseding of the Cross.[11] His Roman allegiance was ready in other instances to align inner conviction uneasily with formal assent. What Paul meant in 2 Corinthians 10: 5 by "the obedience of Christ" was "a captivity which takes us captive".[12] For John Henry Newman, as for us all, the perennial theme of "Christ-learning" is to know ourselves mastered by the freedom of His truth through, and beyond, the perplexing yet mediating means that wait on it. We search in vain for an unattended, un-ecclesiased, unscriptured, unaccompanied Christ. There is no unschooled learning we can come by, yet the lesson is only, and for ever, "God in Christ". It must follow from our captivity to Him that all concurrent loyalties and debts consist within it.

IV

If we have thus concluded from Newman's long biography of Christian self-awareness – if aptly so described – there are features of it still to be explored. It is instructive to relate them to three accents in the "learning" invitation in Matthew 11: 28–30 sounding the whole theme of these chapters. We might think of them as "Newman and the gentleness", "Newman and the yoke", "Newman and the rest". We have seen throughout how these features interdepend. They suggest three queries latent in what he himself presented as his "apologia". Did the urgent focus on Church authority ride with a Christ "lowly of heart"? Was "the yoke" duly known and shouldered? Was "the rest" ever found as "the yoke" promised?

"Labouring" and "heavy-laden" were terms that fitted Newman's ever-toiling, ever-caring years, their intensity, their burdened preoccupations, their wearying controversies, their long sequence. The paradox of a "yoke" as "rest" never suggested relief from "laden-ness". In Matthew's context the contrast was between the "yoke" as symbol of an oppressive legalism[13] and that of discipleship to a "lowly Christ". The latter, freed from the tyranny of the former, meant the unremitting, self-expending toils of ministry as current in Galilee in the very breathing of the words, where "the miseries of the world were misery" and allowed no respite. By the same token they brought a surrender which resolved the question as to where discipleship should be and this was the meaning of the rest, and of the "lowliness", the simplicity of heart, by which selfhood had been recruited into "chartered freedom".[14]

What should be said of Newman's "laden-ness" – so heavily ecclesial, so steadily taken with the truth-question as mental (and romantic) certitude?[15] To the end of his life, on his own admission, he remained the same Tory he had been in 1832. He had had no different politics, no reconsideration of the stance Keble had sponsored in his Assize Sermon as "national apostacy".[16] Even the debt his Roman Catholicism owed to "liberal" emancipation and to Robert Peel did not restrain Newman from sharp attacks on the progressives to whom some gratitude belonged.

His passion for the security of his own dogma, and its inviolate refuge in his adopted Church, set him in resolute opposition to secular auspices of state education, the advance of science and even the notion of "public reading rooms". In his *Discussions and Arguments* (1872) he belaboured (cf. Matthew 11: 28) the Tamworth Reading Room, demanding to preserve a religious monopoly of education that would ensure the Church's vital role in the ordering of society. In this vein he wrote steady letters to *The Times*. Scientific knowledge could only have a fleeting effect like "cold beer". "Who was ever consoled," he asked, "in real trouble by the small beer of literature or science?"[17] The strictures he used were trenchant enough but anxiously bizarre:

> "If virtue be a mastery over the mind . . . we must seek it in graver and holier places that in libraries and reading rooms." He went on: "The pity is that these Christian statesmen cannot be content with what is divine without as a supplement hankering after what is heathen."[18]

He thought Peel was mistaken in commending "devout curiosity", the educative wonders of science, and open access to knowledge. These were like "hunting the slipper" when you should "go to Christianity" which was "the element and principle of all education".[19]

We will have other cause to note the wild intemperance of Newman's language – always a symptom of a frightened mind. If the common folk indulged their curiosity in this world they would leave none for the next. To indulge science was to risk religion. He wanted "truth to come first" and "amusement to follow". Faith – true faith – could only be had by antagonizing its opposite. Newman's theology seemed like a blind rearguard action totally negative in its stance, prejudiced and jaundiced. He protested that he was no politician. He had no measures to propose. He was simply opposing a fallacy and resisting secular "pretence". Blindly he opined: "What science tends to worship when it wonders is the mind that discovers rather than the Mind that creates."[20] Where, in all this bigotry, was the "yoke of Christ", where "rest to the soul"? One of Newman's biographers – such was the spell of his genius or his repute – offers an apologia for this bitter obscurantism in precisely the wrong terms.

> It is beside the mark to wonder at the apparent unconcern with which Newman saw, if he did see, the material conditions under which masses of his fellow-countrymen were compelled to live . . . or at the coldness with which he viewed the first, slight ameliorative activities of the State. The Tractarians were academic clergymen . . . It is useless to criticize them for not being something else.[21]

This entirely begs the question what "something else" they should have been as, in their robust way, Thomas Arnold, Charles Kingsley and F. D. Maurice, might have showed them. Had they let institutional pride of security disparage and preclude both the "meekness", the "earth-possessing" lowliness, of Christ and "the laden rest" it spelled?

A like impatience of stance and language characterized many of Newman's more directly theological strictures in propagation of right authority as he came to espouse it. Was it that somehow the yearning for certitude over-reached itself in the curious capacity he showed – both in the Tracts and in *Apologia* – to make subtle contradiction itself into a refined pro-argument? In his novel *Loss and Gain*, meant to be autobiographical, he had a character say:

> If the Church of Rome is as ambiguous as our Church, I shall be in the way to become a sceptic on the very ground that I shall have no competent authority to tell me what to believe.[22]

Yet he could romanticize about "the Church of Rome as the Face of God" on the ground of his mystical sense of God as transcending all reason. How, then, could an infallible organ be so indispensable? Only "this voice speaking in his heart – "making (him) rest in the thought of two and two only . . . luminously self-evident beings, himself and his Creator" – rescued him from atheism. Did the "luminously self-evident" also turn on the *imprimatur* of an external mentor? Did his sophistry incline to superstition? "We may surely concede a little superstition as not the worst of evils, if it be the price of making sense of faith".[23] Bigotry might be preferable to complacency. Even a bogus relic might legitimately induce reverence and conduce to vital faith. Religious truth being subtle, mysterious and vulnerable, its guardian must be duly authoritarian if it is to survive.

How far away this stance from "fulness in Christ"! Newman's resort to Rome *in those terms* of apprehensive haven-seeking ought surely to have found room and warrant for

> the eager, restless energies of reforming spirits, men who find their way of obedience as a kind of revolt against the institution which they serve in the name of the realities which give that institution its significance.[24]

But Newman's dispute with liberalism was implacably hostile.

For all the mystical "kindliness of the light" he solicited, his own language in controversy could be harshly polemical. It seems to be indicative of absolutisms that they can betake themselves to calumny. There was a telling persuasiveness about his voluminous *Parochial and Plain Sermons*, but elsewhere he might stoop to satire and vituperation. There were times when it seemed that the urgent safeguards against superstition should be relaxed in the interests of a resolute faith. His strictures against the Church that had first nurtured him could become fanatically inimical. "It was a palace of ice and when summer came it melted all away."[25] The Church of England became for him worthless and without a soul. It merely aped Catholic authority and confused the evidence. It fitted the English mood of libertarian fancy and its sluggish soul. Not knowing what it held it nevertheless contrived to hold it vacuously. Its Prayer Book was a mere Act of Parliament and its Cathedrals "the spoils of Catholicism". The animal minds of the English preferred to choose their religion for themselves. Thus they needed a Church that conceded this as their right. It existed with "no article or canon to lean against, sitting on a non-existent chair".[26] He accused the saintly

Edward B. Pusey of "keeping souls in a system which cannot . . . rest upon any authority beside your own".[27] For the rest he – and Rome – "would show these (Protestant) Midianites what Gideon can do".[28]

The evident bigotry in these postures of Newman might be redeemed from evidencing an injudicious temper by the plea that these were the hazards of emotive controversy. Even so, a kindlier light might have chastened them but for his passion round unassailable dogma, suppressing what might call its certitude in question. Even his Roman loyalty, as we must see, required him

> to combine devotion to the Church with discrimination and candour in the treatment of her opponents, to reconcile freedom of thought . . . under a deep sense of the prerogatives of ecclesiastical authority.[29]

Such prerogatives, however, were unilateral. The irony was that Newman's Catholicism came to owe so much to the "liberal" England he despised in respect of a Catholic hierarchy and the opportunity to "convert" with impunity – an opportunity on which his personal magnetism so effectively seized. By the "gentle" criteria of Jesus' Matthean invitation the query presses: What of Newman's "learning"?

V

Answer must be taken further. "Learn of me" the invitation said. Clearly that "me" could not be shorn of question. The very invitation was "reportage" bound over to issues its very existence broached.[30] Newman was right to point out that simple appeal to the Bible as if, of itself, "impregnable", could not avail, seeing that the Scripture was an entrusted thing, an entity only affording truth-to-faith in a context larger than itself. The living Church, albeit Biblically living, was – via doctrine and tradition – the realm of truly comprehended faith. So much was implicit in the very fabric of "learning Christ" – implicit and needing to become explicit in the growing *confessio fidei*.

What Newman did not, believed he could not, allow was that this implicit, become explicit, faith as to "God in Christ" had failed of a guaranteed "edition" safeguarded for evermore in an institution possessing it, inviolate through all ongoing time like some "standing apostolic committee . . . to be its home, its instrument and its guarantee".[31] That claim was as faulted as the simple Biblicism and for the same reason, namely that the instrument itself short-circuited a task and a destiny to be shared with the Holy Spirit of God. The "learning" in the Christ would shape the "school" of his Church: the "school" would need to be perennially in pupil, not managerial, status. "Learn of me" would certainly mean "Learn through mine", never that "mine" equal "me". The situation could not be as Newman perceived it; since "private judgement" would be enlisted in the "learning" as part of faith's integrity. Nor could the "mine" of Christ's "true church" supersede the vocation of personal and corporate faith "as a man out of doors uses a lamp on a dark night and puts it out when he gets home. What would be thought of his bringing it into his drawing room?"[32]

That there was an extra-Biblical fact of "development" Newman sanely recognized and rightly stressed. That "living long and changing much", the Church incurs problems of "development" incessantly is not in question. Newman's alertness to the issue, albeit polity and society-wise inactive or moribund, was mentally valid. His error – out of an ultimate timidity – was to wish its onus monopolized and entirely safe-guarded in a single (western) identifiable Church presiding impeccably in terms of its own impregnable *magisterium*. A monitor of divine truth, however prestigious in the worldly terms of history, could not exempt itself from the menace of its own vagaries nor from the pulsating claims of life, of scholarship, of courage and of hope outside its borders and perhaps its comprehension. Was there not both pretension and danger in the notion of an evolving writ

> the new form, explanation, transformation, or carrying out of what in substance was held from the first, what the Apostles said but have not recorded in writing, or would necessarily have said under our circumstances, or if they had been asked, or in view of certain uprisings of error . . . ?[33]

The concept here saw that "Christ-learning" had a future. Could it have final auspices so immodestly self-appointed? As such ambitious means must they not enter into the equation only as a party to its reckoning, not its unique presiding genius? One could hardly imagine a more timorous analyst and watchman of necessary "development" than so premonitory a mind as John Henry Newman's. Vigilance surely has its part in integrity but an alert theology needs more than a keen fear of heresy. Faith may be impoverished if too ready with anathemas. Even so self-conscious a theologian as Newman felt himself to be could be taken in the pitfall to which all doctrine is liable, namely that of "saying what is meant without avoiding to say what is not meant". For the sake of both truth and clarity it must be alive to its own potential ambiguity.[34] Two examples in Newman relate to the two most central items of his Christian dogma, namely the Incarnation and the Cross.

A *Parochial Sermon* has him saying: "God was taking upon Him her (i.e., Mary's) flesh and humbling Himself to be called Her offspring. Such is the deep mystery."[35] So stating Christian faith – Roman Catholic and non-Roman alike – Newman makes a true statement of doctrine but, doing so, he does not exclude what true faith must exclude, namely that the womb of Mary has given "God" being in giving birth to Jesus – if we are to understand the meaning as in a human genealogy in which, for example, "George Washington was the offspring of Mary Washington". For then, the eternal, ever-real, ever-sovereign Lord of heaven and earth would have come into life out of a prior non-entity. Calling "God" "Her offspring" admits of that interpretation, destroying the very paradox in which the faith – and the "mystery" – stand. To offset that peril-in-words one must say: "The Word was made flesh" and, "in the flesh the Word was God",[36] with Mary as the human means. The credal phrase "God the Son" safeguards this vital self-giving into history of One ever self-subsisting in eternity. The paradox is only safe when it is known and told as such. Otherwise it ceases even to be paradoxical and becomes unwittingly a sort of blasphemy.[37]

The other example concerns the memorable occasion told by J. A. Froude as "an epoch in the mental history of more than one of my Oxford contemporaries" when "for a few moments there was a breathless silence" as Newman said:[38]

> Yes! we shall all . . . one day see that holy countenance which wicked men struck and dishonoured: we shall see those hands which were nailed to the Cross . . . we shall see all this and it will be the sight of the living God.[39]

Authentic, truly! The occasion, recalled by more than Froude alone, had the whole mystique of Newman's oratory, the music of his voice and the near rapture of his hearers in St. Mary's.

Yet it hung essentially on a right perception of his meaning. There was a sense in which it could not be true – a sense which more than ill-will or bare distaste might register. Were the brutalities of Good Friday being "done to God"? Indeed, but to "God in Christ" – not that the Eternal was immune (the "in-Christ-ness" excludes that) but that the participation of the eternal nature happened in the drama, in the history, in the "God-in-Christ" reality of Jesus crucified as the disclosure the Eternal uses to identify Himself. That now known, now proven, identity belongs with a transcendent omnipotence the victim's Cross seems, but only seems, to violate. We cannot right let our preaching mislead those hearers (like Muslims) who might think we had blasphemed or, by their lights, had meant to say what they had taken us to mean.

In his immediate Oxford scene, his pulpit place and 19th-century time, Newman might well be absolved. Yet on his own insistent showing the theological task for ever "develops", and that, not only from the whence of retrospect but into the whither of an open world. Newman, like Rome itself, was always Europe-centred and thought from Greek and Latin.[40]

VI

What of Christ-learning as "rest unto his soul"? The question takes us into his post-conversion experience and finally into the measure of his very soul. Can it be said that Newman found the logic of his great decision truly vindicated? Was his character somehow always at odds with his peace? There were certainly many ironies about his relations with Wiseman and the old English Catholics and about the mischances of his foray into Ireland, then his "heavy-laden" withdrawal to the Oratory in Birmingham. It was possible to claim from his *Idea of a University* and of his *Grammar of Assent* that he could be a formidable exponent of the role of mind and philosophy in the exploration of faith. So could he be "liberal" in some measure after all, though he insisted in his Cardinalate Speech:

> I rejoice to say to one great mischief I have from the first opposed myself. For thirty, forty, fifty years I have to the best of my power resisted the spirit of liberalism in religion . . . an error overspreading as a snare the whole earth.[41]

Was there perhaps a catch in the meaning of the word so that, while "liberalism" must be a deadly foe of faith, it might somehow avail and obtain elsewhere – though, not for Newman, in politics.[42] Who was to distinguish between where necessary religious thought banned all liberty as false (being out of place from the constitution of the human mind) and where the would-be believer could exercise "private judgement" before it was duly superseded in arrival at "the true Church".[43] Or was the enigma resolved in the alleged "rationality" of the submission?

In his time with *The Rambler* he seemed to reach for a way to embrace freedom of thought and manly investigation of themes of public significance. Yet he acknowledged that the journal was "an unmanageable vessel". In any event, Biblical "investigations" should be left to the academics, under a pontifical supervision. And was he, or was he not, Ultramontane, always Papacy-subservient, or did he have reservations? Logically the first, instinctively perhaps the second. Even Infallibility, he recognized, would need – was assumed to need – interpretation. The hierarchical Church, he observed, "would look odd without the laity". For in some way all things Catholic *de fide* needed their *fides implicita*. "Their consensus through Christendom was the voice of the infallible Church." "They were a mirror in which the bishops see themselves", yet to be consulted by the hierarchy rather as a physician consults the patient's pulse, not how the patient consults them.[44] Actual belief was testimony to apostolic tradition, but lay opinion could not be party to its definition.

Distinguishing thus between capacities to possess and warrant to define – so crucial to Newman's concept of authority – must surely suggest some ultimate reference to, or place for, ongoing "private" minding of the faith. The laity, anyway, were divided sharply over wanting, or not wanting, the promulgation of Papal Infallibility. Allegedly the "lay" reservoir welled up to it yet, for many, including Newman, it could only be accommodated by an act of submission. Whatever his instincts, Newman proved quite unable to rescue English "Liberal" Catholics from the Ultramontanes, nor – on his own premises – could he think to do so. Yet this circumstance was an element of the ill-at-ease-ness of his closing years, despite the ultimate benison of being made a Cardinal with its strange antecedent "negotiations".

There was pain for him in the irony that the hierarchy to which his theory looked too often baulked his very case-making. In the days of the Tracts he had undergone this anomaly. The Bishops whose role he invoked refused to deliver the due episcopal order. It was like the Biblicists needing to have the Bible somehow override itself to vindicate their way with it and necessarily failing to do so. Newman's Bishops were not actually behaving in terms of Tractarian views of Apostolic Succession. Newman wrote:

> The Bishop cannot give me a licence to derogate from his authority – he has no self-destructive power. To uphold him and the Church is a plain Christian duty.[45]

The Papacy, too, *a fortiori*, had no "self-denying power". Must the *consensus fidelium* be always compromised by personal reservations and these, in turn, compromised by formal submission, perhaps even as a surrender of conscience?

Newman's numerous papers, diaries and correspondence through his long Roman years are sombre evidence of the "heavy-laden" heart he carried through them. The logic of his loyalty meant there was no "de-conversion" but the price was ongoing travail. "I wish to make friends with it, it will not make friends with me." As an Anglican "religion had been dreary but not my life". As a Roman Catholic "life was dreary but not my religion". The very authority he was exalting was also taking him where "he had so few things to sympathize with him".[46] He could only leave the onus on the responsible authority that duly occasioned what he underwent but the undergoing was his alone. The pathos in the oft-quoted passage on "the parting of friends" is unmistakable.

> On the morning of the 23rd I left the Observatory. I have never seen Oxford since, excepting its spires as they are seen from the railway.[47]

The railway was no place to possess the spires. That the pain was the chosen price only made the cost more heavy. In Rome prior to his second Ordination he wrote of lacking "a practical, lively and present faith" to counter "the evil spirit in my heart". His state of mind was a gloomy sort of despair.[48] "I have a load of care," he wrote later "and no one to take pity on me." These soul-privations may well explain, if not justify, the frequent acerbity of his case-making and his disputings. He had surrendered himself into a harness whose ordering was not his own – or his own only by once-for-all decision. Did he brood long for the opportunity Charles Kingsley blunderingly afforded him? Cardinal Manning thought the *Apologia* a masterpiece of spiritual deceit.

Newman was oppressed by intrigues around him inside and outside his chosen Church. Just as in his Anglican days Canterbury and his Bishops had not believed the Tractarian thesis about them, so Newman's Papacy failed to conform to the theology he held for it and he was caught in the dilemma of outer surrender and inner disquiet, experience somehow interrogating his deepest and costliest act of allegiance. Did the long, explorative labour on his *Grammar of Assent* owe itself to impending Infallibility?

Was there an even deeper "labouring" still in his latent scepticism about humans at large? The intense moralism of his *Parochial* – indeed of his *University Sermons* – has often been remarked: their heavy emphasis on sin and the sense of it. It could have been that he equated the "liberalism" he loathed with something like a "scepticism" of the sort, that is, that loves to have truth ever sought and never found. His was a sharper moral scepticism noting how "human nature remains what it was though it has been baptized".[49] In *The Idea of a University* he had written:

> Quarry the granite rock with razors or moor the vessel with a thread of silk – then you may hope with such keen and delicate instruments as human knowledge and human reason to contend against these giants, the passion and the pride of man.[50]

Was it finally this "burden" that made him the absolutist he required himself to be and, so being, only weighted the burden the more?

VII

If in his anguished story he finally emerges as a figure of profoundly religious pathos a final irony persists. Was there something in his temperament that yielded the biography he traced, even as that biography reacted on his set of soul? There was a deeply rooted egotism in his sense of John Henry Newman. We have noted those "two realities" – God and himself – in that order of their statement. There was a sense of personal theatre about the very sincerity of his self-image. His Oxford career, his gifts of eloquence in the pulpit and magnetism in the student arena, all ministered to it. He could be fastidious, opinionated and exacting in his patterns of relationship, yet with a charm and charisma that might make his advancement serene. Few things in his time and place proved so emotive and dramatic as his conversion to Rome, reinforced by the disciples he drew into the emulation. His capacity for intellectual subtlety, even plain casuistry, inspired awe in admiring circles and a sense of treachery in others. Either way, his writing served to fascinate, if unwittingly, as a stage-production might.[51] Newman's mode of genius allowed the soul no respite from an ever demanding, exerting and exacting self, and "rest unto the soul" proved ever elusive, or had to be conjured out of motives and doings that contrived only to defer it. Had he turned to Rome in some psychological retaliation against a disappointing Anglicanism, not for the latter's "dubious apostolicity" but for its disallowing of his ecclesiology?[52] Did he then allow a legend of persecution to develop when he wanted the Thirty-Nine Articles to be read as "not anti-Roman"?

A "yoke" he certainly carried but was it "the yoke of Christ"? "If I looked into a mirror and did not see my face . . ." what then? His own brother, F. Newman, found him a self-centred "puzzle" to whom he ceased to go for counsel, religious intercourse or sympathy.[53] It might seem that the downrightness of his theology, embodied in an institution that had stood the test of time and was "free from vagaries and excesses", matched the romanticism and the impulses of his mind.[54] What he sought and found was a structure of security and an assurance of religious certitude. In its terms the abiding mystery of human selfhood remained unresolved, if also passionately and painfully underlined.

It is well to leave a study of Christ-learning in John Henry Newman with his famous classic, *The Dream of Gerontius*. Its lyrical beauty gives pause to all the strictures his story invites. In measure, its poetry breathes the same ardent egotism we have noted in Newman's polemics and discourses, the same yearning for the soul's well-being, but now transferred to what lies beyond death. Here is the same reverence that had often reproached the mentality that drew near to truth without homage and presumed to handle things divine with intellectual bravura. The eternal sphere of *The Dream* brought Newman to the most hauntingly sacred realm of faith – his soul's eternal destiny. He was now beyond his visceral hatred of "secular education", free from the vanity in the driving force of his arguments, beyond the trauma of "assent within dissent", rid of the scorn that despised the Protestants, exempt from the incessant urge to strike a figure and be appreciated. Now, with all these attendant dimensions of his mortality, he stood on the threshold of what should purge them. "It was a dream" – that of an old man – "I have said what I saw". He was facing "that masterful negation and collapse of all that makes me man", and asked: "What is this severance?" It is the same Newman who had looked into the mirror for assurance that his selfhood was, indeed, self-warranted. But now, led by his ever guardian angel, he knows, with a new wonder and a deeper awe, how he has been God's "viceroy in the world of matter and of sense". Present before his Judge, "severe e'en in the crucifix", he learns "that the flaming of everlasting Love doth burn 'ere it transform".[55]

Even in shifting the centre of gravity of his "certitude" so squarely from "Christ-learning" to "Church-sure-havening" he had been right about how "Christ comes not in pride of intellect". Indeed, one should "look hard at all pretentious gifts in silence", whether the pretence be personal or institutional, and "ask for the print of the nails".[56]

His contemporary, the poet Robert Browning, would be coming to these like many other Victorians, with a liberty of doubting faith Newman could only have deplored.

SEVEN

Through the Reach of Poetic Doubt – with Robert Browning

I

"I cannot doubt that I am doubting," wrote the 17th-century philosopher, René Descartes, musing in his *Discourse on Method*. He was right enough proceeding that way to reach an indubitable self in cerebral activity. Plainly – no doubter, no doubting. He might thus reach his "I think and so I am" conclusion, though the formula is a very dubious one. It can more pointedly be reversed into: "I am and so I think." That way round, one might well need to be doubting one was doubting, or maybe we should rather say: "doubting one's doubting".

If that sentiment is relishing a certain subtlety, how the poet Robert Browning would have savoured it. He was eloquently given to doubting doubt and is often found stating Christian faith that way. So he is, on that score, an admirable choice on which to measure, beyond Newman, the reach of doubt in the soul's "learning Christ". No modern English poet has more tellingly identified and voiced the heart-significance of "God in Christ" and yet housed his personal conviction of it in more teasingly questioning terms.

Often thought of as a boisterous optimist, he had a radical realism about the depths of human depravity and a lively inquisition into the foibles and fantasies of believers. There is no more spirited example of the tasks Christian conviction has with its own assurance.

> . . . I doubt at every pore,
> Head-doubts, heart-doubts, doubts at my fingers' ends,
> Doubts in the trivial work of every day:
> Doubts at the very bases of my soul
> In the grand moments when she probes herself . . .

He has his Bishop Blougram say.[1] When public feeling demanded that Browning be buried in Westminster Abbey in "Poets Corner", his contemporary, the novelist Henry James, remarked:

> A good many oddities and a good many great writers have been entombed in the Abbey . . . but none of the odd ones have been so great and none of the great ones so odd.[2]

If it be "odd" to have a poetic mind, and a style, like a laboratory, probing, analyzing, measuring and refining both belief and doubt, and doing so with an enormous appetite for life and society, then Browning qualifies.

There is something inherently private about faith and the doubt of faith. That must be our reason for centring this chapter and its theme around a single personality – appropriately a poet – who, for reasons that will appear, provides the keenest personal frame in which to set our exploration of Christ-learning in the constraints of accompanying anxiety. For Browning's was a perpetually enquiring quality of doubt, fully open to the mental world that brooded with it. It was a questioning quite contrasted with the firm agnosticism of a Thomas Hardy. Hardy's poems and novels showed a strong emotional and compassionate identity with the victims, as he saw them, of an often malign and always inscrutable divinity playing with a remorseless jesting on human wistfulness. He was able to convey that situation with an urgent pity and a lyrical mastery of landscape description and character discernment. He rarely ventured, however, into the intellectual reckonings his ironies demanded. His emotions drew the Christian bearings, not from Biblical scholarship or metaphysics, but from a youth he perceived as rawly done by in the rustic privations he begrudged and from memories of village fiddlers accompanying old hymns or the fascinations of the church architecture he had studied in his apprenticeship to life. These associations, it might be said, comprised an existential accusation of mortal injustice which did not delve below its own data for the reasons that might have tempered its despairs and balanced its ambiguities.

Nor would A. E. Housman, for all the telling pathos of his *A Shropshire Lad*, serve us better than Browning in the weighing of doubt. For Housman allowed himself to be at odds with God in the wake of a bitter failure in his youth which soured powers that might have sweetly reversed the entire logic of his retrospect. He persuaded himself that, in his own words: "Hope lies to mortals and most believe her, but man's deceiver was never mine." Biblical imagery was there only to register a negation.

> I never over Horeb heard
> The blast of advent blow.
> No fire-faced prophet brought me word

Which way behoved to go.
Ascended is the cloudy flame,
The mount of thunder dumb,
The tokens that to Israel came
To me they have not come . . .

. . . The heart goes where no footsteps may
Into the promised land.[3]

Housman measures what faith needs to undertake: he is no mentor for doing so. Certainly Robert Browning did not begin adolescence with a wry bitterness assessing the world in dark terms. His nurture was relatively serene and his family well endowed. Though his abilities brought him no pupil honours in the usual terms, his mature poetic fame secured him an Honorary Oxford Fellowship which might be read as one of life's compensating tricks. He was educated, for the most part, by his own avid reading in his father's well-stocked library. He became, with the arguable exception of John Milton, the most erudite of English poets. One of his last poems, "Development", tells the story:

My Father was a scholar and knew Greek.
When I was five years old I asked him once:
"What do you read about?"
– "The siege of Troy."

With chairs and tables, a Troy was conjured and "Hector put to flight". Browning was a highly theatrical thinker in that movement, gesture, vigorous exchange became the hallmarks of his style. Truths, he would insist, have to kindle and possess the imagination, yet not at the expense of "mental fight". Scholars, as he later learned, who queried the very existence of Troy –

Neither besiegers nor besieged – nay, worse!
No actual Homer, no authentic text,
No warrant for the fiction, I – as fact –
Had treasured in my heart and soul so long . . .[4]

would become an analogy for the New Testament critics "taking away the Lord", and the faithful not knowing "where they had laid Him".

In early youth, however, growing sophistication had genial themes. There would seem to have been nothing distinctive about the dispassionate religion of the parent Brownings. They were cultured, musical people in their – then rustic – suburb of Peckham, who unsuccessfully tried to steer their precocious son into a settled profession, until law, medicine, music were all abandoned for a life pursued as a poet at leisure, fired by mentors like Shelley, Byron, Coleridge and the impact of the famous actor, Edmund Kean, playing Shakespeare.

His first long, lyrical poem, "Pauline", reflects the indulgent parenthood he had enjoyed and the harvest of exciting impressions he had reaped and with which he turned to poetry as their exploration. It was himself at the heart of them he must learn the truth of.

> I cannot chain my soul, it will not rest
> In its clay prison . . .
> It has strange powers, and feelings, and desires,
> I cannot account for, nor explain,
> But which I stifle not, being bound to trust
> All feelings equally – to hear all sides.[5]

There, already, is the authentic Browning. Shelley may have called "the God-dimension" into question but what for ever returns us to it is a lively awareness of our own mystery. "I intend to get to God", as Browning later had his "spokesman" say,[6] was the crux of all his versifying, the impulse in his characteristic use of the dramatic monologue.

For this allowed him to turn his interior debate into a graphic interplay of pro and con, though – as in "Bishop Blougram" – Browning thinks the other's thoughts the better to confront his own case-making. The device makes for a most lively casuistry, in which the poet's mind anticipates its own weaknesses and makes his will to honesty effectively discursive with itself. "He notes and watches all and struggles to insert himself into the heart secret of all lives."[7] The agility of his mind and the elusiveness of his verse make for the liveliest learning of Christ in faith, and of faith in Christ. There are few angles of Christian comprehension of humanity and God that escape his exploration, whether scholarly about the evidences of faith, or realist in the reading of "original sin", or philosophical in the quest for intellectual integrity. Some readers, however, are deterred by what they take for verbosity, or over-subtlety, or a suspect romanticism, or an ostentatious egoism. Or they are minded to reproach the privileged leisure of his days and dispute his warrant to be a monitor of Christ-discovery. Where, they may ask, was his Damascus road in the scenic environs of Florence? Where the *imitatio* of that city's sainted son? Such reservations have their place – to which we will return. Meanwhile, our best proceeding will be to take Browning's most eloquently Christian conclusions, know them for their penetration, and then try to situate them in the experience of his soul, remembering the cryptic warning:

> The rest may reason, and welcome –
> 'Tis we musicians know.[8]

Are we being warned that we are not dealing with a dogmatist?

II

We have seen earlier that the central themes of Christian faith are the vicarious and the sacramental, the Cross and the Incarnation, and these together as the clue to the reality of God and the heart's reading of humanity, and these two as one. Even those most distrustful of Browning's voluble and elusive style can hardly fail to note the fascination Christianity holds for him, the frequency with which Christ-themes recur, the place of Christian imagery in his handling of secular concerns, and the fervour of his debate with theological "deconstruction". Sharply alert to natural beauty, he is no Wordsworth, no Keats, complete in nature-mysticism alone. He is as aware as George Eliot of Victorian erosion of faith but does not follow her into a moralism at odds with doctrine. On the contrary, his finest poems belong with "Christmas Eve" and "Easter Day", with the enigma of Lazarus and the last words of the dying John.

His versatile genius and his endless facility with classic themes and European heritage could amply have sufficed without excursion – with all that cargo – into the cares of Christian honesty with Christian meanings that poesy could have been blithe to dismiss or ignore. We must posit some genuine enthrallment. For his exacting subtleties both of thought and language were not those of a propagandist responding to his own believing public. Yet, for all the eloquence of his *confessio fidei,* we must be circumspect. Could he have been making a case without sharing it? He called his last publication: "Asolando: Fancies and Facts", the word being taken from "Asolo", a place-name but also a verb meaning "to browse around at random". Many of his finest statements were in the interrogative – which, no doubt, is how he wanted them to stay. He could always exempt himself from the voices discoursing in his monologues. Yet his they were and, at their most Christian, they sound as if he meant to mean them. "The acknowledgement of God in Christ accepted by thy reason, solves all questions for thee . . ."[9] If not, the onus stays – and stays where it most belongs – in the soul of every self.

For the first of Browning's most Christian credos many will turn to the lines in "Saul":

> 'Tis the weakness in strength that I cry for, my flesh that I seek
> In the Godhead! I seek and I find it. O Saul, it shall be
> A Face like my face that receives thee:
> a Man like to me,
> Thou shalt love and be loved by for ever. a Hand like this hand
> Shall throw open the gates of new life of thee!
> See the Christ stand.[10]

In "the Face" Browning invokes the most telling of Biblical imagery, reverting to the "blessing of Aaron" and Paul's echo of it in the "lifting upon us of the divine countenance" in "the face of Jesus Christ".[11]

The young David has been summoned to soothe the mood and the madness of the King. He muses as he plays. There lies the King – the tallest in Israel – broken and distraught, a ruin of a man. David's whole soul goes out to him in a love that grieves for him and yearns for his healing. It is the profound core of Browning's Christianity that such human love is, has to be, a paradigm, a case made, for no lesser love as within the nature and competence of God. For, otherwise, "the creature would outdo the Creator". Tradition, indeed reason, are full already of the sense of divine omnipotence. "It is the weakness" in this "strength" that Browning's imagination cries for and finds with a sure confidence via the creaturely "image" of it in the human.

"Crucified through weakness" was precisely how Paul understood the Cross of Jesus, as emblematic of exactly that dimension of self-giving love in God as the very form of divine power. Elsewhere it is defined in the single term *kenosis*, the quality by which the divine is known, not in economizing power but in lavishing grace, in vicarious "bearing" of human failure as the only ground of redemption. Browning, keenly alive to verbal hints, was well aware that "bear" means not only "endure", but, thereby, "carry" and "give birth".[12] It is of this vicarious *kenosis* that Browning exclaims: "See the Christ stand", as the end and warrant of "weakness" in the very strength of God. No poet has taken the perception more eloquently. He is moved to a New Testament *parrhesis* in asking:

> Do I find love so full in my nature, God's ultimate gift
> That I doubt his own love can compete with it?
> Here the parts shift?
> Here the creature surpass the Creator – the end what began?
> and dare doubt He alone shall not help him,
> who yet alone can?[13]

In "Saul", as David stumbles "home in the night", all nature seems alive with his vision, its enormous wonder, its strange gentleness. He is both drained and rapturous. "Even the serpent that slid away silent" – "felt the new law". Tiny flowers, the vines and the cedar "witnessing murmured . . . with hushed voices: "E'n so, it is so!"[14]

Later in "The Ring and the Book", Browning, rhetorical as ever, pleads for the same truth.

> What lacks, then, of perfection fit for God
> But just the instance which this tale supplies

Of love without a limit? So is strength,
So is intelligence. Let love be so,
Unlimited in its self-sacrifice.
Then is the tale true and God shows complete.[15]

He returns again with passion to the "face" imagery in the final lines of "An Epistle of Karshish, the Arab Physician", to his teacher, Abib, to whom he is reporting a strange encounter with Lazarus, a man back from the dead, reportedly, and so puzzlingly fascinating as to crowd out all the exotic data on which, otherwise, Karshish would be discoursing. The Letter-form and the elusive, questioning, fashion of the poem have led critics to wonder how seriously the poet took himself. Yet his words are not phrased as if they expected the answer No! The story of Lazarus has entailed the story of Jesus, "A Nazarene physician of his tribe". What will the pundit make of his subordinate's tale – a tale he is embarrassed to be telling?

The very God! think, Abib: dost thou think?
So the all-Great were the all-Loving too –
So, through the thunder comes a human voice
Saying: "O heart I made, a heart beats here!
Thou hast no power, nor mayest conceive of mine,
But love I gave thee with Myself to love,
And thou must love Me who have died for thee!"
That madman saith He said so: it is strange.[16]

Again, the case is "incarnational". The "heart" we humans have from God's "making" it so, is clue to "the hearted-God". Again, the imagery of "the Face": this human countenance we all carry, where flesh and spirit co-inhabit, has its replica in God. Power beyond conception is identified in suffering love, Christ in his dying being the pledge and proof. "He said so."

Indeed, in the poem's final words, "It is strange!" But it is not Browning only making this conception of the vicarious the hallmark of love both divine and human. It is the unique genius of Christianity to have always done so.[17] He is also moving from what must surely be seen as a necessary rubric in theology, namely that "spectator" and "God" are mutually incompatible terms. Divine "indifferentism" would be divine abnegation of all that must appertain to "Godhood", in any intelligible theism, but certainly in any serious concept of creation, any "Let there be" entailing human creaturehood and "dominion".

Browning makes the point with characteristic verve:

Pure faith indeed! You know not what you ask!
Naked belief in God the Omnipotent,

Omniscient, Omnipresent, sears too much
The sense of conscious creatures to be borne . . .[18]

The transcendent can only be such, intelligibly, in self-mediation and engagement. For, otherwise, there must lack all register of transcendence. It is not only that the creaturely may not credibly outdo the only finally creative One: it is that the One consists by the inclusiveness of which love is sign and proof.

The loving worm within its clod
Were diviner than a loveless God
Amid His worlds, I will dare to say.[19]

III

It is precisely the forthrightness of these vigorously Christian passages in Browning, with their sharp instinct for the heart of things central to Christian faith, that must keep us wary, if we would be honest with him. This is the very reason why he is such an excellent foil in the task of learning Christ through lively doubt. Contrary to some easy impressions, his is no sanguine optimism. His Christianity is no wishfulness of mind. Such could find no corner in the keenness of his intellectual quality. Yet he is alert to aspects of faith that must leave intellectualism behind. So doing, however, belief must not think itself out of the wood.

For there is a big issue about credulity itself or, rather, about whether the grounds of faith can legitimately change. Browning is believing in the same Christ as the first apostles but not in the same way. He is not another Ignatius of Antioch, nor a monk of medieval Athos, nor a Savonarola. He portrays in Paracelsus and Cleon men of proud mind who find crude faith repellent, unworthy of attention. In "Christmas Eve" he travels from the bare and vulgar chapel, to the ornateness of Rome, and thence to the reductionisms of Göttingen where the critics are

. . . inquiring first
Into the various sources whence
This myth of Christ is derivable,
Demanding from the evidence,
(Since plainly no such life was livable)
How these phenomena should class?[20]

"Christmas Eve" not only explores different forms of worship but also the great disparities within Christianity – always a preoccupation of the sceptic. There are clearly enormous disparities between believers as to why they believe and what they find their faith to signify. The perspectives from which they answer necessarily vary sharply if the earth is seen as in a geocentric or heliocentric universe, or on the periphery of immeasurable infinity. Since Browning's time, with his robust invitation to courage in duty, genetic knowledge has come to serve for many as an alibi for moral liability and an invitation to a fatedness he would have scorned.

These are issues more broadly suited to CHAPTER EIGHT following. Here two concerns in particular emerge where alert believing realizes that it is not believing in the same terms as earlier generations in the same Scriptures and Creeds. They have to do with the credulity that was based on "miracles", and with the way faith must reason with history. In both realms, Browning proves a very salutary touchstone of integrity.

The first problem might be described as a growing minding of superstition. Without doubt, many have trusted in terms that needed deeper perceptions than they brought. They may have relied on what they read as sheer marvel, not comprehending the nature of a "sign" or misconstruing the purpose of metaphor or mishandling "myth". Sincerity is not at issue, only intelligence is. A faith that avails fully for the one needs refining by the other, lest a marred significance does duty for a full one. This is no plea for an arrogant sophistication but only for a livelier believing.

Thus Browning, in "Christmas Eve", is dismayed by "the preaching man's immense stupidity" and the befuddlement of the unsuspecting congregation, yet – later in his musings – he returns to share the company they are "in Christ". Finding them "harmless as doves", he wants them "wiser as serpents", if the Gospel analogies may be strained. Preacher and people alike have a market-soiled religion and yet must be acknowledged in "the communion of saints".

According to Bishop Blougram, there may well be a point in ecclesiastics "marketing" a superstitiously viable religion, since the people want *sancta simplicitas*. But, Browning asks: "How *sancta* can it then remain?" Is there some necessary crudity about popular faith? If so, all the more need for refining mentors to care for where, hopefully, our believing can learn to be mature. For the grounds on which any act of faith relies will necessarily decide its quality. To believe on the basis of reported "miracle" is to opt for a different kind of "veracity" from that which would satisfy and reward the most "right" faith. We have to look for "faith beyond the forms of faith" and one of the feebler forms is the sort that Jesus might have engineered by descending unscathed from the pinnacle of the Temple. If we want to be credulous the incredible will be our due reward.

I say, that miracle was duly wrought
When save for it, no faith was possible . . .
So faith grew, making void more miracles
Because too much: they would compel, not help.[21]

So it is argued in "A Death in the Desert". To have come to find in Christ divine personality operating in the lives of men and women, transfiguring and enkindling their love is to acknowledge – but no longer to need – the further evidences that earlier pre-scientific generations found compelling but only did so at the price of a livelier discernment of how, more ultimately than any "miracle", "God was in Christ". The Incarnation cares more inclusively than all. This persuasion has Browning asking whether – in effect – we are still the "same" Christians as our long forebears. Indeed we are, since love unites us and always will. For live perceptions are not the prime criterion of Christian faith. Even so he still needs to ask with the Pope in "The Ring and the Book":

As we broke up that old faith in the world,
Have we, next age, to break up this the new –
Faith in the thing grown faith in the report –
Whence need to bravely disbelieve report
Through increased faith in thing report belie?[22]

That question merges for Browning into the discourse between history and faith. How far must faith tie together "what happened" with "what what happened meant"? In a letter to his wife-to-be Browning wrote that "Christianity is a worthy myth and poetically acceptable".[23] But was its whole content historically verifiable? How far so? If not, did that matter? That learned critic of the Gospels – what of him?

Why must he needs come doubting, spoil a dream?
But then, "No dream's worth waking", Browning says.[24]

This issue of faith and history he explores in "A Death in the Desert" where the aged John, the last of those who had known the face of Jesus, nearing his end, is catechized about the truth of things by his perplexed disciples. The poem is a tender, yet puzzlingly elusive, study of whether, how or why to place one's existential trust in what comes to us as a story that may be vulnerable to time and query and, by its very nature, cannot constitute guarantee. Yet the very necessity – and invitation – to *trust* its power to underwrite all meaning, for all its sometime dream-like quality, has to be the hallmark of its authenticity. The very nature of "evidence" is somehow reciprocal to an imaginative grasp that reads it aright. Such "reading" may itself be subject to the "development" central to Browning's whole discourse. We have to be ready to let "the proofs shift". "A Death in the Desert" takes part of its impulse from the European critics of the Gospels, Renan's *Vie de Jesu*, in particular, who had figured in "Christmas Eve". Though indeed those "parts have shifted" since, Browning's poem remains a foremost text in the Christian tasks of doubt and issues reviewed in CHAPTER FOUR.

Disciples are gathered anxiously around the dying John and "would not lose the last of what might happen on that face". The mood is tense: persecution knows where they are. Browning creates the atmosphere cunningly, as John's "dull members, done with long ago", are fitfully aroused to tell the whole. Is he really John, "trying to taste afresh the truth of things"? He rehearses all his pilgrimage and strives against the fear that those around him, in new years, can never know "what truth" he sees, "reduced to plain historic fact". For "the Christ in God" is not a truth akin to how Prometheus came by fire and after always knew it. Bitterly John recalls his own betrayal –

> Even a torchlight and a noise
> And sudden Roman voices, violent hands . . .

Love overcomes his betrayal. He writes his Gospel to deny the gnostics who would despoil the living Word. But he fears in his own monologue the wistful doubts of lapsing time, when there is no longer any "seeing Christ" except in the love that accepts the fading story. Do we need more than that by which alone we recognize what history tells us? The seer muses allusively around the mystery of power comprehended supremely as love – love that defines itself in the being of the Christ. Taken to the soul, it is as if we no longer need the story as miracle, confiding in it as truth by our love's own responding kinship, "where law, life, joy, impulses are one thing". John expires and his five listeners bury him that very eve. There is "no tarrying longer", as some thought his Gospel hinted. "Believe ye will not see him any more . . . and now the man lies, as he lay once, breast to breast with God."

As in "The Epistle of Karshish", Browning sets the whole poem in the guise of a Greek manuscript accredited to one Pamphylax of Antioch, making the sense of distance greater from the fact of things. It is as if Browning's theme, of "truth out of history" and yet eluding the historical to belong finally with love, is conversing with the very generation of Renan's readers with their querying minds. He leaves aside immediate problems of "John's" identity, making him both the author of the Gospel (including its epilogue in Chap. 21) and the prisoner of Patmos. While the Gospel has "John" present at the crucifixion, the poem has him say: "I forsook and fled." The first immediacy, Browning insists, with a variety of analogies, is prey to time:

Whereby truth, deadened of its absolute blaze
Might need love's eye, to pierce the o'er-stretched doubt.[25]

"Faith in the thing and faith in the report" – these were the poet's constant, fascinated concern. "Stand before that fact, that Life and Death, stay there at gaze", yet know that love, not proof, will be your final learning, ever to gain and ever to keep through all the flux of failing years. Without the text, the lesson could not be. The text throughout is the Christ in the history. Nowhere is Browning citing moral codes or static dogma.

He finds truth, not "absolute, abstract", but "only truth reverberate . . . made pass, a spectrum into mind". So he has the Pope say in "The Ring and the Book".

Nor do I much perplex me with aught hard,
Dubious in the transmitting of the tale –
No, nor with certain riddles set to solve.[26]

Such is his response to the critics of the Gospels. There "remains the doctrine, love", while the school of time abides – its ever learning place.

IV

"A Death in the Desert" might be taken as a sinister title, with the Bactrian camel hard by the cave in the noon-day heat. Readers have to be alert to the endless fertility of the poet's imagination and his range of imagery, the root faith and "a dry ground". What, though, of "a life in the mellow"? Browning was no stranger to plenty, ease and elegance, "linking our England to his Italy".[27] He was well aware, too, of a prosperous Christianity, Protestant or Papal, and of the subtle temptations of the religious institution, clerical and "established". If we are learning Christ we must be wary of office in the Churches. What of clerical doubt itself and the integrity of faith-dispensers? How do they align their authority with the credulity, the adulation or the yearning for honesty, of those to whom they minister? How safe is faith with its custodians?[28]

These were the questions to which the poet turned in "Bishop Blougram's Apology", among the finest examples of Browning's monologue debate with a problem. The interlocutor, Mr. Gigadibs, is a silent auditor, as the poet makes his case the better to engage with his own mind. Was he portraying Cardinal Wiseman and the newly created Roman Catholic hierarchy in England? Blougram concedes that he enjoys his perquisites, that doctrine has its problems and that there are vested interests in his show of faith. "Believing" is a good option: Rome has the absolute form of faith: obedience can be rightly born of fear and awe. To be sure, he is "successful". "What can I gain on the denying side?" he asks. Gigadibs, he muses, wants Blougram to "decrassify" his faith, to purify it of excrescences. Where should such a process end, "experimentalizing on sacred things"? Blougram is happy to combine his robustly told allegiance to Christianity with a prudent tolerance of all the givens Roman institution holds. This is the wise course *vis-à-vis* "the rough purblind mass we seek to rule".

Blougram is unashamedly epicurean about his life, his office, his prestige, in terms that must make most readers reluctant to credit the powerful eloquence with which he is made by Browning to tell his faith's Christ-centredness, seeing "how narrowly and grossly" he "views life". He has a subtle power of casuistry to turn arguments back upon his critic.

> In truth's name, don't you want my bishopric,
> My daily bread, my influence and my state?

He dares his listener, a writer for journals, to go public with a bishop's hypocrisy. The conversation has never been one – only a soliloquy that "rolled out a mind long crumpled, till creased consciousness lay smooth", with the listener a feeble foil for the fine episcopal assurance.[29]

A "creased consciousness, long crumpled" is a strange analogy for a soul's belief. The very playfulness and self-indulgent wit of Browning make his poem an enigmatic exploration of the nature of integrity itself. Doubt is compounded by its own frivolity, while faith is compromised in the temper of its avowal. It is, indeed, "hard to be a Christian", because the very heart "requires instruction how to beat",[30] and more – because language, creed, office and ritual turn on human soul. That truth itself is vulnerable is proven in our broken human holding and our being held.

Browning's tuition in the school of doubt takes us further into the endless stress faith registers around the mystery of human evil. The impression many have of his geniality and sanguine "God's-in-his-heaven" mood is far from the whole. Bishop Blougram may be a self-esteeming knave but his creator's perception of the reach of human wrong is deeper far. "The Ring and the Book" has a panoramic quality in realist examination of "deceiving and being deceived", decrying and being decried, in a society locked in contention around a sordid tale of conspiracy, murder and chicanery. Literature has few surer or sharper juries of the human on the human than Browning's "Ring and Book", the supreme product of his genius.

All has to do with a gruesome tale of child-fostering, fraud and greed in marriage, wife and "parents'" murder, the incrimination of an innocent priest, popular gossip, official trial and papal denial of clemency. Class, prestige, chatter, special pleading, corruption, innuendo, people-passion, privilege and dark hatred brood in Browning's story and tell their naked souls in his judicial monologues, each in their case-making exhibiting the depths of human register in guilt and pride and passion. Fear, cruelty, exoneration, cunning, misery, defiance and despair – all speak themselves with the armoury of Browning's rich array of bold metaphor and fertile imagery. The passionate contradictions and confusions in the sequence of self-searchings and expostulations, each probing the same (?) facts, call in question the very virtue of language itself. Browning has anticipated a chronic anxiety of the succeeding century.[31] Are words themselves not a fiction to distrust seeing they may be so discordantly employed?

There is nothing morbid in this tuition of philosophy into an honest realism concerning humankind. Here is no picture of something mere law or exhortation or reproof could control, still less redeem, no situation amenable to better counselling or sound advice. Pompilia, the victim child-bride, and – to a less degree – the befriending, suspect priest, Caponsacchi, are not vulnerable to mere bad manners or discourtesy. They suffer chronic, deliberate, vicious malice, the prey of human guile and social crime in a scheming, conspiring, gainsaying and degrading world. The Sermon on the Mount would, indeed, break in on the evils as on "guilty things surprised"; only the Cross can measure how basely wrong they are and where their final pleas must turn.

May this human realism be the reason why, in his theology, Browning concentrates so pointedly on the vulnerability of love, the incarnational expenditures of grace, as clues to the divine? For the human paradigm of these which he celebrates in his keenest poems could have no purchase in a guileless world where no Sauls sought the vain solace of music in the vexing of the soul and no Christ came to his Gethsemane. If, as Blougram opines, religious faith is "the most potent of all forms, for working on the world", it must penetrate the dark places. The murderer, Count Guido, in "The Ring" says:

> I have gone inside my soul
> And shut its door behind me.[32]

as he cries: "Take your crucifix away!" in a welter of anger, recrimination, exoneration, frustration and passionate defiance.

Why, then, was Browning so given to this taxing work of twenty-one thousand lines through four long years unless out of faith, on his part, "working on the world"? He had proposed the data of that "Old Yellow

Book", his quarry for the story, to Tennyson and Trollope fruitlessly. It is fair to wonder what they would have made of it.

There are many other facets of his total work that ponder the wrongness of the human world. The early poem "Sordello" contains a vivid image of mob-savagery fuelled by malice and hysteria.[33] In "Mr. Sludge, the Medium", Browning presents a creature of endless self-conceit, a cheat caught in the act as he preys on his gullible clients, lovers of lies enticed by the perversion of spiritual mystery into spiritualist trickery. Sludge is committing the ultimate sin of "darkening the eye that is in him", but truculent through all. There is a lie at his heart. For, in the very making of his case, he deprives his accuser of the means to prove him false. There is "original sin, the corruption of man's heart".[34]

Thanks to the form of his dramatic monologues, Browning's *dramatis personae* are all given to self-analysis. They contrive the image of themselves and consciously survey it. They find highly self-conscious poses which – as it were – propose to themselves the self-problem they are. Paracelsus wrestles with the incompleteness of poetical ambition, a veritable man of the Renaissance. Pauline interrogates the high intentions of youth. The Grammarian reflects on his life's significance. Throughout, a keen self-perception makes a verdict on biography. It was sequential to his entire artistry that Browning should search the human reality and find its depths of guilt as well as its heights of aspiration. In "A Forgiveness", a tragedy of passion, comes this arraignment:

> I . . . brought my mind
> To bear upon your action, uncombined
> Motive from motive, till the dross, deprived
> Of every purer particle, survived
> At least in native simple hideousness,
> Utter contemptibility, nor less,
> Nor more.[35]

There was no possibility of exempting that "dross" from contempt, "no love remaining to cast crown before." Popular sentiment associates the Brownings, Robert and Elizabeth, with the utmost romance – for them unsullied and entire. That experience did not blind him to the wretchedness in human betrayals of the good and the pure. The author of "Grow old along with me", of "Pippa Passes", might be thought to have few affinities with Thomas Carlyle and his "Everlasting No!" Yet they were fellow travellers not only across the English Channel[36] but in the awareness of human degradation and things sinister in society. The dubious may refer to "Holy-Cross Day", where Browning pillories the annual obligatory sermon to Jews – "this bad business" he called it, or "The

Heretic's Tragedy", and "the good sappy bavins" that burn him amid acclamations. Thus

> . . . heart refrains
> From loving's acknowledgement.
> Whole losses outweigh half-gains,
> Earth's good is with evil bent;
> Good struggles but evil reigns.[37]

In "Imperante Augusto Natus Est", two Romans, waiting in the baths, muse on the rise and fate of imperial power

> . . . soaring thus to glory's summit . . .
> . . . the crown all too demonstrative for human wear –
> – One hand's employment – all the while reserves
> Its fellow, backward flung, to point how, close
> Appended from the car, beneath the foot
> Of the exulting up-borne Conqueror,
> Frown – half-descried – the instruments of shame,
> The malefactor's due. Crown now – Cross – when?
> Who stands secure? Are even Gods so safe?

In "Caesar Augustus' reign", the grey Sibyl wrote: "one shall be born in blind Judea . . . to master him. An old wife's tale"?[38] Browning was fascinated with the seeming ultimacy of power – power sooner or later shamed by its own logic in a world perpetually vulnerable to wrong. Hence the indubitable ultimacy of love alone.

V

A "Browning agonistes" with doubt has one further point for our learning. Being always at alert with itself, his Christianity learned the necessity of humility – a humility which informs a patient tolerance. Worship – Christian or other – distorts itself if it claims to capture mystery or monopolize the conditions of divine cognizance of its intention. Significantly, it is "Christmas Eve" which teaches him this perception. Like Bunyan's pilgrims, we need skill to look through our perspective glass. "Christmas Eve" affords it best.

Graphically Browning describes the bedraggled congregation filling the Zion Chapel – motley, uncouth, suspecting the odd stranger, communicating a palpable aversion he is minded to make mutual. Dismayed, affronted, by all that is tawdry, arrogant, ugly, in the decor and the preaching, he finally storms out, only to return later, chastened by the itinerary he has made meanwhile to Rome and papal rite, borne in imagination and clinging to Christ's garment hem – a boon bestowed on his struggle to love those chapel-folk – he crosses the world to St. Peter's, Rome and "the rapturous moment" of "the altar's consummation". He, the poet, is still outside – with Christ himself. For

Though Rome's gross yoke
Drops off, no more to be endured,
Her teaching is not so obscured
By errors and perversities,
That no truth shines athwart the lies
And He, whose eye detects a spark
Even where, to man's, the whole seems dark,
May well see flame where each beholder
Acknowledges the embers smoulder.[39]

Christ's "vesture" still leading him, he comes upon a lecture hall in Göttingen, "decent, symmetrical", "grave, virgin-minded, studious", for a dissecting of the Gospels, and "this Myth of Christ", reducing the Christ of faith to "a right true man". Browning leaves. The atmosphere had grown "nephitic". Recoiling, "talking with his mind", he opts for no "further tracking and trying".

This tolerance is a genial mood! . . .
A value for religion's self
A carelessness about the sects of it,
Let me enjoy my own conviction,
Nor watch my neighbour's faith with fretfulness.

But "the lazy glow of benevolence" frightens him. Should he not seek out, and then enjoin, "our chief best way of worship"? Puzzling, he finds himself back in Zion Chapel. Has he slept all the while? As for the preacher, Pope or professor –

I praise the heart and pity the head of him
And refer myself to Thee . . .
May Christ do for him what no mere man shall,
And stand confessed as the God of salvation.[40]

With his passion, his erudition, his wide charity and his agile versatility, Robert Browning serves us well as a monitor of doubt, warm with enthusiasm yet searching in his scrutinies both of psyche and mind. He exemplifies what seeking is "in the realm of anxiety". Throughout, the human, rightly received, is the clue to the divine. It is not simply that faith must be chosen. Unbelief is "chosen" too with no better ground. Power is forever inferior to love. Therefore love is the ultimate – the divine – shape of power. So much is explicit in the experience of humankind.

The arena – and so the proof – of love is here with us in the grim vulnerability of life, our precarious exposure to one another: in family, society, nurture, and community.

Intelligence must be alert and pupil-like but, in its learning, truth must yield itself into the humility of the trust that is responsive to love's readiness to bear and care and do, so "full in God's nature". All is thus incarnational. Truth indwells the phenomenal world but is not ensured infallibly. For, then, it would have de-phenomenalized its legible place. Selfhood is never static. Consciousness must ever explore, disconcerting old dogmas, living in the drama of being, conversing with its innermost counsels, just as a Browning monologue is ever in dialogue with life and time and tradition and experience. There is in God an infinite and gentle patience. Reverent doubt is liberated into riper wisdom, "soul of mine . . . by the hem of the vesture".[41]

EIGHT

Down Among the Human Dregs – with William Faulkner

I

Usually in the plural adds the dictionary in defining "dreg", with "dregs among the population" as a ready example of the meaning. Whence, it is well to ask, was the "weary heavy-laden-ness" in the invitation from Jesus in the Gospel? The verses in Matthew 11: 28–30 lack all identifying incident before and after, and seem to stand in a gentle completeness of their own. With the "yoke" crucial to the promise, could it be that the sense of "burden" belonged with the toils of discipleship, the hard-going of the kingdom's way in the world, the stresses and yearnings Messianic thoughts had given to his willing hearers?

Perhaps, but – if so – pent up behind all such wistfulness of the good and the hopeful lay the haunted masses of the hopeless, the self-abused, the deprived and depraved, the "wastelanders" of human society. If there were such in the tensions of cosmopolitan Galilee and sanctity-beleaguered Jerusalem in Jesus' day there are massively more so in the sloughs and swamps of western consumerism and spiritual apathy in the ebb-time of the 20th century.

These have been mirrored and even strangely celebrated in a stream of novelists – the Nabakovs, the Martin Amisses, the Norman Mailers of our time and their kindred. Lacking redeeming literary graces they have regaled their readers with the sordid and the vacuous, unwittingly portraying a world matching the intention of Jesus' invitation.

The American Nobel Prize winner, William Faulkner, might be numbered among them had his grim portrayal of a "dregs-society" not been served by a quality of near-poetic and strangely evocative literary style. This compels the reader, by its idiosyncracies, to register in sharp realism the emotions and anguish of his stricken families in his scarred landscape. It might be said that his novels depict as ruthlessly as any in a century the human darkness of degradation, the insanities, the perversities, the savageries, that defile the mortal world.

This suffices to explain the choice of William Faulkner as index to the most grim and sombre context of any "Christ-learning" in this human world. Nowhere more aptly than in the Yoknapatawpha County he created as the locale of almost all his fiction[1] could the words of Matthew 11: 28–30 have fitted, even if they never found, their audience. The point is the more memorable in that Faulkner, while abjuring all committed belief in Christian faith and the person of Jesus, left numerous tokens of his wistfulness about the Passion story. These we must explore, as most apt to "Christ in the learning". For this must include the "unlearning", or rather, "the never learning" of the redeeming reality of His Gospel as the very measure of the condition it addressed.

Of its constant fascination there is no doubt. Faulkner, with his own alcoholism as a sort of cumulative suicide, his dark measures of human guilt – familial and historical, the lusts and passions of the flesh, the torment that warps and wastes the human mind and the legacies of mutually vexing generations, and his uneasy writing modes – knew only too well what shapes the patterns of crucifixion. He took ten weary years between 1943 and 1953 over what he conceived would be his ultimate work.[2] To be sure, it was involved with film scripting and the Warner Brothers, and could have been no more than – the temptation of all literary folk – a money-spinner. For long he was unsure what to call it and finally settled on *A Fable*. How might the First World War be understood in the trauma of the Second? Faulkner thought that the heroism of soldierly sacrifice might be fitted into the pattern of Jesus' crucifixion, the supreme paradigm of self-giving.

A corporal protesting against the futility of war by promoting a mutiny against the commanding officer – who was his father – linked the primary motif of sacrifice with the sort of inter-generational crisis Faulkner had depicted in "The Bear".[3] *A Fable* suffered from a strange astigmatism in its whole concept and might be seen as evidence of failing, or frustrated, powers, the writing being laboured and at time turgid and the thread losing itself. Nevertheless, it responds in its own secular terms to the tradition of Christianity. It senses a place of relevance but fails tragically to reach it as it might have been reached. It is well for a believing theology not to presume literary alliance where it does not exist. By the same token it is well not to ignore the interplay that truly obtains. Faulkner, through all his desperate converse with the wrongs of humankind, is entirely frank about both the fact and the limits of his "Christ-learning". Hence his eloquent fitness here for inclusion in the regard and the disregard of Christ's "Come unto me". He himself wrote, when questioned about the Christ-image in his work:

> Remember the writer must write out of his background. He must write out of what he knows and the Christ legend is part of my Christian background, especially the background of a country boy, a southern country boy . . . I grew up with that, I assimilated that, took that in without even knowing it. It's just there. It has nothing to do with how much of it I might believe or disbelieve. It's just there.[4]

Elsewhere, of *Light in August*, perhaps – for all its tragic human ruinations – his "lightest" work, he wrote:

> That Christ story is one of the best stories that man has invented, assuming that he did invent that story, and, of course, will recur. Everyone that has the story of Christ and the Passion as part of his background will in time draw from it. There was no deliberate attempt to repeat it.[5]

His proximity to Christian tradition is the measure of his distance from it. At least we can be sure that this frail tether with Gethsemane warrants us in dismissing the suspicion some have harboured that Faulkner's unrelenting scenario of human lust, rapine, rape, murder, lunacy, incest, suicide and grisly dying was mere indulgence in the melodrama of the so-called "Gothic novel". He had seen and he had believed and knew his *mise en scène* without illusions, in its very depths. If so many of his families, in Paul's words, were "sold to sin", Faulkner was not merchandizing their condition. What shocks for him is what is, and what is is what shocks, and much of his own state of shock was in his pen.

II

The "heavy-ladenness" of Yoknapatawpha might be grimly likened to decomposition in some silo cylinder, a human compost heap where nemesis is steadily at work. It is a nemesis at work through three social factors, namely blood, race and time, and – to retain the metaphor – fermenting in three human forces, namely deceit, decay and guilt, with all of these uncountered by means or motives of redemption. The decomposition analogy, though true and vivid enough, can never suffice for things human, being wholly negative. The yoke metaphor could serve us better, which is doubtless why Jesus chose it. For the yoke that is heavy, our human self-burdening, is only lifted by the yoke that "lightens", by the onus to be forgiven and to forgive which works in a vicarious world to retrieve the evil and restore the true.

It is, with some precarious exceptions, the absence of such redemption in Faulkner's world that makes his human tragedies go unrelieved. All the ingredients are there for the learning of what is explicit in the

Passion story of Jesus, in what Christians know as "the Christ-event", but "the coming" always falters and fails. Wrongs breed and blight in the inter-meshing sequences of deed and circumstance, making for a vicarious tribulation of mutual wretchedness. The forfeiture of hope and sanity, finds no reversal in vicarious capacities for hope and pardon and recovery that could have availed through the will to love.

Things vicarious are for ever present in the human story. In the web of family and township, of parents and siblings, of passions and relationships, of birth and death, there is no eluding them. Life is a traffic of affairs from which no party can escape the risks. The bundle binds all in their Yoknapatawpha. Society is all bruisings, bruisers and bruised. The clue has to be that what we undergo from each other, in each other, we might positively undergo for each other, turning the vicarious-anti into a vicarious-pro, transforming and transmuting by the antisepsis of compassion and forgiveness. Such, it would seem, was the meaning of "the lightening yoke". For "yoke" such costliness must be. Yet there is "ease" in its bearing – ease that is both its gift and its reward. Only rarely and dimly was there such grace in Yoknapatawpha. The hints and glimpses we must note. That they were no more than hesitant returns us to the decomposition analogy for this suffering territory where minds forego their sanity and wills unhinge and souls rebel and death preys on the living.

In accepting his Nobel Prize in 1949, Faulkner saw his entire productivity as "a life's work in the agony and sweat of the human spirit", creating out of that human spirit "something that did not exist before".[6] For all his concurrent confession of faith in the human future, that seemed a wry summation. His novels, to be sure, had "not existed before", but "the agony and sweat" were as old as the hills. What he portrayed with all his idiosyncracies was his poignant local search for the perennially elusive clue to the human condition, pursued as Dostoevsky had interrogated it on the other side of the world. But the Russian had a far deeper perception of the redeeming reality of divine grace. They were one, however, in the searing honesty of the quest.

Faulkner's literary style corroborated in a subtle way the texture of his theme. Having written *As I Lay Dying* in the small hours of darkness in six weeks in 1930 while on night-shift as a coal heaver in a power plant, he possessed the sort of "daimon" by which Rudyard Kipling so often surprised himself. He needed no word-processor to amend his text. The flow of words from time to time produced an odd defiance of grammar, with sentences trailing into a whole paragraph of teasingly dependent clauses leaving the reader denied the pauses of normal narrative. The device was deliberate. Life was a tantalus no less than prose. "Where's all this leading?" was the query in the substance also.

"Sentence" has double point and belongs with fate and verdict more than language form.

Faulkner's apprenticeship to writing, moreover, was not academic. It had some origin in money-making as he moved in and out of the University of Mississippi, in and out of flying in the Second World War, through a variety of pursuits in banks, carpentry, commercial fishing in the Gulf of Mexico, other work at sea and then in journalism in New Orleans. His most notable works were the product of his forties. Fame brought him to a more settled life as a rural farmer. It also coincided with intermittent but growing refuge in alcohol which, for some of his characters, was a necessary parable of a deeper stupefaction in recoil from the inexplicables of life itself.

This varied converse with the world was served in his writing by a lively technical skill. He was a master of calculated suspense, littering his narrative with veiled hints that readers were required to recall at the right moment to unravel relationships, explain hitherto quizzical plots and elucidate perplexities. The old cliché about "at the end of the day" took on pointed meaning in his deferred climaxes either of cause or effect. Loose threads abounded in his stories, awaiting what deferment might unfold but always, when it did so, the roots lay far back in a fated past. This quality had more than artfulness in word: it served to intimate the "furies", as T. S. Eliot drew them in *The Family Reunion* grimly attendant on selves in families, on societies in flux.

What William Wordsworth called "the still sad music of humanity" was there in Faulkner yet unrelieved, in human terms, of all that Grasmere kindled in the English "Lake poets". Nevertheless, despite his apocalyptic vision of humankind, Faulkner was capable of a rare descriptive intensity that gave occasion to a truly poetic quality in some of his landscape pictures. Early in *Light in August*, as Lena Groves, an expectant mother, trudges across country in search of the non-expectant father, the sound of a wagon is heard.

> The sharp and brittle crack and clatter of its weathered and ungreased wood and metal is slow and terrific: a series of dry sluggish reports carrying for half a mile across the hot still pinewiney silence of the August afternoon. Though the mules plod in a steady and unflagging hypnosis, the vehicle does not seem to progress. It seems to hang suspended in the middle distance forever and forever, so infinitesimal is its progress, like a shabby bead on the mild red string of the road. So much is this so that in the watching of it the eye loses it as sight and sense drowsily merge and blend, like the road itself, with all the peaceful and monotonous changes between darkness and day.[7]

The scene is not unworthy of Thomas Hardy's "road on Egdon Heath" in his *Return of the Native*. In both cases, though differently, the poetic register of nature heightens the vision of a contrasted pathos in the paradox of the nature that is human. Either way, we are rebuked in our banality, the triteness of our superficial selves.

The senses are alive in Faulkner's prose – sight, smell, sound and colour are vividly allied to his delineation of human vagaries. Where the human heart is in conflict with itself it is in conflict with its environment. Joe Christmas in *Light in August* is travelling down "a street which runs for fifteen years" and all its turns from Mississippi to Detroit and back "beneath the cold mad moon . . . and the brittle stars", run on "in moods and phases always empty . . ." where

> he might have seen himself as in numberless avatars, in silence, doomed with motion, driven by the courage of flagged and spurred despair . . . with each inspiration trying to expel from himself the white blood and the white thinking and being.[8]

It is in *A Fable* that Faulkner sets his most passionate protests against the human desecration of the good earth in exploitation and pollution. He does so with a near mystical fervour. It is a failure in pity that curses and dooms the land. There is a rape of nature like a rape of the womb and both are avenged by the dereliction they bring upon themselves. The will that commits the crime engenders its own ultimate destruction. In *Delta Autumn*, Faulkner laments

> this land deswamped and denuded and de-rivered in two generations . . . where usury and mortgage and bankruptcy and measureless wealth, Chinese and African and Aryan and Jew all breed and spawn together until no man has time to say which one is which nor cares . . .[9]

In *A Fable* he insists that the earth was given by God to humankind to be held intact "in the communal anonymity of brotherhood", "asking only as a fee to pay the will to pity and to humility and sufferance". It is strange that Faulkner should have discerned no related capacity for pity and sufferance in that same divine nature that sought such practice among humans. For creation, by implication, already entailed that measure of divinely generous risk. There lay the partiality of his "learning of Christ".[10]

Even so, he read the evil realistically and measured it ironically against "the American dream". In *Requiem for a Nun* he yielded, with a veiled scepticism, to the myth of a "virgin America" and its "limitless panorama . . . of boundless opportunity". He saw its benison "for the people" like the heavenly manna of old Israel, tending to a nation inured to its own indulgence by a celestial magnanimity. Here, too, nemesis waits on facile illusion. Faulkner read only too well what Reinhold

Niebuhr called "the irony of American history".[11] There was no transoceanic immunity from the evils of old Europe. Rather, it was "the sailfuls of the old world's tainted winds" that had driven the ships all westward ho.[12]

III

It was, however, in war that Faulkner's human readings found their first "sweat and agony" – the First World War in which, still a teenager, he served in the Royal Air Force, and the Second World War of his famed maturity. His first writing was *Soldiers' Pay* (note the plural, making the title a sentence, if we ignore the possessive). Here Lieut. Mahon returns from war, wounded and shell-shocked, to become a symbol-victim among a people either drained of hope or insulated in their own egoism. "Things rank in nature" – and grotesque – beset him in successive episodes that shift the point of view from character to character until Mahon lapses into oblivion and death. Faulkner thus early showed his hand in the art of narrative infused with "heavy-laden-ness" both in the telling and the told.

His instinct for pathos reached backward to the memories of the native American "War between the States", in which his great-grandfather, "the Old Colonel" of two Civil War regiments, William Clark Falkner (if was W. F. who inserted the "u" in the family name) had come to high local renown. Faulkner was keenly aware that he was the firstborn son, of a firstborn, of a firstborn. Lineage ran deeply in his veins. There is much that is auto-biographical in several of his novels that trace the flux of generations among local families in decline. *Sartoris* is the story of a returned soldier of a doomed family, with characters from preconflict days but now accused by present forfeit of their noble memories. It was not the most successful of his ventures but the familiar themes begin to emerge – the toll of the past, violence, guilt, and seeming fatedness ensuing haphazardly and leaving the reader puzzling for the logic of their traces.

It was in the novels of the height of his powers – *The Sound and the Fury; Absalom, Absalom!; As I Lay Dying; Light in August* and *Sanctuary* – that his inquisition of southern history came to full maturity. The image Joseph Conrad had of "the heart of darkness" belongs no less hauntingly with these stories of families in moral and physical decay, in social and psychic disintegration. They tempt the question whether the author is portraying "hell" and, in these terms, believes in it. He had, however, become a professional writer. There were negotiations with publishers, calculations of market-mind and – perhaps with *Sanctuary* – a conscious will to horrify and amaze, to deprave taste in the act of serving it.

These are always the temptations of 20th-century novelizing. If Faulkner, in part, was not immune, there is no doubting that he writes in the confessional, seeking – to be sure – no absolution since none avails, yet "coming clean" about what he sees of evil being expiated in its own consequences, wrong broken on the wheel of its own perversity. There was, brooding over all, the trauma of the South's defeat, the ignominious affliction of the carpet-baggers, the misery of a passionately indulged identity undone by the deep compromise of its own nobility – "honour somehow rooted in dishonour", by the fact of black slavery and blood enmity.

It follows that so many of Faulkner's characters are under the curse of their own antecedents. They are hapless heirs to a past which overtakes them in a fate of vicarious guilt under which some surrender sanity itself. Despair or disgust sap the will to atone or that saving grace wilts and withers under the press of circumstances or the blight of cynicism. Frustrations multiply on all hands and generate the compound interest of brutality and chronic neurosis. *The Sound and the Fury* embodied the Faulknerian world in what was also a literary *tour de force* in that it involved the reader in the bafflement of a half-wit's long opening efforts after recollection. The device of telling the same story from the angles of the several participants was not new and Faulkner used it again in *As I Lay Dying* and other stories, but never with the bewildering impact he achieved in *The Sound and the Fury*.

Yoknapatawpha's decaying families, the Snopes, Sutpens, McCaslins, Armstids and Bundrens all evoke Hightower's cry in *Light in August* – "Poor man, poor mankind".[13] But the Compsons are most pitiable of all in a "stalemate of dust and despair".[14] Their minds and wills seem caught in an inward hostility, a state of insurrection against what the world has made of them, and memories from which no mercy brings relief. Hence their vindictive hates, their bitterness of soul, the futility of their fevered conflicts.

The Sound and the Fury opens with the babblings of Bengy, the idiot son among the Compsons. The father Compson is already an alcoholic and the mother a neuresthenic. His mind fitfully aroused by sense impressions, Bengy broods dimly on what may be the tale of his brothers, Quentin and Jason, and how their sister became pregnant by a stranger, the tally being elaborated in a second narration by the said Quentin who, madly jealous of his sister's marriage, claims he has committed incest with her. It is on him the family's hopes are set but he bungles his chances in Harvard and ends a suicide. In the third part, the brutal worthless Jason persecutes his sister's child. Divorced, she gives herself to a succession of lovers. Bengy is castrated and consigned to an institution. Jason sells the family home and the saga of degradation is complete.

Among the images Faulkner employs here that of "the diceman" is prominent. Dice presides at our nativity and is loaded with our every breath. We try to counter with all kinds of wild expedients, not even deceiving ourselves, for risk and chance will, we know, devour them. With dicing supreme, there is no final relevance in remorse, still less in despair. Life succumbs to a final pointlessness. Faulkner's "stream of consciousness" remains utterly unrelieved by the spontaneity of young love or the exuberance of the pure in heart. The doom is the doom of obsession.

It is significant that Faulkner felt himself in a near ecstatic state of dream-like concentration when *The Sound and the Fury* was in writing. He wrote of the urge within it as almost an epiphany where: "I who never had a sister and was fated to lose my daughter in infancy, set out to make myself a beautiful and tragic little girl."[15] If his Quentin was to have the "alleviation of oblivion" and his Jason that of rage, his Bengy would never come where "bereavement would be leavened by understanding".[16] There was, therefore, a paradox of dark compassion in his deeply self-conscious artistry. His dark epiphany did not exclude deliberate composition and it was necessary for him to explain his bizarre technique.

His strange achievement in this his most famous novel has aroused fertile speculation about its hidden meanings and, maybe, its sources in the Faulkner family tradition. Our purpose is not served here that way. The one reality bearing for us on all else is the rigorous inter-connectedness of human society as family conditions it. Whence do obsessions come that have a brother perceive all womanhood in his own sister and make her marrying an abhorrent thought? A parenthood, cold and inadequate in earlier years? The augury of a brother imbecile? The legacy of an ancestry read as present reproach? Are these the ingredients of suicide when Harvard is reached to make all vicarious hopes critical? Yet the elder Compson, for all his lapsing culture, could still quote Horace for his purpose.

The ramifications are endless. What is plain is that "no man liveth to himself" and that even alienations allow us no isolation, since we make them in a vain effort to escape their making. There is no rest in narcissism. Only the figure of the black "mama" Dilsey relieves the darkness of the Compson scene. To her we will return.

If *The Sound and the Fury* was written in a rare "privilege of time", *As I Lay Dying* was the rapid product of interludes by night of physical labour as a navvy. Faulkner used the same technique of shifting narrating viewpoints through a sequence of some sixty episodes in the long effort of the Bundrens to bury the body of Addie, the deceased farmer's wife. Jefferson, the fictive county town of Yoknapatawpha, is cut off by a swollen river. All family narrators are psychologically abnormal and their fifty-mile journey is the progressive revelation of a disaster-prone humanity. The central interest is their inner self-disclosure. The power-plant was noisy in the background as Faulkner wrote, but his imagery was of the road, of river, flood, bridge, mules, wheels, wagons and of death and fire. In one vivid scene the barn burns down in which the coffin lies. There is a certain rough homage in filial mother-love. The very road makes inroads into their crude resources of luck and love.

They are poor whites, like figures elsewhere in Faulkner. Their very mules share an apprehension of lurking danger. The log of destiny which pitches its way down-river towards their wagon casts the coffin into the stream, confounding their troubled efforts after dignity and troth. Some have detected an influence of Robert Browning in Faulkner's play with a sequence of separate voices reacting in a flurry of philosophies on the vagaries of time and torrent with behind them the enigmas of a world inscrutable. He is intimating that guesses after truth bear the stamp of the souls that reach them and only son Darl among the struggling Bundrens has wit enough to be the Quentin Compson among them.

We are not spared the putrid stench of Addie Bundren's rotting corpse, though it somehow fails to register with the family members. Is the putrefaction intended as a parable of the adultery in her story, the desecrations in her last journey a symbol of things familial brutalized into so much dead weight? What is the clue to this sheer, broken, tedious, oft-times callous, "delivery of the goods"? Should the "dying" in the title be read as a sort of extended post-mortem experience of life's entail as "mother" undergoes the ongoings of her brood? Or perhaps as the "death-in-life" of the whole human condition?

IV

Sanctuary followed *As I Lay Dying* a year later and *Absalom, Absalom!*, five years on. The former, so oddly entitled, plumbs the darkest depths of Faulkner's world, with brothels, a brutal rape, two murders, a lynching and an execution. The blood and race themes mingle grimly with that other "laden-ness" of Faulkner's world, namely the "monstrous regiment of women", meaning the arousal of lust and the malign power of the female, made the more theatening by the perversities that instigate its incidence. The only "sanctuary" discernible in the novel is the body of Temple Drake, so named, the blond damsel, nubile and vulnerable, raped by the villainous Popeye and doomed to prostitution. Again, Faulkner holds his plots in multiple suspense with constant shifts of perspective, by silences that signify and hints to throw the reader off the scent. His well-intentioned lawyer, Horace Benbow, is flawed by cowardice.

The whole is as if Faulkner meant to ritualize a dark abyss of irredeemable humanity. Caprice, cumulative sin, a weighted past, hypocrisy, ravage society. The narrative mirrors how grimly the author was appalled. Yoknapatawpha lay in hell.

Absalom, Absalom! echoes the anguished cry of David the king: he at least was not killed like old Tom Sutpen, by a rusty scythe. Faulkner's vision cannot find release from "things rank and gross in human nature". His literary devices are as subtle as ever, with hidden secrets belatedly revealed to explain the bitter eventualities of ruthless ambition and racial enmity. Old Tom Sutpen, in his distant youth, lived in Haiti, where he married and had a son, abandoning both when he learned that she had negro blood. He arrives in Jefferson with a band of slaves, determined to make his way in white society. By devious means he acquires a large tract of land and begins the construction of his dream mansion, exciting vague suspicions around his antecedents. He marries a local white woman, through whose sister's eyes we read the thickening plot. Judith and Henry are born to him. In due time Henry makes a friend in university to whom his sister Judith becomes engaged, none other than the son, Charles, whom Sutpen had long before abandoned. Sutpen expels him but Henry refuses to believe that Charles is his half-brother. When, later, he discovers it to be true he murders Charles. This horrific tangle of ritualized racial pride, is partly related by Sutpen's white sister-in-law, the very soul of bitterness about miscegenation and duplicity. Faulkner also introduces the Quentin of *The Sound and the Fury* as narrator, reminiscently of Joseph Conrad. He thus mingles a portrayal of civil war legacies, family inbreeding, and the tyranny of social culture, making a grim tapestry of all the threads of Yoknapatawpha.

When the tangled web of fatedness is finished the mansion of life's passion and intrigue lies burnt in ruin and the Sutpen quest for blood purity is utterly thwarted. The convoluted story, via the introspective malice or trauma of the narrators, has something of the urgent incommunicability of "the ancient mariner" of Coleridge's haunting poem. Self-hatred, status-complexes, dark antipathies and the guilts of history are revealed in their tragic destiny, not only in the saga of a family but in the texture of a writing imbued with metaphorical life and power. The told and the telling bridge areas of southern history. Tradition is in conflict with the will to its supersession. The reader's mystification in the sundry grindings of the Sutpen mill only serves to sharpen the impact of its unrelieved despair – a despair that defies its own bitterness in Quentin's final cry in the ending. He is replying to his Harvard friend, Shreve, who asks him: "Why do you hate the South?"

> "I don't hate it," Quentin said quickly, at once, immediately, "I don't hate it," he said. I don't hate it, he thought, panting in the cold air, the iron New England dark."[17]

On that insistence, sixfold, the novel leaves an ominously empty silence. The negation is plainly at odds with itself.

Despite its Biblical title *Absalom, Absalom!* languishes in a morass of fated evil in total remoteness from the consolations or the disciplines of religion. It is not so with *Light in August* where one of the *dramatis personae,* the derelict preacher Reverend Hightower, finds himself destroyed by his own egotism. Perhaps he, of all Faulkner's characters, had means to know of Christ's appeal to "heavy-laden souls", but his practice of his pastoral role has been blunted and silenced in the frustrations of his own rigorism and his marital wrongs.

However we understand the "lightness in August", this story might be called the lightest of the violent in the author's crowded canvas of the broken, the sordid, the lunatic and the defeated. It exhibits all the familiar Faulknerian devices – hidden hints, backward glances, teasing connections and inter-meshing tangles. It opens on the road, with Lena Groves, a poor white and pregnant, in quest of the father in the "August" that will "make light" her womb. There are more saving graces than elsewhere in Byron Bunch who befriends her. But she is "light" in a sheer femininity, carrying no clinging history with her, in a sort of quiescent acceptance of wombing day succeeding wombing night.

Elsewhere time holds inexorable fates – the history of the South, "the womb of the present big with the meaning of the past", the bitter entail of racial bigotry and the hoarded suspicions in undying prejudices and cruel enmities. The "miss" Joanna Burden, blighted by time, the McEarchens brutalized and brutalizing and, most Faulknerian of all, the – query – mulatto, Joe Christmas. Of all it might be written:

> A man will talk about how he'd like to escape from living folks. But it's the dead folks that do him the damage: it's the dead ones that lay quiet in one place, and don't try to hold him that he can't escape from.[18]

Joe Christmas is Faulkner's most telling characterization of mixed blood

– if mixed it be. He is for ever trying to elude the stigma of his own identity and being ever more mired into it, with nought but hatred from the cruelty of the McEarchens. Their violence is perversity itself, as if branding on Joe the enmity within themselves. The street becomes the symbol of his living, pursuing and pursued. Yet it is in his lair that Lena's child is born.

The brokenness of Reverend Hightower stems from "his dead grandfather" to whom he lied, the onus of his wife's death, scandal-mongering among his congregation, his own repressions and the gossip around his accidental "delivery" of the infant in the hut. Irony deepens in that he, the self-confessed failure, is the counsellor to whom others come in futile wistfulness. Pre-doomed as it seems to him, he is the articulate mouthpiece of the novel's sharpest lament on mankind.

The hunt for Joe Christmas after the brutal murder of Joanna Burden – focus of blood enmity, passion, lust and sheer thrust of power – brings in the Hines family and a further inter-lacing plot in which there is proof that Christmas was, in fact, their daughter, Millie's baby. The coincidence concealed as much as it revealed. Nor does it avail to lift the curse – the curse of birth and fated life – that lies on Christmas. What men will never undo holds them in a doomed mortality – Hightower's bitter impotence, McEarchen's degenerate religion, and the tyranny of a heartless past. Only in conclusion does Faulkner turn again to "a yoke that is light". It consists in the care-shedding feminity of Lena Groves, still travelling on in a sweet naïvety of mind, babe at breast, in blithe recipience of the gentle favours of a viable and humane world. Does she even know or care for the antecedents of her pregnancy?

> I think she was just travelling. I don't think she had any idea of finding whoever it was she was following. I don't think she had ever aimed to . . .[19]

Lena, the orphan, the mother on the road, the artless exponent of the art of being human – un-accursed, free of history, innocent of race, and the curse of "thorn-in-the-flesh" grandfathers – is Faulkner's perfect foil to the "dark in life-long" that is the other journeying of his Yoknapatawpha. But what of Lena's child and what is "the end of the whole matter", the reading of the map of "Faulkner country"?

V

It is well for Christians to be wary of finding in literature allies that do not exist. Art intends to portray and not to preach. Faulkner, as we have seen, was ambivalent about his theology, perennially unsure, suspicious of the often pseudo-consolations of belief. Yet, "Christ in the learning" being our theme, there can be no reproach in measuring his human scenario as a school. "In" the learning is a different preposition in this context from "by" or "through". We are concerned, not with any positive *confessio*, any deducible discipleship, but with the potential for reaching these, independently of the novelist. None could deny that it was within the capacity of Yoknapatawpha to be in direct range of Matthew 11: 28–30, knowing full well the desperate hardness of its native yokes. Faulkner has no illusions about the burdened humanity to which he brings his searching, probing genius, his ruthless realism.

Nor, when occasion allowed and with perfect timing in 1950, did Faulkner forebear to preach. His Nobel Acceptance Speech, to be sure, voiced passionate faith in the human future. But faith it was and could not escape inclusion in his own scenario. In those terms and for that saluting of his literary fame, he became a passionate believer. His vibrant humanism invited into reckoning all the cursings, the depravings and deprivings, the lunacies and legacies, the lusts and damnations, the tale and tally he had enshrined in his vivid prose.

> Victims "of a useless and elaborate practical joke at the hands of the prime maniacal risibility".[20]

could hardly ride with:

> The writer's duty . . . his privilege (is) to help man endure by lifting his heart, by reminding him of the courage, and honor, hope and pride and compassion and pity and sacrifice which have been the glory of his past.[21]

unless those qualities search for a metaphysic by which they may be verified.

We are a far cry from *Sanctuary* and the deliberate shock to its too too squalid world. Maybe Faulkner himself had matured in two decades or perhaps the thrill of the Prize-occasion fired his incipient mysticism. That there must be values even in defeat, that sacrifice for love's sake is at the core of being human – these are the tenor of Christ's "Come unto Me": they are the open secret of the Cross where stood the ultimate meaning of the words.

Faulkner baring his soul in Stockholm leaves us with no claim as to a Christ "learned". It certainly belongs where there was a "Christ for the learning". How far, then, was that potentiality evident within the novels as he shaped and left them? To that final question must be gathered all the grim delineation of humankind we have surveyed in Yoknapatawpha.

It is evident enough that the famous county was not to be rescued from its wrongs by good advice, nor yet by the memory of faded ideals. Faulkner plainly shares two fundamental perceptions lying at the heart of the Christian Gospel – the "bound-into-oneness" of human life and the reality of evil, self-aware in guilt. He has concluded, with William Golding, that

> Man is sick – not exceptional man but average man . . . a morally diseased creation.[22]

The theme of nemesis, the toll on the present of the burdening past, the social entail of "the sins of the fathers" (or the grandfathers) – all these work their condemnatory will through every story. Humans are desperately bound up in the bundle of life and there is no eluding, in family, or heritage, or marriage, or sex, or the clash of identity through race or blood or class, the entail of wrongs that "find us out". Religion itself, in its practitioners, is possessed by some of the same demons. All is a Hobbesian sort of world from which Hobbes' remedy of absolute capitulation to total power spells no redemption, seeing that politics also are bedevilled by human passion and government itself becomes a terrain of strife and brutalizing enmity. All is written large across Faulkner's world. Nor is his depiction of society relieved by any gentle courtships, any youthful gaiety, any blissful sexuality.

Thus his diagnosis is Christian in its moral realism, not Christian in its bleak exclusion of all gentle graces. Yet, if the central clues are recognized, how close the whole is to – as Paul named it – "the mind of Christ". We have in the Yoknapatawpha saga what theology would call an "incarnational" experience of things human, enfleshed in inescapable mutuality through time and place, via birth and lineage, by history and social bonds. But its "inter-animation" – in John Donne's term – is almost all negative, downward, with a gravitational pull in which each degrade all, all bruise each. It is a thoroughly vicarious world in which the generations, the habits, the legacies, the doings, all waylay each other like some persistent ambush or a conspiracy of almost karmic victimization. "Man," says Hightower, "engenders more than he can or should have to bear. That's how he finds that he can bear anything . . . That's what is so terrible."[23] But the "bearing" is only inward and stoical, a misery of endurance. Where, readers might ask, is the "bearing" that is vicarious, a lifting by another on behalf of the afflicted?

If life is cruelly vicarious in that we carry society's nemesis, may it not counter-contrive – by human goodness – to be vicarious in redemption, so that what is "engendered" is a reconciling forgiveness and a glad emancipation, reversing the karmic law of some inexorable destiny into an authentic "newness of life"? The question is in truth the other side of Faulkner's entire realization that all the wrongs we suffer are the "incarnation" in our story of humanity at large.[24]

In the main, Faulkner will not allow himself to think so. As William Golding observed: "The novelist is God of his own interior world . . . he is of all things an artist who labours under no compulsion but that of his own creativity."[25] It must follow that a theology – latent or avowed – will determine the literary construct. Writers externalize their own imagery. The bleakness of a human landscape will argue, but in no way prove, the bleakness of its metaphysics. To allow oneself to discern, and so depict, a vicarious human kindness will be reciprocal to finding the image in the divine nature and that nature in "the Word made flesh".

With Faulkner it is never confidently so. There are, however, occasions and characters in whom he is searching for the Christ-figure. They are least convincing where they are most deliberate, namely in *A Fable*. There the effort after a Christ-mysticism chooses the wrong context in an army corporal and also loses its way in a writing that contrasts poorly with the tension in his maturest works.

Nevertheless, there are situations in which life is allowed – if only tentatively – to be vicarious in positive, gentle, saving terms. Wrong may not be overcome: it is at least tempered with compassion. Burdens, not decisively lifted, are alleviated by dint of human kindness and these gestures are in some measure referred back to a tradition, a whisper, a hint, of the Christ-principle of "incarnation" participatory where the anguish lies. Faulkner had been familiar with Methodism in his youth and his blacks were devoutly religious in his early world. But he seems to have allowed the darkest Calvinism to obscure the joy of faith. The naming of his arch-victim, Joe Christmas, with the initials J. C. may, or may not, have meant more than the satirical. The struggle between Jesus and God which he sought to develop in *A Fable* took him far from the New Testament bearings of both.

Yet, when he can let the Christian subdue the Stoic in him the dark ideas of curse and expiation suggest, beyond them, the hope of redemption. Expiation of wrong is pointless in a world where hope has no register at all. There *is* "light in August" in the protective solicitude of Byron Bunch around Lena's child, set against Hightower's tormented cry: "Poor man, poor mankind".[26] At least the need is evident for the individual to struggle towards "the better human being that his nature wants him to be".[27] Faulkner has maximized the odds against that struggle and so aligned himself with the very realism of the Gospel he distrusts, though we may find Nathan Scott too facile in enlisting Faulkner by concluding that:

> The terms in which experience is analyzed are such as to make the historic Christian answers to the questions raised seem implicit.[28]

In all Faulkner's productivity the strongest ground for that conclusion is the figure of the old black servant, Dilsey, in *The Sound and the Fury*. When the novelist has rounded out the clues and unravelled the multiple telling of the imbecile, the student, the wastrel, of the Compson sons, Dilsey invokes the Passion mystery in a thrill of exultation at the Easter Day service in the black church: "I seed de beginnin an now I sees de endin." The novel is nearing its close though Jason has still to come to his ultimate mortification. Can we think that Faulkner, via the little black preacher, Shegog, is himself wrestling with what is common to preachers and novelists alike, namely the fusing of meaning with the emotion of its recognition. That Easter Sunday coincided, to within one day, with General Lee's surrender to General Grant sixty-three years earlier at Appomattox when the old ante-bellum South entered on its demise.

That traumatic moment, and the gathering eclipse of the Compson family, are set by Faulkner in the Passion story of Christ – how His bitter Gethsemane emerges, through the Cross and the grave, into resurrection life. But, in a kind of self-exemption – as we must assume – he makes the association through Dilsey, the long-suffering servant in the Compson household. It is often interpreted as no more than a presentation of the irony in black Christianity of a subjected and abused people finding consolation, through their masters' traditional religion, in a compensatory eternity reversing the sufferings of this oppressive world by identifying the sequence with the suffering and the resurrection of Jesus. "I seed de power an de glory" is the vision of the fruition of "de blood of de Lamb" in a glad eternity.

That reading, however, is only half a story. Dilsey has been a sort of Christ herself, bearing with the trials of Mother Compson, the helpless idiocy of Benjy, and the sundry aberrations of his contrasted brothers and their burdened sister. She is thus herself a Christ-figure. We may read her self-effacing, long enduring, ever constant personality as the redemption of the story – not that its tragedy is retrieved or the logic of its evil cancelled, but that it has been bathed in "de power and de glory" all the while by dint of who Dilsey is, and how she cares, beyond the categories of race, enmity, legacy and perversity by which the Compsons are – otherwise – doomed and damned. Faulkner gives us a Christ-like Dilsey who is much more than a suitor at "the pearly gates".

For the sort of confidence which the rhetoric of Faulkner in Stockholm voiced in the human future is vindicated only in the human qualities born of Dilsey-like faith, the compassionate integrities that had their ground and fibre, their divine counterpart, in the suffering Christ, the "holy Lamb" of Shegog's sermon. Faulkner reads in the Compsons "the dark diceman's hand" that deals them only petty chicanery, blind violence, and a rank disgust for which no remorse could ever avail. Such a world is only countered from within by a vicarious suffering that rebukes in judgement by its very contrast yet, in the very accusing, points beyond its stark depravity to the patterns of redemption. Dilsey's is "the yoke of the heavy laden" in the double sense of her own patient bearing *for* those Compsons and *of* their destiny into doom. Only so, in the human world, is there "light in the dark".

Whether consciously or not on the author's part, this "light" – whether the luminous or the loadedness – is in significant contrast to "light in August". For there, Lena's soft leaning upon vicissitude and fortune has an almost pagan quality. Nor do her benefactors invoke "the bleeding Lamb". That Faulkner's irony leaves to the blacks in his Yoknapatawpha county. There, in "the sound and the fury", Dilsey's "salvation" "signifies" what without her and hers would be "nothing", the negation of nemesis and the nemesis of negation. But we the readers are free to think that Dilsey is no more than a deluded candidate for heaven. Faulkner keeps his distance but somehow stacks the cards strongly against that odd conclusion.

Nancy, in *Requiem for a Nun*, may be claimed as a supporting witness. For she is a feebler sort of Dilsey. In depicting a negro servant woman who was also a dope-taker, a prostitute and a child murderer, standing a bitter and contentious trial, Faulkner produced a hybrid piece of work that may reflect tensions in his own life and art. Who is the nun, this black Nancy Mannigoe or Temple Drake (reverting to *Sanctuary* twenty years earlier) mother of the murdered child? And what is "requiem"? A novel in the form of a play, *Requiem* has the tangles of a Dostoevsky without the Russian's genius. In her condemnation and execution, Nancy finds some mystique of "redemption" and bids both Temple and her lawyer "Trust" in her Christ. In the sordidness of her being the Nancy she was, she had, in some still enigmatic sense, found "a Christ for the learning". Yet the question lingers whether Faulkner intended us to think thus of her. The enigma remains in which he wraps his Yoknapatawpha lying, albeit fitfully, within earshot of Jesus and the Cross.[29]

NINE

In the Pride and Prejudice of Empire – with Rudyard Kipling

I

"It's no use your talking about waking him," said Tweedledum, "when you're only one of the things in his dream."[1] There were many fictional things in the fertile dreams of Rudyard Kipling. He was a master of the eerie and the supernatural, a creator of "madonnas of trenches" and of bridges grimly surviving through floods of fantasy. But popularly, for many in his time and since, he was thought captive to a single dream – that of undisputed imperialism and the myth of "the white man's burden". He was captive, his critics thought, to a vision so engrossing that there was no disturbing its inclusiveness.

The cartoonist, Max Beerbohm, for example – ruthless as his kind are in every direction – was grossly so in respect of the ballad-writer of British India, the Poet Laureate in the Sussex countryside. According to Beerbohm, Kipling, forever draped in Union Jack, had "Britannia" for his paramour, drooled over his beer with John Bull and peered from bleary eyes over myopic spectacles and a menacing moustache. "Genius" Kipling might have been but he was, cartoon-wise, a disreputable "jingoist".

This – of the author of "Recessional", one of the most honest poems in the literature of empire! It warned Britannia of the fate of Nineveh and Tyre while "holding dominion over pine and palm". It gave currency to the "Lest we Forget" of numberless war memorials across the state.

> Still stands Thine ancient sacrifice,
> An humble and a contrite heart.[2]

The year was 1897. The poem was written – it would seem – in a mood of dark despair about the sanity of nations and the blandishments of distant wars. The poem, hymn-like in its shape and diction and couched in strongly Biblical terms, with deliberate intent resembled an ecclesiastical "Processional" as sung by exiting choirs. It arrived first in the writer's wastepaper basket beside his writing desk, whence it was retrieved by a friend by whom Kipling was persuaded to stand by it. In *The Times* that year it became immediately a celebrated sentiment.

Yet at the very point of its appearance, Kipling was visiting at Spithead the largest pageant, to date, of British naval power under royal review and lyrically enthusing over it. This was the irony of the man and his theme, a perception of empire that was at once celebratory and anxious, a confidence that exulted in its momentousness and feared for its deceits. "Christ in the Learning" is no arbitrary gloss upon the deeply religious agnosticism of Rudyard Kipling. His poems and stories bear all the evidences of a pen "in the school of Christ", and the more incisively for the elusiveness of his religion.

There is no intention here of recruiting him for a role he never shared. It is true he was a "preacher", a man with visions to declaim and an urgent case to make. But he was in no orthodox pulpit. The only "establishment" he served was that of his own reckoning with allegiance, political and national and imperial.

Yet there is no mistaking the Biblical and Christian source of his vocabulary and the very sound of his voice. Nor is it only the most familiar of Biblical image and verse that he quotes. He draws on the most obscure allusions which – in these days – must surely be lost on readers in times more remote than his own from the economy of the Bible. Registering readers will spot them everywhere in both prose and poetry. Here are a few at random: "Sought out many inventions" (Ecclesiastes 7: 29); "poison of asps under their lips" (Psalm 140: 3 and Romans 3: 13); "Bowing in the house of Rimmon" (2 Kings 5: 19); "His banished be not expelled from Him" (2 Samuel 14: 14); "mint and anise and cummin" (Matthew 23: 23); "the dog returns to his vomit" (2 Peter 2: 22); "One glory of the sun" (1 Corinthians 15: 41). In "The Craziest Road of All" he recalls the story of Saul (1 Samuel 28: 7) "consulting" the dead Samuel by courtesy of the witch of Endor – the poem's title: "Endor: 1914–18".[3]

"Gehazi" is a powerful verse-narrative of the servant of Elisha (2 Kings 5: 20–27) making a superb indictment of deceiving to covet. "The Gardener" must stand among the most powerful, yet compassionate, studies in human self-deception. It ends in a telling fusion with Mary Magdalene in the garden of Jesus' resurrection. The poem is profoundly Christian on all counts by its sheer elusiveness.[4] "The Sons of Martha" celebrates the "bearers of the burdens" and indirectly the whole Christian secret of vicariousness – by a loan theme from the Jesus' story.

Readers of the short story: "The Church at Antioch" and of the poem that, as so often with Kipling, sharpens the moral, can be in no doubt of his admiration for Paul the Apostle of the Lord.[5] The things in Kipling's dreams were well fitted to keeping him awake. The vision he saw may have been like a heady wine but a strong affinity with Christian realism kept the brew in check.

II

His house of verse and fiction was eminently a school whose "lessons" had to do with deep and dramatic themes in the human story. There was, in the Indian stories, the clash of alien cultures. The expatriate British, administrators, barrack-room lads and warriors on the borders, registered the mysteries of India, but only in their own mindset of personal courage – or sloth, their sense of "duty" and the snares and perquisites of power. They celebrated their masculinity – or puzzled over their cowardice – as those who sang their own song in a strange land where animals might talk like humans and spirits, far from wholesome, walked abroad.

Kipling's whole scenario before he turned his genius to the spirits and gnomes of rural Sussex shaped for him the entire complexity of what we now would call "inter-faith". His poems and stories, as we must explore, found their own negotiation with the tolerance of pluralism, perhaps the more validly by dint of his penetrating eye and his agnostic readiness for the mysterious and the exotic. He was contemporary with the author of *The Golden Bough* and knew at first hand one salient arena of "the many and the one" vexing all particularities.[6] Nor was his handling academic or arcane but descriptive, allusive, even chatty and mischievous. There are few volumes of verse that alert the reader more cunningly to how deviously we humans take the transcendent to our souls.

Looming over all, both within his Indian sojourn and his entry into British fame and imperial spokesmanship, was the meaning and the destiny of empire. He belonged with the generation of Cecil Rhodes, Milner, Smuts and other paragons of aggressive empire-building. For all his susceptibility to doubt long before the bitter waste and carnage of the First World War, Kipling shared the deceptive persuasion of something in the English calibre that could sustain, and even embellish, the otherwise corrupting pretensions of empire. The "burden" and "the lesser breeds" somehow warranted each other.

Among fellow novelists of his time was Joseph Conrad, by no means a kindred spirit. It fell to him, a Briton only by adoption and long a deckhand on the high seas, to paint in his *Nostromo* and *Heart of Darkness* the corrupting, sordid measures of western expansionism, their gruesome cost in perverted agents forfeiting dignity and sanity in the thrust of Europe's pride and gain. Kipling's was a different idiom. He was beset with the idea of "betrayal" and "treachery", and could fit imperial destiny into the analogy of a church "that had a Gospel" and could still "rationalize" discipleship into fatal acts of treason. "It is His disciple shall make His labour vain". Yet such "going to Calvary", as Kipling strangely phrased the zeal that did so, was quite other than Conrad's Kurtz rotting on his trading station, besotted in the upper reaches of the Congo forest.[7] Kipling's literary "daimon", as he liked to call it, was of a different order.

For, after the early and phenomenal success of his Indian stories, Kipling grew steadily more confident of his vocation. He felt himself possessed of powers which had been duly rewarded by popular acclaim. To be sure, he had proved himself in a hard school but the proving of his powers was satisfyingly evident. His keen eye for detail, his assiduous zeal in – at first – hack reporting, his instinct for the imaginative word and his facility with rhyme and dialect – all these ensured an expectant audience and convinced him of his destiny. India and the British Raj were the making of his mind. When he returned to England via the Far East and America, still only in his mid-twenties, in 1889/90, he was already fusing into one this growing sense of literary standing and an imperial world view. The two would amply corroborate each other as Joseph Chamberlain became his political hero and his pen, in prose and verse, the anointed celebrant and monitor of empire.

Yet this *élan vital impérial* would come to know how close any life-fulfiling passion lies to its opposite. His later years, when personal tragedy befell him in the death in arms of his son John and he had perforce to give voice to a nation's anguish, his muse darkened as it learned "the twin damnation – to fail and know we fail".[8] Here, indeed, was "a Christ in the learning", no less than for Browning in his poetic doubt or Faulkner in his ruined and ruinous Yoknapatawpha. We can well begin with the ambiguities of Kipling's racialism.

By a strange paradox, it was at once robust and quizzical, assertive and self-questioning. The rest had "better be warned" "when the English begin to hate," yet "We and they" breathes a lively sense of sheer human community in the realization that a perception of things strange and people alien is always reciprocal.

Father, Mother and Me,
Sister and Auntie say,
All the people like us are We,

And every one else is They.
But if you cross over the sea
Instead of over the way
You may end by (think of it!) looking on We
As only a sort of They.[9]

He knew that "the world was wondrous large", holding a vast array of various kinds of men

And the wildest dreams of Kew are the facts of Khatmandu
And the crimes of Clapham chaste in Martaban.

Corporate self-love was bound up with soil-love which Kipling celebrated with lyricism in his adopted Sussex even as he had done so with vigour in his Indian memories of Bombay and childhood prior to the self-pitying trauma of his "Baa, baa, black sheep" and banishment from them. "God gave all men earth to love," he wrote:

But, since man's heart is small,
Ordained for each one spot should prove,
Beloved over all
That, as He watched creation's birth,
So we, in God-like mood,
Might of our love create our earth
And see that it is good.[10]

This was, indeed, a far cry from the bantering bravado of some of the barrack-room ditties and the legend of arrogance so long associated with his name. The ambivalence, it could be said, belonged with the implicit irony of his whole persona, kindling to splendours regal yet burdened with misgivings as mood or times prevailed. There was – no doubt – an invitation to the heavy-laden in the entire cast of his mind and his experience. But it was a laden-ness that derived from the very capacity he ardently attributed to his own race and culture. The attributing belonged with accidents of time and history which very few in his generation were able to transcend. In the crucible of great war it was easier for him to be nostalgic about India than to be perceptive about Germany.

The agnosticism in him which may be the surest clue in both directions of his vision inspired his ready tolerance of religious diversity by freeing him from any urge to explain its meanings intellectually. His sympathy was open to admire, if not explore, the tokens of humanity at worship. There came an intriguing number of poems and stories dealing with the shrines and rites of India. They are innocent of the kind of sardonic treatment characteristic of E. M. Forster's mystification of the caves of Marabar in *A Passage to India*. Forster had, as he wrote:

> thought of . . . a little bridge of sympathy (the novel) between East and West, but this conception had to go, my sense of truth forbids anything so comfortable. I think that most Indians, like most English people, are shits, and I am not interested whether they sympathise with one another or not.[11]

There is no mistaking the contrast in Kipling's

> My brother kneels, so saith Kabir,
> To stone and brass in heathen wise,
> But in my brother's voice I hear
> My own unanswered agonies.
> His God is as his fates assign,
> His prayer is all the world's and mine.[12]

Elsewhere he wrote:

> In faiths and food and books and friends
> Give every soul her choice.
> For such as follow divers ends
> In divers lights rejoice . . .
> Each must find his own sufficient for his reckoning,
> Which is to his alone.[13]

"Jobson's Amen," the poem-prayer that closes the story "In the Presence", in *A Diversity of Creatures*, and the pathos of the short story "The Jews of Shushan" and their tragic, inexorable demise, are moving witness to the writer's capacity for human compassion. Or, witness his impression, in 1892, of "Buddha at Kamakura":

> And whoso will from pride released
> Contemning neither creed nor priest,
> May feel the soul of all the East
> About him at Kamakura . . .
> But when the morning prayer is prayed
> Think, 'ere ye pass to strife and trade,
> Is God in human image made
> No nearer than Kamakura?[14]

He was well aware that the "real gods are those of the marketplace", and his "Rhodesian" imperialism was never averse to "strife and trade". Yet an essential reverence was ready to break through – when admissible – to temper even his most blatant zealotry.

Nowhere is this paradox more evident than in the famous – and infamous – lines "Take up the white man's burden". It was not "Britishness" on this occasion he was celebrating. For that extended to a sort of Anglo-Saxon Churchillian fusion of "English-speaking peoples". It was America's acquisition, in 1899, of the Philippines, Texas, Cuba and Hawaii that he was saluting in the poem. It was riddled with paradox, deliberate no doubt yet also perhaps only half aware of its implications – "the savage wars of peace," "fill full the mouth of famine," "to serve your captives' needs," and "the blame of those ye better . . .". There was the utmost racialism in the very notion of "white men" uniquely burdened, yet the "burden" was veritable, as he wrote elsewhere:

> Clear the land of evil, drive the road and bridge the ford,
> Make you sure to each his own,
> That he reap where he hath sown.
> Be the peace among our peoples,
> Let men know we serve the Lord.[15]

The tone was darkly condescending. "The best *we* breed" were "to wait in heavy harness on fluttered folks and wild," "half devil and half child". "The judgement of your peers", to which Kipling appealed, was certainly not that of the "captive peoples," but of British kindred in the same – hoped for – Pax Anglo-Saxonica.

Removed from the illusions and the constraints of Kipling's times, one might query whether the poem was not all high satire: "Ye dare not stoop to less" when power reared itself to pride. The poem's brazen hymnic rhythm (cf. "The Church's one foundation") "cloaked no weariness" in ardently parading the pretence of it. There was little "whispering" in this exuberance. Yet those "subject peoples" were "weighing all" if only in their "sullen silence". The verses borrowed their ruling concept of "burden" from the words of Jesus but they failed in "lowliness of heart" by the ambivalence of their praise of it. Imperial power could perceive itself vicarious, "weighed" with "the hate" of those thus "guarded". But it remained a remote vicariousness beneath the cloak of the human aloofness that sustained and conceived it. "Never forget" Kipling wrote in "His Chance in Life" that

> unless the outward and visible signs of our authority are always before a native he is as incapable as a child of understanding what authority means.[16]

"The white man" was "burdened" with more than the pains of empire: he was enlightened in its "native" incidence. Kipling was unable to bring to politics and power the register of things human he brought to his treatment of religions. His ready assumption of Anglo-Saxon community of will *vis-à-vis* the world at large was scarcely shared in the United States. The writer's own sojourns there might have made him sceptical of his grand vision. For they were tense and awkward enough during his many travels there, despite the pleasure he derived from the beauties of New England and the wealth of the American spirit. He resembled Dickens in the tussles he had over American copyright, or lack of it, and the ambiguities of his relationships.

In *The Strange Ride of Rudyard Kipling*, Angus Wilson finds a clue to Kipling's "poetry of imperialism" in a parallel he discerns between the writer's sense of his "daimon" in creative literary powers and this imperial theme. There was a "trust" enshrined in each. What his "daimon" enabled him to do was a gift of the gods that might always be withdrawn. He had no necessary lease upon his powers. He must fulfil them as a mysterious liability. It was likewise with the accidents – or the providence – of history that had bestowed the implements of a *Pax Britannica* the due discharge of which demanded scrupulous fidelity.[17] In both lay a deep romance conferring the hazardous obligations of genius.

Kipling's "English" racialism, it might be argued, was more a thing of destiny than a doctrine of "blood and seed" of the Nietzschean order as later boasted in the doctrine of *Mein Kampf*. The distinction may, at times, be difficult to sustain and Kipling was well aware of the ambivalent character of Anglo-Indians cherishing their "whiteness" among those enjoying "the real thing", as in the story "His Chance in Life". Even so he had a lively mind for the patriotic identity of other folk where the asperities of war had not intervened. Thus, his poem on "Naaman the Syrian", in the Biblical world, at first disdaining the waters of Jordan for his cleansing.

> But Pharpar, but Abana – which Hermon launcheth down –
> They perish fighting desert sands beyond Damascus town,
> But yet their pulse is of the snows,
> Their strength is from on high –
> And if they cannot cure my woes, a leper I will die.[18]

It is almost as if Naaman could have been "an Englishman".

Indeed, Kipling was able to identify in common human bravery a sort of "blood-kinship" across frontiers and through kindreds not – race-wise – of one's "kind". This experience of a unitive courage, even where inter-feuding belonged, was the theme of "O East is East and West is West" – a first line so often quoted as if affirming irreconcilable antipathy – a notion completely excluded by the words following: "Never the twain shall meet till . . .". There follow two conditions – "meeting at God's great judgement seat" and "two strong men standing face to face" in the common denominator of courage. In the school of Christ we would have to ask whether Kipling rightly held together those two uniting factors across all races? For bravery, *per se*, may well be a shared calibre, yet hardly so if emboldening and toughening these in mutual slaughter.

Kipling thought he had learned that "there is neither East nor West, border, nor breed, nor birth," from an incident in the Khyber Pass, from which he drew the poem. A brigand chief of the Pathans had stolen the horse of a Colonel of the Guards, whose son, forthwith, rode up the Pass to retrieve it. His daring so earned the chief Kamal's respect that the Britisher returned not only with the horse but with Kamal's own son to be enlisted in the Guards. The double gesture surely suited Kipling's soul but strife in the Khyber, its politics, legitimacy and bravery in wastage, remained all unretrieved.

The question follows whether Kipling's romance of a kinship of sheer human courage, absolving him of the reproach of blood-style racialism, did not finally miscarry. The second so readily cancelled out the first as any Christian realism could have warned him. Indeed, was it not for him, as for all romanciers of war, that the very courage-in-common excited, and was excited by, the hostile heat of race? Wilfred Owen understood more poignantly the perjury of war. Few could dispute the cold, calculating courage of Napoleon yet there was justice in Kipling's haunting lines:

> "How far is St. Helena from a little child at play?"
> "I cannot tell – I cannot see – the crowns they dazzle so."

In the same poem he came to "God's great judgement seat" where – in the other poem – he had believed all the brave were absolved only to conclude that "no one knows how far from St. Helena to the gate of heaven's grace".[19]

Christ's "learn of me" could have given pause to thought of war as transcending race when race proved so regularly the subverter of peace. Of 1914–18 Kipling wrote: "When the English began to hate, it was not part of their blood. They came to it very late." For "they had long arrears to make good", presumably arrears of enmity. Are not "arrears" required by a past that does not "begin"? "They were icy-willing to wait" has a menace in its patience.

The point is even clearer in "Cold Iron . . . the master of men all". This was a harsh contrast from the unifier in "the twain shall meet". This military song of swords and sieges and guns denies in its conclusion that confidence from the Khyber Pass. Doubtless the Somme and Paschendaele were less romantic.

> Crowns are for the valiant – sceptres for the bold –
> Nay! said the Baron, kneeling in his hall,
> But iron – cold iron – is master of men all . . .[20]

Perhaps on the North-West Frontier it was the one-to-one situation that could prove redeemable by bravery alone. When "iron" girded the vast collectives – nations, races, peoples, prides and hates – then the "iron" "mastered" all the combatants.

Before we turn to the more directly theological aspects of Rudyard Kipling's mind, it is this correcting honesty in the cast of his soul that must give pause to the sharp, if understandable, hostility to him of so much Asian thinking. For example, Coomaraswamy writes:

> The English-speaking peoples have laboured under one great handicap – that of their domination by Rudyard Kipling . . . whose irresponsible and uninstructed mentality represented all that an Englishman ought never to have been. He, by giving free expression to his resentment of his own inability to synthesize the East and the West in his own experience has probably done more than any other one man to delay the recognition of their common humanity . . . You gave him a place in your literary pantheon where, in fact, he held up the mirror to the adolescent imperialist mentality . . . Your confidence in him . . . goes far to account for the sterility of his Anglo-Indian manners during all the years in which the little that has been accomplished has always been too little and too late.[21]

The vigour of that indictment deserves both sympathy and dispute. We must hold both together. When Poet-Laureate, Kipling was expected to produce catch-phrases and slogans for the national mood but he was only a twelve-year old when "By Jingo" was favoured,[22] and Oliver Goldsmith had coined it more than a century earlier. We might think him apt for it: in the full event he was too deep for its vulgarity, too subtle for its crudity.

III

The "Cold Iron" poem thought, allusively, that "Iron out of Calvary is master of them all". What could he have meant? Such allusions were frequent. Some were ill-contrived and dubious but with the passing of the years they became more wistful and intense. We will not take their measure if we disallow the inner tension which their contrasts, belligerent and weary, gallant and grief-laden, register. For these are also the pressure of the years through which Kipling's mind-set passed from the exuberance of the eighteen-nineties to the heartache of his closing years.

There is no doubt that Kipling shared the thrill of battle, knew the pulse of – strange paradox – eager conscripts for the flush of fight. Yet often in his proud bravado there was a subtle hint of irony.

England's on the anvil – hear the hammers ring –
Clanging from the Severn to the Tyne!
Never was a blacksmith like our Norman King –
England's being hammered, hammered, hammered into line.[23]

"Anvils", iron apart, are an odd metaphor for hope. One could shout "Rule Britannia" and "kill Kruger with your mouth" well enough and yet still pray to "build . . . an undefiled heritage".[24] The coarse vulgarity of "Barrack Room Ballads" shared his pages with the stately hymn-rhythms he so loved to borrow as in "Hymn of Breaking Strain," in 1935.

We hold all earth to plunder –
All time and space as well –
Too wonder-stale to wonder
At each new miracle,
Till, in the mid-illusion
Of Godhead neath our hand
Falls multiple confusion
On all we did and planned.[25]

"Mid-illusion" might aptly describe Kipling's ambivalence but there is no reproaching his militarism if we obscure his reverent fears. Wrapped in his national flag we could still register the Empire's dubious recruitment of Gurkhas and others who "knelt beside us at altars not our own". "Lord, let *their* faith atone" might suggest that "ours" could not, or that, either way, "patriotism was not enough".

There is no doubt of Kipling's urgent imperialism during the Boer War at the turn of the century, nor of his "Kaiser" hate in 1914. The constraints of "Christ-learning" had to wait until they duly came. His poem in 1902 for "The Burial of Rhodes" was brazen enough about "a dreamer devout", "by vision led beyond our grief or reach", and Kipling reached out all the way with the dreams. He thought the dead soul of Cecil Rhodes would, "immense and brooding", be the life of the land that bore his name . . .

The imperious hand
Ordaining matters swiftly to bequeath
Perfect the work he planned.[26]

The verse was indifferently feeble and the sentiment illusory. Reverse in the Boer War he took in his poetic stride. "We've had an imperial lesson," he wrote by 1902, "let us make an empire yet". Comparable gallantries in tenacity did not make a unison where the Afrikaaner was the foe.

The tales which he wrote in Sussex in later years breathed more gently the fervour of land-love and war-pride that he celebrated with a Kitchener-like ring of the recruiting sergeant, in "Who dies if England lives". Unready or unable – as so few were – to penetrate behind the tangled factors of pre-1914, not least the African dimension, he transformed an ardent patriotism into a virile war-warrant. His mind was not unlike that of Dickens' Mr. Podsnap in *Our Mutual Friend*:

> No other country is so favoured as this . . . this island was blest, Sir, to the direct exclusion of such other countries as – as there happen to be.[27]

Hence his validation of the animus about "Kaiser Bill", and his impatience with the pacifists. For "the strength of the Pack is the Wolf and the strength of the Wolf is the Pack," where "kin was cleaving to kind."

It was in this way that his reputation of dire racialism got caught in its toils. "Sea constraining towers" had guarded the English heritage while the waters had bestowed on "navies that sank far away" the empire of the oceans. In the desperate time of 1914–18, with the death of his own son, John, whom he had encouraged to seek a Commission, and the accumulating madness of the slaughter across Flanders, Kipling turned his poetry to more anguished norms. He began to be preoccupied with Gethsemane and Calvary, with the comprehension of the Cross at the heart of Christianity. Something about the dire costliness of war drew him to the uneasy contemplation of sacrifice. The Cross, however ungainly (were we to borrow from gait in walking), seemed to yield a paradigm by which to interpret the desperately vicarious world of the slain and the surviving. In "For All We Have and Are", he wrote:

> To meet and break and bind
> A crazed and driven foe
> No easy hope or lies
> Shall bring us to our goal.
> But iron sacrifice
> Of body, will and souls . . .
> One life for each to give.[28]

In "The Garden called Gethsemane", he likened it to "English soldiers" enroute to Picardy with "masks in case of gas". The imagery extended to a "let this cup pass" – a plea that went unheard "where we met the gas beyond Gethsemane". Celebrating in verse a visit of George V to

War cemeteries in France, he saw the logic of the "all they gave" turning only on whether

. . . after all was done,
We they redeemed denied their blood
And mocked the gains it won.[29]

This chastened, deeply Christian, perception of age-long human interdebtedness, grimly sharpened by the carnage of the trenches or when – later – air raids spelt a kind of inclusive "conscription" from the clouds, was a far cry from the optimism of "An Astrologer's Song".

Then doubt not, ye fearful the Eternal is King,
Up, heart, and be cheerful and lustily sing:
What chariots, what horses, against us shall bide,
When the stars in their courses do fight on our side.[30]

There came for him a Christ-learning that compelled him to drive home the ceaseless lesson of all the living as desperately liable.

Brethren, how shall it fare with me
When the war is laid aside
If it is proven that I am he
For whom a world has died,
If it is seen when the battle clears
Their death has set me free
Then how shall I live with myself the years
That they have bought for me?[31]

Even so, this reaching for clues in Christ's crucifixion went only part way – as perhaps war for its provenance was condemned to do. There were times when despair overrode all thought of redemptive issue or of a post-war mind-set that could live out of debt duly and justly. "The Only Son" theme on one occasion he turned awry so that the fallen soldier had slain his own mother in her dying grief. How deep the satire in "Shock":

My home, my speech, myself I had forgot.
My wife and children came – I knew them not.
I died. My mother followed at her call
And on her bosom I remembered all . . .[32]

"Madonna of the Trenches" might be thought the most gruesome of all his stories. It told of stiffened corpses in the trenches serving with the sandbags like buffers in the cross-fire. Why not one serve also for a sexual fantasy as Mary Magdalene? There were poems too in which

Kipling registered an almost total abeyance of faith with a vehemence, worthy of a Bradlaugh or a Sartre, about a world "a blackguard made". Those "fated to be born could stand witness to God's shame".

It might be fair to link Kipling's themes of despair with his insistence during the First World War on the all-embracing guilt of Germany. "A people and their King" he thought were "sold to evil". They "set no bound to wrong", and now, defeated – "incarnate evil held at last to answer to mankind". They had to relearn the law "a people with the heart of beasts" had wantonly defied.

The partiality of Kipling's "Gethsemane" might be gauged also from how he drew on John Bunyan's *The Holy War*, an epic of "Mansoul". Attracted by the title, he borrowed from it in 1917, claiming that Bunyan "knew and drew the lot," meaning that his "Diabolus was "the Kaiser and his Gott".[33] It was a gross distortion of all that Bunyan had meant concerning the steady strife within the soul of the believer against the besieging machinations of a spiritual Satan. "He who would valiant be", though probably some sort of brief soldier in the 17th-century Civil War, was never in that mode. Kipling had quite misread the pilgrim allegorist. Or should we blame the appalling anguish of those years?

By the nineteen thirties, when Kipling had more ground for an adversary bestialized, his mood grew more gently sombre. He died before the storm broke. In 1934 he wrote his "Non Nobis Domine", these being the opening words in the Latin Psalter of Psalm 115 – the words Shakespeare has Henry V invoke after his victory at Agincourt. Kipling had a humbler purpose.

> And we confess our blame
> How all too high we hold
> The noise that men call Fame,
> That dross which men call gold.
> O power by which we live
> Unfoldingly forgive . . .[34]

How should we read that adverb? Of mysteries within that hardly knew themselves – the enfolded stresses and perceptions of crowded decades fulfiling a daimon in a turbulent world? Or the sense of where "all hearts are open and all desires known"?

IV

What then, in sum, was Rudyard Kipling's experience of a Christ for "the weary and the heavy-laden"? The answer must be circumspect, for he was, despite his notoriety, a very private person. That he could be ribald and vulgar we know well enough from his Ballads and his yarns. He wrote a rollicking satire in the mood of that Gallio, in Acts 18: 17, who confronted by a Jewish riot, "cared for none of these things,"[35] and was evidently well able to share the mood. Yet reserve and reticence were his hallmark when it came to the proper privacies about faith. It has often been remarked that when, somewhat minimally, he wrote *Something of Myself*, the silences were ampler than the substance. "The Committee of Ways and Means" was an odd way of describing decision-making in his marriage. And what did he mean by the cryptic inscription: "For my Friends Known and Unknown"? It was the work of the last year of his life and breathes the partial air of despondency that, on many counts, beset him – retrospect to the pyrrhic victory over the Boers in the field and the politics that foiled it; the burden of the griefs of war in his fifties and forebodings in his seventies; the unease attendant on the mystery of – as he called it – his daimon; the weight of the legend he had become as, often venomously, the cartoonists saw him; and dogging him constantly the trials of ill-health.

That there was "a Christ in the learning" he would have had no doubt. For repeatedly, he hinted so. Yet it is sure he would have shrunk from being recruited to explain it. "Young fellar, How's your soul?" the great General Booth asked him at a Doctoral Degree Ceremony in 1907 which they were sharing together in the Sheldonian Theatre, Oxford, with Mark Twain a third.

> I conceived great respect and admiration for this man with the head of Isaiah and the fire of the Prophet . . . I have always liked the Salvation Army . . . They are, of course, open to all the objections urged against them by science and the regular creeds but . . . when a soul conceives itself as being reborn it may go through agonies both unscientific and unregulated.[36]

Kipling had earlier encountered William Booth on a P&O liner en route around the world. How he answered the pointed question he does not record. What of "the regular creeds"?

There was also reticence. Perhaps the clearest outlines of an answer come in "His Apologies", a poem that offsets its genuine seriousness by the analogy of a dog making "His Apologies". He has "had the time of his life", with numerous pranks and some disgraces and now,

> Master, pity Thy servant
> He is deaf and three parts blind.
> He cannot catch Thy commandments.
> He cannot read Thy mind.
> Oh, leave him not to his loneliness,
> Nor make him that kitten's scorn.

He hath had none other god but Thee
Since the year that he was born.
. . . His bones are full of an old disease –
His torments run and increase,
Lord, make haste Thy lightnings
And grant him a quick release.[37]

If Kipling's agnosticism was understandably morose it could afford to be also jocular with itself. He was now a long way from what a man knows – as he put it – "'ere his lip-thatch grows".[38] His moustache was notoriously ample and drooping. Life had both liberated and chastened his soul and his inner verdict remained ambivalent.

We have noted the frequency of his Biblical references. They feature still in *Something of Myself*. He shared with Robert Browning, whom he deeply admired and sought to emulate,[39] the imaginative stimulus of the Christian tradition. His most notable poems and stories originate there and bear a by no means reluctant witness to the Incarnation and the Cross. Even in "Cold Iron", earlier cited, he reckoned, albeit wearily, with the nails at Golgotha.

He took the wine and blessed it,
He blessed and break the bread
With His own hands He served them, and presently He said:
"See! These hands they pierced with nails, outside My city wall,
Show iron, cold iron, to be master of men all."[40]

Here he stayed with the irony, leaving the victory.

The association of war with the suffering Jesus kindled, but often miscued, his imagery. Take his handling of Martha of Bethany in "The Sons of Martha", they – like her – of "the careful soul and the troubled heart."

To these from birth is belief forbidden:
From these till death is relief afar.
They do not preach that their God will rouse them a little
Before the nuts work loose . . .[41]

Kipling was fascinated by engineering, notably in "The Bridge Builders", a story of "Gothic" type about the high risks run by those on whose tireless techniques the lower world relies. As for Mary's piety, Kipling noted how prayers were continually offered almost *because* they went unheeded. Did not God deserve to be defied? "The Prayer of Miriam Cohen" was to be spared over much reality.

The path Thy purposes conceal, From our beleaguered realm,

> Lest any shattering secret steal Upon us and o'erwhelm.
> A veil 'twixt us and Thee, good Lord, a veil 'twixt us and Thee,
> Lest we should hear too clear, too clear,
> And unto madness, see![42]

The zest and exuberance with which the young Kipling seized on the human world of his Indian journalism, relishing the sheer speed and thrill of assiduous reporting, passed through the many vicissitudes of his British dreams and dramas into a sharp and sombre reflectiveness, eased – it is true – by the rural privacies of his beloved Bateman's in the hills of Sussex but brooding with all the pains of retrospect. "The Storm Cone" in a poem of 1932 played on an imaginary foreboding.

> This is the midnight: let no star delude us,
> Dawn is very far,
> This is the tempest long foretold,
> Slow to make head but sure to hold . . .
>
> Only the darkness hides the shape of further perils to escape . . .
> But till she fetches open sea
> Let no man dream that he is free.[43]

In the story "The Wish House" he painted the sorrows of decay in old age and in the briefest of his tales "Jews in Shushan" he fused a cumulative tally of adversity with a rare pathos.

There were stories from these years which played around the theme of redemption. In "Dayspring Mishandled" he brought a diabolical scheming of revenge into an issue of contrition and pity. Even haunted houses, as in "House Surgeon", could be delivered. But these "restings of the weary" struggled with the heaviness within. Yet his pen and his mind were now – it might be said – surely "not far from the Kingdom of Heaven".

Maybe the most telling story of "release by and into truth" was "The Gardener", with its strange mysterious allusion to the "Madonna of the Trenches" in the resurrection garden, now, of the Fourth Gospel. The central figure, Helen Turrell, has lived for years with the deceit that her son (out of wedlock) is her nephew. Coming to visit his grave she haps upon another mother living in a like falsehood. Their fleeting conversation gives the reader sharpened suspicion of their self-deceit as subterfuge collapses into revelation when the pseudo-"aunt" enquires of a workman in the cemetery the location of the sought-for grave – "supposing him to be the gardener". In words almost as singular as "Mary" on the lips of Jesus, the "gardener" says to her: "Come with me and I will show you where your son lies."[44]

One critic has thought the ending "ill-judged" or mawkish. It would have been "truer" without the Gospel reference allegedly making that "Supposing him to be . . ." an extraneous text inauthentically wanted by Kipling in a tale final in itself.[45] Yet want it he did and followed the story – as was often his wont – with a poem the title of which was "The Burden". We might judge that Kipling knew what he was doing when he linked a woman's release into integrity – into newness of life – with Jesus' resurrection. Conjecture is all that he has left us with – supposing we have due regard for where he placed it. "Burden" there was. Was there not "unlading"?

TEN

At the Madman's Bell Ringing the Death of God – with Friedrich Nietzsche

I

What "Christ-learning" we must ask could possibly belong with Friedrich Nietzsche (1844–1900), the passionate philosopher of ambiguous nihilism, famed announcer of "the death of God"? What is he doing in these pages? His inclusion must seem quite incongruous, if not utterly naive. His contemporary, Robert Browning, wrestled with doubt in quite contrasted terms. The dregs of William Faulkner's fated families have some distant kinship with Nietzsche's wild insanities in the trauma of his final collapse at the age of forty-five into tragic death-in-life. He was worlds away from John Henry Newman's assured selfhood guaranteed in Mother Church. For Newman exemplified by the very thoroughness of his religious scruple the entire falsity Nietzsche denounced and abhorred. On every count, the author of *The Antichrist* and *Ecce Homo* must be declared *persona non grata* among the poets, writers, novelists we have taken here as educated – and educators – into Christ.

Yet those two titles – his final works before the silence of dementia in his last eleven years[1] – are evidence of a mysterious fascination with the figure of Jesus. The passion of Nietzsche's poetic prose and the sting of his aphoristic style make him a sharply enigmatic figure, fated to be invoked and travestied in distortions he never meant. More than most, thanks to his vehemence, he comes to mean what readers take him to mean. It would, therefore, be well to suspect any reaction to him that misread the terms of his rejection of all things Christian.

For, paradox though it be, it was the temper of his rejection that emerged as positively significant. He had profoundly understood the Gospel's measure of the human being and the dimension of the divine nature by the very criteria of his repudiation. His entire life-work thus becomes a telling, if negative, education into the Christ-event. He signals its whole character by the shape and the force of the antithesis he formidably arrays against it. To appreciate him, therefore, can be a powerful initiation into the truth of it. That role is warrant enough for his presence in these pages, if we can discern him wisely.

II

The celebrated passage which suggests this chapter's title comes in *The Gay Science* which Nietzsche published in 1882 and expanded in 1887. It has all the marks of a Biblical prophetic scenario – a madman as he seems to his incredulous hearers. These are taken aback, bewildered and dismissive. Their heedless indifference intensifies the "madman's" urgency. There is a strange reversal of roles. The seemingly mad preacher demonstrates the blind madness of the undiscerning crowd. His errand is vindicated by its very failure. To warn is only to accuse.[2]

A "Gay Scientist", this herald of the supreme wisdom, unwanted in the hapless world, not only senses his prophetic role. He experiences it inwardly in the unaccountable, passionate flow of his own rhetoric. His conscious identity as one "sent" confirms itself in the sublime fervour of his eloquence, an eloquence which, a year later, reached peerless climax in *Thus Spake Zarathustra,* the most resounding of Nietzsche's literary achievements. Was he, then, somehow reproducing as harbinger of God's demise the patterns he had imbibed from his early Lutheran piety rooted in the Isaiahs and the Micahs of that Hebrew world? They, too, had confronted the incredulous and been despised as fools. Ezekiel, indeed, had behaved at times in bizarre scenes that almost invited such discounting of his wits. Muhammad, too, for his part, had been taunted by his Meccan hearers as deluded or distraught, while Jesus' own family thought he was "beside himself".[3]

It seems, then, that though Nietzsche was savagely decrying all things Biblical and Christian he contrived to do so by a *mise en scène* that borrowed from their provenance, paying indirect tribute to the meanings he maligned. Even to announce that "God is dead" required prophetic voice just as "the Lord lives" had wanted ardent mouthpiece. Nietzsche did not outlive his hidden debts in being set so assertively to their denial. The rhetoric and the enigma are one.

> Must not lanterns be lit in the morning? Do we not hear anything yet of the noise of the gravediggers who are burying God? Do we not smell anything yet of God's decomposition? Gods too decompose. God is dead.

> God remains dead. And we have killed him. How shall we console ourselves, the most murderous of all murderers? The holiest and the mightiest that the world has hitherto possessed has bled to death under our knife. Who will wipe the blood from us? With what water can we cleanse ourselves? . . . is not the magnitude of this deed too great for us? Shall we not ourselves have to become gods, merely to seem worthy of it?[4]

The entire thrust of Nietzsche's thought is in the wild vehemence of this famous passage, full of passionate anomaly. "God is dead", yet we – who do not know it so and must be urgently informed of it – are also his very "murderers". Could a deed so desperate have been unwittingly committed? Is it not incongruous that we should need alerting to our own crime – that crime, meanwhile, being our very liberation?

Before what we might consider a rational, normal sanity dismisses this lunacy, it is well to pause to register the writer's origins, the view of all things human which he inherited and against which his emerging genius remorselessly rebelled. Both his father and his grandfather were Lutheran pastors, while his mother was a pious devotee of that Christian tradition, as were two unmarried aunts, sisters to his father. He grew within this godly, female society, with his sister Elizabeth, just a year and a half his junior, abetting its circumscribing influence. Or such it came to seem to him in his later teens. During these, his mental powers, notably in the realm of philology, began to serve notice on the academic world of a brilliant future. There was the usual adolescent revolt against paternal faith. It rapidly developed into a much more fervid rejection of all things Christian as his mood proceeded and his perceptions girded for ardent controversy. He was appointed Professor of Philology at Basle University at the age of twenty-four. Shortly thereafter, he naturalized as Swiss. It is noteworthy that, despite his debts to Schopenhauer, the German philosopher of radical despair, and for all his fascination with Wagner, Nietzsche was no admirer of his native Prussia or of Bismarck. What has been made of him by a Nazi Germanism may seem to have his imprint but only by gross distortion of his meaning.[5]

He formally renounced Christian faith in 1865 when he reached his 21st year. His father had died in 1849 when the only son was a bare four years old. He was thus exempt from the strictures the self-assured neophyte scholar levelled against his domestic, female Christian "captivity". Indeed, he thought of his father in their village of Rocken as a perfect model of a country parson whose life was peaceful and simple, trusting implicitly in divine Fatherhood and exemplifying all the traditional virtues of the honest Christian.[6]

Whether the absence from young Nietzsche's boyhood nurture of those paternal qualities could account for his rejection of their faith-sources or whether he became obsessed with the fear of early death, looming for him also, are questions open to conjecture. There seems to have been a sharp issue around his sexuality arguably stemming from home circumstance. Syphilis certainly afflicted him and may have contributed to his final insanity. Through crucial years he avoided normal attitudes to society while resorting to prostitutes until, in something like a panic about relinquishing the very hope of authentic sexual commitment, he developed a passionate infatuation impossible of fruition. It may be doubted whether his ideology had ever been compatible with the mystique of authentic sexuality sealed in self-surrender and mutual coronation.[7] For the meaning of sexual love inherently contradicts the "supra-human" pretensions of Nietzsche's system, his reading of the mortal scene. It must be doubted whether he was ever marriageable, given what he himself was to entitle "the genealogy of morals".

III

Between 1872 with *The Birth of Tragedy* and 1889 with *Twilight of the Gods* and his final entry into total dementia (through which he survived until 1900) a copious stream of torrid pen-eloquence flowed from his ardent mind. Titles like *Ecce Homo* and *The Antichrist* betrayed his constant preoccupation with Jesus whose very captivity – as he saw it – in Christianity he was urgent to denounce, if only at the cost of an entire misreading of how "Beholding the man" had given rise to the community of faith.

Clearly Nietzsche understood Christian faith only too well – and that, precisely in the terms in which he rejected it. Yet its rejection issued from a complete misconstruing of what made that faith authentic. This is the heavy irony we have to measure. If his home and village nurture in part contributed to this paradox of keen perception and perverse abhorrence, the irony is the more profound.

One could readily derive Nietzsche's whole indictment of Christian faith directly from Matthew 11: 28–30. Exactly, "you who are weary and heavy laden"! Here is comfort, solace, ease, respite. "Rest" is what you seek: you can have it from "the meek and lowly in heart." The secret is to let yourself succumb to your frailty, surrender to your lust for consolation, opt to have the easy illusion of external "means of grace". "Take this yoke!" – precisely! Christ and his religion will enslave you in a fiction of deceit, a web of inhibition. Such, manifestly, is what the Gospel offers. Be beguiled into the "perspectivism" of ascetic practice and craven delusion which will cramp your personhood and foreshorten all your horizons, making you the unwitting slave of *ressentiment*, of world-weariness.[8] You will be drugged into a complete incapacity to know your own bondage, caught in a net of creed, ritual and morals entangling all your native powers, your "Dionysic" urges, in hopeless, hapless atrophy – an atrophy the more entire for your unawareness of it. Your only salvation is to repudiate the whole illusory scheme, the figment of a religious "saviour".

It was thus that Nietzsche traced "the genealogy" of morals, the factors in human weakness conspiring to establish a human psychology that personified nature and read behind the phenomena of experience "agencies" with grudges, vagaries and enmities – as well as precarious benevolences. These needed to be placated, humoured, propitiated, implored. Fear having "made the gods," only fearlessness could unmake them. Their "genealogy" – their mythical ancestry – had to be undone. For they were a false progeny. Nietzsche was in part in debt to Feuerbach for this ideology, though giving it a passion and a rhetoric far beyond his tutor's turgid reach.[9] One could well liken it to the "archaeology" of the more recent Michel Foucault[10] or, if grammatically minded, "etymology" would do as well for the basic notion of religion constructed solely from psychic origins of a vain hope and an age-long wistfulness. Christianity, supremely, with its "other refuge have I none . . . let me to Thy bosom fly," had grossly and criminally fostered this "birth of tragedy", this conspiracy to death-in-life.

Deferring Nietzsche's counter-salvation, let us first measure how darkly he had missed the whole thrust of the Gospel and, indeed, the terms of Matthew 11: 28–30. There was nothing craven about *prautes*, that "meekness", with its steely quality of staying power and noble tenacity, like the supple trees which are the only ones to outride the storms. As for the "laden heavily" could not even John Keats have told him of those "for whom the miseries of the world are misery and will not let them rest."?[11] Thus the yoke of Christ had nothing to do with burdens of self-pity and commiseration, nor did "rest unto the soul" intend some escapism that demanded, like Newman, to come into some safe harbour.[12]

But the immediate "Come unto me" passage apart, Nietzsche's "genealogy" of Christian faith had quite overlooked its full Biblical dimensions, had excluded how human personhood could see itself entrusted, by the whole ordering of a created world, with a lively "dominion" dignifying human nature and truly evoking and requiring a responsive mastery. Being "bound in the bundle of life," as humans are, could spell a gentle heroism the truer for its acceptance of social compassion and its horror of the self-confined "supra-human" ideal which Nietzsche enigmatically proposed. If there were paradox, then, in the "the yoke of the Saviour" it did not have to do with a bridling asceticism but with an imaginative discipleship and a "service spelling perfect freedom". As we must see, there were certain elements of Nietzsche's discourse that could comprehend such Christian humanness – or humanism – but only at deadly odds with the philosophy by which he reneged on them. Or was it simply the vehemence of his own "prophetism" that demanded he should incriminate his godly origins?

IV

Accumulating vexing issues this way, it will be well to trace further Nietzsche's logic and the dramatic prose in which he told it. His avoidance of all Aquinas-like coherence, his reliance on the skill of aphorism, left him open to be read "as in a glass darkly." Readers can repay him with his own impatience. They have to be alert to constant tensions. *The Will to Power*, not published until 1906 and not authorized, was a collection of random notes and jottings. Especially in *Ecce Homo* he used the term "Christianity" ambiguously and let his passion ride.[13] Nothing could be constructive if not polemical. If satire clothes all stakes in enigma – as in "There was only one Christian and he died on a cross"[14] – then quiet reason in the reader suffers crippling violation. How should one take an author who thinks it cannot be otherwise except mingle uneasy tolerance with heavy scepticism?

Such tolerance must attempt some structuring of Nietzsche's aphoristic wisdom, taking his very proximate analogy of the camel, the lion and the child. The first (though one surmises Nietzsche had never seen or handled one) symbolizes the trouble with unaware humanity. It accepts burdens, its "docility" "puts up with" them. It is reverent towards unqueried values. In a word, it submits and undergoes. Priests, with their dogmas and ritual, are ideal cameleers, organizing to their own ends men's proneness to be "saddled". Or, in due course, "scientists replace the priests". They, too, are "camel-mounters". Their values are no less subjugating. To stretch the analogy, camels function in deserts – tokens of sterile journeyings, to-ings and fro-ings – wherein, as T. S. Eliot opined, "death has undone so many".

In this vein, Jesus is "the least in the kingdom of Nietzsche". For he, too, humbled himself into a yielding harness instead of "grabbing success" that lay to hand. Those who awaken to this camel-truth of things are liable to take on the lion's style, the "no-nonsense" rebels, set to depredatory ways in defiance of all laws but their own. For these, there are no categorical imperatives beyond their private hunger.[15]

This, too – as we must see – has to be superseded by a "transvaluation of all values" in the Nietzschean Gospel. Yet – and despite the camel-style, crowd-mind, of craven conformity – Nietzsche takes a very harsh, Hobbesian view of human life as brutishly competitive and harshly aggressive.[16] "Being" – that toy of metaphysics – is an empty fiction, seeing that there is only "becoming", and in "becoming" humanity can have no confidence in any regulatory "human nature" to which moralists and pragmatists make sanguine appeal. In terms of "the lion" there can only be precarious "contracts" by which impulses are crudely enwebbed in "checks and balances" until the true "gay", not the false pseudo, "science" is revealed.

This third stage Nietzsche strangely images under the analogy of "the child", neither camel nor lion, neither dragooned into supine timidity nor wildly destructive, but innocently "open to new worlds". The usage is odd indeed. Was it a throwback from Jesus setting "a child in the midst", as Nietzsche had once learned at his mother's knee in Rocken? Now he took the child as symbol of a *tabula rasa*, free of an indebting world, on the far side of dogma and ready for an unreserved Yes to self-hood.

Could it be that, in his exuberance for this metaphor spelling the uninhibited luxury of Nietzschean self-creation, he had overlooked how childhood is also, inherently and inevitably *in statu pupilari*, at first totally, and only later diminishingly? Boyhood is no fit arena for "the gay science" finding supra-human being. Rather than being, in Nietzsche's phrase, "condemned to innovate", it is obliged to imitate. If not camel-like, it takes its paniers to school, and needs a pedagogus.[17] Nietzsche had to betake himself beyond inapt analogy.

V

Far at risk to readers as Nietzsche made himself by his passion and his rhetoric, it is the more necessary to take special pains to get scrupulously to the heart of him. A lively sympathy can help to this, kindled by a realization of the constant ill-health under which he laboured and the tensions of his mental world.

Systematizing what, for him, could only be in aphorisms, the Nietzschean scheme would seem to be "taking one's world by the fore-lock" in "an innocent becoming". The only world that matters, or that signifies, is the world of our own determining. For there is no "set order", no metaphysical truth of things. He took from Schopenhauer the conviction that irrational striving in the inter-human scene makes belief in a moral order pointless and illusory. So to realize, however, could only lead to nihilism and absurdity if one let it do so. The alternative is "to will power", but only in the subtle sense that Nietzsche intended by the term.[18] He seems to have meant an inner vitalism which despises the inferiority mindedness which religions fostered and traditional moralities imposed. Since there was no metaphysical "given order" and no teleology or pattern of purpose – not even in the realm of the natural sciences – wide-awake selves found themselves summoned to a world-creation of their own. This alone could endow an otherwise worthless existence with significance and engender zeal.

Such would have to be "the philosophy of the future" – that future whose prophet "ahead of his time" Nietzsche claimed to be. By its very nature it would be essentially selective, seeing that ordinary mortals would never register the destiny nor rise to its fulfilment. Only "the new free spirit" could take in the reality that was out from under the constraints, the rubrics and the boundaries of a given world – given as religion and philosophy had hitherto presumed to structure and affirm it. There were echoes in Nietzsche of 19th-century notions of "stages" in human consciousness, progressing – or at least moving – from pluralist spiritualism, demonic powers in a divinized world of natural phenomena, on to theological concepts of a world unified under God and, therefore, rationally intelligible and calculated to sustain a responsible humanism in intelligent custody, so warranting culture, cities, civilization and rational fulfilment.

That stage had largely given way, in turn, to a self-sufficient, if not self-explaining, scientism presuming to dispense with the God-dimension but still – in Nietzsche's view naively – clinging to rationality and the rule of order in a scheme of human hope. Nietzsche's "futurism", however, saw all these as due to be superseded by power relationships striving for an amoral enhancement of life, "beyond good and evil".

That phrase might make him seem no more than grossly libertine. Many readers have so taken him, therefore, as plainly mad. But, by "beyondness" he meant "the goods and evils" of a stultified society in which "free spirits" were eclipsed by "slaves". He seems to be meaning that any "truth-value" could only be "life-value" but by criteria sublimely other than those of a crude pragmatism, itself still imprisoned in consensus inferiority and the decadence still caught in self-deception about transcendence.

Such is the tenor of "the gay science – the science that is beyond familiar referents for conduct, like justice, pity, love and truth, and exalts the sheer quality of the will that moves the self. What is repudiated as absolute truth via reason and moral order is replaced by "aesthetic judgements".[19] If one can allow that the artist makes inspiration his own law – which non-Nietzscheans must deny – then art becomes the paradigm of the free creative spirit. Hence the place in Nietzsche's thought for "Dionysian inspiration", "the agony and the ecstacy" of a Michaelangelo. In art and music by the will to affirm, to create, to assert, absurdity is countered and opposed but only in terms of the expressing self, proposing a world willed wholly from within. If we see the sanctions of art as interior to the will of the artist, then it serves to illuminate Nietzsche's theme of "the over-will" that takes even perversity in its stride insofar as that perversity has been identified as such by moral restraints drawn from reason or faith. For then it ceases to be perverse. Perversity itself is "trans-valued", in being tied to criteria, namely in the will, that are no longer those of an answerable ethic.

Art, furthermore, signals spontaneity and zest. It pursues a self-mastering mastery. We are misfits in a rational, dogma-ridden universe: we are free spirits when art inspires us. It is only in aesthetic terms that existence itself is justified. This emphasis may explain why Nietzsche's scheme of things is so energetically couched in poetic prose, whereby his very language – even in English translation – indulges a kind of rapture and cannot content itself with weary argument. It offers itself as a thing inspired. At its most intense in *Thus Spake Zarathustra* and *Ecce Homo* it brought his genius to the very precipice of final collapse.

That may not commend it as a case being made: it does enshrine it as a vision being lived. Beset with contradictions, as we must see, his theory of art, as clue to how "power" in Nietzsche waits on the "will to it", captures his meaning well enough. His philology attests his fascination with language and he moved always in the thrust of inspiration "I taught them all my poeticization and aspiration to compose and collect into unity what is fragmented in man and riddle".[20] If the artist indeed creates his own world, then, as Nietzsche held, even despair can be reconciled to life through beauty.

VI

This, essentially, is the context in which to seek an understanding of Nietzsche's notion of *übermensch*, often translated as "super-man", but, more usefully as "supra-man", or still puzzlingly, "over-man".[21] It is surely criminal to invite mis-comprehension, as Nietzsche did, the more so if blithely so doing is a token of disdain for vulgar throngs who will lack all discrimination. Saving Nietzsche, as it were from himself, there is in *übermensch* no racialism, no ethnic selectivity. What is selective belongs in personal will. Yet it certainly intends a kind of aristocratism, somewhat akin to that of Aristotle's intellectualism – a thing fated to exclude those for ever disadvantaged by accidents of birth and culture.

Nietzsche perceived a slave mentality in society irretrievably caught in that camel-burden pattern of docility, unable for his vision of "the will to power". Indeed, it was the prevalence of such slave mentality that obscured and impeded the progress of his prescriptive futurism. Hence the thrust of his denunciation of the theism, the Christianity, that conspired to perpetuate popular captivity to norms, duties, ascetic with-holdings and dogmatic stultification of their "values".

He was not, as he said, "in the business of improving mankind". His message would select hearers worthy of it – a stance which allowed him the cruel ironies, the extravagant pen-gestures, in which he provoked easy verdicts of madness concerning him. In the Foreword to *Ecce Homo* he taunted readers with his "greatness", his "seduction", his majestic "loneliness". He chided and bludgeoned, charmed and teased them with "Why I am so wise". He could afford to let the old clay idols (ideals) learn of themselves that they had feet of clay.

> I now go away alone, my disciples! You too now go away and be alone. So will I have it . . . one repays a teacher badly if one remains only a pupil.

He reviewed his mind autobiographically as exemplifying the path to "over-manhood", "dancing" – as he put it in exuberance – "right over morality".[22] What he called "the eternal return" – the future open to infinite possibilities – would be the fruit of hearkening to his vision, the art of outwitting the past and so setting the human story towards its given, but too long frustrated, destiny. In the preening of his "wisdom" he did not reckon with how perversely the "human all too human" that was "down among the dregs," would distort his eloquence into the raw material of fascist tyranny and racial arrogance. Fearing, in *Ecce Homo*, lest he should be thought "holy", he contrived to be seen malign.

To ask why snatches of autobiography should be entitled *Ecce Homo* is a telling way to reach his case against Christ, Christology and Christianity. The scene in Pilate's Judgement Hall dramatizes the entire question: "What is truth?" and Nietzsche has been turbulently making his own answer. He is also having us "behold" his theme of a humanity shackled to false values and doomed to despair over an irrational world. He is summoning us to perceive his "supra-man", liberated from illusion and open to the Nietzschean kingdom. But he is also setting "Dionysius against the Crucified".[23] In the "silence" of Jesus he might discern a hint of "transvaluing value", but he must cancel that suspicion by deploring the failure to resist, the sequel of desperate victimization. Perhaps, above all, he is half-consciously envious of the Jesus-role in the long reach of time and space. In all else he is "presenting" himself.

Be the Nietzschean relevance of *Ecce Homo* what it may, there is no mis-reading the passion and the animosity in *The Antichrist*. The cry is to anathematize "Mercy, Pity, Truth and Love" to which – as William Blake sang – "all pray in their distress". These Christianity discerns in "the throne of God and of the Lamb" as being the doxological heart of New Testament theology. By the light of *The Antichrist* none should be so praying who rightly read the world. For "pity", available or sought, is no remedy for what is only "distress" for having never known, or cravenly distrusted, "the gay science" of Dionysian bravado. It should be as Nietzsche has it: "I tell myself my life and that, not as penning its story, but ordering its goals."[24]

To be sure there is a kind of "pity" which, offered, ministers to a condescending pride and, received, enervates a cringing will. But there is a "pity" which knows these things only too well and subdues them as crucial to the succour it brings. Nietzsche is right if he means that bland "do-gooders" never redeem: he is wrong in excluding "redemptiveness" from the whole orbit of his mind.

The issue between him and Christ, we might say, has to do with the onus of the past. In Christianity it is a vital reality. Self-hate – or self-love – may strangely make a sense of sin obsessive and guilt a weird indulgence. In Nietzsche's world there is no absolution – a verdict only reached by having no mind for the wounds and wrongs of the vulnerable world. On the "over-man" hypothesis, one has no criterion for conscience. For, one's action done, one does not "leave it in the lurch afterwards". Any evil consequences have no place in evaluation, nor do they entail on other parties. The past has to be taken in the stride of one's persona even *because* it went wrong. Remorse could have no place and redemption, retrieval, no relevance.[25] "Sinfulness" is somehow elided in the revaluation of value.

In this realm "the Antichrist" is truly so named. For this ignoring of how vulnerable to one another humans are rides oddly with Nietzsche's perception of a Hobbesian world where there is only competitive "becoming" and no "order" or "being" except, perhaps, if we go with Hobbes, some covenant to erect an absolute political power to police the whole. That paradox apart, Nietzsche's *Ecce Homo* may be indicted as having never, pitifully or otherwise, perceived the human as the human is. Given the Christian understanding of what is reciprocal between the human and the divine, it also means that he has forfeited, or never registered, the heart of Christology, namely the divine stake in human tragedy and its understanding in an intervening pity as the inclusive index to the divine nature. Such is the meaning of Incarnation. Its quality of gentle deference[26] takes care of all that was legitimate in Nietzsche's antipathy to crippling "do-goodism": it passionately denies his concept of a human loneliness in vaunting self-sufficiency. In his dismissal of the onus of the past, Nietzsche seems a total stranger to the ravages – political, legal, social, religious – of human hypocrisy, to the mixed motives by which cunning disguises itself and lust, cupidity, pride and passion work their unconfessed evils. These cannot be subsumed into some unrepentant future. They demand to be recognized in self-damning retrospect and redeemed in the adequate riddance of an active forgiveness replying to a genuine self-accusation. It is as the correlative of this human reality that Christology exists, finding in the confession of veritable ("very God of very God") Christhood and the Cross "the image of God". It was a sound instinct of Nietzsche's *Antichrist* to align human moral exoneration with the negation of "the Christ of God".

That theological vision-in-event, as it might well be termed, belongs, of course, with the whole Biblical, indeed also Quranic, understanding of the created order. Incarnation corroborates creation, as both the Fourth Gospel and Paul insist.[27]

There are two aspects of this theme of human creaturehood which Nietzsche in his crisis of faith throws, by misconception, into sharper controversial focus. They have to do with human "dominion" and, more intimately inside personhood, with the human body.

The first may be broached in querying Dionysius by a mind for Prometheus. Traditionally a demigod, the latter has been an apt symbol of technology, of that other science that Nietzsche saw as on the wrong side of a final irrationality.[28] The mythical Prometheus was chained to the rock after presuming to grasp the fire from heaven. The human creature in "dominion" does the one and is spared the other. Whether it is by the early plough or the lowly wheel, humanity masters, manages, recruits and exploits environment, does as it does with what there is.

Theists – and Christians in distinctive terms – acknowledge this "dominion" as entrusted for reverent, responsible custody as the matrix of all moral, and ultimately political relationships, simply by its delivering us into the economic order. Fertility in the good earth is partner to the enterprise of humankind. Through agronomy via technology we know both survival and society, civilization and the realm of value. This evident reality of human life, culture and "being with becoming" – in the Christian view – makes us "priests" in having us be "kings", i.e., it bestows a power of possession in order to propose a habit of consecration. The sciences that enable the social scene call upon the arts to celebrate its meaning in experience. The two are one privilege – the privilege of humankind. So much the interplay of creation and creaturehood presents to our experience.

It seems ludicrous, therefore, to postulate that the God whom faith perceives in these terms must be "unwarranted incubus" on our due liberties, a piece of indelicacy against us thinkers,[29] an outmoded fiction, an entity to be appropriately "murdered" in order that the human may be free. Nor could it credibly be claimed that the notion of some divine Lordship had arisen, as Nietzsche alleged, from hidden malignancies that needed to be placated, humoured, bribed by abject worshippers and assumed to replicate the basest human passions.

More primitive and environmentally precarious times, to be sure, had ample reason to be awed by thunder and storm, to dread the onset of drought, the miscarriages of the womb and the grisly incidence of death. Superstition had its deep pathetic warrant. To be sure, technology has shattered that superstitious world and made ever more evident the privileged "dominion" a pre-science had not known well how to handle. Yet the pagan awe and gratitude felt towards Nature remained deeply relevant. Had not Nietzsche made science instrumental? But for whom – the "over-man" or the trustees? And what of the history that had accommodated this incredible theatre of the human dignity? There is very little trace in Nietzsche's writings of concern even for a possible teleology of historical time. Truth is a long way from his thesis in *The Antichrist*, misreading Genesis 1–3, as of a deity "regretting" the venture with the human creature, then perceiving us "rivalling" himself and so forbidding we should think to take up "science".[30]

That, on the contrary, humankind has been given a mental "latch-key" to enter on the *imperium* in external nature was underlined by the vital clue of the capacity to "name things" (Genesis 2: 19–20). Taxonomy has ever been the means to the ends of science. In this way Promethean humanity, reaching into light and fire unhindered, finds indeed "a will to power", but one which obligates and, read historically, constrains to wonder, awe and gratitude. The sense of these is no part of that "philosophy of suspicion" which Nietzsche reads in Christian – and every theist – concept of deference towards God. Why should not the evidences on every hand of a strangely concessionary dignity be trusted as authentically ours?

Rightly so acknowledged, it surely gives the lie to fondly Dionysian ideas of self-prescribed exemption from its credentials in a self-asserting pursuit of private ecstasy which "transvalues" all the disciplines and sanctions of a rational response to experience.

There is one intriguing feature of Nietzsche's mind-set relating to the human body. The body, via procreation, is plainly the locus of all else, while procreation is the most immediate, intimate sphere of the human *imperium* we have discussed, a crucial arena of our power in life to give life, to "renew the eternal creation". Nietzsche's fascination with the body, its functions and senses, recurs throughout his vocabulary. It may stem from his many illnesses, physical and psychic distresses, especially after the end of his tenure at Basle in 1876 and the chronic consequences of his syphilis and other sickness. He sees a sort of suicidal anorexia in Christianity. Nausea has a place in his verdict-making. Theology "smells". The Christian is "a sick, animal". Pity wants to keep what is "ripe for a multitude of abortions".[31] A philosophical contempt can couch itself in terms of vomit and excrement. Nietzsche would have appreciated the recent English jargon about "a gut reaction", so much of his anti-Christian writing being about what is wretched retching. "Canst thou not minister to a mind diseased?" was Shakespeare's graphic way of capturing the tragedy of the Macbeths, man and woman.[32] The irony of Nietzsche's indictment of Christianity and Christians is that he opted for analogies which turn their tables on him. That clue deserves a fuller exploration.

VII

In what lapses into chronic diatribe he can nevertheless be uncannily discerning, when he is not engaging in misogynism. Thus for example, in *The Joyful Wisdom* he could be describing the New Testament situation when he says: "The founding of a religion always becomes a long festival of recognition." Indeed, there was in its Epistles, and in the Gospels that ensued from them "A consciousness raising", "a social communalizing of conviction . . . giving a religion its style".[33] He aptly sums up all we have studied earlier in CHAPTERS TWO, THREE and FOUR.

But all, for Nietzsche, was focused on "No!" – no to life, to power, to freedom and to "supra-humanness". We can ignore his version of the old canard that "Paul invented Christianity". It has been sufficiently exposed in the foregoing. He adds nothing to the discussion except the venom of his hatred of "the Jew of Tarsus".[34] This betrays him, however, into undermining his basic thesis about getting "beyond good and evil". In *The Antichrist*, he reads Jewish "chosen-ness" under Yahweh as their tribal God as a valid example of "the will to power". Their "God-partnership" is the subtle, and effective, shape of their own ethnic virility. Describing Christian "priestcraft" as "an anarchic form of Jewishness", – "the Jewish instinct over again" couched in terms of grace for all peoples but under Church control – he castigates it as "hieratic power lust". There is "a will to power", utterly reprehensible, in the enslaving of naive believers in the church system.

If it is pleaded that such "wills to power" are in no way to be classified with the Nietzschean sort, seeing that the latter pursues "revalued values", the plea plainly discriminates between the moral quality of the several "power wills". So doing, Nietzsche is in no way "beyond good and evil". His reproaches, and their utmost bitterness, proceed, however scornfully, within moral criteria. Moreover, the quest he has for innate superiority, out from vulgar mediocrity, is no less a self-engendered pretension than the *superbia* enshrined in the Jewish Yahwism and the hieratic priestcraft he berates in its Old Testament and New Testament embodiments.[35]

Indeed, his whole indictment of Christianity as "perversity", "loathsome" and "conspiratorial", becomes pointless if what is so passionately accused is not blameworthy and "shameful". These characterizations cannot obtain "beyond good and evil". The vehemence recoils upon its own "genealogy of morals". Nietzsche, like the idols of the pagans, discovers he has feet of clay. Or is it that only his readers do?

There are times when open-hearted ones are at a loss to know how his wildest strictures are meant to be taken. Is there some subtle strategy in the sense of outrage they provoke? How, for example, are we to understand his seeming commendation of the Governor Pilate as "the only New Testament figure one can help respecting." He "had the noble scorn of a Roman," set never to "take any Jewish quarrel seriously", thinking one Jew more or less did not matter. "Every book becomes just, after one has read the New Testament." There is so much pitch there that "One puts on gloves on reading" it. "In vain have I sought for a single sympathetic feature in the New Testament." Christians "simply smell bad".[36] Elsewhere he wrote:

> I regard Christianity as the most fatal seductive lie that has yet existed, the great unholy lie . . . I reject every compromise position with respect to it.[37]

"Lies at any price" is the prescript by which Christians live.

Christian faith and ethics are seen as the most reprehensible form of "the genealogy of morals," namely the creation of morbidity, ascetic suppression of the laughter of life, and the cult of deity as spelling a perpetual régime of backward looking guilt. They harbour a deep misunderstanding of the self, and constitute "the most sinister form the will to destruction can take." Christian doctrine libels life, its morality "a principle of calumny."[38]

"A moral order of the universe" being "lies", it follows that the classic doctrine of the Cross is delusory. "Jesus died for his sins . . . there is absolutely nothing to show that he died for the sins of others." The disciples conjured up the idea of "the resurrection" in psychic mitigation of their own despair.[39] Christianity is thus the most heinous shape of that human cowardice that fashions all ethical norms to compensate for its own refusal of authentic "becoming", that calls up fear and fantasy to make its world falsely tolerable to the "decadents" these Christians are.

VIII

If there is here in Nietzsche a radical faith-crisis at least it is clear that he "learned Christ" perceptively in the very terms of his vociferous rejection. How should we then read his indictment, subtitled as *The Antichrist* was, with a rare modesty, "An attempt at the criticism of Christianity"?

A medley of migraine and mischief, mockery and madness, might be the cynic's answer. Nietzsche certainly suffered painfully from the first. There were deep psychosomatic factors in his entire authorship. Mischief and mockery were certainly elements in his practice of "serious humour". *The Antichrist, Ecce Homo* and *Thus Spake Zarathustra* were written on the brink of his final collapse into helpless lunacy so that, in the assessments of many, they anticipated its onset. Or was it all, like the "pity" of those "decadents" a matter of "bad manners"? [40]

Taking him in the riddle of his own "seriousness", a counter criticism might well begin with the puzzle about the "demise" of God as also his "murder". By Nietzsche's "genealogy of faiths", his was "the mind that brings the thaw", i.e., the perception that theology and ethics are the progeny of human wistfulness arguing a benign "personification" of some "transcendent" whereby fears are allayed, solace is had, a paradise may be awaited and society with its "priests" ensures a due will to subservience. When "the thaw" comes, i.e., a Nietzschean realism, this frozen "perspectivism", with all its falsehood and fantasy, melts away and the authentic "will towards power" comes at last into its own – for its élite.

But how is a melting "murder"? A thaw simply happens and is surely to be seen as beneficent. "Murder" is something that wilfully destroys what deserves to live. It is no ebbing of life: it is its cutting off. As such it is presumably heinous, an act of treachery and deeply reprehensible. Nietzsche's "madman" tells us we have slaughtered God and urges it on us as an alarming crime. How then has a bare awakening to an illusion merely let him die?

Some might explain this enigma in Nietzsche's scheme of things as anxiety that we should realize the sort of world we are to know deprived of all the illusory comfort, certitude or peace of soul to which we were clinging to make existence bearable and fend off the call to naked courage. Does he then resemble Charles Darwin, hovering for years over the disclosure of a secret that would go hard on credulous believers and be potentially shattering to public order and tradition? To see

Nietzsche so, however, still leaves the riddle of how "natural death" in heaven qualifies as earthly "murder".

Is not the "murder" language perhaps the clue to Nietzsche's own wanting it so? The divine demise that is allegedly the outcome of a mature humanity that has left behind its "ages of faith" is, in fact, what has to be contrived by hate and venom. The paradox is evidence of "the will to power", to power over against reverence and a genuinely human modesty aware of the incredible magnanimity to be read in the *imperium*, the *tüchtigkeit*, which, in the natural order of the good earth, we manifestly possess.[41] So to think would go far to reinstate, *contra* Nietzsche, the whole classic humanism of Christian faith.

Nevertheless, there is a certain "ministry of correction" which Christian thought might welcome in Nietzsche's scheme of things. It is always well to wonder what a philosopher is reacting against, since it plainly conditions what he aims to propose. There can be point in the negation even if there is no valid case otherwise. The psalmist's prayer: "Let not those who seek Thee be confounded through me" is one disciples always need to pray.[42] For believers, by their crudity, silence, or stridency, have often occasioned sad misconstruings of the things they held.

If Nietzsche, explaining "How I became what I am," could write: "As my father, I have already died, as my mother, I still live and grow old",[43] he is tracing his thought to his story. And the end is reproach. He is in revolt. He feels he has known effete "pity" and only survived "decadent" theology and Christian piety by "seeing through" its frailty and – for him – its "untruth". His corrective may be salutary insofar as the charges are honest. His insistent distinction between what is true and what is thought true,[44] has point. Credulity, not least in religion, can contrive a false reality. When it does so it deserves to be accused. Courage, a readiness to "consider" despair, an honest openness to question, an instinctive resistance to self-deception when identified as such – these are desirable qualities. Faith may well conspire against them. There *is* a kind of "pity" which degrades, induces dependence and cripples the will.

But if, in this way, Nietzsche can be salutary in checking vain religiosity, what he misses is the way in which love learns to practice what love most soundly has to be, knows to undeceive and discipline in the "learning" that ends in "a yoke" and not a couch. It is well, at times, to be discerningly subversive but in a world where there are no ultimate values he contrives, none the less, to be monumentally judgemental.

Yet he was evidently preoccupied with Christ and with Christianity, if in sometime parody. He understood them if only through the very animus of his rejection, nowhere perhaps more cogently than when he opines: "The Gospel of the lowly lowers".[45] It was the conviction of *Magnificat* that it magnifies, renders truly great. Can one, as some think Nietzsche meant, experience nihilism in order to transcend it? Is it not rather in the acceptance of our actual creaturehood, as birth and time and place have "perspectified" it, that we come by genuine courage and an honest will?

Such a posture requires us to "take in the decadents" – into a lively compassion. The question which presses on the readers of Nietzsche is: What of those masses? Can we expect to find release or absolution from the backward drag of society's debris and dregs? Given that "there has never yet been a superman" are Nietzsche's "arrows of desire" mere arrow-heads, the forefront of superior humanity fired in the lack of the back-stretching shaft without which no arrow flies? Do we ignore the pathos of our common vulnerable human situation? What was the real lesson of Nietzsche's own long tragic need of family's care?[46]

The questions multiply and their answer turns on the potential for resilience that lively Christian faith can demonstrably sustain around those "growling bells". For it is not – always – that crippled, static, hollow thing Nietzsche sees it as being. It grows, adapts, responds, admits of liability for its own expression. Its ministries are not an ordination to a closed mind or a hidebound soul in some "monotono-theism".[47]

It knows that we cannot contain or comprehend our humanity exclusively in aesthetic categories. Nor can we rightly live regretting nothing as "supra-man" purports to do.[48] The arts themselves, via their public media, have obligations to society. They do not exist merely to be indulged. *Homo sapiens* is more than a Dionysius. The arts alone are no sufficient answer to the mediocrity Nietzsche deplores. By some artistic criteria they aid and abet it.

Philosophising – as he said – "with a hammer," Nietzsche destroys too much. The wind that brings the thaw hottens into a drought. "He doth protest too much." His faith-crisis heads towards dementia. Yet it moves with uncanny instincts even in its deepest throes. At the end of *The Birth of Tragedy* he wrote: "I have the right to understand myself as the first tragic philosopher."[49] He was claiming to be the first to measure the reality of the God-demise and the burden of the loneliness of man under necessity to prove heroic against impossible odds. "Tragic" indeed he was. But there had long been, in the Christian faith he renounced, an utterly different, because inclusively redemptive, "tragic theology". The Cross of Jesus told the full measure of human "heavy-laden-ness" in terms of how it might be exchanged for discipline and peace in the gift of grace.

With a keen insight, if with no glad assent, Nietzsche wrote: "In order that love may be possible God must be a person." A single sentence comprehended the nature of the Incarnation. When he added, still dissenting: "The answer was to discover a religion in which it was possible to love" he had identified the New Testament. Could there be a sounder reason for a Christian allegiance?[50]

ELEVEN

In the Homo-Erotic World – with Oscar Wilde and De Profundis

I

"A Mon Locataire" read the solitary inscription on a wreath, and that artificial, in the funeral of Oscar Wilde. It came from the proprietor of the Hotel in Rue des Beaux Arts where the poet, playwright and prisoner had spent his last wandering days after release from Reading Gaol – the erstwhile renowned, now broken, C.3.3 of that scandal-laden confinement.[1]

There is large risk, yet poetic justice, in deciding to have homosexuality take its place in a school of Christ-learning via the tangled career of a famous Irish man of letters. For while he proved a *cause célèbre* in the public history of "love between men", his imprisonment and the vilification he endured remain harsh evidence of the malicious retribution with which it could be stigmatized by a vindictive society. If there was a perversity a dominant culture identified as guilt there was no less a perversity in the mood and manner of its revenge. "Perversity", it may be argued, is a cultural construct and, therefore, Wilde's "fall" and early death at the hands there and then of the verdict it passed makes his tragedy a bitter indictment in reverse.

What is more significant, however, is the writing the experience drew from this supremely articulate man. The flamboyance in which he had revelled in talent and epigram gave way to an eloquent register of despair and the discovery of pity.[2] There are those who would dismiss *De Profundis*, the long prose-poem of vicarious suffering that came from his prisoned soul, as only the same Wilde in a new pose of humbled self-projection invoking a Jesus in the image of his own persona.[3] But this is crudely to misread the depth of Wilde's own Gethsemane and the convergence of his "wrong-done-ness" with the central theme of the Christian Gospel, where the vicarious and the vulnerable are seen to belong with the story of divine love.

Wilde was preoccupied in the restless months after his release with an embryonic play about Judas. We may read it as symbolic. He was too far broken to survive into a future of narrative redemption but he had seen its contours and the secret of its cost. The *emathen epathen* we earlier followed in Christ in his own school in CHAPTER ONE could truly be written across the art, both of pen and personality, that moves through "The Picture of Dorian Gray" to "The Importance of Being Ernest", from a Newdigate Prize Poem to "The Ballad of Reading Gaol". The final suffering was the more incisive for the youthful hedonism and the conspicuous, effortless success that had paved the treacherous way to it. The learning told itself in chastened but undiminished powers of pathos and irony.

Finding access to the homo-erotic world by the biography of Oscar Wilde in no way implies that the gay and lesbian scene is all assumed to be susceptible to exposition by the lights of the pathos and mystique of Wildean proportions. He was as unique as the theatre he presented both in his person and his plays. There was that risk in the option to think with him, since all of these CHAPTERS from FIVE to TWELVE have linked a broad theme with a personal exemplar. There is potential wisdom nevertheless, inasmuch as the story of Oscar Wilde sets the broad double scenario of how selfhood and sexuality are patterned in homo-eroticism and also how society is itself on trial in reckoning with its claims and meanings.

II

The terms "gay" and "lesbian" are quite maladroit. The former was arbitrarily commandeered – only in the 1970s – to displace the odious attribute of "queer". "Gay", however, now irreversibly monopolized by male homosexuals, is grievously lost to wide and joyous meanings stemming from the Latin *gaudium*, "joy". What, now, of Wordsworth "gay" in the breeze among his "jocund daffodils". Such thieving of meaning is criminal and needs to be denounced. Was the implication that only certain patterns of life and style discovered *joie de vivre* and that all the rest were deplorably sombre, joyless and forlorn? Words at times have doubtless to be yielded to their privatizers but surely not without protest and dismay at gross verbal injustice. "Gay" ought to keep its one authenticity.

As for "lesbian", it seems odd that a hilly island in the Aegean should be landed with a unilateral identity when there is much more to its story.[4] There is no clear evidence that the intellectual coterie of girls and women around the charm of Sappho, the poetess, with her Sapphics six centuries before Christ, were uniquely, or even habitually, involved in genitalia. The Greek tradition, to be sure, savoured the endless mystery of touch, of sight and form. The body was esteemed and cherished as a realm of life and beauty. But there was also esteem for the character of restraint, of discipline and self-control. The appreciation of corporeal joys did not insistently require the bed and the orgasm.

The point is one to which we must return. For the moment, it suffices that "gay" and "lesbian" cannot properly be denominators held to connote a particular shape of human-ness exhausting personal reality, in the way the terms themselves now admit of no wider meaning. Are those that choose to use them, as with Biblical "idolators", "like unto them" in such confining of their range and their acceptance of their being human? For all of us must comprehend our being as inherently open to meaning beyond the prescripts which we write – or think written – for ourselves, whether ethnic, sexual, cultural or preferential. When we start to admire or aggrandize an idiosyncrasy it is well to suspect it and be "involved in mankind".

Pursuing that thought, must it not be conceded that gay and lesbian preoccupation puts all friendship in danger, not least in these days when homosexuality insists – for its own good reasons – on "outing" itself? There are endless forms and occasions of association between the two, or more, of the same sex – relationships honest, mutual, lasting and benign, thanks to talent, interest, profession, and habitat. Must an obsessive, even prurient, interest from the context bring them into suspicion via conjecture or innuendo, so perhaps forcing them into single-style patterns and the forfeiture of community?

There may have been ills and evils in an earlier ethos of "no questioning" or tacit non-investigation. These made the case for the explicitness that a changed climate now demands. But the new paradigm of the homosexual style contains a menace to that largesse of friendship which has its sufficient fulfilment in a spiritual and social sincerity that never had "the name it feared to speak". Harassment, explicit or implicit, militant or mischievous, implying that friendships have always something hidden, is not only destructive of their innocence: it is a violation of the very integrity to which homosexuals themselves must plead.

The "companion" word comes from the Latin *panis* (not *penis*) and means "taking bread with", hence "company". Interhospitality is at the heart of all human society and, by his "You spread a table before me" the psalmist set it also as the clue to a divine guest-making of us humans in the meaning of creation. Christian faith took that confidence further into the bread and wine of redemption so that a "holy table" is the physical focus of Christian worship of "the God of all grace".

By these lights it is the more unhappy that genuine – we could say sacred – hospitalities among us, the converse of two kindred minds, the bonds of mutual awareness, should be in jeopardy to readings, or misreadings, of eroticism in the only terms that such suspicion has in mind. There is a kind of sordid thinking that wills to make it so. Society needs to be capable of friendships, maybe closer than brothers may attain, with an integrity of love free from the kind of inquisition that surmizers bring. Their quality deserves to be immune from cavil and erotic surmise. What some homosexuals like to call "outing" presumes to require no credentials but their own.

The point emerges endlessly in literature. There is bawdy aplenty in Shakespeare and doubtless the groundlings loved it. It would be folly to pretend it away. But need it be incessantly identified as such so that the action is innocent of all grace and honour? The speaker being Graziano and the play heavy with sexual overtones, we take the point when the curtain falls on *The Merchant of Venice* about "keeping safe Nerissa's ring".[5] But must it be the same with Julius Caesar where Brutus, being "honourable", says of Caesar: "I loved him well", and Antony finds Brutus "dearly loved" by Caesar? Is it the innocent, or only the naive, reader that takes this language in terms, not of *eros* but of *agape*? In Shakespeare's military plays it is clear that there is eroticism even in death and wounds. Some 20th-century war poetry carries the same intent. Yet to find the erotic everywhere, or require that it must be paramount, is to consign both life and letters to crippling partiality.[6] There is for our humanity an inwardness that no "outing" can succeed to violate. Certainly the desire of some in the gay and lesbian communities to have their style blatant and aggressive has contributed to an eroticization of society in general, away from the modesty and reticence once thought implicit in the nature of sexuality itself.

It has, however, to be acknowledged that this drive to the self-advertisement of homosexuality owes much to decades of hostility and social reproach. The suspicion that wills to conjure all friendships out of their "innocence" has its provocation in the suspicion that relishes the register and the indictment of guilt. Homosexuals have found themselves "despised and rejected",[7] "queered" in the human equation, harried and persecuted, harshly intimidated into loneliness, anonymity or self-contempt. The infamous "Trials of Oscar Wilde" had aspects peculiar to their incidence, but his vilification and sentence to imprisonment were nevertheless representative of the vindictiveness and acrimony inflicted on homosexuals by a retributive society.

History may make only tardy amends for its injustices but it would have been surpassing strange had a slow sea-change in perceptions not at length disqualified a long story of distortion and oppression. That in no way argues an uncritical validation of all that has ensued upon the change or of the sexual anarchism to which – in some quarters – claim is made. Extravagant, even mindless, assertiveness is liable to requite the bigotry that earlier matched it in disproportionate self-warranting. At long range, the saga of Oscar Wilde enshrines the whole plea of homosexuals to society, the whole waywardness of society and homosexuals.

It was a tragic saga deeply "theatred" – we might almost say – in a cultural milieu that sundry other human cultures would have found bizarre, if not incomprehensible. Yet it would be false to suppose that all the issues of homosexuality could be left in the relativity of culture. Wilde, until *De Profundis*, was always liable to subdue the ethical to the aesthetic, to confuse the true with the beautiful, the good with the pleasing. Study of Christ-learning in this chapter must come later to the sacramental principle of the body's inherent holiness where the elements of flesh, its form, its touch, its glow, its sweet embrace – that of it which lust perverts – find the due experience of their authenticity. For present purposes there is the immediate issue thrown up alike by gay–lesbian libertarian assertion and by a traditional rejectionism, namely how, beyond claim or prejudice either way, we can think we know what is "natural" and what "perverse", and by what criteria we presume to decide.

III

The cultural is everywhere the form in which we receive and transact the natural. There is a tendency in many quarters to think of culture as wholly determinative of how the natural order should be assessed. More careful reflection promptly indicates how untenable that view is. The very diversity of cultures – a diversity bewilderingly wide in this very area of sexuality – must mean that how and why cultures differ sets an open question about them all. They will always be conditioning our experience of things natural: they can never exclusify themselves in our experience nor imprison us in their control. Western 19th-century awareness of the Greek world, via aesthetes like Walter Pater or Gustave Flaubert, fell athwart the Judeo-Christian tradition of sexual perceptions and, so doing, generated the sort of prolonged debate and tension in which Oscar Wilde was tragic prey. It followed then, and follows still, that issues are joined where culture, far from being arbiter, is itself *sub judice*, the reach of which compels us to wrestle with "nature" *per se*. It is in a reading which incorporates culture as only relevant not absolute that we must reach for what nature herself arguably finds perverse.

At a later point we shall find this task conveying us to the Christian sacramentalism about our human sexuality with which the chapter must conclude. Meanwhile there are more immediate duties.

It seems incontrovertible that nature intends male for female. The vagina is a different aperture from the anus. The mechanics or, better, the physical functions of procreation manifestly belong with organs calculated to perform them. It is presumably agreed that "insemination" otherwise is "artificial". The natural is the normal, the normal the natural. That far nature is unequivocal. The point holds without any implication that male-with-female sexuality belongs only with procreation. The truth is quite otherwise. That such intercourse has dimensions of inter-personhood far beyond the incidence of parenthood can underwrite a case for homosexual transactions as equally and significantly interpersonal, despite the same-sex situation isolating them into those terms alone.

Yet, though sexuality in exchanges fulfils, delights, admonishes, explores and engrosses the parties either way, there must for ever remain the question whether it does so authentically when the physically natural pattern is absent or disdained? Without what nature herself bestows on male with female, female with male, are we left with more than reciprocal masturbation?

Infinitely more, gays and lesbians will want to say, and say with vehemence, querying, too, that "physically natural" language. Nevertheless the most ardent among them cannot gainsay that there is a physically authenticated naturalness and that it is not theirs.

But should that reading of authenticity, by that physical right of the way human genitalia are, resolve all issues categorically? What of psychic criteria? What of impulses others, for all their simply physical identity with the rest, find or discern within themselves? While, to the anatomist, we are all by bodily count – as the ugliest of words has it – "heterosexual", what if, on other no less arguable counts, we are not so? By what authority, and what criteria, do we then adjudicate the deep contention?

IV

Whatever our allegiance to Scriptures, it will not suffice merely to cite them. For those who are indicted by them will refuse to be accountable to a tribunal which, they will say, is itself on trial. Leviticus 18: 22 and

20: 13 prohibit homosexual acts between men. Romans 1: 27 abhors and reproaches them; 1 Corinthians 6: 9 likewise. As it stands in the texts the anathema is complete. Yet even acceptance of it must discriminate since Leviticus 20: 13 calls for the killing of those who indulge. At least, in Britain, since 1861, adherence to that injunction would itself be a crime and could in no way be Christian even so. Since that part of the dicta has to be taken into responsible revision maybe the other part must also. The same would apply to Islamic Scriptures.

If we cannot read religious authority, in textual form, categorically – what of reading nature? In what range, from what angle, with what lights, for what clues? Disallowing – as already argued – the total writ of culture, how should the insistent phenomenon of homosexuality be understood? No longer shamed, or content to be secretive, it is now vocal and even clamorous about its legitimacy.

That there has been a growing review of former attitudes against that claim is not in doubt. Should we now be thinking that God is no more angry with gays and lesbians than with diabetics? Or, healthily away from any "sickness" analogy, ought we to say that their "condition" – a neutral word – might be likened to being left-handed or liable to baldness or tone-deaf? The homosexual orientation may then be seen as genetically contrived and, therefore, in no way reprobate and every way legitimate for those so discovering. The evidences seem to require "natural" and not "perverse" as now the due and proper term in such cases. If so, there needs to be a radical shift in the response and the reckonings of the wider community.

However, "those so discovering" is a moot expression. Science, not least in the sphere of the psyche, all too readily supplies easy alibis for those who want to take them. It is too trite, in many many cases, for an individual blandly to announce: "I am homosexual", or "I realize that I am gay", or "Sure! I'm an islander on Lesbos". It might not – or never – be confidently so, apart from the contributory, if not decisive, factor of environing persons and occasions. The parallel must not be pressed but there are homosexuals, like alcoholics, who are more "made" than "born", more shaped by people than by genes, or if by both then in a connection that inter-acted.

It is this that makes often naive, and sometimes culpable, the allegedly comprehensive conclusion that "one is gay and gay one is". The verb "is" has always been elusive, and there is much that is subtle about its being, or coming to be, truth-telling. If a growing literature of self-narrative, the annals of day-to-day eroticism, may be trusted, it is evident that they present a scenario of psychic negotiation, manoeuvre, suggestion, appetite, experiment, dominance, submission and seduction, where homosexual experience transpires, is discovered, comes to be assumed and, by engagement affirms its alleged naturalness, and so, perhaps, fatedness.

Male/female relationships, to be sure, may be known in similar ways, and sundry "devices and desires", but – by our earlier argument – with different sanctions of mind-in-body. Thoughts which we must later develop in due place suggest that those detecting an innate homosexual condition do well to be alert to the link that surely exists between first behaving and then belonging. For the sequence is often that way and an orientation which has merely been adopted comes to seem a proud or problematic determinant for which birth could be thanked or blamed.

It is clear that it takes a gay to find a gay, a lesbian to make another. There is always an initiative to feel for a response, an "innocence" (in the strict sense) in line for an initiation. The process may stem from any of the subtle motives that make for every kind of bonding – attraction, self-imaging as in timid awaiting or active triumphing, achieving and being achieved.[8] It would be fondly naïve to exclude this factor and simply assume a "condition" obtaining in a neutral world. That being so, any notion of being helpless or passively acquiescent, or yielding to an alleged inevitability, is futile and negligent of the responsible task that all sexuality imposes.

Whatever the genetic and psychic "givens" that are believed implicit, there is always in homosexuality a becoming explicit by virtue of social rapport and the environments of personhood among persons. This being so, the theory of something ineluctable, though it may be conveniently exonerating, is false when it atrophies self-control and makes the self a hostage in a realm of whims or fates.

Nowhere was this situation more shadowing and shadowed than in the career of Oscar Wilde near the turn of the last decade of the 19th century. He had been married for six years, was father to two sons, and confirmed in a brilliant society as the wittiest of conversationalists, the owner of a fertile pen. For ever afraid, as he said, "of not being misunderstood", it was clear that he was cutting a theatrical figure that might compound its brilliance with brittleness. Few, however, could have been prepared for the tragic denouement of a homosexual entanglement with Lord Alfred Douglas, the provocateur of the disaster that ensued.

The circumstances of Wilde's charge of libel against Douglas' father, the two trials and his own final sentence, were doubtless exceptional both in notoriety and scandal. But the root of the tragedy was the "gay" equation (as the term would now be) between the two younger men. There seems no doubt where the initiative lay and how what we are calling a "condition", not a "malady", had initiation. The personal "politics" involved are always complex and necessarily private – a fact which makes the cult of finding and being found not only a possible intensification of experience but certainly a loading of uncertain dice. The same, yet not the same, could doubtless be said of the enterprise of marriage. "I grew careless," Wilde wrote in *De Profundis*,

> of the lives of others. I took pleasure where it pleased me and passed on. What the paradox was to me in the sphere of thought, perversity became to me in the sphere of passion. Desire at the end was a malady, or a madness, or both.[9]

Deliberately he uses the contentious word. Despite the strenuous will to forgiveness in his last writing, there is no mistaking the vehemence of Wilde's reproach of Alfred Douglas to whom the entire *De Profundis* is addressed. "An unintellectual friendship" had been allowed entirely to dominate Wilde's life. "Sterile and uncreative", and "intellectually degrading," Douglas' "persistent grasp" "stereotyped" Wilde's temperament. "Blindly, I staggered as an ox to the shambles", he wrote. The friendship "was entirely destructive of everything fine in me".[10]

> The froth and folly of our life grew often very wearisome to me: it was only in the mire that we met: and fascinating, terribly fascinating though the one topic round which your talk invariably centred was, still at the end it became quite monotonous to me.[11]

There have been few more articulate and desperate protestations of the victim-making fate of homosexuality than that of Oscar Wilde. The tragedy was only the deeper for the fact that there had been no inevitability about it, only the hazard of circumstance. His witness is the more eloquent for its being firmly unvindictive. It deserves to be heeded in a climate where homo-eroticism is trivialized as harmless or commended as innocuously self-fulfiling. That there are fatal friendships is not in doubt. They "twist the ordered issue of vicissitude to suit some whim or appetite of their own".[12]

V

Situations are neither fully measured nor readily retrieved by the language of warning. The tobacco companies carry them untroubled on all their brands. *De Profundis* is too authentic to be in the business of deterrence. Moreover, it would be naïve to imply that the Douglas/Wilde bitter fiasco is all that should be said (though said it should be) about the physicality it transacted. What of the *In excelsis* which practitioners claim to find in relationships, gay and lesbian, they take "natural" to them and therefore socially acceptable in being personally "true"? The question deserves due heeding.

But first, there is the issue of "years" and their "discretion". There must be "the age of consent" or we are in to paedophilia, so strangely so-named which most societies would disallow and condemn. For it violates personality and forestalls the precious fruits of self-awareness in their due time and dignity. However, is consenting-ness – if we may so speak – a matter of calendar measure only? Consent can hardly be comprehensively given if the dimensions of the invitation are half unknown, the invasion of rights scarcely discerned.

So much is already evident from the Oscar Wilde scenario, in the sense that it was only a stunted and inveigled consent he ever gave. The awesome reservations that properly make paedophilia so abhorrent need to extend to expropriation of the other, riper though the years may be. The point is at issue in the classical Greek tradition of the *erastes* and the *eronomos*, the older man and the youth, the former initiating the younger, and at the same time exciting and indulging his own purposes. It could be warranted as a form of sexual education by intercrural copulation. There could even be, or be pretence of, a certain elegant dispassion about the ritual.[13]

Whether formalized as a social norm, or engaged in other terms, what the *erastes/eronomos* relation makes plain is a heavily ambiguous notion that often begs its own question and is, therefore, no adequate safeguard of integrity for either party. Nor can consent be decided by calendar alone. Bitterly, after it has been either tacit or assumed, it may wish itself either withheld or deferred. What was done cannot be undone and regret is barren. Then, sadly, Wilde's frequent dictum: "What is realized is right" is altogether wrong.[14] Rather, the "right" was not "realized", but usurped.

But leaving the heavy problematics of consent, what of the positives of homo-eroticism as being, for those who find them so, natural, legitimate, authentic and intensely fulfiling? The lively sense of beauty can be their patron, the visual delight of young limbs, the love of beauty, the sheer pulse of physical being, the impulse to belonging – need these be disavowed as fit for censorship because they are only erotically employed? Are only male/female relations in the flesh susceptible of an integrity otherwise denied? If we say that these too are liable to perversions for which they are reproached, must the gay and the lesbian couplings be allowed no assessings other than condemnation, all qualities subject to instant veto and anathema? Is not the embrace, after all, the supreme gesture being human has?

What cannot be in doubt is that *all* copulation (shall we call it, using a limiting word for an inclusifying deed?) is the theme of – or the prey to – a wealth or a welter of attitudes, intentions, attentions and desires. The question for the gay and the lesbian might, on some counts, be said to turn on what is seemly. It is certain that the anus is not normally or naturally a place for sexual penetration, nor the mouth an organ for the orgasm. They have other physical functions and, these apart, are physically perverted, i.e., turned away from the justice in them.[15]

"Seemly" and "unseemly", however – despite the force they truly have – may be overridden by passion, disavowed by culture, or ignored by liberation – as pretension has it. Their bearing on behaviour needs lifting into sanctions higher still. These will turn on principles and perceptions transcending, yet also underwriting, simply physical criteria. For love is ever more than sex and sexuality more than bodies in embrace. The word we need is "sacramental". In its fulness (*pace* "Christian Gays and Lesbians") it requires the housing it gets in the Christian theology of "the Word made flesh", of the divine hallowing the human, the human implacing the divine, in the meaning of the Incarnation.

There is, necessarily, some measure of that sacramental situation in all faiths when what is done transacts what is meant as in the simplicities of a kiss, a salute, a handshake, a wreathe-laying or a kneeling. For, as Wilde wrote: "Love is a sacrament that should be taken kneeling."[16] He did not have sexual positions in mind – an observation which weirdly captures the whole distinction between what may be physically had and what can be spiritually received and known. Not apart from, nor against, but always within the sexuality, the sacramental enshrines – and only so doing safeguards – its full dimensions and, with them, the whole integrity of personhoods engaged.

It is this sacramental reading – and receiving – of our human sexuality that redeems it from mere animality and, more, fulfils or achieves it in the measure of its inherent worth. We are taken here beyond, perhaps at times into scorn of, mere legalism and platitude, the rigorism of Levitical, or other, prescripts. The prohibition these impose has place but only in the consent a deeper perception brings – and brings only by premises that could not avail if they were only negative. For what is, or would be, entailed in heeding prohibition belongs with larger, and positive, dimensions of selfhood and humanity. To have refuge only in "Thou shalt not" may secure a certain innocence and, indeed, fulfil a precious end, but will not engage the health of the heart nor register the true mastery of love.

The radical error is if, and when, the sensual is isolated from the sacramental. "Sensuality" is often turned into a word of reproach and the indulgent are then up in arms. It needs to be rightly discerned. For we are indeed creatures of senses and they have their right not merely in the mechanics of existence but also in the wealth and wonder of relatedness, of intimacy and passion. The interpersonal transactions they bestow and empower deserve – may we not say expect? – the reverence, the reticent modesty, the grateful alertness, that take them for the mystery they are. Sexuality binds its parties at least physically, perhaps only momentarily, in the utmost self-awareness via body-exposure and mental abandon, keenly aware of otherness and inwardness in a coincidence of persons, limb to limb and face to face. Such meanings are only truly sensual in being sensitive to awe and wonder as well as the other meanings of coitus.

To know and have it so is the meaning of the sacramental principle in this its sexual realm. To trivialize, commercialize, superficialize is to betray. Wilde's reading of his own homosexual experience from the perspective of his prison griefs brings him squarely to this mind with clear implication for his own abandonment, those three fatal years, of the sanctity of his marriage.[17]

By the time he wrote *De Profundis* it seems clear that two streams in his heritage came together, namely the Greek aestheticism of his culture and the Christian tradition of his Irish roots. Often thought to be at odds when the former stays in hedonism and the latter lapses into puritan rigorism and ascetic rejection of the body, they may combine – to mutual enrichment – in a warm sacramentalism.

He could write of "something wrong in what one becomes" more than in "what one has done". He could enthuse over "the play of beautiful muscles and the moulding of fair flesh," and could speak of

> the outward rendered expressive of the inward: the soul made incarnate, the body instinct with spirit.[18]

Writing there first about art and form, he took it onward into sorrow and, implicitly into a Christian receiving of sex. Allowing for the aestheticism with which Wilde read his New Testament,[19] and despite his self-exemption from its institutional legacy, that "body instinct with spirit" theme belongs with Paul's insistence: "Know ye not that your body is the temple of the Holy Spirit?" Sexual exchange is then understood and entered as into a sanctuary where wonder belongs as well as excitement, and mystery waits on appreciation.

A deeply sensual awareness of the body need not take E. M. Forster's oft-quoted dictum: "Only connect", as if it had to read: "Hasten to copulate". That will be the more so if we are hastening asymmetrically, where parts do not organically correspond. Doubtless we may aver with Bernard Shaw or D. H. Lawrence and their kindred that human life is not the fulfilment of moral law but the satisfaction of a passion that is inherently chaotic. Yet, in body-sanctuary terms, the option of reverence and chastity will reassert itself, and temper with sincerity the transactions it approves.

Doubtless again, we may see the body-sanctuary situation as a conspiracy of repression, the subversion of due appetite by a puritan rejectionism, conniving with what Wilde called "the terror of society". If "society" wears here the mantle of stern parenthood and turns nature to its ends, our resistance is all the more in need of body-hallowing lest we mistake our independence for assertive license. Literature is full of the complexities of adolescence emerging from things familial. It was no coincidence that Oscar Wilde renamed himself Sebastian Melmoth, "riddled with arrows" not only of desire but of slander, scorn and vicarious sorrow. Yet to insist that body is ours alone, its sexual fulfilment our personal "dominion", is not to think ourselves unbridled when extraneous referents have been assigned to our margins.[20]

To have our body and its fulfilments among the sacraments is more surely, more aptly, more pointedly, to rejoice in the blessings of touch, the delights of the eye, the charm of the hearing, the bliss of the surrender. For all these belong with a good creation and the dignity of honest selfhood. It is then no more blessed to give than to receive. For we do neither without the other, only each in their unison.

It is here that Wilde's repeated "Only what is realized is right" proves a quite misleading paradox. His plea was for intensity, not "shallowness". He thought that all life should be somehow, that moment, wholly self-consummated, so that most people, for the most part, rarely ever lived. "Unrealizing" was virtual unreality. Thus far he had a certain logic but only with continuing fallacy. When "sorrow" as he put it, quoting Dante, had "re-married him to God," he "realized" that his flamboyant, fastidious youth, his entanglement with a sordid and treacherous friendship, had been tragically "wrong". What, he has us ask, was "really realized" in his picture of Dorian Gray?[21] "Only what is realized is right" entrusts the proving to the future, whereas it mostly lies in what precedes the proof. André Gide reported in 1895 that Wilde "had grown reckless, hardened and conceited". *De Profundis* is bitter confirmation of the same verdict in Wilde's own prison-redeemed retrospect. He left posterity in no doubt of which "realization" was right.

VI

What of the body-sanctuary in sex-understanding for those who find or believe themselves homo-erotic, meant for single gender sexuality? Answer, for Christians, must turn on a personal – not an imposed –

verdict that can honestly belong with sacramental engagement. It must reckon with the manifest asymmetry, with the exemption from parenthood, with the part-absence of social participation in "the great chain of being",[22] where they found their own being and being awaited continuity. Vocations to celibacy are real and authentic. They serve past and future in terms of a different present. But celibacy, by definition is not homo-erotic except perhaps in its renunciation.

These considerations apart, are male/male, female/female relationships in their contrivable forms of intercourse, among the sacraments? If they can hallow "the flesh" may they not be – more than legitimated – positively vindicated? Were those not actively, or potentially, ugly factors which for so long in our society (unlike Greeks and Romans) read them as damnable? Has hostility not been itself "weird", bigoted, "queer" and malign? Do we still need the urgency of births to offset the infant mortality that used to have us frown on "desertion" in homo-eroticism? If hetero-eroticism is rightly part of intercourse, so that marriage means sacramentally more than procreation and flesh is sweetly the transacting of the love that binds and dedicates into a mutual consecration to fidelity, as the marriage vow affirms, then may the fact of sacrament be no less present in genuine single-sex relations?

The answer has to be personally made. Christians will always find it far to seek in the affirmative, seeing that "flesh" is so differently engaged, so incongruously employed. Yet it would be an improper tyranny which demanded to defy or disown the possibility, if – in some measure – "believing made it so". Yet any such believing needs its own inner caveats that, in our present times, are all too readily renounced. We must resist the vehemence of aggressive homosexuals who see themselves as having much persecution to avenge. Belligerence, however understandable, is no substitute for sanity or patience where we need perceptions that give us pause.

Is there no place for chastity, for "holy abstinence" as obtain in marriage unless it descend into rape? The parallel is not exact but neither is it pointless if the erotic everywhere is subject to discipline and charity, "with tapers bedward", as Shakespeare has it.[23]

One of the pioneers of the study of homosexuality may help our thinking. John Addingtom Symonds was studiously enamoured of the Renaissance in Italy, on which he wrote seven volumes, published in 1879. He read Walt Whitman's *Leaves of Grass* as "a sort of Bible", with its "celebration of the body" in rhapsodic erotic terms.[24] Alive to the beauty of limb and line, he had dreams of naked forms and relished the "desires" he traced in literature and sculpture. He thought that perhaps pre-natally he had led the life of a Greek in the erotic lure of beauty in the flesh.

All this was compatible with normal marriage and was known only within his thoughts where it lived only implicitly, fascinated as he remained, with choirboys and visual nudity. It seemed to him – whether from Plato or from societal demur – that homo-erotic intercourse would have falsified his desires which he avowed were never translated into act. His *A Problem in Greek Ethics* considered that what was sensual in base acts offended what was nobly spiritual, "the flesh (not) providing a fit dwelling for the spirit which controlled and fashioned it".[25]

Symonds must not be claimed for a Christian sacramental ideal of "what we do after the flesh". Yet the "aesthetic sexuality" he represents has a kinship in that virility need be no stranger to chastity nor chastity to comradeship. Love certainly has often been thus across the centuries in the way that Symonds was "in love" with Michaelangelo. Reflecting so, however, does nothing to handle the urges of the living and the lively, unless the option to spiritualize or transmute them is always available. "Consenting", then – the word legally crucial around things homo-erotic – may come to mean adults pausing to deliberate in a total context. Perhaps we can amend Wilde's dictum and say that "only what is sacramentally realized is right". But deciding what is rightly realized must turn on a Christian discerning of the criteria for what they are. For "what they are" makes the possession and the decision ours.

In the context of the Christian ministry there should be no question about the call to homo-erotic chastity. Discipline has never been other than integral to the due care of souls. The case of the well-reputed, saintly Edward King, Bishop of Lincoln can serve us well, the more so since his homosexuality was so closely linked with his "holiness". Had he survived into our different times he would have had the "Stonewallers" and the "Outragers" baying at his heels to "out" him.

With "wild ploughboys" in his curacy at Wheatley near Oxford, and later in Pastoral Theology at Christ Church in the University, he was aware of the erotic no less than J. A. Symonds. Keyed to what might be called "the temptation of occasion", he told himself and his clergy that "lust was the essence of selfishness", that it was no bridge but a bar to honest friendship. "Love we must", he wrote, in his other-worldly way, "but so as to be in heaven together." More down to earth, he asked what the Gospel meant in telling us that Jesus, "looking on the rich, young ruler, *loved* him"? (Mark 10: 21, the verb is *agapao*). Jesus had "loved" Lazarus too. And what of that "disciple whom Jesus loved" leaning on his breast at supper? (John 13: 23).

King was sure that such love was at once both ardent and pure, as when Jesus had the children in his arms. He felt that human hearts had immense capacity for tenderness if also surrendered to God in discipline. In Christian ministry unilaterally obsessive love crippled the ability truly to love all and the disciple must be "servant of all". Human attraction could – and should – thus lead to the divine in the very principle of the Incarnation.[26]

Did not New Testament faith break out radically and finally from divine love via an exclusive covenant into divine love equally and inclusively embracing all humankind in faith and grace? A favouritism crudely conceived had no further place in a divine economy. The personal equation in the ministers of Christ must be comparably unselective and equal in their control of things potentially erotic. Only so could a ministerial hospitality of mind, heart and home to all and sundry, be consistent with the Incarnate Lord.[27]

VII

If that is where we come in the Christ-learning these chapters intend there remains the final query whether – in this area of what "now dares to speak its name" – it was well to come via Oscar Wilde and *De Profundis*. For his talent and his tragedy were as exceptional as his wit and verve. He was an exile repairing to a culture he delighted to unmask and, so doing, amuse and entertain. He remained exotically self-esteeming even in his deepest register of a sordid and folly-laden story. It is true, as we have seen in CHAPTER THREE, that he aestheticized Jesus himself and read his own idiom into the New Testament. Yet his allusions and reflections were deeply Biblical and his "realization" of "pity" – as he loved to call his deepest value – the costliest "learning" of his darkly truncated life.

So it must be this ultimate "learning of the meek and lowly in heart" that deserves the reckoning we have attempted of all else. In adversity Wilde found an un-hardening of the heart. He discovered Francis of Assisi. The very injustice of his ordeal "learned" him (as the King James Bible would have said)[28] the lot of vicarious souls and how their only "real" option is to bear wrong in a forgivingness that is not overcome by enmity and revenge. This became his clue to the reality of Jesus Christ, the Cross in the heart of God.

It was not a "learning" that mastered the quarrel he still had with orthodox belief and the familiar sacraments of "bread and wine". There were idiosyncrasies in his praise of Jesus. His *confessio fidei crucis* carried the marks of his ego in its broken-ness. He did not survive to fulfil his hope of renewing in this chastened vein the passion of his muse. He had understood how Isaiah's words of one "despised and rejected, a man of sorrows and acquainted with grief" Jesus had found pre-figuring himself. "Every work of art," Wilde wrote,

> is the conversion of an idea into an image. Christ found the type and fixed it, and the dream of a Virgilian poet, either at Jerusalem or at Babylon, became in the long progress of the centuries incarnate in him for whom the world was waiting . . .

adding

> For every expectation that he fulfilled there was another that he destroyed . . . He appeals to the temper of wonder, and creates the mood in which alone he can be understood.[29]
>
> Only one God has let his side be wounded by a soldier's spear.[30]

Only so realizing is "the yoke easy and the burden light".

TWELVE

Christ-Learning as Personal Crisis

I

"Academy" was, in origin, the name of a garden in which Plato taught, using the property of Academos its owner. There was a garden also at the heart of Christianity, named Gethsemane. It is fair to ask what the two gardens have in common. For it might be a poetic way of posing the perennial issue between dialogue and discipleship. The former is increasingly *de rigueur* in western theological circles though less readily so elsewhere. The latter may seem to be in some attentuation where inter-faith discursiveness converses in Socratic garden. The form the process takes is subtle.

Practitioners are insistent that allegiances remain intact and loyal. Patterns of worship and confession of belief abide. Membership and identity are not at stake nor are convictions in question. Yet they may appear to have come to be held in openly private terms as denominators of faith community in a discipline disinterested in ready access. It is assumed that such tacit inter-neutrality will be genuinely mutual so that the several faiths, in conversing about their contents, are content to stay conversational, immunizing respective communities from any active recognition of their significance.

The situation may be harshly phrased and needs more probing analysis anon. The immediate issue is that – for the Christian – there is that other garden, that Gethsemane, which was in no way academic. Christians "adore", as Augustine wrote in comment on Psalm 132: 7, "in the place where His feet stood".[1] They do so, as the same writer dramatically realized, because a decision had firmly arrested, or patiently wooed, them into surrender. The disturbing thing, for all dialogue, is that nowhere in the world did the faith of Christ arrive and "establish" except by conversion. Galilee and Jerusalem apart, in no place was it ever native or indigenous. Its enterprise everywhere was a deed of baptism. It was only anywhere found because it had been brought. Its story was mission and mission was its story. New birth, not mother birth, occasioned it. Not as pundits do we "enter into the kingdom of heaven".

May contemporary dialogue imply that this shape of Christian history is now obsolete? that Christian faith can effectively be private to those who already happen to belong? But do *any* merely "happen to belong"? May we thus disown the centuries and the integrity of those who have come to faith, through wind and fire or by "a voice of gentle stillness", because they knew themselves summoned to believe and belong? Is that hallmark, in disciples, of all Christian history to pass into abeyance? Jesus characterized his Gethsemane as "my baptism".[2] Were there such waters in Plato's garden?

These are deliberately pointed interrogatives in preface to this final chapter in study of Christ-learning. For the more we are persuaded of the claims and merits of inter-religious dialogue the more at issue we make our own believing and belonging. Have we, at one and same time, a mandate both to hold, and to withhold, "things surely believed among us"? For withhold we do, if there is no space for accession to conviction, no concern for the discipleship without which we are still academic. Is dialogue where the old ballad sang

> Goodman, you've spoken the foremost word!
> Rise up and bar the door.[3]

For, lingering round that door is the human presence, the *proselutos*,[4] the recruit with yearnings beyond discursiveness. These are the stakes around dialogue. They engage us all in a deep contemporary problematic, namely how religions believe enough in themselves to hold them proper for new disciples, while also relating disinterestedly in a comparing converse. Or, more bluntly, what of commending faith to the other? Is discipling precluded, included, prospective or improper?

II

In its third Chapter the Fourth Gospel introduces us to Nicodemus. He is – we might say – a Jewish Academus. He seeks out Jesus – imagination may allow us to guess – in a garden. He thinks privacy essential, lest he be suspect to his own religious kin. He senses the delicacy of his enquiring of an upstart rabbi, being himself "an eminent Pharisee", a proper "establishment man". All the familiar elements of dialogue are here.

His opening stance is courteous, eirenic, even deferential. Nicodemus would be at home in the Council of Christians and Jews, perhaps even in one with Muslims as well. He makes big concessions to Jesus. He is a paragon of how dialogue may open. But promptly he is in deep waters. Most startingly for any Jew, he is told he "must be born anew", or "born from above". Puzzlement ensues. He may have felt mortally offended. For had not birth to a Jewish mother ensured his inclusion already in "the people of God"?[5] He is confused and misunderstands. "Womb-right" is clearly in his mind when he asks about the mystery of re-entering it in order to be "born anew".

Dialogue is quickly floundering. This "new birth" has to be understood as like first birth in its "newness of life", but not like it in that it is happening – and urgently needs to happen – within a given self that already exists, whose "givenness" of culture, nurture, quality and story, it will not erase but, instead, receive into "the kingdom" of new grace and forgiveness and life. This *is* "how a man *can* be born when he is old".

However, and strangely, this meaning is in no way housed rigorously in an institution, or structured into the sort of orthodoxy that demands adherence to itself. On the contrary, it is likened by Jesus to the mysterious "wind"[6] that "blows where it will", is tributary only to its own mystery. Pressing his surprise that Nicodemus does not already know this, Jesus appeals to a sort of self-evidence already in the field, the ground they share.

How distant from contemporary dialogue that abrupt "You must be born again", yet how close to it are the sequences. An utterly disturbing point is made even where existing insights are enlisted. Judaic birth and covenant, birth with water and from that mother's womb, are required to undergo in universally human terms the "new birth" in the Spirit. The theme is exactly what we explored in CHAPTER THREE earlier around the Mediterranean expansion of the faith of Christ crucified. "Flesh", human nature indiscriminately, "bears" its kind. Only the Spirit makes that nature new in grace. The meaning is told with an authority that claims to "speak of heavenly things", and more credibly because it has been honest about lesser ones.

The inter-religious scene is frequented by numerous Nicodemuses. Let us leave this first one, noticing that the passage gives no clue to where he himself departs. For, like many Johannine discourses, it leaves its original setting far behind. There has indeed been dialogue but it has quite failed to stay only discursive. "You must be born anew."

But if we let Nicodemus go, to enquire about him later, and also leave the immediacies of the passage in John 3, we are not out of our contemporary wood. That "wind" metaphor has to haunt our thoughts lest we pretend to bind it. This "birth anew" is categorically necessary but how should we read its meaning? The language is not uniquely evangelical. Jews sometimes spoke of "Gentiles" who became Jews as *renati*. And there were those many gnostic rituals in which postulants were "born of water" as "of the spirit" in their several cults.

Questions follow as to the author's precise intention in the shaping of his Gospel. For, if nothing else, comparison with the Synoptics makes clear that he is presenting Christhood in the perspectives, partly examined in CHAPTER FOUR, that belong with a received theology, itself the child of faith as to a history. The "dialogian" outside Christianity will be right in wanting to include such relevance in any encounter with Christian reliance on the text. A Scripture which might close the issues for one party may only open them wider for the other. May this mean that widening dialogue surrenders the absolute note of "You must be born again"? Will we do right by all that is involved if we have it less than fully academic, or if we leave it only so?

That burden is confirmed by another consideration still with John 3. The writer draws an analogy, which to modern minds must seem quite incongruous, from Numbers 21: 8. It is appallingly far from the real significance of Jesus and the Cross, having to do with the serpent "lifted up" in the wilderness story of nomadic Israel whereby those who looked at the image were healed of their malady. There is a strong irony in that "lifting up" – factually on the pole, historically on the Cross and metaphorically in "the preaching of the Cross". Aside from the problem of the "miracle", it was only an *argumentum ad hominem* in respect of Nicodemus. At a stretch it might be said to comprise the truth that you must fully "see" your guilt (in penitence) as the condition of being healed from it in pardon.[7] That latent meaning, however, has no measure or place for the realization of the Cross as divine love in a suffering redemption engaging with "the sin of the world". Meanings are not well served by allusions or associations that bemean them. Honest dialogue cannot well invoke its possessed Scripture without conceding the duties its possession imposes here and now. Nor can it rely on *argumenta ad homines* when other *homines* are in the frame. For religions bewilderingly diversify the very humanity we share.

A right perplexity, however, should not mean we lose heart. Given patience, there is a way in which being truly ready for the honest reach of dialogue enables authentic communication. The difficulty sometimes affords the opportunity. A modern Nicodemus may the better be led to the real dimensions of the vicarious Christ of the Cross precisely by *not* going tamely along with an ancient imagery about "serpents". Having right interrogatives or caveats can bring us into the way of right affirmatives. What the evangelist did in his time in the Johannine discourses may be our example in our different time and place.

If, thus far, we have not shirked the tensions, perhaps we can abide them further by a brief return to Nicodemus. For his story is not only intellectual. Whatever the puzzles of his mind we are given to glimpse, by the evangelist, the movement of his heart. For, in 7: 50 we see him in the Sanhedrin, still "being one of them", nevertheless speaking up on behalf of Jesus in terms of common justice. "Does our law judge any man before it hear him and know what he does?" A sympathy with Jesus is emerging out of the rabbi's own lights and, as need requires, against the prejudice of his own circle. It is not seldom that something akin is the experience of sincere dialogue. We become pervious where once we were absolute.

By 19: 39 Nicodemus is helping Joseph of Arimathea to bury the body of Jesus. Again the evangelist does not let him shed that identity-tag, "he that came by night", as if to emphasize that these sequels belong with that origin. Later tradition gives Nicodemus sundry roles. The one that suffices us here concerns things elusively reciprocal between dialogue and discipleship.

The task of exploring them further entails two broad themes. The one is to take onward this clue about frank discourse enabling wiser communication. The other is to study in personal terms the things at stake between truth-meanings found and long communal loyalties staying tenacious in the individual psyche. Can a self respond when he/she is "aged" already even in youth, is religiously possessed by, and subtly possessed of, a pattern of faith and community? To ask how personal movement can be authentic in face of these strong counter-constraints of a given society is to realize how exacting the interpretation of the faith that might anticipate it. Does the individual response to a perceived conviction as to truth not hitherto owned by one's community require formal transfer of one's being from here to there? Does faith have to be corroborated by legal status? More deeply, what is the way of "the wind that blows as the spirit lists" *vis-à-vis* the solidarities of institutionalized belief?

III

Caring for the interpretation of the faith that might anticipate a movement into new discipleship means that people are as much the content of communication as themes and meanings. What we may think of as truth *for* the former is truth *in* witness to the latter. That distinction around the prepositions having to do with truth goes far into all the problems. If there is to be Christ-learning it must mean that the truth *in* Christ, via Islam, via the *Dharma* etc., is becoming truth *to* the new disciples for whom it must follow that the new truth *of* has negotiated with the old truth *for*, since no meanings register on a vacant place and no receptive soul is innocent of culture, no recruit minus nurture and its strong affection.

It has long rightly been emphasized that dialogue is between people even though it must be about meanings.[8] Whatever explains a faith has to contain hearers – and retain them. Prejudice, in a right sense, will be as much entailed as perplexity. For truths to be intelligible requires that they have found cognizance with parties hearing as well as adequacy from parties telling. And always in any anticipation of faith-receiving will be the anxieties of faith-retaining and all the social, psychic pressures the situation arouses.

Agreeing to defer what these entail in the personal realm, we stay with the task of having the Gospel intelligible by patient negotiation with this inter-human, inter-cultural, inter-religious context, making it a task indeed. In the case of Nicodemus, Jesus was able to intercept his preconceptions with immediate relevance to where Nicodemus himself had been minded to begin. The abruptness then was more apparent than real. For the field of discourse was at once in place, namely "birth", i.e., the visitor's Jewish identity ensured from his Jewish mother's womb and implicit in "a master in Israel's" coming to a Jewish "teacher come from God", *and* that teacher's summons to an understanding of another "birth", wombed in universal grace and therefore inviting those in Jewish "birth-covenant" to a new comprehension of God and themselves. "You must be born anew". "Anew", to be sure, was radical but it moved from a perception it needed, namely Jewish sense of privilege. For how is there a "new" except by premiss from an "old"?

In reading the John 3 passage this way we are, of course, taking account of the author's own presentation of the Jesus he has come to recognize in these terms. We in our time can only be "Johannine" in lowlier ways, ways that do not impugn the *magisterium* of the canonical Scripture. Yet it can duly be our guide. For every conceivable Nicodemus, whether from Jewry or Islam, from Asia or Africa or the Pacific, will come with something like a hallmark of themselves analogous to that womb-sense of Jewish identity. If they come at all, it is from their own choice of opening ambit that we also must begin. Their very quest with questions – if so it be – addresses our credentials even if also probably suspecting them.

The assumption here that Christ-learning can be truly dialogical, and that a will to witness can readily be a desire to converse, may well be disputed. There will be those who hold that Christ makes his way into souls by sheer otherness, by the force of an absolute Scripture that claims downright truth and finds any solicitude for existing loyalties mistaken. Yet, if "learning" is the thing in hand, it can only be an enterprise of gentle patience, that probes perplexity and alerts curiosity.

Today's "master in Israel" may come saying: Do not you Christians stake and lose all on one throw? That Cross that was to "save the world" and be followed by the Messianic reign – is not the world still manifestly, still incorrigibly, unredeemed? What happened to that *parousia* of yours, that "love of his appearing"?[9] In truth do you not have a failed eschatology such as we Jews have always escaped by not pretending to define "hope" in any terms that history could verify, while meanwhile we have our abiding *emunah* with Yahweh?"[10]

The Christian's Christianity is thus perceived as facing such a "how can these things be?" and needing to "come clean". Here, as always, what interrogates illumines what must be interpreted. Meanings are only rescued by heeding the mystification they are found to arouse. The Christian is indeed staked on a singular and supreme event, an intense concentration of significance. But that is the way of all drama. Intensity was always the crux of truth-recognition. The Cross can be seen to bring into one telling crisis the falsehood of the world and the responsive, redeeming long-suffering of God. An event in those terms is the very text in which its authorship is known.

The rabbi – as was said – may indeed look out of his window on the world and observe "No difference".[11] But how is there a virtue in an unidentified "hope" which, by the same token, must remain perennially un-realized? What is *emunah* about, if the hope it sustains has no definition, however tentative? If we take history as we experience it, a "vacant" eschatology will be no better than a "failed" one.

But is "failed" an honest word concerning the Christian reading of "God in Christ"? We need not here restate the story in CHAPTER THREE. There were no illusions in the New Testament about the continuity of evil things.[12] For there had been no magic, no wand waved, in the crucifixion.[13] What had happened was a principle of forgiveness, seen as deriving from the heart of God and regnant in the suffering Messiah. As such, it transacted redemption within the souls of all who discerned its meaning. So doing, further, it released that principle actively into the world of human society, as eminently reproducible in all of us. In that way, further, Messiah (always assumed to be in some sense "collective") would be "all of us", a redeeming people in every engagement of which the Cross could be the paradigm. That would be the ongoing of reconciliation in the only terms consistent with the human texture of wrong and the human autonomy of will, seeing that no goodness in this world is other than crucifiable and no wrong undone without the long-suffering of it.

That ongoing redemptiveness, however, required the once-for-all epitome *and* the faith that could recognize it as indeed the way God is. *Parousia*, then, however misread in a first enthusiasm, could be seen to be taking care of itself all the time – as we have seen in CHAPTER THREE – in the ongoing-ness of faith itself via the faith-community.

The choice of just one area, albeit crucial, in Jewish/Christian discourse may at least serve to indicate how an invitation to discovery, a refocusing of awareness, can be offered in the same setting that is striving to tackle mutual rejectionism or obviate crippling misreading. There is no easy assumption that, thereby, it succeeds. For what, definably, could succeeding be? That is part of our whole problem. At any rate, there has been no silent compromise, no abeyance of concern. A perceived task is not ignored by the muting of its own experience, nor by the disregard of neighbour. The desire to be articulate marries with the will to be related and feels the marriage right.

If we were foreseeing an area similarly availing in Muslim/Christian discourse we would be in no way at random if we opted for "God and prophethood", as Islamic *Shahadah*, or faith-creed, joins them. There is in fact no "and" in the *Shahadah*. For Allah as One and Muhammad, as *Rasul* ("apostle") of Allah, are so conjoined there as to make "and" superfluous both in grammar and in faith. "There is no god but God: Muhammad is Allah's message-bringer".

How ought we to understand this "association", so often reproduced in the great medallions in many a mosque carrying on left and right in equal size the Arabic words *Allah*, and *Muhammad*? "Association" is going to be a dubious word. For Islam was urgently set to eliminate idolatry and plural worships were denoted by the term *shirk* since they were making pseudo-deities parties, in some sense, to the worship that belonged to God alone.[14] Everything about Islam's *Shahadah* lays anathema on idolatry. Yet, in a totally different and utterly anti-idolatrous sense, there is "association", i.e., of Allah and His messenger in that very *Shahadah*, as indeed there is in all other, lesser, prophetic agents, including Jesus ('Isa) as Islam perceives him.

For all these, and Muhammad finally and comprehensively in the Muslim faith, are instrumental to that, of God, which is "word", warning, guidance, reminding and *risalah*, cognate word to a *rasul* who bears it. It might be venturesome, though not un-Islamic, to say that all these are proxy for God, in that – on His divine behalf – they relate humanity to Him and Him to humanity. Thus they implement the whole meaning of creation and creaturehood as the divine bestowal of a human liability to duty, praise and responsive custody of the good earth and all its fruitful risks and meanings. All these derive from the divine nature fulfilling the divine Names.[15] It is this inherent relationality between Allah and ourselves in humankind that must be presupposed in all prophetic mission. For such relatedness apart, there would be occasion neither for worship nor for guidance.

Only, then, in prophetic mission to us is the reality of God operative for us. Something, therefore, elemental in the being of God is expressed in the agencies of the messengers. Otherwise, we would be left in that chronic *jahiliyyah*, or untaught "ignorance", in which Islam first addressed Arabian pseudo-worships.[16] To have been so left would have meant, somehow our desertion by God and, in some sense also, God's disloyalty to Himself. In positive ways, then, prophethood serves – and serving vindicates – the divine nature. In that way Allah is "in" their mission, imperatively.

It is at this point, from these common convictions, that the Christian – needing to carry this logic onward – is resolutely forbidden by Islam. Patience, therefore, at this crux of things, has to seek gentle permission to make the further case, which is – that God may be "in" associative message-bearing not only (the word just chosen) "imperatively", but affirmatively. The meaning then would be that such "bearing" – albeit with words – might also live a life in which agency was taken up into "sonship". Then what was "on behalf of God" might mean "God in His own behalf", yet still within the human terms that prophethood had always needed. They would now be terms, however, where "sending" would give way to "coming".[17]

There has long, and sadly, been an Islamic insistence that "such things cannot be". They seem derogatory to divine glory and unseemly compromise of divine incommunicability. This demur – indeed it is much more than demur – this anathema, has to take us into the ultimates of theology. What can appropriately be thought "possible" in Allah, what compatible with God? In those ultimates we must exclude crudities of reference that have not taken measure of the meaning.[18] It is with the divine transcendence the issue must belong, a transcendence not in dispute between us *qua* submission, only in issue between us *qua* character. We may be anxious about what we, as believers, may allow or disallow to God:[19] but what of the lengths God may allow Himself in belonging divinely with us?

There is, then, something deeply convertible in respect of thought on that divine sovereignty in which both Muslim and Christian agree. If thoughts of God are convertible by an inner logic moving from where a religion starts to where it may arrive, will not persons also – finding it so – be themselves discipled by weight of that transition? A soul-transforming discovery may happen via the progression of theology from a divine sovereignty of law and judgement to a Lordship that takes these further into vicarious love meeting us historically.

IV

Any such progression from discernible themes and concepts to persons discerning them in a formal sense was stoutly resisted, for example, by Mahatma Gandhi. His mind and fame are a fitting way to bring into our perspectives here the subtle mind of Asian religion. His reasons for only neutral reckonings were partly those of the politician and partly of the Hindu soul. Indian nationalism in the pursuit of *swaraj*, or independence, required the sort of loyalty to its culture that personal decisions for new allegiance would betray. More importantly, a Hindu sense of the transcendental unity of all religions made any will to faith-change both superfluous and invalid. For they were all partial, and equal, elaborations of the truth-mystery that eluded them all.[20]

Thus it was precisely in repudiating any notion of those not so born ever "becoming" Christians that Gandhi was able, indeed eager, to recruit Jesus and the Gospel for aspects of what became Neo-Hinduism. The very term indicates inward change – change in which, in the broadest terms, Christianity might loosely be said to have played a part. Gandhi, however, proved a very forceful disclaimer of the idea that even lively recognition of meanings could duly lead into Christian community. At best, they could be domesticated into already given loyalties as for ever conditioning their relevance and their survival.

We are here, of course, in the age-old problem of syncretism which cannot, however, be handled by making the word a stigma. In wholesome ways, syncretism abounds and belongs inevitably with the diversity of cultures.[21] Gandhi's adaption of the New Testament with insistent disavowal of its baptism demand deserves better from the Christian mind than simple embarrassment or regret.

Adequate reflection on the issue would take us out of present depth into the complexities of Hindu philosophy. Staying with the practicalities that most concerned him, we discover how vital were his siphonings from the teaching of Jesus – the Christology apart – and his fusing of them with the concept of *ahimsa*, or "non-violence". This, via the Sermon on the Mount, Tolstoy, John Ruskin and others, he deepened from "avoiding to injure by thought word or deed", to a positive state of doing good even to the evil-doer. Beyond not returning blow for blow

> . . . I go further. If we resent a friend's action or the so-called enemy's action, we still fall short of this doctrine. But when I say we should not resent I do not say that we should acquiesce. By resenting I mean wishing some harm . . . If we harbour even this thought, we depart from the meaning of *ahimsa*.[22]

What more need a Christian add? Indeed, how dare the Church think to "Christianize" this more than the "Christian" it already is, having also in mind how Gandhi developed his ashram for the necessary training of this *ahimsa*-capacity shortly after returning to India from his South African experience?

Yet does the Christology of the New Testament and Christian faith have no relevance to where Gandhi arrives, though gratefully alert to what, ethically, he has distilled from them? The question has its place for any right discussion of the dispensability of personal discipleship. Maximize to the full a grateful realization of this positive neighbour-love. Know its nearness to Jesus. Salute its dynamic, superbly self-critical vigilance. Civil disobedience this way does not signify contempt for law, only law's retrieval for its better sake. *Ahimsa* is not for extracting favours, nor is it subtly manipulating the other. It is watchful for its own authenticity. It is bent only on changing things in the heart, its own and the other party's.[23] It shares, we must say, "the mind of Christ". It could shelter at the foot of the Cross.

What then is its shortfall? A Christian theology would have to reply by asking: Is it written into the nature of God? Has it the final measure of human sin and so the radical quality of repentance? Gandhi affirms that "Truth is God"[24] but only as unknowable and eluding all conceptions. There is a similar apophatic tradition in Christendom. However, granted that the divine must always transcend human thought and language, do we then only deludedly rely on those theologizings on which we base any discourse at all? If, even given their proximate nature, these do not truly avail, all else, including *ahimsa* and *gnosis*, is vacuous. For this "love of neighbour" is precarious, tentative, even phantasmagorical unless reciprocal to "love in God".

Does something like *ahimsa* enter into God, so that it may confront us by more than our own warrant? Can it summon us as a moral replication, in ethics, of what is true in the divine mind? Can real history vouch for *ahimsa* as the principle of the divine being by some costly un-self-seeking that "not being overcome of evil" is proven able to "overcome evil with good"? The positive answer is in Christian Christology. Hearing – and heeding – it there, we will be sustained to live by it as being anchored in a will eternally higher than our own.

Undoubtedly, then, there is case for a community "holding this truth" – if not "against the world"[25] – urgently on its behalf. If so again, there must be warrant for that faith patiently recruiting disciples made eager to share its vital witness. It could doubtless continue in its loneliness, in these its defining terms, except that its faith-people have themselves only arrived there by a trusting response of mind, heart and will to its verdict as to God and themselves "in Christ". Verdict and trust alike enjoined on them the gentle persuasion of others.[26] It is not only in respect of God as love, in these Christly measures, that realism is vital. Realism needs to be present also in the human reckoning. Can we take to heart the Sermon on the Mount and not also register its arrival in Gethsemane, with the world of its intention a crucifying place? Did not Gandhi's *ahimsa* itself come into a "garden of agony"? Its very nobility of intent came to experience how grimly wrong our humanity can be.

Its theme of *satyagraha* (positive non-violence for truth and justice) found response but often precariously.[27] It came to learn how far to seek are the victories of love over hate, of truth over wrong. Was it, in the last analysis, too sanguine about our human amenability to the finest ideology, our desperate need of redemption? While Gandhi himself was fully committed to the ending of "untouchability", his *ahimsa* retained *swadeshi*, as its twin concept, i.e., the duty to one's own state of life (including ancestral religion) as circumscribing economic claims. It had a fine positive side in repudiating caste-hatreds. It also fostered local economies in the cause of *swaraj*, while ashrams that nurtured it had profound influence. Yet urgent human pleas against the caste system remained unsatisfied. To bid "each and all be their own sufficient ruler" remains a splendid ethic. Can it, however, be more realistic than Henry Thoreau's ambiguous withdrawal to his Walden?[28]

On the human side, then, as well as for profound reasons in theology, we are driven back on to the central issue of our remaking, its reach within ourselves and its dimensions in the economy of God. The significance of Gandhi in the setting of India and Hinduism only exemplifies a universal theme. That haunting question of Nicodemus: "How can these things be?" rings universally – far beyond the right wombing that was his immediate perplexity. It takes in all that our personal identity embraces and all that nurture and culture have predisposed us to make of our autonomy as selves.

Are we not, in a sense, "old at birth" in being so far already denominated by givens which we cannot reverse? And how far are we "masters", whether Nicodemus-like "in Israel" or in any other heritage in the psyche and the tongue? And, even when we consciously involve ourselves in the business of religious belief, or when we "come by night" to our sundry "teachers", how well are we minded to discern where we are and whither we tend? Staying passive or academic in the presence of the new will always be the easy option because, actively, it is no option at all.

V

What, then, should we make of the uneasy relation between truth perception and movement of faith-allegiance? The familiar term "conversion" begs more questions than it resolves.[29] This is the more so seeing that "belonging" in any collective shape of religion is so far bound up with psychic community, with cultural norms, with social solidarities and even with citizenship and nation. In the last of these, even treason may be entailed in any deviant embrace of authentic truth.

None of our exemplars in CHAPTERS SIX to ELEVEN were in this dire category. Even so, we have had adequate measure of how searching the issues of honest faith can become – the reaching for "right authority" in Newman, the several undergoings of misgiving and of *suspiratio* – as Latin has it – "yearning with a sigh", the restless enquiring what "things" are. If faith – as we are seeing throughout – is "crisis", how can its measure inwardly to the person be rightly realized, made good and viable, outwardly in society? Such is the two-sided question of "conversion".

On the societal side, it must call into question too facile ideas about the feasibility of individual initiatives around the embrace of new believing. Personal baptism, to be sure, has always been central to becoming Christian. The genuine use of personal pronouns has always been the hallmark of Christian discipleship. The self, in self-commitment, is the vital unit within the unity of Christ's people. "The Son of God loved me and gave Himself for me" stands at the heart of faith-confession. In that acceptance, that being accepted, there can be no proxies and no neutrals.

Yet how should Christianity hold that reality *vis-à-vis* the complexities of jealous, or alien, or hostile societies that for religious or political or psychic reasons, reject the premise of individual liberty on which it is based? What of communities prone to read in such liberty an unwarranted violation of their own sanctities, an insult to the nationhood and the tradition that guard them?

The question presses whether Christian baptism assumes too much of what, at the same time, it ignores, namely societal tolerance? For ignore it a ritual transaction does, if it is not effectively alert to the absence of what it presupposes. Perhaps the individual denominator in Christian faith unduly atomizes the personal equation and pushes the private heart into too radical a challenge to the forbearance of public norms round every minority church.

Certainly any sustained Christian dedication to the authentic rule and rite of faith-confession must also dedicate itself to the public establishment in every society of freedom of movement of belief – for its own sake and irrespective of where its availability leads. This must mean a steady engagement with the inner debate of every faith with itself, a concern for the effective deployment of the intellectual and spiritual resources it may possess, or can contrive, towards that end. No religious faith is a monolith, set in remorseless hardness of heart or obduracy of will. All have every reason to query their separate temptations to bigotry and every duty to do so. Only so can any claim to ultimacy fulfil itself. Only so can any heed the tuition that current secularity offers to them all.

The Christian sense of the preciousness of its ancient rubric that "Whoso-ever will may come" requires it to register the heavy ambiguity of that "may" word. For, while the Christ of the open door remains inviolate, the factors that impede its realization persist, so that striving to obviate them belongs with the integrity that holds the rubric to be sound and sure.[30]

There is, here, a strange paradox around what is now widely known as "dialogue". Clearly a critical part of it has to do with the necessary "intolerance of intolerance", i.e., elucidating and serving from within any faith the resources of freedom, the case-making of genuine openness. Yet, when dialogue stays only discursive, or seems to imply that no decisions are ever intended or entailed, it side-steps the thing most radically at stake. It thus ministers – perhaps unconsciously – to obscuring the most crucial dimension of all in the tolerance it purports to pursue, namely the tolerance that allows for an obedience of faith. In cultivating a right mutuality it eludes the ultimate dimension of religion which is discipleship. It is thus in danger of reducing faith to philosophy. Philosophers best continue such by leaving all issues debatable, whereas religions belong with belonging. They may not, therefore, resolve themselves into indifference about indifference. That, inherently, they seek to recruit is, precisely, the whole paradox of dialogue as an exercise in being, for honesty's sake, impartial about themselves. The paradox arises from the sheer fact of pluralism, allowing no faiths to exclusify themselves, while the growing idea of an optionality about them all stimulates in many quarters a determination that exclusive they must be.[31]

It is that determination, reinforced by politics and culture, which bedevils majority/minority situations across the world. Where faiths are perceptively interrelating too often their rapport is élitist, even arcane, and bears only slightly on the passions and prejudices of their societies at large. The struggle for genuine coexistence and for viable personal liberty of faith-decision seems often forlorn. It, therefore, remains central to Christianity that devotion to the age-long "whosoever will may come" reality be upheld only in the utmost, and parallel, effort towards the persuasion of liberty of mind and conscience everywhere. This, if no other factor, would engage Christians purposefully with the self-perception and the inter counsels of religions at large. A secluded, introverted Christian theology can never serve the liberty for Christ-learning across the breadth of the world or in the depth of its confusions.

VI

It must surely follow for what we called "the two-sided question of conversion", that personal movement of faith should preserve within itself, as authentic to its own newness, all that feasibly abides from its first birthing. If we have pleaded for a societal recognition – and occasion for – such Christ-learning, must there not be a reciprocal awareness of the bearing of the new upon the old, the legacy from the old into the new? That sense of treachery to identity and heritage which makes communities resent those who leave them has to be surmounted in the public domain – as we have seen – by conceding the liberty as authentic. No less, then, in the personal realm, does the implication of desertion have to be disowned. The private sphere, no less than the public, can pay tribute to the other. For the option of liberty works both ways. To have it avail and to avail of it would make for something mutual.

That may be far to seek but even under duress and molestation the claim to liberty of faith-obedience can diminish ensuing tensions by knowing itself in debt, albeit in departing. There is much that true Christ-learning must reject but it is never total. There are continuities everywhere in the psyche, some of them positive and honest. The remaking of persons only happens in the persons they are. Their past has residues which their future will ripen and renew. In every case through CHAPTERS SIX to ELEVEN we have found the new meanings in Christ issuing from, and merging with, the shaping of the personal world where they first kindled perception and staked their claim. Is it not on that account that the Fourth Gospel retains that identity tag of one "who came by night"? Was it not out of his capacity as a member of the Sanhedrin and a man of wealth and influence that we find Nicodemus taking his tentative way into discipleship? (John 7: 50 and 19: 39). What we have once been has always to find its maturing as well as its pruning away in what we newly become.

This must be true however dramatic our experience may be. Saul becoming Paul via his Damascus road is – lifelong– the man who "sat at the feet of Gamaliel". There was also a necessary gradualism about his becoming "apostle", witness that sojourn in Arabia and the long tuition of the self that came only with his pastoral cares. Peter's "dark night of the soul" any reader can discern in the humility and the temper of his first Epistle.

Indeed all the foregoing in CHAPTERS THREE and FOUR within the New Testament community is eloquent of antecedent factors abiding in the Christ-learning that transforms them. The Judaic sense of a private peoplehood under Yahweh preserves the incorporation it cherished when it is thrown open in grace to "as many as received Him" empowered thereby to "become children in His Name". The new people of God remain ready to appeal to the old via the *argumenta ad homines* we studied. There is retentiveness where there is revolution. The Jewishness is not "unborn", nor could it be. To think it were would be to imagine grace itself unhoused. If, as we have argued, personhood is where alone discipleship can happen, then, by the same token, the self with its inalienable birthmarks, is where it is fulfilled. The "yoke" metaphor harnesses as well as invites. Since "rest" in the invitation responds to "heavy-laden-ness", where the "learners" are coming from persists crucially in what they find.

It may be said that these New Testament examples of continuity from past to future in the immediate – and the extended – experience of discipling are not relevant to Christ-learning from other antecedents. Obviously, by their place in the Scripture they have a quite distinctive status. Yet the closedness of the Canon – while claiming to be the Scripture of a universal faith – must mean that what it contains has to be precedent for dealing with what it lacks.[32] The silence of the Canon about India or the Chinese, its neglect of Buddhism, its being antecedent to – and so oblivious of – Islam, has to mean that when the Christian mind moves in these other realms it must emulate Paul, for example, in Colosse and the Johannine circle somewhere beside the Aegean. It will need to venture towards all these areas of their Scripture's neglect, the sort of initiatives of mediation the writer to the Hebrews made in that Letter – a letter whose strangeness to us now stems from its strategy for its own audience.

There is no escape from thinking this way about Christian mental ministries *in situ* everywhere. Only so can we proceed upon "the sufficiency of Holy Scripture". It is the very principle of the Incarnation that where truth comes (namely the human scene) yields the means whereby truth tells. "The Word is made flesh" so that "flesh conveys the Word". It follows that the antecedents in Christian discipleship must have their due place in the remaking it brings. The strange invitation in Matthew 11: 28–30 was to folk un-named but who, in their heeding, were by no means anonymous. Their identities were in no way abandoned in their response. There is always that in culture that enters with persons into baptism. The recognition of new meanings rides with the context out of which it happens, in confirmation as well as contradiction. This means that the crisis in Christ-learning carries retrospect into its prospective character and maintains a caring negotiation between them. It may well be that new disciples find what is unlearned concerning the past dominates the heart in the first warmth and wonder of the new. Growth into its meaning, however, may reinstate an adjusted heritage and mitigate the sense of things forsaken and thereby also allow a sense of a people unforsaken from whom one came. The more this is so the more truly may society comprehend the nature of conversion to Christ.[33] An unforsaken people may well stay rejectionist out of old prejudice alleging that a will to new faith spells betrayal of nation, or affront to culture, or surrender of family identity. If such misreadings persist – as for long they well may – only patience can give the lie to them and then the situation stays within the issue of liberty we have discussed. It remains, however, part of faith-crisis in Christian terms that it returns people creatively to their biographical debts and their human milieu. That a man's foes might be from his own household never meant that it was his calling to make them so.[34]

The pain of that situation when it arises is precisely from having been no party to its cause. The ultimate answer to all the tensions and stresses, the "heavy-laden-ness", of minority Christians as persons and communities lies in the evidence they can bring as to the Lord who is at proof in whom and how they are. In the vivid phrase of the Hebrew prophets, they are "the place of the Name", the referent for Him whom they serve. Their burdens can then be known as taken up into the travail of the Lord Himself, the cost-taking of the struggle for spiritual freedom and a partnering of the vicarious Cross. Only so can all the other factors, economic, political, social, that make their situation hazardous, be patiently sustained.

From Nicodemus in this chapter as a mentor, with his impulse for dialogue and the abrupt turn it took in John 3, we have been required to face issues in faith-crisis in terms wider than those involved in narratives from Hooker to Wilde. Reasons for the choice of these were given in the Preface. In the light of all the foregoing it would seem that two themes must occupy a conclusion to the whole. The one is: What is the quintessential Christian reality, the magnetic field of its "attraction" – the "come, take, learn", of that Christ-invitation? The other concerns the mystery of "the will to believe". That mystery is one we can only fully explore by asking also about "the will to disbelieve". For both exist. Otherwise there could be no point in faith ever being a crisis.

VII

What is quintessential in Christianity – some would say – does not exist, given how disparate history's verdicts have been. Yet, if we keep inside the words of Mathew 11: 28–30 and have in perspective Jesus being the Christ both towards and beyond his Gethsemane and if, further, we take in the word "Christianity" itself (via "Christian" via "Christ"), we can hardly be in serious doubt concerning where, and wherein, it lies.

The Muslim author, Muhammad Kamil Husain, at mid-century, saw where it lay. He wrote: "The best Christian in his most sublime moments is a sad man."[35] His insight needs deepening but it is authentic. Christianity consists in a radically serious reckoning with humankind which it firmly associates with a radically compassionate theology or faith about God. The former sees the human world as a crucifying place, where love fulfils itself in vicarious encounter with wrong. The latter grounds this perception in the very nature of God whence alone it could be and avail as the truth it is. In Jesus as the Christ it discerns the human drama where the former took historic shape and where, by the same token, the divine meaning had its substance and criterion in earthly time and place.

There could be no doubt about the depths of human despair out of which, as we have traced in CHAPTERS TWO and THREE, the disciples of Jesus emerged to identify in Him, crucified and risen, the Christ of God. It was not only, as Kamil Husain thought, the trauma of their own craven failure in the crisis that induced "the Christian sadness". It was, far beyond their own immediate broken-ness, the evidences of the inclusive human capacity for wrong placarded so starkly in the public will to crucify as the final commentary on Jesus' ministry.[36] That spelled the end of anything superficial, sanguine or facile about the human situation. What transpired was eloquent, qualitatively, about "the sin of the world".

As such, with all its human significance, the drama had contained, on the divine side, a vicarious, unbroken capacity to love and forgive which was there to be identified as coming, via Jesus and the meaning of his Sonship, from the heart of God.[37] It was this, by its quality, that kindled the faith by which it could be recognized for what it was. Thus the Christian Church was born and thus Christianity came to be, "Very God of very God" – the two dimensions of one event and one *confessio*.

Capable on both counts of its human honesty and its divine wonder, it could "draw all humankind" towards it significance. It was no fantasy or surmise: history contained it. Room had to be made in our thinking for "God the sufferer" as the meaning of "God Almighty".

> . . . a pre-sentiment of recognition and the awed question: "Who art Thou, Lord?" to which He answers: "I am he whom you persecute." It is right to say that He must suffer, not only with us for also for us and *at our hands*. The brunt of our selfishness has fallen upon Him.

History has to be read as the drama of God's life in His remaking of men.[38]

It follows morally and practically from this quintessence of Christianity that a theology, thus imbued with "gentleness", yields a responsive "lowliness of heart", a disposition towards the world as needing to be handled with vicarious care. We might capture this quality in words of Richard Steele.

> An instinct of sorrow . . . seized my very soul and has made pity the weakness of my heart . . . Good nature in me is no merit . . . I imbibed commiseration.[39]

If, with William Blake, God dwells in Christ, then "mercy, pity, truth and love" in God are dwelling too. That Good Friday, with its Easter after, are set to "gentle our condition" where there is both yoke and rest.[40]

But all remains as vulnerable to doubt as Jesus was to enmity in that Gethsemane. The will, no less than the mind and heart, is needed in the option for faith. There has to be "the will to believe". It is open, for example, for anyone to say: "All this about Good Friday as the gathered wrongness of the world turns on a grossly exaggerated reading of what was merely a sorry miscarriage of justice such as happened frequently in that brutal age. Christianity has hopelessly overloaded a single event, made to carry in its ambition, like *The Spire* in Golding's novel, heights it can never sustain." As noted in CHAPTER FOUR, faith can be held precarious on various counts from many sides.

The will, then, has its place – not blind nor craven, certainly not wishful but – with thought and heart in line – ready to affirm, to risk, to venture and to find. Unbelief, too, is a thing of the will. There is a wilfulness in many a scepticism. "Let us hear no more of the Holy One" is the cry of those who find Him inconvenient to their ambition or their lust. If Christ calls us to find the world summoning us to the practice of love in situations making us vicarious, then it becomes expedient to take refuge in agnosticism. Doubts, to be sure, may be as genuine as positive convictions as to "God in Christ", but they may not.[41] "The exclusion of God" from our ken – to borrow a Quranic turn of phrase – suits well our self-centred calculus of ease or prudence or advantage. A bland scepticism can fit the book of the slothful and the proud.

A Christian's faith, then, is always in the making. It holds and it is held. It has aspects which only exist when we will they shall. Friendships are never static but always in the making. We have to bring to them what alone will ensure that they exist. It is so, in measure, with what is credal and confessional. We proceed only upon credentials but we must, in measure, *will* their being such. Only via the will is the mind vindicated in its faith, only so the heart confirmed in its loyalty. "Whosoever will may come" is the rubric, not "whosoever thinks" or "whosoever feels". These have their place but "the readiness is all". Pascal likened faith to a wager. Dostoevsky, already an inveterate gambler, depicted movement into faith as answering the impulse of vicarious love. Only so may "deep call to deep" in the transactions of divine grace. "Heart in pilgrimage", as George Herbert told, exactly fits the personal sagas of self-critical faith. What is quintessential about Christianity is their sufficient logic and their gentle theme.

How Christ's love-encounter
With our world of sin
Counter-signed our pardon
Realised within.

Learn we by the wound-prints
Easter understood
Why the faith of ages
Calls that Friday Good.

Thus with love's perception
Near His Cross we stay
Treasuring the mystery –
God's defining day.

Notes

Chapter one *Jesus in His Christ Experience*

1 The Greek term, *agon*, belonged with contest and its pains in the games, such as boxing and wrestling. (Hence "wrestling with an issue" as a synonym for hard struggle against odds.) The New Testament writers adopted it to tell the toils of true discipleship. In modern drama *agon*, with the derivative "protagonist", brings us to the central themes of human tragedy, with either Promethean defiance, Carlylean heroism, or Kierkegaardian anxiety. "Learning" – sublime or tragic – is never far from the aura of the word. It is intriguing that in Herodotus also (1: 207) there is this same associating between "suffering" and "learning", *mathemata ta pathemata*.

2 Hebrews 12: 3. "That which is against the word", the moral *chaos* and the *logos* it resists, well describes the encounter in Jesus' ministry and its culmination in: "Let him be crucified."

3 Though it is significant that Islam (the Shi'ah apart) has a theism – and a theology of creation – which seem somehow able to exclude the problem and the burden of the historical scene. It would be right also to see in Rabbinic Judaism after the 1st century (CE) a theology that deliberately shut out the riddle in history with which Messianism belonged. A historical, or even an eschatological, Messiah came to seem an unwarranted supersession of the human moral duty. Jacob Neusner writes: "The Mishnah is a statement of goals for the projected life of Israel which was entirely separate from appeals to history and eschatology." in J. Beuken; *Messiah in History*, New York, 1993, p. 55. Cf. A. Neher: "the responsibility of man entails the silence of God", *The Exile of the Word*, trans. D Maesal, Philadelphia, 1981, p. 188. Militant Zionism today, in *Gush Emunim* terms, is a most sharp recovery of an urgent and vital Messianism in the here and now.

4 The term may seem anachronistic here but it conveys suitably to that time and place what it broadly connotes still, namely identity robustly and politically expressed.

5 The thesis is linked with the name of W. Wrede, a German NT scholar who surmised that Jesus had not regarded himself as "Messiah", that the disciples only so identified him after the Resurrection and, therefore, that Mark must have devised the idea of a "secrecy" around it, on Jesus' part, which could explain why recognition of it had come only after Easter. It is a view that runs counter to Occam's law against contriving devious explanations when simple ones suffice. More importantly, it does violence to how crucial throughout is the whole Messianic theme.

6 On this usage there is an enormous literature. In its simplest "the son of man has nowhere to lay his head" might be taken as denoting human restlessness in general. Yet, when it is echoed in the crucifixion narrative ("he bowed i.e., 'laid' his head") a Christ-reference is imperative. The term draws on a variety of prophetic and apocalyptic meanings. It might – and might not – be taken Messianically. Hence its preferability in general, given the tensions. See, *inter alia*, the analyses in H. Conzelmann, *An Outline of the Theology of the New Testament*, trans. J. Bowden, London, 1969, pp. 131–37; and Oscar Cullmann: *Christology of the New Testament*, trans. S. G. Guthrie and C. A. M. Hall, London, 1959, pp. 137–92.

7 Political ambition could certainly be among such factors, "zealotry" being admirably served by charismatic powers. Yet would those of "healing" ride well with conspiracies of subversion? Agitators, however, would certainly covet to recruit such figures and harness their appeal. On the thesis that Jesus was in fact a Zealot see S. F. G. Brandon, *Jesus and the Zealots*, London, 1967; and a critique in A. E. Harvey, *Jesus and the Constraints of History*, London, 1982, pp. 14f.

8 The passage is crucial to an understanding of the Biblical sense of history. The Hebrew text of Exodus 3: 14 is not a philosophic riddle. Only in exodus is the God of exodus known. The event is the meaning. Neither the people, nor Moses on their behalf, can have advance guarantee. With the Cross, thought of by Jesus as "his exodus" (Luke 9: 31) at its centre, Christianity has drawn its theology from that history.

9 The patriarchs between Abraham and Moses are thought of as "anointed" and "prophets" as having the future of the nation in their "seed". It is notable that the Qur'an also sees them as "prophets". Biblically, Psalm 105 apart, it is sounder to reserve the term for those whose eloquence against and fidelity with the nation was authentic prophethood laden with the deepest moral issues as patriarchs never were.

10 Luke 4: 16–21 citing Isaiah 61: 1–2. The native prophet who is denied "honour in his own country town" in conjunction with the theme-items so descriptive of the ministry to come are a striking analogy for what was to ensue.

11 The Talmud (Sanhedrin 98 a) later wrote that the coming of Messiah, if the people deserved him, would be "like the Son of Man on clouds of power". If they did not deserve him, he would be "like a poor man riding a donkey". The Gospels see Jesus as invoking the words of Zechariah 9: 9.

12 Hence, no doubt, the prominence of Jeremiah as the figure brought to mind by impressions of Jesus.

13 Vital words in the Letter to the Hebrews, meaning the "consummator" of a purpose-in-hand which then calls, as the Letter insists, on all who read to receive and emulate (in terms only disciples can) its heart meaning.

14 John 5: 17, in the context concerning Jesus' "violation" of Sabbath rest, in the interest of human rescue.

15 In Matthew 12, 18, for example, the word *pais* is used in the rendering of Isaiah 42: 1, in the synagogue sermon in Nazareth. There are other far more frequent words for both "son" and "servant" but the mutuality may illuminate both. The "child" "servant" unison belongs also with the self-understanding of Israel in general as "children" under God. Theology has always held the instrumental and the metaphorical in close bond.

16 The necessary rendering of Luke 2: 49 where the phrase is, lit., "in what is

to my Father", no explicit noun being used. The familiar "business", or "house", or "will" are all supplied by conjecture. Though not good English, the hanging possessive fits best.

17 John 12: 47. Taken out of the Johannine rationale the words might be – and have been – read as suggesting either a megalomaniac delusion or divine proven-ness. Neither has the meaning: only Messianic sense of mission duly explains. It is odd that John Ashton, *The Interpretation of John,* Oxford, 1991, pp. 244f., tends to minimize the Messianic theme. Cf. A. E. Harvey: *Jesus on Trial, A Study in the Fourth Gospel*, London, 1976, where the whole is read as an aspect of status-confrontation with authorities.

18 In this way the parable breaks out of its own parameters, where, in terms of a vineyard/tenancy equation, aspects of "son-sending" that were beyond legal significance could have no place. The legal criteria could convey the sense in which violent conspiracy had flouted them: they could not carry any redemptive meaning. That precisely registers how sin deepened itself from: "What about the dues from your tenancy?" to: "What of your violation of me, your Lord?"

19 P. B. Shelley: "Queen Mab", lines 134–39, 142–43 and 167, in *Poems and Prose*, London, 1995, pp. 4–5.

20 The issue is deep in the fabric of Islam, where the Qur'an sees "vindication" as crucial to prophethood and finds it in "being proved true", or in "being victorious in the event", or, in Jesus' case, by rapture into heaven out of the plot to kill.

21 With an intensity matched by no other Hebraic figure, Jeremiah endured through more than four decades the toils and traumas of a ministry made all the more agonizing by its unavailing character and his own rustic horror of public scorn and calumny. See his so-called "Confessions" notably in Chapters 15 and 20.

22 Paul's doctrine of "justification by faith" derived itself in a subtle way from a quite different context in Habahkuk and others. There "the just man lived by his fidelity", i.e., he did not succumb to compromise and, so doing, vindicated the righteousness he symbolized, leaving a heartening example. Paul takes "faith" *in* the "righteousness of God in Christ" as bringing about a just forgiveness for the sinner, whose own "righteousness" has no redeeming worth. Paul's interest in Abraham being "justified" by believing (i.e., without works – other than faith) lies in Abraham's being antecedent to the Mosaic law.

23 By the prescripts in Exodus 22: 13, shepherds – even "good" ones – were not required to risk battling with wild beasts: they were responsible only for reasonable care and vigilance (though Jacob reminded Laban that he had borne the cost of "torn" carcases [Genesis 31: 39]). Cf. Amos 3: 12 where shepherds are at close quarter with lions.

24 That is, at Chapter 16: 9, the present conclusion beyond v. 9 being a non-Markan addendum. If (which must be for ever unclear) Mark actually *meant* his Gospel to end in confusion and fear, what other conclusions might be drawn?

25 See, for example, Midrash parallel in G. Dalman, *Jesus-Joshua,* Eng. trans. London, 1929, p. 206.

CHAPTER TWO *In the First World of Galilee*

1 Evidence of the widespread use of *koine*, colloquial Greek in Galilee through the dissemination of Greek culture is becoming more impressive than older generations of scholars allowed.

2 The story of the Syrophoenician woman (Matthew 15: 21–28 and Mark 7: 24–30) and Jesus' reserving of himself to "lost sheep of the house of Israel" have often been read as indicating strong Jewish particularism on his part. Yet the reading that sees him only "testing" the woman is certainly sustained by the sequel. Jesus' attitude to Samaritans and the inclusive humanity of his parables support that view. The word about "the pets" can be read as only teasingly forbidding. Matthew 7: 6 about "not giving what is holy to dogs" is in a different idiom. To be sure, Jesus was not engaged in more than a local mission: the universal one would follow from the Church's reading of his mind.

3 The deep issues of the parable have concerned us in CHAPTER ONE. Concerning the disciples at a late point in the ministry must it not have seemed a strange story full of foreboding? Quite evidently it played a large part in the final climax.

4 Fictitious transactions, concealing loans, were frequent enough. Both those needing capital for ventures, and moneyed folk wanting to make their money work, could have what they sought, despite the veto on "above-board" usury. The lord of the steward could have no complaint, for he had his money back and all parties a wry exposure of their market-manipulation.

5 There was a clear distinction between *douloi*, who had salary and tenure, and *misthioi* (among whom the returning prodigal proposed to be) who were menials by the hour.

6 One can almost see the hand on the shoulder as, laughingly, the boats and nets were left. Analogies ought never to be pushed too far nor refused, where apt, because of their inapt range. As a fisherman, Simon was recruited: fisherman he would always remain. Boats could be utilized for pulpits the better to accommodate a lake-side audience.

7 Notable passages are in Mark 8: 31, 10: 32f. and parallels in Matthew and Luke.

8 Only if the "Iscariot" in his name derives from this Latin word for a dagger. The *Sicarii* were a violent sect of the Zealots. "Iscariot", however may be a place-name or have some other connotation.

9 Like Philip and James, Simon and Jude, in the Book of Common Prayer.

10 Or, as with the old Maccabees, in the thoughts of their mothers. Cf. Matt. 20: 20 with Mark 10: 35. Was it the mother, or James and John themselves, who came asking about the prime places at the banquet, or collusion between them?

11 Film-makers around the Gospels have been prone to this kind of presentation of a regal Jesus often misconstruing the real terms of what faith reads in the Incarnation.

12 The analogy is apt inasmuch as – to use familiar jargon – the "Jesus of history" is the "Christ of faith" as read through the lens of witness "printed" into recollection via the perspective of sequential experience.

13 The problems of the relation of the Fourth Gospel to the Synoptics belong with CHAPTER FOUR. A. E. Harvey, *Jesus on Trial: A Study in the Fourth Gospel*, London, 1976, explores this angle in brief but lucid terms.

14 Matthew's Gospel is clearly at pains to set the ministry of Jesus on the model of the Mosaic "mount of the law", with "the elders" and "the people" in communal audience, while stressing the contrast between "You have heard that it has been said . . ." and his ". . . but I say to you . . ."

15 As in Geza Vermes, *Jesus the Jew, A Historian's Reading of the Gospels*, London, 1973, a salient example of the lively recovery of Jewish scholarly interest in Jesus of Nazareth – too long left to the possession of Christians – in the second half of this 20th century. See below, CHAPTER FOUR.

16 Echoing the *Aeneid* of Virgil – a descent into night.

17 "Hear him, ye deaf, ye dumb your loosened tongues employ", and the rest of the invoked are the retinue of Jesus on Palm Sunday. They are celebrating their own story.

18 In 2 Corinthians 2: 14, Paul repeats the same imagery in saying that the Lord still leads us in triumphal procession but as liberated – not imperial Roman style, enslaved – in demonstration of his victory.

19 It has often been noted that translations vary. While Presbyterians have "debts", and Methodist "sins", only Prayer Book users have "trespasses". It is urgent to note how insistent the Qur'an is on the "seeking of forgiveness" or *istighfar*.

20 In English some noun has to be supplied. "Business" was taken in the 1611 translation as suggested by the Temple where he was among the scribes. "House" might serve too, or "concerns". "In my Father's", simply, is perhaps the best.

21 "Failed" in the sense that where all hopes were, they were comprehensively betrayed. It is a "failed eschatology" that some writers within Judaism see as "premature Hallelujahs" at Easter when, in fact, no *parousia* happened and the allegedly "redeemed" world seemed just as "unredeemed" as ever. This was to misread the Messianic principle of vicarious forgiving love eminently repeatable, having once been historically made real and bequeathable in a once-for-all redemption.

22 For example, Mark 13: 4–31, Matthew 24: 1–51 and Luke 21: 7–33.

23 There is a useful study of the Messianic contours of the Lord's Prayer by D. H. Milling is the *Union Theological Journal*, Bangalore, vol. 3, no. 1, January, 1969, pp. 13–25: "The Lord's Prayer in Terms of Future Eschatology".

24 *Paradidomi*. See the discussion in W. H. Vanstone, *The Stature of Waiting*, London, 1987, pp. 1–33.

25 The word usually translated "upper room" is the one used in Luke 2 for the "inn" at Bethlehem. It means the large guest room as distinct from the family quarters.

26 It is significant that this sense of a guilt-complex in the disciples' experience of Jesus' Passion finds central place in Muhammad Kamil Husain's *City of Wrong: A Friday in Jerusalem*, 2nd edn, Oxford, 1994. Further, he thinks that it is a clue to Christianity's emphasis on human wrong. See p. 228 below.

27 The usual translation "when you are converted" would seem odd in address to a senior disciple. The context also requires the other meaning, as of one surviving from a desperate situation.

CHAPTER THREE *Into Mediterranean Dispersion*

1 Perhaps an improper borrowing. Alfred N. Whitehead's "process

theology", developed in Harvard in the 1920s, decried the notion of "a static God" (if such the "notion" had ever been) and thought of God Himself ever developing in such a way that "de-absolutized" what the divine could be. He resisted what he called "the fallacy of misplaced concreteness". One should not think that "the map was the territory", though – territory apart – it is hard to see how "maps" belong. In present context, the theology of the early Church was *in via*, "on the way", as formulating what it possessed in Jesus.

2 "The uttermost" – as far as New Testament narrative is concerned – is, sadly, all western. A mention of Spain is its farthest bound. What we are to make of the absence of India, Asia and Africa from NT geography will occupy us at chapter end.

3 The critical issues here come later and further in CHAPTER FOUR. The very rise of Judaism, in the strict sense of Rabbinism and "the sages of Yavneh", is in part parallel with the spread of Christianity and, as such, belongs with the inter-Jewish theme we are handling.

4 "Proselytes" were not, of course, the folk current "proselytism" goes after. They were spontaneous "seekers" drawn by aspects of Jewish faith and worship but keenly sensitive – not least in the "public baths society" of Graeco-Roman culture – over bodily subjection. Making it a *sine qua non* was also intellectually disquieting to cultured "Gentiles".

5 The "Messiah-question" on which – as we must argue – all finally turned was also profoundly intra-Jewish and had been so, as studied in CHAPTER ONE, throughout the short ministry of Jesus.

6 As in an Orthodox reading of Psalm 73: 1: "In Jewry is God known." Where the doctrine of "the land" held that "the place of the Name" was local the synagogue movement had to make good the "foreigness" but extra-Jewish worship of Yahweh remained somehow wanting, if not sterile. It was part of the nature of Christian diaspora that "the name of Jesus" constituted "meeting-place" whatever the geography. On exclusive monotheism see also: I. Jakobovits, *The Condition of Jewish Belief*, New York, 1966, pp. 112–13, on *avodah zarah*, "Strange worship".

7 If "You only have I known of all the families of the earth" (Amos 3: 2) means "Only you of all the families . . . have known Me."

8 *Collected Works*, vol. xvi, trans. A. M. Ludovici, Edinburgh, 1911, "The Antichrist", p. 147.

9 For covenant, people and land were bonded together – the whence, the who and the where of identity, story, tribe and territory.

10 The Greek mind needed to move instinctively towards ontology, to pass from "event" to "significance", to enquire how "incidence" related to "essence". Thus Judaic "Sonship" as denoting "agency" and "service" on behalf of God and expressive of the divine nature had to be told in a philosophy of "Sonship" or "Logos". By "hypostatic union" the Greek mind meant what the Judaic faith had been content to understand as the divine action.

11 It is the fervour and the reach of such passages that are so impressive. Cf. also Isaiah 55: 1–6, Micah 4: 2–5, Malachi 1: 11. The motif, however, of a purely Jewish ingathering from among the nations persists, as in Isaiah 60: 1–7.

12 It seems to be "threatening" strong pagan state-powers with dire penalty if they do not salute a new accession in the tiny, yet pugnacious, Judea.

13 Eusebius thought the psalm "extremely enigmatic and darkly uttered. Much turns on how we take the syntax, and decide the order of the verses. It is well, no doubt, to have it mean what we would wish it to mean, namely wondrous universalism, but it could equally be the opposite, namely a calling on the nations to salute a native-born ruler coming to Jewish Sovereignty, as in Psalm 2. Does a double exegesis symbolize the double mind?

14 As, see CHAPTER TEN, on Nietzsche. And cf. Hyam Maccoby: *Paul and Hellenism*, London, 1991.

15 Issues in the formation of the tradition are deferred to CHAPTER FOUR but technical questions about Saul's "mandate" do not affect the fact that there were sharp issues at stake. That they were attended by zeal is not in question. The provenance of the Pastoral Epistles has also to be addressed.

16 The "olive" as a symbol of vocation is clear from, e.g., Jeremiah 11: 16, Zechariah 4: 3–12. Paul's analogy does, however, fit the dilemma inasmuch as that wherein the "grafted" branch goes is itself, as it were, uprooted. In what sense, too, is "the Gentile" "wild by nature" if "all have sinned"? Can there be some collective reintegration if the way of grace is by indifferently personal faith? What is unmistakeably consistent is simply Paul's ardent continuing Jewishness.

17 Does not the very passion behind the exchanges bear witness to this? Where issues are known to run deep feeling runs high. It is not a situation of gratuitous denigration.

18 Not, more obviously: "Why are you persecuting mine?" A little reflection realizes how exactly the exchange captures the situation. Saul's harrassing the community affirming Messiah crucified *is* the form of his disavowing that figure. The implication is deeply heartening for the Church if they are "in him" as both confessing and suffering.

19 The very incidence of the term "Christian" belongs in this context of opprobrium, as well as being needed to denote an identity that was not only Jewish and not only "Gentile" but both in one. (Cf. Acts 11: 26.)

20 The phrasing may well be prior to Paul and a pioneer "creed". It is "codal" only in the sense of a "minding emulation" (v. 5)

21 See CHAPTER TEN. Nietzsche employed many images to denote his "demolition" of both superstition and metaphysics – "the bell", "the thaw", "the undertaker", "the lunatic".

22 "I am that I am" as a bare philosophic riddle could be no assurance to a downtrodden and enslaved people being called to emigrate from Egypt. Egypt, clinging to the one vital river which allows it to exist, is no likely country for such a call, with bare deserts on either side of it. The context on Exodus 3 is evidence that Moses was well aware of this reluctance in asking Yahweh how he is to respond to it. See also Martin Buber, *Moses*, London, 1946, pp. 39–55.

23 Certainly not where Greeks of Socratic mind were around. It is also a viable translation of the Hebrew and underlies the long tradition of the ineffable Name, never to be uttered but denoted by other indicative terms.

24 For it was, in a feasible sense of the phrase "eschatology realized". There was "the Christ-event". In its very happenedness, however, it did have a future tense. "He who is is He that is to come". God would continue consistent with what he had definitively been – a confidence which was able to survive the non-realization of the *Parousia* which had initially enshrined that confidence.

25 Cf. John 12: 32–33, where "being lifted up" refers to the Cross and perhaps also to the preaching of it. "All" must be understood as a universally accessible salvation – one free of all prior conditions of race, birth or culture – not a universally successful salvation. Personal faith-response would, in some form, be requisite.

26 "Staged" in no theatrical sense but only as enlisting place and time which its revelation could occupy and make significant.

27 "Discern" here echoes and takes up the double significance of 1 Corinthians 11: 29 where Paul rebukes ill-disciplined communicants who turned the Eucharist into an ordinary meal. They did not "discern" "the body", i.e., the sacramental situation and – so doing – they failed to appreciate that they were incorporate as "the body of Christ". The two delinquencies went together.

28 But see fuller discussion in P. W. L. Walker, *Jesus and the Holy City, NT Perspectives on Jerusalem*, Grand Rapids, 1996. One has also to do justly by what concerns CHAPTER FOUR below.

29 C. H. Dodd's title *The Founder of Christianity* (London, 1971) was meant to focus an issue as well as make a viable case.

30 The charismatic figure highlighted in Geza Vermes' studies in 1st century Palestinian Judaism as throwing significant light on an understanding of Jesus. See CHAPTER FOUR.

31 He falls into the same unhappy ambiguity we must examine later in J. H. Newman and all uncareful formulating of what is rightly said of "God in Christ". Cf. pp. 111–13.

32 The matter is urgent inasmuch as his baptism means – or ought to mean – that there is a church to receive him. Some readers feel that this part is added to serve later thinking around a precise formula of ritual confession.

33 Taking the title of Edwyn Hoskyns and F. N. Davey's study, London, 1931, dealing with text, theology and narrative.

34 Adapting the familiar usage of legal documents: "by these Presents", i.e., these credentials or referents or indices.

CHAPTER FOUR *In the Cares of New Testament Scholarship*

1 Even *haeresis* (whence "heresy") meant "having one's own thoughts", no doubt often to be disciplined but quite evidently no part of dormant faith. Criteria of "orthodoxy" themselves developed in step with faith-interrogation. Nicholas of Cusa (1401–64) in his *De Docta Ignorantia* counselled believers to be alert to their own ignorance. The 16th century, with Erasmus, marked the beginning of modern textual criticism.

2 Crises of heart about the Qur'an do not seem to have been frequent among generations of Muslims. In any event the relation of allegiance to text has a distinctive quality, for reasons not far to seek, in the Christian case in contrast to Asian sacred texts.

3 Robert Browning, *The Poetical Works*, Oxford, 1940, stanza xv, p. 405.

4 Matthew Arnold, *New Poems*, London, 1867, p. 114. The line about "Ignorant armies clash by night" came from Thucydides on the Battle of Epipolae where the two armies, in the dark, could not distinguish friend from foe. Arnold was in Sophoclean mood. The ebb-tide metaphor was denied its proper range. For tides that ebb also flow back for "A World, so various, so beautiful, so new". Further, *ibid.*, p. 194, "Rugby Chapel".

5 From a letter of the Balliol philosopher and tutor, T. H. Green, a compas-

sionate agnostic himself, to Henry Holland, his star pupil at the time of ordination. The "Holy Orders" he queried, the dedication he could applaud. Stephen Paget, *Henry Scott Holland: Memoirs and Letters*, London 1921, 2nd edn, pp. 65–7. Cf. also George Eliot who no longer had any antagonism towards any faith in which human sorrow and human longing for purity had expressed themselves . . . She never returned to dogmatic Christianity . . . but saw in it the highest expression of the religious sentiment that had yet found its place in the history of mankind.

6 This is in no way to exclude the bearing on Christian origins of research into the Dead Sea Scrolls and other illumination on the milieu in which Christians became such. But the only sizeable source, *in extenso*, of Jesus in his teaching and persona remains those four Gospels if – as argued here – the Messianic theme is held to be the clue. See below.

7 There is a copious literature on these forms of criticism. See, *inter alia*: W. D. Davies, *Invitation to the NT*, London, 1966, C. M. Tuckett: *Reading the NT* London, 1987; N. R. Petersen: *Literary Criticism for NT Critics*, Philadelphia, 1978; M. A. Powell, *What is Narrative Criticism?* Minneapolis, 1990; and sundry Gospel commentaries.

8 Notably the eminent scholar, Geza Vermes, formidably arraigning, yet illuminating, the Christian New Testament. "Wisely open" is right. See below.

9 As in the German terms – Geschichte and Historiche – or crudely the happening as it was and the happening as it was told.

10 That is a central truth of existentialism. Discourse, at best, can only be for the sake of decision. Time overtakes the ever hesitant. Applying this, however, to religions implies that critical intelligence need not monitor "the leap of faith". Bultmann's view has been likened to a theological cul-de-sac.

11 The sources on Bultmann are numerous. See *Kerugma and Myth*, ed. H. W. Bartsch, trans. R. H. Fuller, London, 1953. See also: Braaten and Harrisville, *The Historical Jesus and the Kerugmatic Christ*, 1964. Bultmann built on the thought of M. Kahler who, in effect, bypassed the whole historical quest on the ground that, if and when we ever meet and know Jesus it is in "the Word heard" in the Church. To look elsewhere would be an essay in abstraction. Kahler objected to what he called "the learned Papacy of the historians". Personal faith could not abide the risk of historical relativity. Ernst Kasemann and many others have reasserted historicity as both necessary and fit for faith.

12 Cf. the perceptive remark of Horace Bushnell. "The Gospel is a gift of God to the human imagination . . . His last metaphor". God "types" Himself humanly in creation and Incarnation. See: *Building Eras in Religion*, New York, 1881, pp. 259–60.

13 Geza Vermes: *The Religion of Jesus the Jew*, London, 1993, p. x, quoted also in his: *Providential Accidents*, London, 1998, p. 216. "The wrong thing" was "the commotion", "the wrong place" "the Temple" and "the wrong time" "the Passover". These three blunders apart, "he would probably have escaped with his life".

14 That ". . . of the world" about the Cross in both Christian text and Christian liturgy is vital. It perceives the Cross as "globally human", not "privately" Judeo-Roman. The forces that conspired to its happening are seen as symptomatic of "what we all do" in common compromise and wrong by false counsels – political, religious, social. It is thus in this "eventful" sense that

Christ "bears our sins". In doing so forgivingly he "bears them away". Incurring Calvary was far other than an error of strategy: in such terms its inclusiveness is forfeited.

15 Martin Buber, *Mamre: Essays in Religion*, trans. G. Hort, Melbourne, 1946. "Messianic self-disclosure is the disruption of the Messiahship . . . it stands or falls with its seclusion", pp. 117–18. Also Gershom Scholem, *The Messianic Idea in Judaism and Other Essays*, New York, 1971. No individual is capable of Messianic action. "The Messianic idea has compelled a life lived in deferment in which nothing can be done definitively", p. 35. See also his *Types of Redemption*, New York, 1968, p. 12, "Messianism is bound up with the future".

16 Geza Vermes, *Providential Accidents*, London, 1998, p. 212. It seems odd that he should have thought the venture and idea of "a book on the historical Jesus" should be "a revolutionary idea" even in the 1960s (p. 212–13). David Strauss had been doing it as early as 1835 with a radical scepticism about the very feasibility of any "Life of Jesus". Albert Schweitzer had produced his famous *Quest* in 1906; see below.

17 *Ibid.*, p. 213. The Gospels can be cited for those parts of them that conduce to the view being taken. Should not this selective reliance on them do justly by the rejected dimensions as – perhaps – being more, or other, than "the religious speculations of the primitive church". It might be sounder to dismiss the Gospels completely if failing to wonder why they had brought essentially incompatible elements together – as allegation had it.

18 *Ibid.*, p. 212. But was it "superimposed"? The Book of Enoch, for example, would have found nothing incompatible about a Messiah equipped with itinerating powers of exorcism and healing. Nor can an Messianic "agency" for Yahweh – even on Jewish grounds – fail to incur the relation it has to Him. This is precisely what Jewish/Christian integrity was doing (as we have earlier seen) in needing its Christology. That the Christology, in turn, should attend on the evangelists is nothing strange. Nor does it qualify as "myth-making" Hellenism. Even Maimonides was capable of something like it.

19 Like "the Synoptic problem bored me to tears"; "Romans and Corinthians in no way exciting" though "reconstructing the real world of Paul would be": "I meant to portray Jesus against his genuine historical background." *Ibid., loc. cit.* Outstanding work on Qumran has every right and duty to "get involved with the New Testament" but needs also to relate Qumran more directly to the actual emergence of Christology around the person of Jesus.

20 As, for example, the bearing of "demon-dispossession" on the Sabbath, as a "giving rest to the people of God" but also raising the issue of authority, making the "healer" something more than "healer". And what of the "teaching", as in the parable of the husbandmen in the vineyard, its overtones far more significant than ethical exhortation? Did not popular following in health-seeking – and fascination – imply Messianic hope and/or (for the "healer") temptation? Did it hold no alarm for the hierarchy? Jesus can hardly be circumscribed into a Hanina ben Dosa, having in mind both the scene and its issue.

21 The view was developed by Walter Wrede in 1901 in a short work entitled *Das Messiasgeheimnis* (or "The Secret of Messiah"), holding that Messiahship was "read back" into the Gospels, via Mark, only after the Resurrection yet had also been "true" all the time. To explain why it had

been there, all unrecognized, on their part, the idea of its having been kept "secret" was devised.

22 Albert Schweitzer, *The Quest of the Historical Jesus*, trans. W. Montgomery, London, 1910, pp. 399–401.

23 *Ibid.*, p. 399 and chapter "the Problem". Both credal Christology and "liberal" repossession of Jesus, he considered equally aberrant.

24 That long experience gave rise to his several writings on the significance of "the primeval forest", his philosophy of "reverence for life" and his belief that he had put back Jesus into the ethos of his real time and so rescued him from the tedious "metaphysics" of classical Christology.

25 He uses the analogy in *Quest*, p. 6, and gives examples of what he saw as delusion in the Gospels: the wilderness temptations were there because the desert was the haunt of demons, so Jesus must have been tempted by them there; despite "the Last Supper" "Jesus had nothing to say as to why his blood was shed for many". Even so, Schweitzer saw his missionary service as obedience to Christ. In line with Gandhi, he thought action in/for the world the truest form of selfless withdrawal from it.

26 See John Riches, *Jesus and the Transformation of Judaism*, London, 1980.

27 Like Geza Vermes, Schweitzer thought that early Christianity showed an odd indifference to the actual life and character of Jesus – this despite the very existence of the Gospels! Seen in that way, the situation left everything to be made good by their scholarship. Could not this have been more co-operative with the evangelists?

28 H. M. Orlinksy, *Studies in 2nd Part of Isaiah, Vetus Testamentüm,* Vol. 14, Leiden, 1977, p. 41.

29 Ezekiel Kaufman, whose 8-volume *Toldot Ha-Emunah Ha-Yisrealit* is a monumental Jewish treatise of self-understanding, insists on the singular link between pure monotheism and national Judaism, in total separation from the nations and their ways. People separation marches with a unilateral divine covenantal election. He points out how Roman historians – Tacitus, Juvenal – saw Jews as those who refused to share the universal tolerance of the pagan world in their *odium generis humanum* (Tacitus). See also: Martin Buber, for example, in *Two Types of Faith*, trans. N. H. Goldhawk, New York, 1951, p. 98, where he writes of divine revelation at Sinai "destined to confirm and strengthen the hereditary actuality of faith of the Jewish person who hears it" and stresses how faith as Paul saw it "fundamentally changes" this. Whereas Christians (whether from among Jews or "Gentiles") have to "become" such by act of faith, Jews are "already there" as Jews by fact of birth. Commenting on Song of Songs 2: 7, Rabbi Melbo advises Jews "not to reveal their mystery to the nations". (Cf. Scholem, *The Messianic Idea in Judaism, and Other Essays*, New York, p. 14.)

30 Thanks to "election" and "the Davidic tradition" and retrieving the exile. On Messianism in the great prophets see: Krishan Kumar, *Utopia and Anti-Utopia in Modern Times*, Oxford, 1987, pp. 13f. It later became largely a political emotion. In Rabbinic times, as Jacob Neusner sees it, it becomes not what a Messiah *does* but what Israel *is*. Throughout, of course, Messianic ends are always reciprocal to Messianic patterns.

31 "Jesus the Messiah", in *Mysterium Christi*, ed. G. K. A. Bell and A. Deissman, London, 1930, pp. 70–1.

32 Ernst Bloch (1885–1977). Usually thought of as a German Marxist, he held a teleological view of reality as directed towards an inner goal. Messianism

had to be seen as the secret of all religion. God was "the name of a goal". Cf. Michael Lowry, *Redemption and Utopia: Jewish Libertarian Thought in Central Europe*, London, 1992, one might compare "tears" here with the *Zohar* saying: "The Messiah will not come until Esau has ceased weeping" (i.e., when Esau's tears are dry Messiah's presence will be proven).

33 The theme of "cosmic responsibility" must be central to any and every monotheism ethically understood. That is why monotheism housed in ethnic particularity must seem rather a monolatry, if the inclusiveness of God is unequivocal. Emil Fackenheim in *God's Presence in History*, New York, 1997, argues that, while Yahweh's presence is "universal", Jewish particularlity is "required" because that presence does not "(as yet) transfigure history". Jewry has, therefore, still "to be singled out and made to *hope* for holiness . . . (in) witness to the Messianic future and to remain stubbornly at this post until all has been accomplished", pp. 52–3.
The New Testament held that the transfiguring had happened and that "stubborn witness" to it could be the calling of all who understood it so. Messianic actuality in Jesus as the Christ has its ongoing future in the community living in its meaning. *Extra amorem patiendem nulla salus.*

34 William Wordsworth, *Poetical Works*, ed. T. Hutchinson, Oxford, 1905. The suggestion was made by R. H. Strachan in his *The Fourth Evangelist, Dramatist and Theologian*, London, 1941, pp. 61–2.

35 If the events of Jesus' ministry (out of which – for the most part – he addresses the crowds and his disciples broadly in the terms the Synoptics give us) were truly proleptic, i.e., set toward that divine Lordship which the Church came to recognize, then that "for which all was meant" could be read back into the ministry from which it came. This is what "John" is doing. It would be crass to think of a Jesus "not yet glorified" telling the Galilean crowds: "I and my Father are one" or "I came to save the world" or about "drinking my blood". Yet they belong proleptically with that ministry into which this Gospel fits them. But we must understand what he is doing and why. There has been at times, the strangely misleading argument which runs, roughly: "If Jesus said these things, we have only three options: "Either he was quite insane, or a megalomaniac, or he was God." It comes down on the third option. But the divine-ness of Jesus does not stand in his *not* being the other two. It stands in the whole destiny and meaning of his ministry and his person. It is that the Fourth Gospel tells in what is both narrative and theology.

36 In telling the story the writer lives in its sequel as that to which its significance headed. He does so as only retrospect could. We need not crudely fear that he is "making Jesus say things he never did say". Rather he is having Jesus speak as the one we now know him to have been.

37 Borrowing here from other history-writing and drama need not be suspect as somehow compromising Scripture. Rather it aims to understand how divine inspiration could have a human strategy.

38 The language of the summation of all things in the great prayer of John 17, its "legacy" of finished words and deeds, its achievement of the kingdom, its confidence in the disciples are far removed from the sleeping disciples and the "strong wrestling in tears" of Jesus in the other Gethsemane. Yet the Gospel follows it immediately with "crossing thither over the brook Kedron".

39 By "community" here is broadly meant the whole developing early

Church. But it is likely that the Fourth Gospel derives from a "Johannine community" – perhaps in Ephesus – and reflects a circle of disciples and so a common mind. There is no occasion here to discuss the precise authorship. It has been exhaustively debated in the commentaries.

40 C. F. D. Moule, *The Birth of the New Testament*, London, 1962, p. 95.

41 The strangeness (as the disciples saw it) of the colloquy between a woman of alien origin and Jesus was in line with that "neither Jew nor Greek, neither male nor female" of the view the Epistles took on the "openness of the kingdom to all believers". Also the universal feasibility of "worship" across the world. There is also much subtlety in those "five husbands": Books of the Pentateuch? or tales of the Samaritans? A woman evangelist and the spread of the Word from first hearers becoming witnesses depicts a diaspora situation.

42 On the role of worship in the shaping of the New Testament see Moule, *The Birth of the New Testament*, pp. 11–32. John refers to three Passovers in 2: 13, 2: 23, 6: 4 and 13: 1 with 19: 14. In 7: 2. the Feast of Tabernacles sets the discourse about water and light, while the Hebrew Lectionary for the Feast of the Dedication (Hanukkah) in 10: 22 concerns the shepherd theme in that place. See Aileen Guilding, *The Fourth Gospel and Jewish Worship*, Oxford, 1960. Other arguable parallels are in chaps 15 and 16.

43 "Prolepsis" means allowing what, at long range, ensues, to be anticipated in the telling of what led to it. The Fourth can only be consistent with the other Gospels in such anticipatory terms. Clearly the disciples could never, initially, have known or confessed Jesus in those terms. Only post-Easter did they become aware of the Cross as redemptive. Nevertheless, in following Jesus in their own "apprentice" ignorance, they were – in fact – becoming acquainted with one whom they would attain to know as "the Lamb of God".

44 See the New English Bible text, which owes much to C. H. Dodd in this context.

45 Cf. Hebrews 11: 1 and "substance" (Hebrew: toholeth) – the credentials that make trust sound.

46 As, for example: John Bowden: *Jesus – the Unanswered Questions*, London, 1988; or J. K. Elliott, *Questioning Christian Origins*, London, 1982. No attempt has been made in present context to probe, still less to satisfy, *querelles* and quarrels, rather to set them in the larger experiential business of "Christ-learning". It is one that "reading its map" can find its way through to discipleship. Integrity in believing demands that no caveats be silenced, no misgivings suppressed. Perhaps these are part of the learner's "yoke". Elliott concludes that very little of historical worth can be drawn from the Gospels and the Acts, and that accounts of the sayings and doings of apostolic mission are highly suspect. Yet he is able to add that this should not be disconcerting. Religious truths are not expressed solely (sic) in verifiable history and are not to be subject to assessment in any narrowly (sic) historical sense. Yet what can these elusive adverbs imply? If history is not (as with Bultmann) essentially irrelevant it must be reckoned with diligently as more than virtual legends on which belief chose to hang its meanings.

47 One might say that the very "ethos" or "definition" of Anglicanism enshrines this theme. In the famous Crockford Preface of 1987 Gareth Bennett suggested that theology had better – and ideally – be done by

"churchmen". But see, more analytically, Stephen Sykes, *The Integrity of Anglicanism*, 1978.

48 It is incongruous that a faith for all continents should confine its defining Canon of Scripture to a rim of Asia and a map into Europe when other apostles found their unscriptured way into Egypt, Armenia, India and beyond. When in the early 19th century in India, Henry Martyn in much despair about translation "wondered what Paul would do in his situation" he had, of course, no answer.

49 There is a remarkable parallel between *L'Évangile et L'Église* and the young Michael Ramsey's *The Gospel and the Catholic Church*, London, 1936, 2nd edn, 1958. While the Cross was central to the Gospel, he argued that without episcopacy something would be wanting to it. He also sharply disparaged the distinction – vital to his evangelicalism – between the *esse* and the *bene esse* of the Church. Loisy was striving for the necessity of the institutional Church to the integrity of the faith in "God in Christ".

50 See, further, A. R. Vidler, *The Modernist Movement in the Roman Catholic Church*, London, 1934.

51 A recent discussion is William Horbury, *Jewish Messianism and the Cult of Christ*, London, 1998, who argues that a persistent Messianism did characterize post-exilic, as well as pre-exilic, Israel, so that the under-rating of it in much current scholarship is regretable. He may be less relevant in detecting "Gentile" pagan factors in the "heroicizing" "cult" of Jesus as a factor in Christian expansion – if Messiahship, whether in Jesus or in the *kerugma*, was of a very different order.

52 This continuity is more carefully discussed in my: *The Weight in the Word: Prophethood: Biblical and Quranic*, Brighton, 1999.

CHAPTER FIVE ***In the Ebbings of Ecclesiastical Polity*** **with the Heirs of Richard Hooker**

1 Richard Hooker (1554–1600): *The Laws of Ecclesiastical Polity*, 1841 edition, Oxford, vol. 2, p. 514, being Book viii, chap. iii, para 6. His erudition was disciplined, gentle and based on a robust faith in the principle of "holy reason". Even Pope Clement VIII paid tribute to "a style that expressed such a grave and so humble a majesty . . . in a poor, obscure English priest". Hooker was a master of the telling phrase. "The presence of the King and his retinue maketh every man's house a court"; "his (an opponent's) former sting appeareth again; "framing unto some sores unwholesome plaisters"; "unnatural concepts set abroad by seedsmen of rebellion only to animate unquiet spirits". It is mainly in Book VIII that his argument for "royal supremacy" comes; the word has to be understood as *intra ecclesiam non supra ecclesiam* (vol. 2, p. 507.) He saw the Church as a politic society of men. "Commonwealths" ought to provide for things spiritual and, by every Jewish precedent custodians of God's revelation were obligated to the body politic. Hooker did not agree that pre-Constantinian patterns were meant to be perpetual. His case for "royal supremacy" doubtless owed its urgency to the circumstances of Tudor England, but he saw his advocacy as truly Biblical and logical.

2 *Ibid.*, Book VIII, chap. ii, para 7, p. 493.

3 John Donne, *Poetical Works*, ed. H. J. C. Grierson, Oxford, 1912, vol. 1, p. 158, lines 100–2.

4 Hooker, *Laws of Ecclesiastical Polity*, p. 495. Arguing from Jewish precedent, Hooker seems to have forgotten that whereas Judaic unison of "people" as "church" was ethnic, a Christian "commonwealth" stood in personal faith which could by no means be assumed universal or in any way "foregone".

5 *Regio/religio* neatly enshrines the theme of Church and State, Bishop and King, as purporting to fulfil the duty of either to the other, the body politic serving the faith, the faith guiding the body politic.

6 Antioch was notable among these, while Jerusalem carried its distinctive prestige. Though it spread within an Empire, the Early Church did not become an imperial structure in pagan, Roman hierarchical terms. Its ministry developed in pastoral and sacramental form. Its being "dis-enlandised" was notably claimed in the Epistle to Diognetus, an anonymous treatise in letter form of the late 2nd century, claiming that Christians were "native" to all habitats and nowhere "natively" at home.

7 Surah 90.2, addressing Muhammad, assures him that he is (lit.) "free of this land", or: "This land of your security". The reference may be to "this city", i.e., Mecca, or "this earth" at large but, more likely it signals the Prophet's "habitat-by-right" in Arabia, the peninsula of the Arabs which was always, distinctively, "proper to Muslims". The words are part of an invocation or "swearing" as to human tenancy and warrant to belong in that *kabad*, or toilsome pain which is the human lot.

8 For it was in terms of territoriality that conflicts were pursued and, later, the idea of *Dar al-Sulh*, or "armistice", could develop in which exclusivity was neutralized. See, e.g., James Muldoon, *Popes, Lawyers and Infidels*, Liverpool, 1979.

9 That "public truth"/"private option" issue concerns us below. Faith, dis-identified from power, may seem to be a matter of public indifference. When it enjoys the sanctions of being "established" it may relish a structure which, in fact, weakens its fibre. There were doubtless social advantages and disadvantages *inside* the early Christian communities, depending, for example, on how we read "saints in Caesar's household" (Philippians 4: 22: "retinue" or "menials"?) but Philemon and Onesimus qualified as "brothers in the Lord".

10 Matthew Arnold, *New Poems*, London, 1867; "Dover Beach", p. 113.

11 Yet that phrase conceals the issue to which we must come, namely: Is "spirituality" in any society, the exclusive care, still less the inclusive care, of any single organ of faith or ethics?

12 Hooker held that, without "establishment", the Church would be resolved into a wholly clergy-constituted society. The laity would be excluded. All humans – in Christ – were "associates of deity" for, without humans, we could not see how God could exercise divine power or receive the glory of human praise. In that dual task the whole nation was as His habitation. Vol. 1, p. 612, i.e., Book V, chap. liv, para 6. Somehow, too, when political Rome became "Christian", he thought, "they all embraced the Gospel", vol. 2, p. 488, i.e., Book VIII, chap. iv.

13 See, for example: Owen Chadwick, *The Secularisation of the European Mind*, Cambridge, 1974; or Marcel Neusch, *The Sources of Modern Atheism*, trans. M. J. O'Connell, Ramsey, NJ, 1977.

14 "Franchized", here, meaning variously "warranted" to be and to let others be, subject broadly to public order, via an open tolerance and co-existence – these not prejudiced by surviving legal and historical privilege.

15 The famous passage in Matthew 22: 21 is often misread. In no way are the two "things" separate or mutually exclusive. On the contrary, "the things of Caesar" are within "the things of God". All human *imperia*, political, technological or social, are no more than "entrusted" and "tributary" in liability to what for ever transcends them.

16 Unless, of course, policies of oppression of minorities or a state's forfeiture and violation of "human rights" brings back something of the condition of the first Christians under pre-Constantinian Rome.

17 Hooker, *Laws of Ecclesiastical Polity.*, vol. 2, p. 399 being Book VII, chap. viii.

18 *Ibid.*, vol. 1, p. 227, being Book I, chap. xvi, para 7.

19 *Ibid.*, p. 129, being Preface to Book VIII, chap. ii.

20 *Ibid.*, p. 146, being Book I, chap. i, para 2.

21 *Ibid.*, p. 266, being Book II, chap. vii, para 7.

22 *Ibid.*, p. 240, being Book II, chap. iv, para 6, and p. 264, being Book II, chap. vii, para 6.

23 *Correspondence*, vol. IV, 7, ed. J. A. Woods, New Haven, 1963.

24 Burke stands in horror of the deeds in France but he is clearly in partial retreat from Hooker. He was concerned for the Roman Church in Ireland and, writing on India, he urged that "we should extend ours (ideas) to take in" those of Hindus and Muslims, save only if "all change on their part was entirely impracticable". *Correspondence*, vol. iii, p. 112. He used the "clock analogy". A fool should not take apart, or meddle with, a complex machinery he does not understand.

25 *S. T. Coleridge*, Oxford Authors, ed. H. J. Jackson: "On the Constitution of Church and State", 1985, p. 696.

26 *Ibid.*, p. 696.

27 On Gladstone's inner development in issues of Church and State see *Correspondence on Church and Religion*, 2 vols, ed. D. C. Lathbury, London, 1910; and A. R. Vidler, *The Orb and the Cross*, London, 1945. In *Speeches*, ed.. A. Tilney-Bassett, London, 1916, Gladstone told the Commons: "I have no fear of atheism in this house", p. 600.

28 This situation can be sensed in the strange (mis)fortunes of the noble word "rhetoric". From the Greek *rhetor*, "a speaker", it used to mean "words well spoken that persuaded". Now it tends to connote empty, even pompous verbiage. Oratory, if not somehow obsolete, is now at a discount. See also: *The Bible as Rhetoric*, ed. Martin Warner, London, 1990, being "Studies in Biblical Persuasion and Credibility".

29 London, 1912. Figgis aimed to "defend" by "attack". Intellectual social and moral self-indulgence needed to be arraigned. Only through condemnation could healing come. See below.

30 His main writings on this theme were *Honest Religion for Secular Man*, 1966; *The Open Secret*, London, 1978; *The Other Side of 1984*, Geneva, 1983; *Foolishness to the Greeks*, London, 1986; and *The Gospel in a Pluralist Society*, Geneva, 1989.

31 *Faith and Power*, ed. L. Newbigin, L. Sanneh and J. Taylor, London, 1998, p. 42 quoting *The Gospel in a Pluralist Society*, p. 166.

32 *Ibid.*, p. 37.

33 "Well and truly said – on which you can rely" might be a paraphrase version. It may well be that the formula "a faithful saying" used elsewhere in the Pastoral Letters is the beginning of a credal form.

34 It is intriguing that Muslim measures of the impact of the Qur'an used just

this language of "virtually no alternative". Fazlur Rahman writes of the Qur'an's *sultan* (the warrant of its verses): "*Sultan* has a power that is psychologically almost coercive, in that it might cause those who were fairly determined in their rejection of the truth to accept it anyway." It is "that which overwhelms without leaving any real alternative". *Major Themes in the Qur'an*, Minneapolis, 1980, p. 74. Could the Gospel of the Cross ever be this way?

35 See CHAPTER SEVEN for his meaning and why.

36 Using "negotiation" in its strict sense (from the Latin *neg otium* – "denying sloth") or working towards agreement between two parties.

37 This view of language as only operating "within its cultural norms" (just as a dictionary "explains" by suggesting other "referents") is thought to disqualify it from any other than "conditioned" statements.

38 Is there not always something reciprocal between the claim of an authority to be heeded or trusted *and* its posture towards the parties and the situations its relations handle?

39 H. Wheeler Robinson, *Redemption and Revelation*, London, 1942, p. xxviii.

40 Hooker, *op. cit.* vol. 1, Book I, chap. xi, 5, p. 203 and Book V, chap. xv, 3, p. 463.

41 The concept, *zulm al-nafs,* is central to the Qur'an and figures largely in Hebrew prophethood where wrongdoing is read as a people's "self-destruction" (cf. Hosea 13: 9). It is central to Christian faith that we see repentance as the deepest tribute to self-meaning, paradox though it seem.

42 Arnold, *New Poems*, note 10, pp. 112–13.

43 W. H. Auden: *The English Auden, Poems, Essays & Dramatic Writings,: 1927–39*, London, 1977, "Here on the cropped grass", xvi. p. 142.

44 Philip Larkin, *Collected Poems*, ed. A. Thwaite, London, 1968, "Church Going", pp. 97–8.

45 In the sense that Christian baptism recognizes the crisis implicit in being "me". Unlike Buddhist doctrine it can accept to distinguish between an ego-centric situation (in which we all exist in bodily individuation and identity) *and* the moral ego-centricity that chooses to live only for private ends and interests. This latter has to be renouced in the Baptismal: "You are not your own: you belong to Christ". So, belonging we receive back the possibility of an "unselfish" self-realization such as broadly Buddhism thinks impossible, seeing that – in its bleaker forms – Buddhism holds "our very existence a sin". On this different (Christian) reading of selfhood "the Eightfold Path" of Buddhist discipline (free of the Buddhist grounding – which Buddhism will not permit) can be entirely akin to Christian discipline of life and near; e.g., to Paul's "put on Christ and make no provision . . . for lusts of the flesh", or his listings of "whatsoever things" in Philippians 4: 8 – all uncannily close.

46 Citing Iris Murdoch, *The Sovereignty of Good,* London, 1970, p. 79. She writes: "That human life has no external point or *telos* is a view as difficult to argue as its opposite and I shall simply assert it. I can see no evidence that human life is not something self-contained." Yet, strangely, her main ground for believing that "a human experience has nothing outside it" seems to be that "thinking God" stems from an illusory yearning for "consolation" and expresses a subtle form of egoism. There can be, indeed there is, a "secular form of grace". It consists in a *moral* self-transcendence and the will towards authentic humility.

47 Romans 5: 8, where it is "God's method" in the Gospel. Also Romans 16: 1, 2 Corinthians 3: 1, 4: 2 and 5: 12. The word has a different "feel" from "proclaim". Was it not the habit of Jesus' parables to draw on some ground mutually indisputable and lead then to some new truth? "What man of you etc?"

48 The prime passage is *Carmen Christi*, Philippians 2: 5–11. The translation "he made himself nothing" does not fit well. One has to think, say, of kingship becoming, for truly kingly reasons, a servanthood. The idea is essentially of a stature realized in paradoxical terms, so that even "condescension" will not quite denote "what is still there in seeming not to be". "Disguise", too, is inadequate, just as it is inapt to say of the "Incarnate" "veiled in flesh", seeing that in flesh it is disconcertingly disclosed.

It is important to realize that there is divine *kenosis* in the theme of creation in that something within "Almightiness" is now assigned to humankind concerning the divine purpose in the created order. "God in Christ" culminates this same meaning, and it has been well said of the Holy Spirit: "If the sacrifices of the agonizing, much enduring Holy Spirit were enacted before the senses in the manner of the incarnate life of Jesus, he would seem to make the world itself a kind of Calvary from age to age." Horace Bushnell, *The Vicarious Sacrifice*, New York, 1866, p. 47. "Christ has his Gethsemane within us", p. 43.

49 Iris Murdoch, *Henry and Cato*, London, 1976, pp. 143–4.

50 The theme is very prominent in Murdoch, finding in our human avoidance of its implications a salient evidence of our chronic delusion of ego-hood. She sees art as "a redemption of our tendency to conceal death and chance". *Sovereignty*, p. 87.

51 The place of their coming has been variously pondered in study of the Fourth Gospel, penned – as it was – when "Gentile" inclusion in Christ had been achieved. Was their coming a presaging of the ultimate reach of the death he must undergo?

52 See Arnold Toynbee, *Experiences*, London, 1969, p. 158f. Also discussed in my: *Troubled by Truth*, Edinburgh, 1992, p. 227.

53 Namely that the principle of perpetual hope precludes any identifiable "fulfilment". Jewry clings to trust in Yahweh without hankering after final vindication. There is no point in a "Messiah" whose timing antedates the still urgent tasks. Since evil is never "maximized" it can never be definitively "redeemed" in time. Christianity believes that what its "redeeming" takes may be *qualitatively* achieved for active *anamnesis* ever after. Such is the Gospel of the Cross – the fact and its future in one.

CHAPTER SIX *Amid the Irony of Kindly Light* with John Henry Newman

1 Ed. J. A. Froude, *Thomas Carlyle: The History of His Life in London*, 2 vols, London, 1884, vol. 1, p. 291.

2 The theme of Christian faith is always this "*whom* one has believed", never "*what*". Even so, that Christ-identity, the "Whom" is known and told via Scriptures, witness, confession and these acquire a necessary "whatness" it would be folly to dismiss. The primacy, however, will always belong with the one whence these came and where they return. To know it so is to "believe in the Holy Spirit".

3 He had left his companions by a decision to continue a solitary journey in

which dire sickness beset him from which he was only rescued by the devotion of his Sicilian servant. Thoughts of Oxford, the future and his grasp of belief broke through his bouts of delirium. It was little wonder that on shipboard, homeward bound, his imagination broke into the emotions of a very private poem.

4 So "hands steadying the ark of God" are liable to assume when authentic faith would be more discerning and so more patient. Conscience would have said that the Irish Bishoprics deserved to be curbed, that the sacred institution should heed the secular ethic. To suggest, as by his text from 1 Samuel 12 John Keble did, that "not ceasing to pray" for the errant State was the sum of his response only compounded the wilful moral "apostacy" of the celebrated sermon.

5 He thought there was "some influence . . . isolating me . . . and making me rest in the thought of two only absolute and luminously self-evident beings – myself and my Creator". *Apologia pro Vita Sua*, ed. M. J. Svaglic, Oxford, 1967, p. 18. Was the order significant – "me and . . ."?

6 The hymn, of course, meant one present "step" not prejudicing many future ones in "the dailiness of life", in no sense like the inclusive single step Newman took on 9 October 1845, when an Italian Father received him into the Roman Catholic Church.

7 They all had to do essentially with whether "Church" could or should be prior to "Christ" as the locus of the act of faith. It is intriguing, for example, to note in Owen Chadwick's lively analysis of Newman, how rare is the mention of Christ. "God offers you," he writes, "a Church-bearing truth about Himself" (*Newman*, Oxford, 1983, p. 40). Do not the criteria of "Christ-learning" belong with Him before they pass in to any "church-school"? Only like Mary in "the low estate" of "bearing the Word" is the Church "highly regarded" alike in the divine economy and the perception of faith.

8 The distinction is vital. The way human minds work and wills decide so often turns on moods of soul and determinants of character, via heredity, heritage, disposition and influence. There were elements of Newman's egocentrism (as of all humans – and clerics) readily susceptible to adulation, posturing, impulse and introversion. His long religious travail tells a complex psychic story. See, in part, below.

9 The *pleroma* theme is central in both the Pauline Letters and the Johannine Gospel. It cannot ride with any concept of "development" that purports to enlarge it or to discover what, otherwise, it failed to embrace already. In being what and how it is, *pleroma* makes "complete".

As if echoing Newman's familiar theme of "two – and only two – realities", the French poet/novelist, Charles Baudelaire cried: "I desire with all my heart to believe that an external, invisible being is interested in my fate. What does one do to believe it?" "Do" is not the right verb: rather "Perceive God in Christ". So the Gospel. With the anguish of a true artist, Baudelaire knew how his own depravity demanded some place where a divine "interest" in him could be known authentic by the measure it had of the tragic capacity to love and so to suffice the depth of our human need. The early Church understood Christ as *pleroma* in these terms.

10 Verses from my *Poetry of the Word at Christmas*, London, 1997, p. 3.

11 In a strange way in his *Apologia pro Vita Sua*, Newman insisted on how "the Catholic Church allows no image of any sort . . . no saint, not even the

Blessed Virgin herself, to come between the soul and its Creator. It is face to face." *Apologia*, ed. M. J. Svaglic, Oxford, 1967, p. 177. But did not the Blessed Virgin, in fact, "come between"? And is not this divine/human, Creator/creature "immediacy" ours in the Christ who "comes between" as the meaning of the Incarnation?

12 A familiar Hebraism where the verb supplies its own object making the sense categorical. There is an obvious echo of Psalm 68: 18. That which hitherto enslaved is now itself over-mastered. Such is the de-tyrannizing that is ours in our bondage to Christ and such the inward meaning of his *pleroma* "fulness" in the heart. This does not obviate due authority: it certainly conditions it.

13 "The Yoke of the Law" was a familiar analogy in psalm and prophet. Baruch's Apocalypse deplores "Thy people who have cast from them the yoke of Thy Law" (12: 3). The Matthean passage, in echoing the invitation of "Wisdom", applies the yoke metaphor to the whole appeal of Jesus to an interpersonal discipleship.

14 Borrowing Wordsworth's "Me this unchartered freedom tires", *Poetical Works*, ed. E. de Selincourt and H. Darbyshire, Oxford, vol. 4, 1947, p. 85; "Ode to Duty", line 37.

15 See later the "romantic" element in Newman's stance, the aestheticism of his character and the "wishful thinking" measure of his concept of "faith" as "illative sense".

16 Down to his death in 1890, he remained a Tory of 1832, constant in an impossible loyalty. "Since 1832," he wrote to a friend, "I have no politics." Bernard Newman, *Newman*, London, 1925, p. 42.

17 *Discussions and Arguments*, p. 266.

18 *Ibid.*, p. 268.

19 *Ibid.*, p. 274.

20 *Ibid.*, pp. 293f. Far from predisposing the mind towards God, science, he considered, had little religious significance, being so dogma free. We cannot be Christians "by implication". Life was too short to admit of mere inferences and, in any event, there was the issue of the vulgar masses who needed guidance that was specific and incontrovertible, unless society was to be subverted.

21 Bernard Newman, *Newman*, p. 68. It sufficed that "all who came under his spell" found religion "invested with a new austerity and a new beauty".

22 *Loss and Gain: The Story of a Convert*, London, 1848, p. 203. Note also pp. 198f.

23 *Via Media*, London, 1877, vol. 1, p. 69. There was also a notorious sermon which concluded: "I will not shrink from uttering my firm conviction that it would be a gain to this country were it vastly more superstitious, more bigoted, more gloomy, more fierce in its religion than at present it shows itself to be". *Parochial Sermons*, vol. 1, pp. 311f.

24 D. M. Mackinnon (with J. D. Holmes), *Introduction to Newman's University Sermons*, London, 1970, p. 17.

25 *Verses on Various Occasions*, London, 1868, p. 256.

26 *Essays Critical and Historical*, London, 1890, vol. 1, p. 302

27 *Letters and Diaries*, ed. C. S. Dessain, and others (1978–84) 31 vols, Oxford and London.

28 *Letters and Diaries*, vol. v, p. 263, the grim reference being to Judges 8.

29 *Letters and Diaries*, vol. xix, p. 38. He was writing in 1859 concerning the affair of *The Rambler*. See below.

30 If we take the words of Matthew 11: 28–30 as what Jesus personally uttered, we still have to wrestle with attendant matters – why only noted by Matthew?; the aura of invitations from "Wisdom"; the quality of "labour", the nature of "yoke" and the meaning of "rest". A literal confidence will not absolve us of taxing duties implicit in it.
31 *Letters and Diaries*, vol. xxv, p. 418.
32 *Loss and Gain*, p. 203.
33 *Certain Difficulties felt by Anglicans in R.C. Teaching Considered*, London, 1898, vol. 2, p. 314.
34 There is serious ambiguity, for example, in saying: "Jesus is God" (which the Gospels and the creed never do say) if it is like saying: "Caesar is God". For then, in either case, the word "God" is in the predicate (where it should never be) so making the noun generic and shareable by many subjects. An alert Christology must say: "Jesus is God the Son", and the words are no longer susceptible to wrong reading. The vital point was well made by an evangelical contemporary of Newman when James Denney wrote: "In the formula: 'Jesus is God the Son' 'the Son' introduces the very qualification of God which makes it possible to apply it to Jesus. 'God manifest in the flesh' serves the same purpose." (Denney was writing in a letter to W. R. Nicholl, as quoted by John Baillie, *The Place of Jesus Christ in Modern Christianity*, New York, 1929, pp. 145–6.) Jesus is God within the meaning of the Incarnation.
35 There is the same serious double possibility here. *Plain and Parochial Sermons*, vol. 2, p. 127.
36 It needs to be noted, in the Greek of John 1: 1, how the third clause: *kai Theos en ho Logos* "and God was the Word", *Theos* lacks the article it had in *pros ton Theon* ". . . with God".
37 There is a similar instance of inviting misconstruction when in the 12th century a Frankish knight in Jerusalem asked Amir Mu'in al Din: "Do you want to see God as child?" When the Muslim said: "Yes" he was shown a picture of Mary with the infant Jesus in her lap. The Frank said: "This is God as a child." From the Memoirs of Usamah ibn Munqidh, *Kitab al-I'tibar*, trans. Philip Hitti, Beirut, 1964, p. 164.
38 J. A. Froude, *Short Studies in Great Subjects*, New York, 1910, vol. 4, p. 188.
39 *Plain and Parochial Sermons*, vol. 6, p. 76.
40 For all his unease about the Ultramontanes, he allowed himself a strange animus against his own nation in his strictures against the Church of England, as somehow wanting in simply being that, and culpably "English".
41 *Letters and Diaries*, vol. xix, p. 141.
42 Witness his hounding of Robert Peel and his intransigence over "liberalism" as undermining a "faith and polity".
43 *Loss and Gain*, A Novel, p. 203.
44 *On Consulting the Faithful*, ed. J. Coulson, London 1961, p. 72.
45 *Letters and Diaries*, vol. iv, p. 221.
46 *Auto-Writings*, ed. H. Tristram, London, 1957, p. 138.
47 *Apologia*, Part VI, p. 213.
48 *Letters and Diaries*, vol. xii, p. 73.
49 *Ibid.*, vol. iv, p. 154.
50 *The Idea of a University*, ed. C.f. Harrold, London, 1947, vol. 2, p. 121.
51 The paradox of Newman, both doctrinally and personally, belongs with this shape of things.

52 It is clear that deep psychological factors affect the mental attitudes of theologians. Newman was remarkably fitted to register their incidence.
53 F. W. Newman: *Phases of Faith*, 6th edn, London, 1860, p. 7.
54 *Idea*, p. xxxviii.
55 *The Dream of Gerontius*, London, 1866.
56 John 20: 25.

CHAPTER SEVEN *Through the Reach of Poetic Doubt* with Robert Browning

1 Robert Browning: *The Poetical Works*, Oxford, 1912, "Bishop Blougram's Apology", p. 444, lines 604–5. Lines (not included in the 1912 edn) are cited here for reference use in other editions.
2 Henry James, *Essays in London and Elsewhere*, London, 1893, "Browning in Westminster Abbey", pp. 233–41. Citation, p. 236.
3 A. E. Housman, *Collected Poems & Selected Prose*, ed. C. Ricks, London, 1988, p. 148.
4 *Works*, "Development", p. 684, lines 1–4 and 70–73. Included in the last volume, it was published on the day Browning died. In the little family "theatre" the five-year old R.B. was Priam, King of Troy, Helen was the cat and Achilles the pony. Two or so years later Browning Snr. came upon his son reorchestrating the siege of Troy, so gave him Pope's translation of *The Iliad*. He studied Greek in the original. The episode lights up the boyhood delightfully, while the analogy between a dubious Homer and a doubt-laden New Testament is intriguing. But is it flawed?
5 *Ibid.*, "Pauline", p. 8, lines 593–98.
6 *Ibid.*, "Johannes Agricola in Meditation", p. 426, line 6.
7 Henry Scott Holland, cited in: Stephen Paget, *H.S. Holland, Memoirs and Letters*, London, 1921, p. 277.
8 *Works*, "Abt Vogler", p. 480, line 88.
9 *Ibid.*, "A Death in the Desert", p. 489, lines 674–6.
10 *Ibid.*, "Saul", p. 231, xviii, lines 308–12.
11 Numbers 6: 23–27 and 2 Corinthians 4: 6 where "the face of . . ." means ". . . in Christ as in a face", or ". . . the face being . . ." The "face" of Yahweh is a frequent usage in the Psalms.
12 Browning's *The Ring and the Book*, London, 1972 edn, might be said to be, in its entirety, a study in guilt and its consequences, innocence and its burdens, the whole liability humans bear by their birth into humanity, personal and universal.
13 *Works*, p. 231, xvii, lines 206–10. *Parrhesia* is the New Testament term (yielding rhetoric to English – *rhesis*) meaning "freedom with a theme and freedom to speak it", also "boldness" and "frankness" implying confident commending not inconsistent with rhetorical questions.
14 *Ibid.*, pp. 231–32, xix, lines 334–35.
15 *The Ring*, pp. 513–14, x, lines 1367–72.
16 *Works*, "The Epistle of Karshish", pp. 425–6, lines 304–12. Karshish has travelled up from Jericho and encountered Bethany. En route, Browning has him "stripped and beaten" by robbers – reminiscent of Jesus' parable of the same road.
17 "Unique" is a dubious word to use in religion. There is a deep strain of divine "pathos" in Judaic prophets, especially Hosea. Isaiah 43: 24 has Yahweh saying: "You made me a burden-bearer with your sins". There is

also the thought that the divine "presence" goes into exile with the people. However, only Christian faith associates this divine pathos with a place and point in history that engages it with the utmost expression of human sin in the shape of the Cross of Jesus. It might be argued that "historicalness" does not matter: the mere "idea" suffices. Christianity does not think so. The issue is involved for Browning. See below.

18 *Works*, "Bishop Blougram", p. 444, lines 647–50.

19 *Ibid.*, "Christmas Eve", p. 399, lines 285–86. See further, pp. 133–4.

20 *Works*, "Christmas Eve", p. 405, xv, lines 857–62.

21 *Ibid.*, "A Death in the Desert", p. 489, lines 663–64 and 672–73. It is immediately after these lines that Browning goes on "I say the acknowledgement . . ." cited in note 9 above.

22 *The Ring and the Book*, p. 527, x, lines 1863–67.

23 *Letters of R.B. and E.B.B. 1845–46*: ed. Kintner, Cambridge, Mass., 1969, vol. 1, p. 43.

24 *Works*, "Development", p. 684, lines 83–84. The situation as it was for the boy with Homer and Troy can be transferred for the man to the Gospels.

25 "A Death in the Desert", pp. 483–92: the passages in sequence are: lines 310–11, 664–67, 312 and 323–24.

26 *The Ring*, p. 515, x, lines 1407–9.

27 *Ibid.* The final line, i.e., xii, 870.

28 This has always been the issue for the institutions of religion. Clericalism, punditry, guru-ship, have been endemic where creed, code or rite have been entrusted – as they must needs be – to officiants, authorities, exegetes and interpreters, all of whom acquire, or expect, prestige thereby and, by and large, material sustenance. Thus doubt engendered by the forms of faith is no less urgent than doubt of faith itself.

29 *Works*, "Bishop Blougram", pp. 437–48. The lines in sequence are: 380, 732, 765, 903, 979–80.

30 *The Ring*, p. 565, xi, line 1825.

31 "What do you mean?" was the familiar question: it sounds naïve when thought about language compels itself to enquire: "what *can* you mean?" "De-construction" – so-called – has put in question, via things like "reader-rendering", the assumed trustworthiness of words and our using them.

32 *The Ring*, p. 597, xi, lines 2289–90.

33 *Works*, "Sordello", Book i, p. 98 lines 88–97.

34 *Ibid.*, "Gold Hair", p. 474, xxx, last two lines.

35 *Ibid.*, "A Forgiveness", p. 542, lines 322–26.

36 See Edward Dowden, *The Life of Robert Browning*, London, n.d., pp. 140–1.

37 *Works*, pp. 351–55, and "Reverie", p. 687.

38 *Ibid.*, p. 683.

39 *Ibid.*, "Christmas Eve", pp. 396–409. Stanza xi.

40 *Ibid.*, Stanza xxii.

41 *Ibid.*, Final lines Stanza xx.

CHAPTER EIGHT *Down among the Human Dregs* with William Faulkner

1 Named for the Yocon Rover, Yoknapatawpha was symptomatic "Faulkner country", in terms very different from Thomas Hardy's "Wessex", or George Eliot's Warwickshire. In the State of Mississippi, it corresponded with Jefferson and was defined by its creator as his "sole ownership and

property", listing its population as 6298 whites, 9313 blacks and having an area of 2400 square miles. Almost all his characters and their families belonged there. The whole constituted a sort of way map of his imagination on which the tally of events could be located by the "geographers-in-residence". Thus it became an inclusive world of Faulkneriana.

2 The idea stemmed from Faulkner's interest in the tomb of the "Unknown Soldier" under the Arc de Triomphe in Paris. Christ might be a paradigm of young men "sacrificed" in war, though the theme was blurred for him by his desire to set Christ in dissociation from "the Father", thus entailing a familiar concept of his thought – the tangled father-son issue evident in his own story.

3 "The Bear" is among the stories gathered in *Go Down Moses* that concerns a son's initiation into the heroism of the hunt at the hands of his father. The awesome quarry in the forest, "the bear", is somewhat reminiscent of "the white whale" in Melville's *Moby Dick*, the quest which will either make, or break, the "hero" lured by its fascination.

4 Ed. E. L. Gwynne and J. L. Blotner, *Faulkner in the University*, Richmond, Va., 1959, pp. 85–86.

5 *Ibid.*, p. 117.

6 Cited in Frederick R. Karl, *William Faulkner, American Writer*, London, 1989, p. 815.

7 *Light in August*, Modern Library edn, New York, 1968, pp. 5–6.

8 *Ibid.*, pp. 210–11.

9 "Delta Autumn" was published in *Go Down Moses*, London, 1942. In the spirit of *A Fable* or "The Bear". Faulkner, by this time increasingly fearful for the human future in the throes of war, reads in the "trust" of nature a paradigm of the whole "duty of man" *vis-à-vis* history at large. Penguin edn, p. 275.

10 Or perhaps he *did* discern. See below.

11 Reinhold Niebuhr, *The Irony of American History*, New York, 1952.

12 The theme runs through all American literature – the reproach of a European connection disallowing the "newness of American man".

13 *Light in August*, p. 93.

14 *The Sound and the Fury*, New York, 1929, p. 143.

15 See David Minter, *William Faulkner, His Life and Work*, Baltimore, 1980, p. 95.

16 The terms Faulkner used of the three brothers in his Introduction to the novel. See *A Faulkner Miscellany*, ed. J. B. Meriwether, 1974, p. 159.

17 *Absalom, Absalom!*, 1936, Vintage edn, 1995, p. 378.

18 *Light*, p. 69.

19 *Ibid.*, p. 480.

20 Houston in *The Hamlet*, 1940, p. 215.

21 Cited from Karl, note 6, p. 816.

22 William Golding: *The Hot Gates*, London, 1965, p. 87.

23 *Light*, p. 283.

24 Thus Quentin Compson, in *Absalom, Absalom*, sees "childhood full" of presences from the past. "He was not a being, an entity, he was a commonwealth", p. 12 (chap. 1).

25 William Golding: *A Moving Target*, London, 1982, p. 200.

26 *Light*, *op. cit.* p. 93..

27 Faulkner's comment in ed. J. B. Meriwether and M. Millgate, *The Lion in the*

Garden, Interviews, 1926–1962, p. 247.
28 Nathan A. Scott, *Tragic Vision and Christian Faith*, New York, 1957, p. 322.
29 There is a subtle under-play between Nancy's "faith in grace" though herself condemned to die, and Gavin Stevens' effort, in strange lawyer-guise, to draw Temple into a consciousness of guilt.

CHAPTER NINE *In the Pride and Prejudice of Empire* with Rudyard Kipling

1 Lewis Carroll: *Through the Looking Glass*, London, 1872, 1962 edn p. 51.
2 Rudyard Kipling, *Definitive Edition of His Verse*, London, 1943, "Recessional", pp. 328–9.
3 *Ibid.*, p. 366. Saul's journey – "the craziest road of all – to Endor", Kipling's repudiation of the false trail of the dead, through occult practices, so fascinating to many in the years 1914–18 and beyond.
4 Rudyard Kipling, *Short Stories*, ed. A. Rutherford, 1971, Vol. 2, 1994, pp. 203–13 and *Verse*, "The Burden", p. 766. See below, and notes 44 and 45.
5 *Ibid. Stories*, pp. 236–54. *Verse*, pp. 774–5.
6 James George Frazer (1856–1941). His *The Golden Bough* published in the opening decade of the century, gave powerful currency to the study of primitive society, the folklore of tribes and the fields of anthropology at large. It had a deep impact on the popular mind and ideas of culture and religious belief and the nature of myth. Ironically, Frazer himself drew all his material from the findings of others. He was no field-researcher, but his encyclopedic pages were a contemporary fillip to – in his highly contrasted style – the interest in social mores that Kipling fostered with his Indian and Sussex stories.
7 *Verses*, p. 774. Joseph Conrad, by birth a Pole, acquired a total mastery of English language and narrative. *Heart of Darkness*, published 1902, has come to be seen as epitomizing in personal terms the degradation of agents of exploitation drawn ever deeper into the farthest reaches of the forest.
8 *Verse*, "Hymn of Breaking Strain", p. 385.
9 *Verse*, "We and They", p. 764.
10 *Ibid.*, "In the Neolithic Age: The Seven Seas", and "Sussex", pp. 215–16.
11 Cited, without reference in P. N. Furbank's Intro, to E. M. Forster, *A Passage to India*, London, 1942, pp. xix–xx.
12 *Verse*, "The Beginnings", p. 673.
13 *Ibid.*, "The Glories", p. 813.
14 *Ibid.*, "The Buddha at Kamakaru", pp. 92–3.
15 *Ibid.*, "Song of the English", p. 170.
16 *Plain Tales*, ed. 1981, "His Chance in Life", p. 81.
17 Angus Wilson, *The Strange Ride of Rudyard Kipling, His Life and Works*, London, 1977, p. 205.
18 *Verse*, "Naaman's Song", p. 777.
19 *Ibid.*, "A St. Helena Lullaby", p. 530.
20 *Ibid.*, "Cold Iron", pp. 508–9.
21 Coomaraswamy in *Cross Currents*, vol. vi, i, p. 35.
22 As a parody in 1878 by some rhymster when Malta was under threat and Indian troops, it was rumoured, were to be sent there to help the British.
23 *Verse*, "The Anvil", p. 713.
24 *Ibid.*, "The Absent-Minded Beggar".
25 *Ibid.*, "Hymn of Breaking Strain", pp. 384–5.

26 *Ibid.*, "For the Burial of Rhodes", 1902, pp. 209–10.
27 Charles Dickens, *Our Mutual Friend*, chap. 11.
28 *Verse*, "For All We Have and Are", 1914, p. 329.
29 *Ibid.*, "The King's Pilgrimage", p. 806.
30 *Ibid.*, "An Astrologer's Song", p. 591.
31 *Ibid.*, "The Question", pp. 327–8.
32 *Ibid.*, "Shock", p. 387.
33 *Ibid.*, "The Holy War", 1917, p. 290.
34 *Ibid.*, "Non Nobis, Domine", p. 512. In "unfolding" was he perhaps recalling "the folded meaning of your words' deceit" in Shakespeare's *Comedy of Errors*, Act 3, sc. 2, line 36.
35 *Ibid.*, "Gallio's Song", p. 542.
36 Rudyard Kipling, *Something of Myself*, ed. Thomas Pinney, Cambridge, 1990, pp. 61–2.
37 *Verse*, "His Apologies", pp. 816–17.
38 *Ibid.*, "The Conundrum of the Workshops", p. 337.
39 See: *Something of Myself*, pp. 22, and xxx–xxxii.
40 *Verse*, "Cold Iron", pp. 508–9.
41 *Ibid.*, "The Sons of Martha", pp. 382–3.
42 *Ibid.*, "The Prayer of Miriam Cohen", p. 614.
43 *Ibid.*, "The Storm Cone", p. 824.
44 *Stories*, p. 213 and *Verse*, "The Burden", p. 766.
45 Angus Wilson, *Strange Ride* (note 17), pp. 317–18. Is this an instance of "Judge not and you will not be judged" or "the opinions I hold tell you about me"? Wilson can register how a woman emerges from a life of self-deception, finds the story "perfect" but wants it to turn on mere logic and be devoid of mystery. Mary's "happy" mistake of identity belongs well with Helen Turrell's bitter/glad attainment of a true one.

CHAPTER TEN ***At the Madman s Bell ringing the Death of God*** **with Friedrich Nietzsche**

1 The significance of this – one fifth of his years – has been variously interpreted. Was it an index to the ultimately intolerable ambitions of his philosophy for the human psyche? Was it the final collapse of a mind unduly weighted with the perpetual tension of paradox? Was it the delayed reaction to the radical rebellion he underwent against all that had natally shaped him? Or was it simply the debacle of a physical frame exhausted by disease, chronic dyspepsia and persistently poor vision?
2 The irony of the Biblical association with a prophet's scenario is evident enough. Or, at random, cf. T. G. Long in *Hebrews, A Commentary*, Louisville, 1997, p. 7: "Revelation is . . . a shout in the street crying news that could not have been anticipated". The scene is reminiscent of the startling occasion in the life of the New England poetess, Emily Dickinson, when, in a sudden onset of passion, her father rang the church bell in Amherst to arouse the townsfolk for no reason but his own impulse.
3 Mark 3: 21.
4 *The Joyful Wisdom*, 1883, tr. Thomas Common, 1910, vol. 10, *Complete Works*, Edinburgh, Sect. 125, pp. 167–9. Questioned, the madman always gave this reply: "What are these churches now if they are not the tombs and monuments of God?", otherwise entitled *The Gay Science*.

5 Cf. his denunciation of Germans in *Ecce Homo* (1888), tr. A. M. Ludovici, London, 1911, "Why . . . Wise", pp. 33, 43 and 47. "Wherever Germany spreads she ruins culture", ". . . a large German city . . . that structure of vice in which nothing grows". See also: *The Twilight of the Idols* (1889) tr. O. Wilde, London, 1911, pp. 50–9.

6 See *Ecce Homo*, Sect. 3, "Why I am so Wise", p. 15.

7 In *Genealogy of Morals* (1887), tr. H. B. Samuel, London, 1910, p. 135. "A married philosopher belongs to comedy". His infatuation with Lou Salome in 1882 seems to foreshow the ensuing madness, accompanied as it was by strange behaviour and illusions of victimization. "Are you visiting a woman"? he asked in *Ecce Homo*, 11: 6. It would seem impossible for the entire mutuality of sacramental, Christian love in marriage to find place in Nietzsche's ideology. In any event, his affair with Lou Salome had all the features of a panic obsession. "Coronation", *iklil*, with exchanges of crowns, is central to the ritual of Christian marriage in the Orthodox tradition of the East.

8 The term is borrowed from "the coming on again of a pain or disease" to indicate the idea of a chronic proneness, or submission, to what disallows your true condition as religion does. See below.

9 Ludwig Feuerbach (1804–72) taught that theology should yield to an all-inclusive humanism, seeing that "we are on our own" and that religious acts and attitudes have their meaning and relevance within nature, the soul and society.

10 Michel Foucault (1926–84) with his "perspectivism", tracing the factors from which what we find has arisen, excluding transcendent reference.

11 John Keats, *Poetical Works*, ed. H.W. Garrod, 2nd edn, Oxford, 1958, "The Fall of Hyperion", p. 513, lines 148–9.

12 Taking an analogy from J. H. Newman, or rather a "character" of his in *Loss and Gain*, Pt. 1, Chap. vi, p. 22: Faith was "like coming in to Port after a rough sea, when a vessel, after much tossing, finds itself in harbour". To ask for the solace of security at any price is to play right into the hands of Nietzsche's argument.

13 Sometimes it is "the religion of Jesus" (as in Matt. 11: 28–30) deplored for its flouting human selfhood. Elsewhere it is the religion fabricated by the miscreant, Paul. The first Jesus is the patron of "decadents", blending the sublime with the pathological, while Paul made Jesus into a monstrously "redemptive" Christ. It would seem that there was an element of Jealousy in Nietzsche's attitude to Jesus, as if – the prophet of "the gay science" in a latter day – he was baulked by a great haunting "original". The suggestion is made in H. de Lubac in *The Drama of Atheistic Humanism*, p. 180, citing André Gide. In his last work. *Ecce Homo*, he set himself up as the victorious rival of him whose teaching he proposed to supplant.

14 *Ecce Homo*, "Why . . . Wise", p. 39.

15 *The Joyful Wisdom* (1887), trans. Thomas Common, London, 1910, para 346, p. 284. "Either do away with your venerations or with yourselves", i.e., religious scruples inhibit crude self-assertions (but these also have to be despised by the authentic, Nietzschean "Over-man").

16 In *Human all Too Human* (1878), trans. Helen Zimmern, pt. 1, sect. 92, p. 90 "Justice" can only be negotiating over one another's demands, given a built-in egoism compelled to make means for any social self-preservation.

17 Nietzsche would doubtless not recall Paul's use of the analogy in Galatians

3: 24 when he wrote: "The law was our *paidagogos* to convey us to Christ".
18 *The Will to Power*, a compilation of notes and jottings, was only published after Nietzsche's death. Trans. A. M. Ludovici, London, 1900.
19 These are not in any way *a priori* like those in Kant's *Critique of Pure Reason* where mind is categorizing sense data. They are quite arbitrary, only that the "arbitariness" of "taste" on the part of "supra-man" is achieving, or set to achieve, the "supra-value" of "the will" that is alerted to its destiny.
20 *Thus Spake Zarathustra* (1883), trans. Thomas Common, London, 1909, "Old and New Tables", LVI, No. 3, pp. 241–2. He adds: "As composer, riddle-reader and redeemer of chance did I teach them to create the future . . . to redeem by creating . . . until the will saith: 'So did I will. So shall I will it.'"
21 If we complained earlier about Newman involved in unhappy ambiguity by words tending to confusion in the reading, the offence was vastly more serious in Nietzsche's case. Yet it was his mission to shock as well as to teach. The inspired are not drawn to verbal caution or scruple.
22 As in *The Joyful Wisdom* (1887) Sect. 3, 24. "The Assassin's motto: 'Nothing is true, everything is permitted' could easily become everyone's motto".
23 *Ecce Homo*, "Why I am a Fatalist", Sect. 4, 9, p. 143.
24 See the Foreword and first two sections of *Ecce Homo* ("Why I am so Wise", "Why I am So Clever"), pp. 9–54.
25 It is almost as if he was reversing the karmic "law" of Hinduism and turning it into a plausible positive. By that "law" a rigorous determinism prevails in human life and the past prescribes inevitable "fates" into the present. With Nietzsche it is as if "the will to power" prescribes its own "supra" goal in some self-ensuring way.
26 How it took the long way round and how it always waits to be recognized. It has no "will to power" except the patient attraction of its own mystery. There are no "press-gangs" into "the kingdom of heaven".
27 The link, so obvious, in John 1: 1 and 14 between the "light" "Let be" at creation and "the Word made flesh". Similarly in 2 Corinthians 4: 6 where "the light" at creation "shines . . . in the face that Christ is".
28 Seeing that "science" in the usual sense was tied to the "rational" whose ways and means could never be identified with Dionysius.
29 Nietzsche was given to language drawn from "taste" and manners". See below and cf. *The Joyful Wisdom*, Pt. iii., Sect. 132, p. 173. ("Our taste . . . no longer our reasons.")
30 *The Antichrist*, Sect. 48, pp. 197–9. ("God's infernal panic" about science in human hands.)
31 *The Antichrist*, Sect. 13, p. 139. In this context it seems incredible that Nietzsche should have so far missed the central theme of "the sacramental" in Christian faith, "the body as the temple of the Holy Spirit" (1 Corinthians 6: 19 *et al*.). He includes that verse in a cluster of New Testament verses he scorns (*ibid*., p. 193) but comments: "One cannot have too much contempt for that sort of thing." The conviction, central to the doctrine of the Incarnation, that the body is "the soul's book", where – as in authentic human love – spiritual dimensions transact themselves, seems altogether to have eluded him. Awareness of it, via Liturgy and Communion, might have saved him much passionate distortion.
32 William Shakespeare, *Macbeth*, Act 5, Sc. 3, line 42.
33 *The Joyful Wisdom*, Sect. 353.
34 Paul is pilloried in many places, e.g., *The Will to Power*, Vol. I, Par. 167, pp.

136–8 Paul re-erected what Christ had annulled through his life: "invented the Saviour": and Vol. I, Par. 224b, p. 183f. "Rabbinic impudence characterizes all his doings." Cf. *The Dawn of Day*, trans. J. M. Kennedy, London, 1911, para 68, p. 71.

35 *The Antichrist*, Sect. 25, pp. 157–61.
36 *Ibid.*, Sect. 46, p. 194, cf. Sect. 47, p. 196.
37 *The Birth of Tragedy*, Cambridge, 1999, ed. R. Geuss and R. Speirs, p. 9.
38 *The Antichrist*, Sect. 38 pp. 161 and 177. In *Human All Too Human*, Sect. 113, p. 122 he writes: "When we hear the ancient bells growling on a Sunday morning we ask ourselves: 'Is it really possible? – for a Jew crucified 2,000 years ago?'"
39 *The Antichrist*, Sects. 27–29 pp. 162–4 and Sect. 42 p. 184. "Died for his sins . . ." meaning he led "a small insurrectionist movement rising against established order" and paid the price. Further, Sect. 35, p. 174, however, he writes that "Jesus died to show how one ought to live", not in order "to save mankind".
40 As he said in *Ecce Homo*, Sect. 1, 4, p. 18: "It is only among decadents that pity is called a virtue".
41 The German term used in *The Antichrist* for all that enhances and girds power. It might be translated "efficiency", "adequacy to ends", or even physical fitness. It fits the point earlier made about having "the latch-key" to nature – whence technology. The issue is whether such "power-in-exercise" is an end-in-itself in individual terms (as, apparently in Nietzsche) or whether it invites to diffident gratitude and a sense of liability towards society, including society's "weary and heavy-laden". That issue is not susceptible of proof either in Nietzsche or in theism.
42 Psalm 69: 6, though in a different sense. The psalmist is worried lest his adversity reflect badly on his "patron" Yahweh. It can be "with a kiss" that "the Son of Man is betrayed".
43 *Ecce Homo*, "Why I am so Wise", Sect. 1, p. 9.
44 *The Antichrist*, Sects. 22–24, pp. 150f. where Christianity is said to hate the senses, to despise hygiene and cleanliness, to bring knowledge into bad repute and so, in short, to live in a wilfully falsified world. See also the powerful concluding paragraphs of *Twilight of the Idols*, Para. 5, p. 127: "I once more come . . . where I once set out . . . my first transvaluation of all values".
45 *The Antichrist*, Para. 27, p. 162 (or: "the lowest of the low"). See also Para. 29, pp. 169–71.
46 The bosom of which he had forsaken. It is unwise – and un-Christian – to exploit his utter need and brokenness of mind in treating of his philosophy, but the relevance of its pathos is irresistible. He, too, seems to have thought Christian compassion (with its "unreal" theology) would still be necessary, for a while, among the masses, pending "super-man". He also seems to hold with natural instincts "like marriage and the care of the sick".
47 *Ibid.*, Para. 19, p. 147.
48 *Thus Spake Zarathustra*, Sect. viii, pp. 45–8. "Regret", "remorse", even simple "penitence" are backward looking. We have to change every "It was" into "I wanted it thus . . ." and move on. See *Thus Spake Zarathustra*, Sect. 8.
49 *Ecce Homo*, "The Birth of Tragedy", Sects. 1 and 2, pp. 68–71.
50 *The Antichrist*, Sect. 24, p. 153.

CHAPTER ELEVEN *In the Homo-Erotic World* with Oscar Wilde and De Profundis

1 C.3.3. was Wilde's number as prisoner. His friend, André Gide, who recounts the story of the lonely funeral, adds: "Seven persons followed the hearse . . . On the coffin were some flowers and some artificial wreaths." In *Oscar Wilde, A Study*, trans. Stuart Mason, London, 1905, p. 88.

2 Wilde told Gide: "During the first six months, I was dreadfully unhappy, so utterly miserable that I wanted to kill myself, but what kept me from doing so was looking at *the others* and . . . feeling sorry for them. O what a wonderful thing pity is! And I never knew it . . . I went into prison with a heart of stone . . . I have learned now that pity is the greatest and most beautiful thing in the world." *Ibid.*, pp. 63–4.

3 Bernard Shaw certainly thought so. See Terry Eagleton, *Heathcliffe and the Great Hunger: Studies in Irish Culture*, London, 1995, p. 341. Eagleton agrees. "The Wilde of Reading Gaol . . . has simply discovered a fascinating new persona. *De Profundis* is all about how deeply its author has changed and how utterly self-identical he remains," p. 340.

4 It is intriguing to reflect that Paul was briefly there, Mitylene being its adjacent port (Acts 20: 14) en route from Troas to Ephesus.

5 William Shakespeare, *The Merchant of Venice*, Act 5, Sc. 1, line 307.

6 William Shakespeare, *Julius Caesar*, Act 1, Sc. 2, line 84 and Act 3, Sc. 2, lines 19–20: "I say that Brutus' love to Caesar was no less than his." See also more generally: Paul Hammond: *Love between Men in English Literature*, London, 1996.

7 It is significant that homosexuals should have wanted to associate their victimization with this haunting language of Isaiah 53 and "the suffering servant". The phrase was the title of the novel published in 1918 under the pseudonym of A. T. Fitzroy who was a woman, Rosie Allatini. Evading the escapism of E. M. Forster's more famous *Maurice*, it depicts the struggles of its main hero to recognize and affirm his "difference" and the dark passages of relationship and adversity through which he goes.

8 As Shakespeare might have phrased it, echoing *Henry V*, Act 4, Sc. 3, line 92: "Bid them achieve me and then sell my bones."

9 *De Profundis* (Penguin edition), London, 1986, p. 152.

10 *Ibid.*, pp. 99, 100, 102, 105, 109.

11 *Ibid.*, p. 108.

12 *Ibid.*, p. 123. He even uses the word "outrage", though in a sharply opposite sense from that of the outfit now so named. "I was outraged with you . . . my sense of the outrage . . .", p. 146.

13 The terms meaning "lover" and "loved one". The notion of "falling in love" may well be absent – or sequential. Given the disparity in years the "luster" and the "lustable" might translate the words.

14 Wilde was fond of saying so. See pp. 98, 130, 155, and 206. "Shallowness" was the ultimate vice, i.e., not entering into all experience to know it for "real", whether in bed or in prison.

15 "Justice" is here the right word. Or, in Islamic terms, there is point in the idea of *hudud*, or "limits" appropriately circumscribing the realms of our legitimacy, while – by their inherent generosity – leaving these bounds, and their active acknowledgement, to our free assent and conformity.

16 *De Profundis*, p. 175.

17 1890–93. He refers to the kindness of his wife and there is deep pathos in

his being judicially deprived of the care of his sons. *Ibid.*, pp. 142 and 149: "infinite distress, grief without end or limit".

18 *Ibid.*, pp. 154, 156 and 161.

19 Thus he spoke of Christ "fascinating and dominating art as no Greek god ever succeeded in doing", and wrote of him as "this palpitating centre of romance". *Ibid.*, pp. 171 and 173.

20 "To margins" in that family ties, public bearings, maybe envies, conjectures, gossip, will still be around us despite the autonomy we act upon.

21 The title of his early novel, depicting the steady moral decline of its hero registering on a hidden portrait of his beauteous youth, to be revealed at the climax in hideous guise.

22 Using the old phrase about the unity of the worlds for the saga of human generations.

23 William Shakespeare, *Coriolanus*, Act 1, Sc. 4, line 32.

24 Walt Whitman (1819–92), the robust poetic embodiment of the 19th-century American persona, despite the trauma of the Civil War through which he lived. His verse celebrates his sense of the thrill of human being and is replete with erotic imagery. Whitman, however, assured J. A. Symonds in 1890 that "his loves were not physical". A century later he might have felt less minded to say so.

25 J. Addington Symonds, *A Problem in Greek Ethics*, 1883, p. 71, cited from Paul Hammond, *Love between Men in English Literature*, London, 1996, p. 170.

26 See Lord Elton, *Edward King and Our Times*, London, 1958, pp. 54–7.

27 *Ibid.*, p. 57.

28 "To learn" in the sense of "causing me to learn", is usual also in Shakespeare. Witness Caliban to Prospero "my profit on it . . . learning me your language". The usage bears illuminatingly on our whole topic of these chapters.

29 *De Profundis*, pp. 172–3.

30 Oscar Wilde, Poem: "The Sphinx", *The Complete Works*, London, 1993 edn, p. 812.

CHAPTER TWELVE *Christ Learning as Personal Crisis*

1 Meaning "the holy ground", not of physical place but of the Incarnation and the Passion. *Enarrationes in Psalmos*, cxxxi.13.

2 Luke 12: 50 and Matt: 20: 23 with Mark 10: 39. The first ritual connotation of the word clearly ripens into a larger personal event or crisis. Keeping water associations one might think of a Rubicon-in-faith such as the Cross was in anticipation and in fact.

3 *The Oxford Book of Ballads*, ed. James Kinsley, Oxford, 1982, "Rise up and bar the door", p. 630, No. 133: "Johnie Blunt".

4 Thanks to the distorted recent sense of "proselytizing" as soliciting converts, while the original Greek word simply means the opposite, i.e., one asking, seeking, to be enlightened.

5 The point is often made by Jewish writers, e.g., Martin Buber, in stressing that whereas Christians have to "be made such", Jews belong in Judaism by right of birth in "covenant". See: Martin Buber, *Two Types of Faith*, trans. N. P. Goldhawk, New York, 1961, pp. 9–11.

6 John 3: 8, the word *ruah* in Hebrew (Greek: *pneuma*) may even mean a hurri-

cane or the gentlest whence and whither of the breeze, before the connotation of "breath" and "spirit".

7 "Case-making" with a view to the mind-set of the audience (*argumenta ad homines*) is a familiar device and has always to be borne in mind in reading any Scripture. The incident in Numbers 8 followed complaints of the people about their hardships. When punished with serpent bites, Moses was required by God to erect the brass serpent on a pole. Long after, it became a symbol in the heraldry of medicine and healing. Doctrinally the imagery is quite incongruous when applied to the meaning of Messiah crucified, even though the "lifting up" is echoed in the far richer setting of John 12: 32. Examples abound in Christian language and metaphor – as in any other faith-speak – where a sort of *non-argumentum* occurs for mind-sets that are only puzzled, if not appalled. In wise dialogue it is vital to tackle, disentangle and hopefully elucidate these situations.

8 As, for example, in the World Council of Churches' Commission for Dialogue with *people* of other faiths", and comparable units within separate member churches.

9 The phrase occurs in the Pastoral Epistles, notably 2 Timothy 4: 8, also 1 Timothy 6: 14 and Titus 2: 14. Cf. also 2 Peter 1: 7. As with horizons at sea, the future is always a near contemporary. Expectation has always been a near cousin of faith. That the Church readily survived the non-fulfilment of the near form in which it first anticipated Christ's presence in glory only helped to explore that glory's real dimensions.

10 Here citing a very familiar Jewish questioning of Christian meanings frequent in, e.g., the writing of Martin Buber, Franz Rosenzweig, André Neher, Gershom Scholem, Jacob Neusner, Emil Frankenheim and others. See Tony Bavfield and Marcus Braybrook (eds), *Dialogue with a Difference*, London, 1992.

11 A familiar way of laconically combining realism with scepticism and both with undeluded honesty. Christians, as Leo Baeck perceived them, were taken in by sheer romanticism. See his *Judaism and Christianity*, trans. W. Kaufmann, Philadelphia, 1958, p. 291.

12 For example, I John 5: 19: "We know that the whole world lies in wickedness . . ." nearly the last words written in the New Testament. The quarrel with gnosticism in the context of the Epistle must be understood in tandem with its confidence in "the victory that overcomes" that world.

13 No wand-waving" indeed, but it is intriguing that one possible rendering of "Hosanna" in the entry of Jesus into Jerusalem is "Lift high the psalm", as a cry of crowd enthusiasm. The day itself revealed how deeper than waving foliage were the issues in hand.

14 The root term, *shirk*, means "sharing" and so "belonging with" and gives rise to a cognate meaning both "company" and "fellowship". The problem theologically arises from a right and categorical distinction between the kind of alignment in worship which idolatry makes between Allah and any pseudo deity *and* the sense in which, by creation and prophet-sending and law-making, Allah is certainly "associated" with the human scene.

15 The *Asma' al-husna* frequently found in the Qur'an by which Allah is denoted. They are both adjectival and nounal and often go in pairs – *Al-Rahman al-Rahim*, *Al-'Aziz al-Hakim*. As words deriving from human currency, Islamic theology requires them to "mean" only in the sense in which they can be true of God – a sense always categorically "other".

16 *Jahiliyyah* denotes the state of deprivation of truth characterizing Muhammad's hearers prior to – and by resistance during – his mission with the Qur'an.

17 The movement from the lesser word to the greater is basic in Christian faith, though – to be sure – the "sending" term rides well with the "coming". The Gospels have Jesus using both words and would have us know that there is truly a "coming" of God in the "sending" of the Son, while "sending" alone obtains in prophethood and messengers.

18 Muslim/Christian debate or polemic in the early centuries could often take misconstruing to bizarre lengths. How, for example, could bodily functions, like excrement or sweating and digesting, be thought compatible with the divine allegedly "made flesh" in Jesus? Such crudities had no place in how via personality in critically human situations of healing, teaching, suffering and serving, the divine might be self-giving and self-given in our sort of world. See, e.g., David Thomas, *Anti-Christian Polemic in Early Islam*, Cambridge, 1992.

19 "Anxious", no doubt, over what we falsely attribute. Islam had a zealous vigilance against all that is wrongly "associated" with God (cf. note 14). Yet we need to beware, in that zeal, lest we might be disallowing to God what patterns His will might take, to what lengths freely go.

20 In 1934 in *Harijan*, Gandhi wrote: "I believe in the fundamental truth of all great religions of the world. I believe that they are all God-given . . . and were necessary for the peoples to whom these religions were revealed . . . at the bottom all one and all helpful to one another."

21 The term meaning the tacit, or wilful, acceptance of elements from another faith or tradition in one's own. For the purist it is reprehensible, confusing and disloyal. Yet for the realist it is in some measure inevitable in the interplay of cultures. Few Scriptures are exempt from it.

22 Gandhi addressing the YMCA, Madras, in 2 February 1916.

23 In this way *ahimsa* may closely resemble Jesus' word on "turning the other cheek". It has kinship also with the Shi'ah Muslim tradition of *taqiyyah*, a stalwart "piety" that refuses to concede that wrong is right while patiently undertaking the consequences.

24 See note 20.

25 Echoing Robert Browning's query in "A Death in the Desert", *Poetical Works*, Oxford, 1905, p. 486.

26 For truths that may not be accepted may need, for that very reason a community in trust with them *on behalf of* the unpersuaded. A faith is not "held" only for its "holders".

27 Conjecture has sometimes wondered whether Gandhi would have achieved *swaraj* had he and the Congress been striving with a Nazi Raj not a British one.

28 See the classic narrative of a Massachusetts venture into the woods to learn a simple self-sufficiency in an American *swadeshi*, albeit within easy reach of social succour.

29 It is intriguing to note how rarely the word (or verb) occurs in the New Testament – only five times in the Gospels, three in Acts and twice in James' Letter. It has the sense of "to turn (or be turned) around". Given cultural suspicions and social prejudices, "convert" too often connotates "pervert", whereas "the new birth" language not only allows but requires what natural birth has constituted. Otherwise, the "newness" lacks all personal

territory to occupy. There is no "baptism" without a "baptizand", a self in transformation not deformation. It is urgent to have Christian "conversion" understood in its spiritual dimension.

30 Or, in other terms, the accessibility of Christ-faith has to mean not only its own unconditional invitation, but also its firm resistance to whatever factors would circumvent it. The New Testament's insistence that faith was freely open to "uncircumcized Gentiles" required Paul and others to "take on" all those who actively frustrated that conviction or denied its right to be so.

31 Witness the hard-heartedness of all so-called "fundamentalisms". What the Qur'an calls *ikhlas*, or "integrity" in religion, has often its largest task about the bigots within. We do not rightly counter the menace in the notion that "truth" is no more than "private option" by requiring that "truth" be brutally coercive or imprisoned in its own duress.

32 There were good *ad hoc* reasons for the closing of the Canon and it is well it should not now be challenged. Yet the issue – so frequently quite unrecognized – is thereby the more urgent. Only by adducing precedents from apostolic thinking in its own setting can Christian thought, in every generation, surmount what time proves to be the "incubus" of the Canon itself, i.e., its lack of geographical spread and contemporary sophistication. Is not this situation the reason why we have to "believe in the Holy Spirit guiding into all truth".

33 The principle here must be: "Let not your good be evil spoken of" (Romans 14: 6) Misunderstandings will be wilful and culpable, but it is urgent to obviate all that makes them so, insofar as lies within the Church's power.

34 The case made here does not overlook those many passages in the New Testament that urge, for example: "Come out from among them" (2 Corinthians 6: 17). These concern loose ethics not communities, though these, of course, interact. "Hating one's kin" (e.g., Luke 14: 26) is surely "priority via hyperbole" just like "plucking out one's eye". The "hate" disciples have to know is that inflicted not a hate harboured.

35 Muhammad Kamil Husain, *City of Wrong*, trans. Kenneth Cragg, Amsterdam, 1959, p. 224, reissued, Oxford, 1994, p. 233. See also discussion in Pierre Cachia, *An Overview of Modern Arabic Literature*, Edinburgh, 1990, p. 142. Husain surmises that crucial qualities in religions derive from collective, psychic trauma – Jewry and Exodus, Muslims and critical victory at Badr; while Christians take their self-image from the bitter self-accusation of the disciples of Jesus around Calvary. His insight is too drastically focused and needs ripening into a more inclusive "serious realism" concerning "us humans", as Christ's being crucified in our world underscores our *zulm*, our wrongness. "Sadness" in this context leaves room for the kind of "gladness" that has first refused all facile "solace". Kamil Husain is more fully studied in: Y. Y. and W. Z. Haddad (eds) *Muslim-Christian Encounters*, Gainesville, 1995, pp. 411–25: *Religious Pluralism in the Thought of M. K. Husain,* Harold Vogelaar, and also in: Kenneth Cragg: *The Pen and the Faith*, London, 1985, pp. 126–44.

36 The end was climactic but the Gospels clearly present it as a cumulative rejection, slowly building up during the brief years of Jesus' ministry. It is vital not to isolate the teacher from the sufferer, nor the climax of the Cross from the career in Galilee. The integrity of things said and things suffered was in line with the whole precedent of costly prophethood. Cf. my *The*

Weight in the Word, Brighton, 1999.

37 Cf. "The cup my Father gives me" (John 18: 11) The "Sonship of Jesus is most achieved – and so substantiated – in the Cross. He undergoes it reciprocally to the "Fatherhood" of God. That "Fatherhood", accordingly, is proven in his words and so attested in its meaning.

38 William Ernest Hocking: *Human Nature and Its Remaking*, New Haven, 1923, p. 423. Italics his.

39 Richard Steele (1672–1729), *The Tatler*, no. 181 (1710), "On Recollections of Childhood". He is writing about an early indelible impression of grief at the death of his father and what he saw his bereaved mother undergoing. His words are transposed here into another key, as music may.

40 It is legitimate to enlist Shakespeare's idea of "common" folk ennobled into "gentility" by shared fortunes in battle, for the making "gentle" of our souls in response to the Matthean invitation.

41 The case for the element of "will" in "belief" was memorably made by William James. The "will" is certainly an arbiter of "unbelief" also. Iris Murdoch's *The Sovereignty of Good*, London, 1970 (for all its splendid ethics) is simply content to "assert" its veto on traditional theological faith, p. 79. The only stated ground for this "bare assertion" is that she *wills* to counter what, for her, is the only point in theology, namely a *will* to be comforted, to pretend solace. That we might indeed be meant for "rest via a yoke" is willed out of court.

Index of Names and Terms

Index of Themes

Scriptural Citations